ERRATA

Page	Line	error	correction
any		area of supervision	area of jurisdiction
24		*delete* lines one and two	
27	14	joint prosecution	collective responsibility
66	36	ovides	provides
96	19	役	流
103	40	joint prosecution	collective responsibility
160	15	*after* ancestry	*add* (*kuan* 貫)
295	13	*delete* proper	

The T'ang Code

Studies in East Asian Law
Harvard University

The T'ang Code

Volume I, General Principles

Translated with an Introduction
by
Wallace Johnson

Princeton University Press
Princeton, New Jersey

Princeton Legacy Library edition 2019
Paperback ISBN: 978-0-691-60632-3
Hardcover ISBN: 978-0-691-65647-2

Published by Princeton University Press, Princeton, New Jersey
In the United Kingdom: Princeton University Press, Guildford, Surrey

Library of Congress Cataloging in Publication Data will be found on the last printed page of this book

Publication of this book has been aided by a grant from The Andrew W. Mellon Foundation

This book has been composed in Varityper Bembo

Clothbound editions of Princeton University Press books are printed on acid-free paper, and binding materials are chosen for strength and durability.

Printed in the United States of America by Princeton University Press, Princeton, New Jersey

The typesetting and paging of this book were done under the supervision of the author

The Harvard Law School, in cooperation with Harvard's East Asian Research Center, the Harvard-Yenching Institute, and scholars from other institutions, has initiated a program of training and research designed to further scholarly understanding of the legal systems of China, Japan, Korea, and adjacent areas. A series of publications has been established in conjunction with this program. A list of the *Studies in East Asian Law* appears at the back of this book.

In memory of my parents
Wallace and Ellen Johnson,

and for my teacher
Derk Bodde.

Contents

Preface

The field of Chinese law first attracted my interest during a two-year seminar on oriental law at The University of Pennsylvania with series of lectures by such persons as the late Ephraim A. Speiser on Akkadian law and S. N. Kramer on Sumerian law, as well as by Derk Bodde on traditional Chinese law. Some of the material that Bodde presented at that time was later further developed by him and Clarence Morris in a book on Ch'ing dynasty (1644–1911) law.

As a result of this introduction to Chinese law, I decided to attempt a complete translation of *The T'ang Code*, a text that has never been translated into any western language and yet which is certainly the most seminal legal work to have appeared in the whole of East Asian history. The first three chapters were submitted with an introduction as my Ph.D. thesis. Now, with extensive revision, they, together with the rest of the General Principles section, appear here in book form. I hope within a reasonably short time to be able to publish the remainder of my translation.

I also hope that this translation will be read not only by specialists but by the broader scholarly community interested in the history of law and the study of comparative legal institutions—persons such as historians, anthropologists, and sociologists. Therefore I have written an introduction to the translation that is aimed primarily at those who have not been trained in the field of traditional Chinese studies. Before proceeding with the translation, the general reader would do well to read the first two chapters of the introduction, which offer him a brief historical and philosophical background into which he can fit the *Code*, as well as further suggested readings on specific topics related to this book.

In the translation itself, I have tried to supply adequate notes for the specialist, while at the same time making the notes generally intelligible to those who do not have Sinological training. Thus when reference is made to other Chinese texts, I have also given a translation where such exists for the benefit of the reader who may not be competent in classical Chinese.

I am glad to have this opportunity to acknowledge the support afforded me while working on this translation by an American Council of Learned Societies Study Fellowship, a Harvard Law School Liberal Arts Fellowship, The Kansas University Endowment Association's Elizabeth M. Watkins Faculty Summer Fellowship, and The University of Kansas' Graduate Research Fund. Publication of this volume has been supported by a generous grant from the Andrew W. Mellon Foundation.

The translation could not have been completed without the willingness of others to offer criticism, and I am grateful to Derk Bodde of The University of Pennsylvania and L. S. Yang of Harvard University for their time spent in carefully reading through it and making numerous and valuable corrections and suggestions. Jerome A. Cohen of Harvard Law School and Michael Dalby of The University of Chicago gave their help in making the introduction more accurate and hence more useful. I also wish to thank Yin-lien Chin, with whom I first read the *Code* in Taiwan, and my students, Mark Allee and Rex Niswander, who made several useful suggestions. Any errors that remain are my own responsibility.

Abbreviations

Biot	Edouard Biot, *Le Tcheou-li ou rites des Tcheou*
Deloustal	Raymond Deloustal, "La Justice dans l'ancien Annam," *Bulletin de l'Ecole Française d'Extreme Orient*
KHCPTS	Kuo-hsüeh chi-pen ts'ung-shu 國學基本叢書 [Basic Sinological Series]. Shanghai: Commercial Press, 1933, 1936
SPTK	Ssu-pu ts'ung-k'an 四部叢刊 [Collected Reprints of Works in Four Categories]. Shanghai: Commercial Press, 1920–1936

Weights and Measures

Length

10 *li* 釐	equal 1 *fen* 分
10 *fen* 分	equal 1 *ts'un* 寸
10 *ts'un* 寸	equal 1 *ch'ih* 尺 (slightly less than the English foot)
10 *ch'ih* 尺	equal 1 *chang* 丈
1,800 *ch'ih* 尺	equal 1 *li* 里 (approximately one-third of the English mile)

Area

1 *mou* 畝	equals approximately one-sixth of an acre
1 *p'i* 匹 or 疋	equals a piece of cloth 1.8 *ch'ih* by 40 *ch'ih*

Weight

1 *chin* 斤	equals approximately one and one-half English pounds

NOTE: These weights and measures are taken from Balazs, "Beiträge zur Wirtschaftsgeschichte der T'ang-Zeit," *Milleilungen des Seminars für Orientalische Sprachen zu Berlin*, 36 (1933), 49 ff.

PART ONE
Introduction

CHAPTER I

Background

The T'ang Dynasty

The T'ang dynasty (A.D. 619–906) was one of the most important periods in Chinese history.[1] The preceding Sui dynasty (A.D. 589–618), it is true, must be credited with the reunification of a China that had been split into small states since the fall of the Han dynasty in A.D. 220. But the Sui triumph was short-lived. It was under the T'ang, then that the empire won political and cultural supremacy in East Asia, a position that it held for nearly three hundred years.

Once the House of Li was securely upon the throne, a vigorous policy of territorial expansion sent Chinese armies across half of Asia. Within a short time T'ang China was recognized as the most powerful and prestigious state in the Far East, and embassies began to come from foreign countries bringing tribute to the Son of Heaven. When they returned home bearing gifts and resounding titles for the rulers of their own countries, these envoys often took back Chinese ideas as well.

But not only armies went out beyond the borders of China. Many pilgrims, the most famous of whom was the Buddhist priest Hsüan-tsang, journeyed to Central Asia and even to India to visit holy places, study, and bring back Buddhist scriptures.[2] During the T'ang dynasty Buddhism attracted many of the best Chinese minds, and students even came from other countries to study in the great Buddhist monasteries. The best known of them, the Japanese monk Ennin, has left us a valuable picture of ninth-century China in his diary.[3]

Ch'ang-an, the capital of the empire, with more than two million inhabitants, was the greatest city in East Asia. Because of the wealth of T'ang China, its markets were filled with merchants and goods from as

[1]There exists no general, book-length treatment of the T'ang period. A good introduction for the non-specialist reader can be found in C. P. Fitzgerald, *China: A Short Cultural History*, pp. 291–374. Edwin O. Reischauer's *Ennin's Travels in T'ang China*, about a Japanese Buddhist monk who visited T'ang China, might also be useful. Among Edward A. Schafer's numerous publications on the period, *The Golden Peaches of Samarkand* gives a good picture of the wide variety of goods either brought as tribute or imported into China during the T'ang dynasty.

[2]Hsüan-tsang's life and career have been treated briefly by Arthur Waley, *The Real Tripitika and Other Pieces*. However, no one with an interest in China should miss reading Waley's excellent translation of some of the episodes in the magnificent picaresque novel about Hsüan-tsang's journey to India published under the title *Monkey*.

[3]Reischauer, tr., *Ennin's Diary*. Reischauer's *Ennin's Travels* is based on this book, but contains additional material and has a broader interest.

far away as Java and Iran. Its streets were crowded with both Chinese and foreigners come to seek wealth, position, or learning. In seventh to ninth-century Asia, all roads led to Ch'ang-an.

Much of the brilliance of the period is due to its literature. But the renowned poets Li Po, Tu Fu, and Po Chü-yi were only the tallest trees in a dense forest of writers. Han Yü, the essayist, led a movement to revitalize prose. At the same time, he denounced Buddhism and called on his countrymen to look to Chinese philosophers. Interestingly enough, it was this "foreign" religion that inspired the invention of printing. The desire of pious Buddhists to gain merit through the reproduction of scriptures was responsible for the world's first printed book.[4]

The arts flourished, as well. From the few examples of T'ang painting that still survive, we can acknowledge the talent of such artists as Yen Li-pen and Chou Fang. It seems probable also that true porcelain appeared for the first time during the T'ang dynasty. The superb ceramic portrayals of horses and camels, made originally to be grave figurines, are much prized by museums and collectors today. In short, the three hundred years of the T'ang dynasty were culturally extremely rich. Not only was its prestige immense during its own time, but later Chinese dynasties and foreign countries as well were greatly influenced by T'ang achievements.

Supporting this luxuriant growth of cultural life was a solid economic and political base.[5] Many of the institutions that originated or reached full development during the T'ang period lasted throughout imperial China. Indeed, some of them survive even today.

Administratively, the empire was divided into prefectures and counties responsible to the central government in the capital. At the base of this pyramid was the county magistrate—the lowest official in the bureaucracy—who heard criminal cases, collected taxes, and managed a hundred and one other matters. It is he who is the hero in countless Chinese detective stories, who plays the role assigned to Sherlock Holmes or Hercule Poirot in the West.[6]

The emperor was at the head of the government. But obviously he could do no more than set the main lines of state policy. The offices that

[4]This is the *Diamond Sūtra* of 868 described in Thomas Francis Carter's *The Invention of Printing in China and Its Spread Westward*, pp. 65–66. Because of the professional quality of the printing, Carter considers it likely that the book had some precursors. Nevertheless, the *Diamond Sūtra* is the world's oldest extant printed book.

[5]The most recent work on economic developments during the T'ang period has been done by Denis Twitchett. Interested readers should consult his *Financial Administration under the T'ang Dynasty*, as well as his numerous articles on the subject that have appeared in *Asia Major*. The standard work on political organization in the T'ang dynasty is Robert des Rotours, tr., *Traité des fonctionnaires et traité de l'armée*.

carried out these policies, or sometimes frustrated them, were staffed by a bureaucracy partly recruited through the examination system. This system had its roots in the earlier Han dynasty (206 B.C.–A.D. 220), but really began its development only during the T'ang period.

There were many types of examinations, and among them one that led to a degree in law.[7] To gain this degree, students had to answer satisfactorily seven out of ten questions on criminal and administrative law. However, the study of law was not so popular in T'ang China as the study of literature, and only a small minority of the candidates sat for the law degree.

Above this governmental machinery stood the censorate. The censors were not so much concerned with the actual administration of the government as with its quality. It was their duty to denounce the corruption or maladministration of officials to the throne. When they felt it necessary, individual censors even criticized the actions or policies of the emperor himself, sometimes at the cost of their lives.

T'ang Legislation

In the first years of the dynasty a series of criminal codes and administrative statutes were promulgated in order to govern the empire effectively. Though based on earlier sources, T'ang legislation has been more important historically than that of any other dynasty. The names of many important officials of the early years of the dynasty are connected with these legal compilations. The great criminal code entitled *The T'ang Code* (*Ku T'ang-lü shu-yi*, 故唐律疏議, hereafter referred to as *Code*) is always associated with the T'ai-tsung emperor's (reigned 627–649) brother-in-law, Ch'ang-sun Wu-chi (?–659), one of the most powerful statesmen of the time.

Though only the *Code* has survived in entirety, we know from historical sources, as well as from still extant fragments, that there was a large body of written law in effect during the T'ang period.[8] There were four main divisions: the *Code* (*lü* 律), the *Statutes* (*ling* 令), the *Regulations* (*ko* 格), and the *Ordinances* (*shih* 式). The *Statutes*, the general

[6]The detective story flourished in China long before Edgar Allen Poe started the genre in the West. The late Robert van Gulik, the well-known Dutch scholar, published a whole series of excellent detective stories in the Chinese style starring Judge Dee, a famous magistrate of T'ang times.

[7]See des Rotours, tr., *Le Traité des examens*.

[8]A list of at least the major compilations and revisions is given in Karl Bünger, *Quellen zur Rechtsgeschichte der T'ang-Zeit*, pp. 238–245. A good discussion of the different kinds of law operative in the T'ang dynasty can be found in Twitchett, "The Fragment of the T'ang Ordinances of the Department of Waterways Discovered at Tun-huang," pp. 23–36.

administrative rules for the central government, were the most important of these latter three.

While much of the *Statutes* has been recovered,[9] only portions of the *Regulations* and *Ordinances* have been found. In a recent study, Professor Twitchett has concluded that the *Regulations* served as a means through which new provisions and rulings could be introduced as supplements to the *Code* and *Statutes*.[10] The *Ordinances* seem to have been administrative rules concerned with limited areas of law, in contrast to the *Statutes*, which were general.[11] Other, less important groups of laws have survived in name only.[12]

The imperial government was primarily concerned with the prevention and punishment of crime. Other forms of conflict resolution were left to private means. Mediation and guild law were probably the effective agents here; we have no records. Yet commercial law was of great importance during the T'ang dynasty. This has become known only in the present century through the mass of contemporary manuscripts discovered at Tunhuang and Turfan in western China.[13] Most of these manuscripts preserve works of literature or religious texts. But a sizable number of them consist of tax rolls, household registers, contracts, bills of sale, and even parts of the *Code*, the *Statutes*, and the *Regulations*. Although a great number of the manuscripts are housed in the Bibliothèque Nationale and the British Museum, very little work has been done on them by Western scholars.[14]

The *Code* had many precursors in Chinese history. But how early did written law or codified law exist in China? According to the *Tso Commentary* (*Tso chuan*), laws were inscribed on a bronze vessel in 536 B.C., more than a thousand years before the T'ang dynasty. Hithertofore, this has been assumed to have been the first time that laws were ever written down in China.

[9]One of the outstanding achievements of modern Japanese scholarship on China is Niida Noboru's recovery of a great portion of the T'ang statutes by searching out quotes of the statutes in *The T'ang Code* and other works of and on the T'ang dynasty. The results of his research were published in his *Tōryō shūi* (The T'ang Statutes Re-collected).

[10]Twitchett, "A Note on the Tunhuang Fragments of the T'ang Regulations (*ko*)," pp. 380–381.

[11]Twitchett, "The Fragment of the T'ang Ordinances," p. 36.

[12]A discussion of these various legal compilations is found in Twitchett, "Tunhuang Fragments of the T'ang Regulations," p. 375.

[13]Twitchett, "Chinese Social History from the Seventh to the Tenth Centuries," recounts both the history of these documents and how they can be used to advance our knowledge of the period.

[14]The obvious exception is Denis Twitchett. But Jacques Gernet has also made use of the material in his "La Vente en Chine d'après les contrats de Touen-houang (IXe–Xe siècles)."

Recently, however, Professor Creel has asserted that written law was in existence during the first half of the first millennium B.C.[15] His evidence comes from certain documents of that time, and a particular Chinese character used several times in those texts to mean law or statute. Professor Creel further believes that at least some of these laws were organized in a systematic way. That is, that they formed a code.

The first actual reference to a code is to one supposedly compiled in the fourth century B.C. by a certain Li K'uei. It is stated that Li, who was the tutor to Marquis Wen of Wei (reigned 424–387 B.C.), brought together the laws of all the states existing at that time and formed them into a code, the *Canon of Laws* (*Fa ching* 法經). This story, however, is first recorded in the seventh-century A.D. *History of the Chin Dynasty* (*Chin shu*). And the existence of a law code so early as Li K'uei's time is at least questionable.[16]

However, the prefatory remarks in the first chapter of the *Code*, which were written by Ch'ang-sun Wu-chi, do assume the existence of this *Canon of Laws*, stating that it was transmitted and expounded by Shang Yang (d. 338 B.C.).[17] Shang Yang, or the Lord of Shang, rose to be prime minister in the state of Ch'in, and is credited with a reform of that state's laws *circa* 350 B.C. It was this state of Ch'in that later unified China for the first time, and during the short period of its rule instituted a great number of political and economic changes, some of which were to last throughout the imperial period.[18] In 1975, as a result of an archeological excavation in Hupei Province, portions of the Ch'in code were found. These laws, which are written on bamboo strips, and which do indeed seem to have formed a code, are the earliest that we definitely know to have existed in China.[19]

During the following Han dynasty, Hsiao Ho, who was chancellor to its founder, is said to have selected from among the Ch'in laws those he thought suitable, and added others to make a code. But only a few of these provisions have survived. They have been aptly described as remnants by Professor Hulsewé in his excellent book on Han law.[20] It is only by having read laboriously through the histories of the period, contemporary authors, and surviving records that Professor Hulsewé

[15]Herrlee G. Creel, *The Origins of Statecraft in China, Volume One: The Western Chou Empire*, p. 165.

[16]See Timoteus Pokora, "The Canon of Laws by Li K'uei, a Double Falsification."

[17]See p. 52.

[18]See Derk Bodde, *China's First Unifier*.

[19]Study Group for Ch'in Bamboo Slips from Yunmeng, "Yunmeng Ch'in-chien shih-wen" (A Transcription of Ch'in Dynasty Inscribed Bamboo Slips Unearthed at Yunmeng, Hupei Province).

[20]Hulsewé, *Remnants of Han Law*, Vol. I.

has succeeded in giving us at least a partial picture of law at that time.

The later, pre-T'ang codes are supposed to have been based on that of the Han, but only individual articles or fragments of articles are still extant.[21] Hence, the T'ang dynasty is the earliest time from which we can obtain an accurate picture of the range of Chinese criminal law during the imperial period and the structure of ideas that underlay its provisions.

The T'ang Code is divided into two parts: an initial section expounding the general principles of criminal law, and a second section setting forth the specific offenses covered, together with the punishment for each such act. Though the section on general principles contains only 57 of the 502 articles of the *Code*, it comprises nearly one-third of the whole work. Such a division between general principles and specific offenses seems to have been used in all the previous Chinese codes. Even in Li K'uei's supposed *Canon of Laws*, the last chapter is entitled "Generalities."

This method of organization for a law code is not uncommon. Indeed, the present day German criminal code, the *Strafgesetzbuch*, has the same two divisions as *The T'ang Code*. In our Western tradition, however, the origin of a separate section dealing with the principles of administration seems to go back to Roman law. In the long history of East-West contact there is no evidence of the exchange of legal ideas until modern times.

Unfortunately, none of the case records of court hearings has survived from the T'ang period. Neither do we have any condensed reports of cases such as the *Conspectus of Criminal Cases* (*Hsing-an hui-lan*), which has proved such a fertile source of legal material for the Ch'ing dynasty (1644–1911).[22] However, a group of decisions (*p'an* 判) written by eminent scholars in response to legal questions put to them in examinations is still preserved in the encyclopedic *Collection of Literary Masterpieces* (*Wen-yuan ying-hua*), which was brought together at the end of the tenth century.[23]

Moreover, many actual cases must be recorded in the two T'ang histories. The late Dr. van Gulik suggested that one way to begin would be to search out the cases contained in the biographies of famous judges in the histories. But we must wait for someone with the patience and

[21]The best work on pre-T'ang law in a Western language is Etienne Balazs, tr., *Le Traité* juridique du "Souei-chou." Ch'eng Shu-te brought together a large portion of the fragments of pre-T'ang laws in his *Chiu-ch'ao lü-k'ao* (Research on Law during the Nine Dynasties).

[22]Derk Bodde and Clarence Morris, *Law in Imperial China, Exemplified by 190 Ch'ing Dynasty Cases*.

[23]See the discussion and references to articles on this subject in Twitchett, "The Fragment of the T'ang Ordinances," p. 25, note 1a; and Hulsewé, *Han Law*, I, 4.

ability of Professor Hulsewé to read through the 455 chapters of the histories and bring the legal material to light.

The *Code* had great influence on later Chinese criminal legislation. The following dynasty, the Sung (960–1270), accepted the *Code* with only minor changes. All too little is known of Yüan (1279–1368) law, but that part which is still extant shows great resemblance to the *Code*.[24] During the Ming dynasty (1368–1644), there was a major reorganization of the criminal code and the number of articles was reduced. Further revision was ordered in the Ch'ing period. Yet one scholar has estimated that thirty to forty percent of the Ch'ing criminal code consists of articles taken over unchanged from *The T'ang Code*.[25]

The *Code* also strongly influenced the development of criminal law in other East Asian countries.[26] T'ang China served as a model for the then emerging Japanese state in many ways, and both the *Code* and the *Statutes* were adopted by Japanese emperors intent on the reorganization of their government.[27] Later, in the tenth century, Korean law was also influenced by the *Code*. And even as late as the fifteenth century, a large part of the *Code* was taken over either without alteration or only slightly modified by the Vietnamese Le dynasty.[28] Indeed, it can be safely asserted that the *Code* has been the single most influential piece of legislation to appear in East Asia.

Philosophy of Law in *The T'ang Code*[29]

In other civilizations law has been seen as the gift of some god or gods; not so in China. The *Code*, and indeed other writings of Ch'ang-sun Wu-chi, are quite specific in ascribing the creation of the law to the great sage rulers of antiquity.[30] It is stated that during the reigns of the (legendary) emperors Yao and Shun there were very few crimes owing to the high moral standards that were followed in those days. The view of society expressed in the *Code*, and which is a main theme of Chinese thought, is that those ancient times were a golden age from which there has been a steady decline.

[24]See Paul Ratchnevsky, *Un Code des Yuan*.

[25]Hsüeh Yün-sheng, quoted in Bodde and Morris, *Law in Imperial China*, p. 63.

[26]Yang Hung-lieh, *Chung-kuo fa-lü tsai Tung-ya chu-kuo chih ying-hsiang* (The Influence of Chinese Law in East Asia), is the earliest study on this subject. The latest serious work is Niida Noboru's *Chūgoku hōseishi kenkyū: keihō* (A Study of Chinese Legal History—Criminal Law), pp. 301–596. Niida has summarized his views in English in "Chinese Legal Institutions of the Sui and T'ang Periods and Their Influence on Surrounding East Asian Countries."

[27]There is an enormous literature on this subject. Most of the important works are listed in Twitchett, "The Fragment of the T'ang Ordinances." See also the discussion and books and articles listed in Mitsusada Inoue, "The *Ritsuryō* System in Japan."

With this decline, standards of morality were no longer sufficient to maintain order, and so laws became necessary. Thus morality and law are the two principal supports of society—morality first, but if it fails then punishment is the answer. The punishments are intended to inspire awe and to be dreaded, hence they are modeled on the thunder and lightning. Certainly one of the aims of the *Code* is to act as a deterrent; to fill the prospective law-breaker with fear for the consequences of his act.

But the primary purpose of law is to maintain a balance in society and a harmony between the human and the natural worlds. In this, the *Code* reflects the thought of the Han philosopher Tung Chung-shu (179?–104? B.C.).[31] His view of the universe was holistic, that is, the human and the natural worlds are linked together so that actions in the human world will bring about a corresponding reaction in the natural world. The universe then is anthropocentric, and the most important connection between the human and natural worlds is the emperor, whose actions can have either a beneficial or harmful effect on both the human and the natural orders.

Tung attempted to explain all phenomena in terms of certain general principles. The most important of these were the *yin* and *yang*, the alternating negative and positive forces in the universe; and the five elements (earth, wood, metal, fire, and water). The sun, man, imperial grace, spring, and summer are all dominated by the *yang* principle. But the moon, woman, death penalties, fall, and winter are under the *yin* influence. Then there are five basic notes in music, five colors, five important human relationships, and five directions (the center is the fifth) to correlate with the five elements.

An offense is regarded as a disruption of society that must be restored by the proper punishment. But punishments in the human sphere that are too heavy can bring about a reaction in the natural world—epidemics, floods, and droughts are commonly mentioned. In such cases the emperor must take steps to reduce punishments and so alleviate the sufferings of the people.[32] This belief in the connection between human

---

[28]There exists a French translation of this code by Raymond Deloustal which was made in the early part of this century. However, Vietnamese scholars at Harvard Law School are presently making another translation into English.

[29]The basic work in the field of legal philosophy has been done by Derk Bodde. His views are given in the first section of Bodde and Morris, *Law in Imperial China*. But see also the articles listed in that bibliography.

[30]*Sui shu* 25/1a; Balazs, *Traité juridique*, p. 29.

[31]A good discussion of Tung Chung-shu's thought is found in Yu-lan Fung, *A History of Chinese Philosophy*.

[32]See T'ung-tsu Ch'ü, *Law and Society in Traditional China*, pp. 213–218.

activity and the occurrence of natural phenomena is probably one of the reasons for the lack of flexibility afforded in sentencing by the *Code*. Once the magistrate had an understanding of all the facets of the case, he had no leeway in sentencing; the exact sentence provided by the *Code* had to be given. Thus throughout the empire a particular crime would be met with precisely the same punishment. The theory behind this is that if a certain punishment had been decided upon for a crime, then assigning a lesser punishment would not be a sufficient response and a heavier punishment might provoke some natural disaster.

With such a theory serving to temper the administration of punishment, there was concern about the validity of accusations. If the accuser had made a false accusation he would receive the same punishment that would have been administered to his intended victim. This would serve to restore the social balance that had been affected by the false accusation.

Confession of crimes such as robbery, and return of the stolen goods, could also repair the damage done by the crime, and in such cases the thief would not be punished. Indeed, the *Code* states that even if crimes such as rebellions were confessed before any action had taken place, the rebels could escape the severe penalties for that offense.

The *Code* also reflects the position of the emperor as the most important link between the human and the natural worlds as well as the head of the government. Offenses that involve the emperor or the imperial house are on a different level from those against other persons. In such cases not only the criminal but also his family members would be executed and their possessions confiscated by the state. Such crimes head a list of ten categories of offenses that were regarded as particularly heinous. Not only were the punishments especially severe for persons who committed such offenses, but certain other procedural protections, usually available to those convicted of other crimes, were not allowed to them.

Another dominant theme expressed in the *Code* is that social and political status affects a person's liability for punishment. The followers of Confucius in the first centuries before Christ were opposed to both a written law code and to liability for punishment, at least for ordinary offenses, for those persons who were of higher social or political standing than the ordinary person. The guiding principle for such favored classes should be morality (*li*); law was for the common people.[33]

[33]"Ritual does not extend down to the common people, punishments do not reach up to the officials." *Li chi*, "Ch'ü li"; Seraphin Couvreur, *Li ki ou Mémoires sur les bienséances et les cérémonies*, I, 53. See the very good treatment of Confucius found in Creel, *Confucius, the Man and the Myth*.

The Confucians likewise advocated hierarchical distinctions within the family group. Fathers, and indeed all elders, should have the loyalty and obediance of the junior members of the family. The *Code* institutionalizes this idea by allowing family members to conceal each other's offenses. Offenses by superiors against inferiors should be punished less heavily than those against equals in status. Similarly, offenses against superiors by inferiors should be punished more heavily.

In this, the Confucians were opposed to the Legalists, who stressed the need for a written law code that would be applicable to everyone and emphasized the state as the highest object of loyalty. The *Code* represents a harmonizing and a compromise of the views of these two opposing factions.

It will be apparent from reading the next chapter that much of the section of the *Code* on General Principles is devoted to guaranteeing some classes of persons a reduction of punishment for certain types of offenses, and/or the right to pay a fine instead. But all such provisions for leniency are extremely specific both as to the offenses that are covered and the degree of leniency allowed. Moreover, in certain cases those in official position or who were heads of families would receive more punishment than ordinary persons.

But none of the legal benefits allowed to various types of persons could be invoked in cases that endangered either the emperor or the state. Neither were relatives permitted the right of concealment of such offenses by family elders; indeed, if the elders did try to conceal such a crime, they were likely to become involved in that person's punishment.

The *Code* also reflects an attempt by a centralized, bureaucratic state to extend and protect its power throughout all of China. This is certainly another reason why the local magistrate was permitted no discretion at all in the sentencing of cases. He had to provide for each case some relevant article of the *Code*, the *Statutes*, the *Regulations*, or the *Ordinances* to justify his decision. Failure to do so would result in being punished himself. Moreover, any case that required punishment beyond beating had to be reviewed by higher authorities—in the case of the death penalty, permission had to be given by the emperor himself. The emperor could also, if he felt circumstances justified it, increase punishment as well as ameliorate it.

In order to make the administration of justice as automatic as possible, the *Code* attempts to foresee all possible circumstances that would have to be taken into consideration for any particular case. Take, for example, the crime of robbery, which is not only distinguished by whether or not force was used but, in addition, has separate articles dealing with the theft of government documents, Buddhist images, articles connected with national sacrifices, and weapons, each with a different punishment. And if no article could be found to fit exactly a given offense, there is provision for making a judgment by analogy with some crime that is covered in the *Code*.

The status of the defendant is also covered in detail, since it has relevance to the punishment assigned for any particular crime. Mention has already been made of provisions that favored certain classes of persons. Certain others, who may be called the inferior classes, were punished more heavily for some crimes than were the largest group of the population, who may conveniently be called commoners.

But in addition to social status, there were other factors of youth, age, sex, and mental and physical condition that could lessen punishment for many offenses. Moreover, these factors were operative in all cases, so that even members of the inferior classes could benefit from them. The recognition in a law code that such personal factors should be taken into consideration in sentencing seems to be the outstanding positive feature of traditional Chinese law.[34]

These basic ideas formed the theoretical base underlying the individual articles of the *Code*. After the fall of the T'ang dynasty, the *Code* continued to dominate Chinese criminal legislation until the end of the imperial period. Then, with the collapse of the Ch'ing dynasty and the founding of the Republic of China in 1912, Western law gained favor, as it had earlier in Meiji Japan. Later, when Mao Tse-tung came to power in 1949, Russian law became influential. So the *Code* has now been pushed into the background. Despite this, certain of its concepts—confession, for instance—are very much alive even today. Thus for some 1,300 years *The T'ang Code* has played the dominant role in East Asian law, a period of time rivaled only by the *Corpus Juris Civilis* in Western Europe.

[34]These ideas, in fact, can be traced back to the *Rites of Chou (Chou-li)*, a constitutional document of approximately the third century B.C., which has been translated by Edouard Biot, *Le Tcheou-li ou rites des Tcheou*. Creel, *Statecraft in China*, p. 478, does not think that this represents any actual practice at that time, and I agree. But see also the opposite view in Sven Broman, "Studies on the Chou Li."

CHAPTER II

General Principles of *The T'ang Code*

Harmony of Law and Nature

The provisions of the *Code* attempt to reinforce harmony with the natural world through compliance with the *yin-yang* and five elements theories. Indeed, the *Code* itself represents the *yin*—the dark side of social control—in contrast with the *yang* influence of ritual, morality, and education.

The best example of the importance of the *yin-yang* theory is the restriction on carrying out the death penalty.[1] Death was under the *yin* or negative power. Thus there were two death penalties—strangulation and decapitation—two being a *yin* number.

Because of this, executions were carried out only during that part of the year when the *yin* influence was in the ascendant, the fall and winter seasons. Should criminals be put to death during the seasons when the *yang* power was rising, a poor harvest might result. In addition, there were other auspicious days, such as the equinoxes and the solstices, as well as Buddhist fast days, when executions were banned. Altogether, there were so many of these forbidden days that it has been estimated that fewer than sixty days of the year were available for executions.[2] Should an official violate one of these taboo days, he could be punished by as much as one year of penal servitude.[3]

The influence of the five elements theory in the *Code* is well illustrated by the preference for groups of five. It was traditionally supposed to have contained 500 articles, though there are 502 as it is now constituted. There are also five punishments. The subcommentary to Article 1 of the *Code* states that the sages created the five punishments in imitation of the five elements.

The Five Punishments

1. light stick: 10, 20, 30, 40, and 50 blows
2. heavy stick: 60, 70, 80, 90, and 100 blows
3. penal servitude: 1, 1½, 2, 2½, and 3 years

[1]A general discussion of this practice is given in Bodde and Morris, *Law in Imperial China*, pp. 46–48. The details as they pertained to T'ang law are based on Hulsewé, *Periodieke executie- en slachtverboden in de T'ang tijd en hun oorsprong*.

[2]Bodde and Morris, *Law in Imperial China*, p. 47.

[3]Article 496.

4. life exile: 2,000, 2,500, and 3,000 *li*
5. death: strangulation and decapitation

As can be seen, there are also subcategories of fives for the light stick, the heavy stick, and penal servitude. Then there are three distances of life exile and two death penalties, so that these major punishments also total five.

Other instances of categories of five are the five important degrees of family relationship, the division of official privileges at the fifth rank, and the particularly serious crimes punished by the five kinds of life exile. Not all of these may have resulted from conscious attempts to correlate the *Code* with the five elements, but groupings of five are certainly numerous and suggestive.

False Accusation, Reparation, and Amnesty

In a society which believes that punishment of the innocent can cause natural disasters, there is justifiable concern over false açcusation. During a trial, every effort, including even torture within specific bounds according to the offense, was made to get the accused to confess his guilt of the charge against him. But if the accused would not confess, the next step was to interrogate his accuser for the possibility of false accusation.[4] When it then came out that the accusation was false, the accuser was punished with the penalty for the crime of which he had accused the innocent person.[5]

If the person falsely accused was a commoner or a member of the inferior classes, reciprocal punishment did not present a problem. Were the offense punished by two years of penal servitude, the person who made the false accusation was so sentenced. But the case was more complex when officials or members of the Buddhist or Taoist clergy were involved as the original accused. Officials who were found guilty of certain offenses would be forced to resign from office. Monks and nuns could be required to return to lay status. A table was given for such offenses, which equated resignation from office or forced return to lay status with so many blows of the heavy stick.

The *Code* is also concerned with balancing injustice that has already resulted in punishment either through wrongful conviction of the innocent or too heavy a sentence for a guilty party. When the person who suffered unjustly was known and the facts were clear, such a person received reparation from the government. But if natural disasters oc-

[4]Article 478.

[5]Article 342; Deloustal 501.

curred that could not be linked with any particular person, more general remedies were used.

Reparation was limited, however, to sentençes of penal servitude or life exile. Apparently a mistaken beating was not serious enough to warrant any reparation. But it seems strange that no provision was made for mistaken execution. It is possible that this was because no one could be executed without the emperor's consent, and the *Code* cannot consider the possibility of a mistake by the emperor.[6]

For each year of penal servitude served either by someone who was, in fact, innocent or who was guilty but whose sentence was too heavy for his crime, two years of taxes and labor services would be remitted.[7] When less time had been served, fifty days was considered to be the same as a year. For still shorter periods, relief from certain taxes was granted according to a fixed scale.

Such exemption from taxes and labor services was not affected by other factors. Thus, if a person had a year's relief from taxes and labor services, and there was a flood or drought in that year so that there was a general exemption from taxes and labor services by imperial decree, the person's private relief would be carried over to the next year.

The emperor also had other means at his disposal whereby he could counterbalance the effects of too-heavy punishments.[8] Amnesties, in particular, were announced at the beginning of a reign, on the emperor's birthday, or at other auspicious occasions, and not just because of fear that too-heavy punishments might bring famine. There were 174 great amnesties during the almost three hundred years of the T'ang dynasty, and certainly many more less general awards of imperial grace.[9] Great amnesties reached throughout the empire, while others were limited to particular regions or particular offenses. Thus the sentence of almost any criminal had some chance of being lessened or even canceled by amnesty.

There were also decreases of sentences and revisions, most often

[6]I am indebted to Dr. Fu-mei Chang for this suggestion.

[7]Article 44.

[8]A general treatment of ways to balance the effects of too-heavy punishments is found in Ch'ü, *Law and Society*, pp. 213–218. The famous memorial of Ch'en Tzu-ang to the Empress Wu on this subject is translated in Bünger, *Quellen*, pp. 108–118. See also Eugene Feifel, *Po Chü-i as a Censor*, p. 225.

[9]Hsü Shih-kuei, *Chung-kuo ta-she k'ao* (Researches into Great Amnesties in China), p. 94. Hsü gives lists and official explanations but has very little analysis. There is also a discussion of various types of amnesties in Tai Yen-hui, *T'ang-lü t'ung-lun* (General Principles of *The T'ang Code*), pp. 330–344. However, the best treatment is found in Shen Chia-pen, *Shen Chi-yi hsien-sheng yi-shu, chia-pien* (Bequeathed Writings of Mr. Shen Chi-yi [Shen Chia-pen], first series), I, 230–357.

because of natural disturbances, such as plagues of locusts. Decreases of sentences were general, but revisions concerned individual criminals.[10] The cases of these persons were examined to determine whether or not their sentences were proper. The officials then memorialized the throne as to what action they favored.

The Ten Abominations

Most of the offenses covered in the *Code* are simply set forth in the appropriate part of the section on specific articles. But certain crimes were considered so heinous that they were listed also under Article 6, entitled "The Ten Abominations." Since the criminal acts brought together here were held to be especially reprehensible, an examination of them will help to throw light on the values of T'ang society.

The Ten Abominations

1. plotting rebellion	6. great irreverance
2. plotting great sedition	7. lack of filial piety
3. plotting treason	8. discord
4. contumacy	9. unrighteousness
5. depravity	10. incest

It might now be advisable to read through the translation of Article 6 in order to become familiar with the particular crimes covered under these ten categories. Here it is sufficient to state that the crimes included within the ten abominations are those that endanger the emperor or the state, those that are committed by subordinate members of the family or bureaucracy against their superiors, those that threaten the existence of the family, and those that involve black magic.

The procedure in dealing with crimes that came within the ten abominations was markedly different from that ordinarily used. None of the privileges allowed special groups, such as members of the bureaucracy, was permitted in cases of violation of one of the ten abominations.[11]

Not all of the crimes included within this category were punished by the death penalty. However, they were commonly all explicitly exempted from the provisions of amnesties.[12] Even in special cases that were pardoned, the criminals were deprived of whatever rank they had, and any goods or real property that had been confiscated by the state were not returned.[13]

[10]Shen, *Bequeathed Writings*, 1, 353–354.

[11]Articles 8, 9, 10, and 11. Privileged groups are discussed in the fourth part of this chapter.

[12]See, for example, the amnesty of 635 quoted in the subcommentary of Article 488.

[13]Articles 18 and 32.

execution could take place.[14] And if the death sentence were approved, it would be carried out immediately. The continued existence of such criminals was reckoned a greater threat to society than the violation of one of the taboo days.[15]

The above procedural factors operated to make punishment of the criminal more certain. Moreover, for some of the crimes that came under the ten abominations, not only were the criminals themselves punished, but their families also. And their goods and real property were confiscated by the state.

Collective Prosecution

The most serious crimes covered by the *Code* are the first two of the ten abominations, plotting rebellion and plotting great sedition.[16] I say the most serious, because the extent of punishment is greater for these two crimes than for any others in the *Code*.

Plotting rebellion is defined as plotting to endanger either the ruler or the state. The plot is sufficient of itself; there need not have been any attempt made. But some act was required in the case of great sedition. This consisted of destroying the ancestral temples, tombs, or palaces of the reigning house.

The penalties for plotting rebellion or actually committing great sedition are the same—decapitation for everyone involved. The distinction between principals and accessories commonly made in the *Code*, which afforded these latter a reduced sentence, is not allowed here.

Punishment also reached a great number of persons who had no involvement in the crime whatsoever. The fathers and sons of the criminals were strangled. If the sons were fifteen years of age or less, they were enslaved by the state instead. Enslavement was also the punishment for the criminals' mothers, daughters, grandfather, great-grandfather, and great-great-grandfather in the male line, grandsons, great-grandsons, and great-great-grandsons in the male line, his brothers and sisters, his and his sons' wives and concubines, and any retainers or slaves belonging to the above. Moreover, all of their goods and real property were confiscated by the state.

Further, the offenders' paternal uncles and nephews in the male line would be exiled for life to a distance of 3,000 *li*. But their goods and real property would not be confiscated.

[14]Niida, *Statutes*, p. 761.

[15]Article 496.

[16]Both of these offenses are covered in Article 248; Deloustal 410.

Plotting treason was considered to be a less serious offense, and included smaller numbers of relatives in the criminal's punishment.[17] This offense is defined as betraying the imperial house or a city, or turning over territory under one's control to rebels. If the plot is already underway, all those in it are decapitated. Their wives and sons are exiled for life to 2,000 *li*. And should the criminals have gathered more than a hundred followers or have done deliberate harm, their parents as well as their wives and sons would be exiled for life to 3,000 *li*.

The least serious of these offenses against the state is informing the enemy of attacks by the army.[18] Though not placed within the ten abominations, the crime of giving such information is still punished by decapitation. However, no one except the wife and sons of the criminal are involved in collective prosecution, and they are only exiled for life to 2,000 *li*. If the criminal is a foreigner, he is strangled instead, and no other members of his family are punished.

Collective prosecution would also be invoked for killing three members of one family, a crime that was included under depravity.[19] The criminals would all be decapitated, again with no distinction being made between principals and accessories to the crime. Their wives and sons would be exiled for life to 2,000 *li*.

The definition of a family was very broad. It comprised all those whose names were on a single household register, whether or not they were kin. Even if they were on separate household registers, if the three victims were within the second degree of mourning relationship, they were considered to be members of a single family under the relevant article. The only limitations were that the three victims had to be of at least the same social status as the murderer, and that none of them had committed a capital offense. Thus if one of the three victims were a member of the retainer or slave class and the murderer were a commoner, the crime would not come under the ten abominations, and collective prosecution would not be applicable.

The last category of crime involving collective prosecution was that of making or keeping *ku* poison, which was considered to be black magic.[20] This crime was classed as depravity, the fifth of the ten abominations, and linked there with summoning spirits and other forms of magical practice that were considered especially reprehensible. One way of making *ku* poison was by putting poisonous insects together; the

[17]Article 251; Deloustal 411.

[18]Article 232; Deloustal 254.

[19]Article 259; Deloustal 419.

[20]References to articles on *ku* poison are given in note 130 of Chapter I of the translation. The offense is covered under Article 262; Deloustal 423.

one that killed the others was termed the *ku*. If the excrement of the *ku* was added to food, it was supposed that the victim would go mad or die. In the *Code*, making *ku* poison is associated with women and, in fact, was the only crime specifically associated with women that would involve their families in collective prosecution.

The offense itself was punished by strangulation. All those who had goods and real property in common ownership with the criminal were exiled for life to 3,000 *li*. But their goods and real property were not confiscated by the state.

The subcommentary to the *Code* gives the reasoning behind such extension of punishment for offenses against the emperor or the state, or for black magic. In the subcommentary to Article 248, the emperor is placed on the same level of importance to his subjects as heaven and earth. In the subcommentary on plotting rebellion in Article 6, he is described as the father and mother of the masses who are his children.

Moreover, rebellion against the imperial house is compared to natural calamities. The intent of the *Code* toward those who plot either rebellion or great sedition is clearly stated in Article 32: "Plotting rebellion and great sedition are criminal to the utmost degree of censure and extermination. They defile the whole family and property and the eradication of evil must reach to the roots." Clearly, then, the purpose of the law in such cases was not merely to punish the criminal, but rather to exterminate his whole family. In traditional China, with its great emphasis on the continuation of the family, there could be no greater punishment than to end a family's name.

With regard to *ku* poison, Article 28 states: "Making and keeping *ku* poison falls within what is intolerable and women who do so are expelled to the frontiers of the empire in order to cut off this evil." In fact, the person who actually made *ku* poison was strangled, it was those who held goods and real property in common with the criminal who were exiled for life. But the meaning is clear: all of them were to be expelled from China permanently.

Other offenses involving the emperor are listed under great irreverance. There mislabeling, or not following the prescription when making medicine for the emperor, making mistakes in preparing the emperor's food, or making boats that will carry the emperor not strong enough are brought under the ten abominations, together with stealing the objects belonging to the great sacrifices, stealing the carriage or possessions of the emperor, stealing or forging the imperial seals, criticizing the emperor, resisting messengers carrying imperial edicts, or simply "lacking the manners a subject owes to his emperor." Concerning the first three, the *Code* states that if these crimes are committed deliberately and not by mistake, they are considered to come under plotting rebellion. In such cases, punishment would also include the relatives, as described above.

Offenses against Superiors

Though offenses against superiors in the bureaucratic and family hierarchy do not involve the family members of the criminal in punishment, they are regarded very seriously in the *Code*. Five of the ten abominations list such crimes: contumacy, lack of filial piety, discord, unrighteousness, and incest.

So many offenses are covered that it is not possible to treat them all here. But a comparison of the punishments meted out for offenses against persons of a higher status in either the family or bureaucracy with those given for the same offense when committed against a neutral person will effectively show the intent of the *Code*.

A plot to kill a parent or paternal grandparent, or the chief of one's department in the government, was punished by decapitation and life exile, respectively.[21] The same plot against a neutral person was punished only by penal servitude.[22] Similarly, anyone who actually hit a parent or paternal grandparent was decapitated.[23] And any official below the fifth rank who struck an official of the third rank or higher would serve a year of penal servitude.[24] But ordinary blows against a neutral person brought the offender only forty blows with the light stick.[25] And, of course, offenses classified under the ten abominations placed the offender under the procedural disadvantages that have been outlined above.

Within the family, the children were legally obligated to support their parents or paternal grandparents. If these latter complained to the court that their children or grandchildren were not supporting them, the punishment was two years of penal servitude.[26] Division of goods or separation of households were not allowed while the parents or paternal grandparents were alive. Either of these offenses was punished by three years of penal servitude.[27]

Further, a series of laws enforced the mourning regulations for parents and paternal grandparents very strictly. If a child did not go into

[21] Article 253; Deloustal 415; also Article 252; Deloustal 417.
[22] Article 256; Deloustal 414.
[23] Article 329; Deloustal 474.
[24] Article 393.
[25] Article 202; Deloustal 464.
[26] Article 348; Deloustal 505.
[27] Article 155.

mourning upon learning of the death of his or her parents or paternal grandparents, the punishment was life exile to 2,000 *li*.[28] Then, if during the twenty-seven months' period of mourning for the parents one wore any festive clothing or made music, the punishment was three years of penal servitude.[29] The same punishment was given to those who married during that time.[30] All of these crimes were classed as lack of filial piety.

More distant degrees of relationship, as well as that of the wife to her husband were covered under discord. A plot to kill a relative of the fifth degree of mourning was punished by life exile to 2,000 *li*.[31] And a woman who struck her husband was punished by one year of penal servitude.[32]

Closely linked with the ten abominations were certain provisions of Article 11, which is called "Those Entitled to Deliberation, Petition, or Reduction of Punishment." The last four of the five kinds of life exile named in that article were applicable to those persons involved in a violation of certain of the ten abominations.

The Five Kinds of Life Exile

1. life exile with added labor
2. life exile for collective prosecution for rebellion or sedition
3. life exile for sons and grandsons in the male line for accidental killing of their paternal grandparents or parents
4. life exile for lack of filial piety
5. life exile despite amnesty

Life exile with added labor, that is, three years of labor instead of the usual one year does not concern us here. But the last four are directly connected with the ten abominations. After giving this list, the article states that persons sentenced to these five kinds of life exile may not have their punishments reduced or make redemption of the punishment by payment of copper. If they have any noble rank or office, they will be stripped of it and sent into life exile.

Furthermore, the subcommentary then goes on to state that while reductions of sentence may benefit those sentenced under categories one, two, and four, persons sentenced under categories three and five will not have their sentences reduced.

Essentially then, this part of Article 11 acts as a corollary to Article 6. It takes up almost all of the cases that would be punished by life exile rather than death, and disqualifies criminals whose punishment comes

[28]Article 120; Deloustal 130.
[29]Article 120; Deloustal 130.
[30]Article 179; Deloustal 316.
[31]Article 253; Deloustal 415.
[32]Article 326; Deloustal 480.

under life exile from any legal privileges that they might possess.

Personal Status and Liability for Punishment

Under the provisions of the *Code*, the personal status of an offender could have great effect on the conduct of a case, the sentence given, and, indeed, whether or not the offender were punished at all.[33]

The most important classification of privileged persons in the *Code* is of those who possess the qualifications that place them within one of the eight deliberations. As is pointed out in the subcommentary to Article 7 entitled "The Eight Deliberations," these categories are those that were first set out in the *Rites of Chou* (*Chou-li*). They are:

1. deliberation for relatives of the emperor
2. deliberation for old retainers of the emperor
3. deliberation for the morally worthy
4. deliberation for ability
5. deliberation for achievement
6. deliberation for high position
7. deliberation for diligence
8. deliberation for guests of the state

Several of these are quite vague, and I do not know how persons qualified themselves for numbers three, four, five, and seven. Neither is number two definite beyond stating that those included had served the emperor "for a long time."

However, categories one, six, and eight are very specific. Category one includes all relatives of the emperor through the sixth degree of mourning—a degree beyond that affecting other persons—relatives of the emperor's paternal grandmother and his mother through the fifth degree of mourning, and relatives of the empress through the fourth degree of mourning.[34]

Category six is composed of officials on active duty of the third rank or higher, titular officials of the second rank or higher, and nobles of the first rank. These different types of rank and title are dealt with in detail below.

Guests of the state, referred to in category eight, are the descendants of the two previous imperial houses. Certainly there cannot have been

[33]A very good general treatment of the relationship between status and punishment is given in Ch'ü, *Law and Society*, pp. 170–206.

[34]The mourning system in traditional China was incredibly complex. An analysis of the terminology, together with the relevant historical changes can be found in Han-yi Feng, "The Chinese Kinship System." Those persons in each of the five T'ang dynasty categories are listed in Koei-hing Ou, *La Peine d'après le code des T'ang*, pp. 105–115.

Guests of the state, referred to in category eight, are the descendants of the two previous imperial houses. Certainly there cannot have been great numbers of persons in any of these categories. The significant point is that, except for categories three and four, all of the persons included under the eight deliberations are either connected with the present or previous ruling houses, or have served the state with distinction.

If anyone included within these eight categories committed an offense punished by life exile or less, their punishment was automatically reduced one degree. For a capital offense they could not be punished through the ordinary criminal process. Instead, the Board of Punishments had to memorialize the throne for permission to deliberate on the case. If such deliberation were permitted, the Board of Punishments then decided which article of the *Code* was applicable to the case, and sent up another memorial requesting the emperor to fix a punishment. The implied, though not necessary, result would be that the emperor would decide for a punishment that was less than the death penalty.[35]

The second highest privilege was that of petition. This was allowed to three classes of persons: relatives of the crown prince through the third degree of mourning, officials and nobles of the fifth rank and above, and the grandsons in the male line, as well as the relatives in the second degree of mourning of all those persons who were allowed deliberation.[36]

Should any of these persons commit a crime punished by life exile or less, again the sentence was reduced one degree. But were the offense capital, the Board of Punishments did not have to request permission to discuss the case. Rather they sent up the facts of the case, the punishment for the crime, and the reason for the person having the right of petition in a memorial to the emperor. He would then decide the punishment.

The right of deliberation was allowed in all cases except those involving the ten abominations. But the right of petition was still more circumscribed. Again it was not permitted in cases of violation of one of the ten abominations, but neither was it allowed in cases of murder, theft, or illicit sexual intercourse. Nor could it benefit officials who committed the crimes of robbery or kidnapping, or of taking bribes and subverting the law within their area of jurisdiction. But where no goods had been taken in the robbery, nor had the intended victims of illicit sexual intercourse or kidnapping yet been seized, a lesser right, that of reduction of punishment, was allowed the criminal.[37]

[35]Even if sentenced to death for a crime other than one of the ten abominations, officials were allowed to commit suicide or were strangled in a secret place, as were members of the imperial clan and women. See Niida, *Statutes*, p. 764.

[36]Article 9.

[37]Article 10.

Reduction of punishment for sentences of life exile or less was permitted to a still broader range of persons than those permitted deliberation and petition. The group included officials of the seventh rank and above, as well as the paternal grandparents, parents, brothers, sisters, wives, sons, and grandsons in the male line of all those persons who had the right of petition.

Furthermore, those who had the rights of deliberation, petition, or reduction of punishment could not be tortured in order to obtain their confession during a trial.[38] Instead, the evidence of at least three witnesses was needed to convict them of any accusation.

The last and most general of these legal benefits was the right to redeem punishment by payment of copper. It was granted to everyone in the above three categories of privilege and, in addition, to officials of the ninth rank and above, together with their paternal grandparents, parents, sons, and grandsons in the male line.[39]

This extension of the legal right to privilege to certain of the relatives of officials and nobles was known as protection. It also included the right of official rank for sons and certain other relatives of the persons who could give such protection.[40] In this way, it was possible to have the benefits of office without having to go through the rigors of the examination system.

Official Privilege and Responsibility

Several kinds of rank and title existed during the T'ang dynasty. The *Code* grants the most privilege to those officials on active duty who served in the civil and military branches of the bureaucracy. This civil service was composed of nine ranks; ranks one through three having two grades each, and ranks four through nine having four grades each for a total of thirty. Civil-service officials often had titular offices as well, which had the same thirty grades, and such titular office might carry a higher or lower rank than an official's active-duty office. Then there were also honorary offices with six ranks and twelve grades given for such reasons as bravery in warfare. Finally, there were hereditary titles of nobility, with five ranks.

Depending upon their rank, officials had the rights of deliberation, petition, reduction of punishment, and redemption of punishment by

[38]Article 474; Deloustal 664.

[39]Article 11.

[40]See Karl Wittfogel, "Public Office in the Liao Dynasty and the Chinese Examination System"; and E. A. Kracke, "Family vs. Merit in Chinese Civil Service Examinations under the Empire."

payment of copper. But, in addition, official rank could be exchanged for punishment.[41] The extent of such replacement of punishment by rank depended upon the type of offense and the official's rank. Officials of the fifth rank and above could replace as much as two years of penal servitude by their positions, while those of lower rank could replace only one year. Moreover, if the offense were connected with official duties rather than having been committed by an official in his private capacity, his rank replaced one additional year of penal servitude.

Further, cumulative replacement was specified. Currently held active-duty offices, office in the imperial guard, and titular office in most cases were lumped together as constituting one type of office, and only the highest of these could be used to replace punishment.[42] But if this office were not enough, then concurrently held honorary office could be used. In the unlikely event that all currently held positions were insufficient to replace the punishment, those offices that the official had previously held might also be used. And when all offices had been surrendered, one or more years of penal servitude could be redeemed by payment of copper.

The offender was given no choice between the punishment being replaced by office or being redeemed by payment of copper. Only if the official's office was more than was needed to replace the punishment might he keep his office and completely redeem his punishment by payment of copper. Each of the five punishments had a set value in terms of copper. However, redemption of punishment by payment of copper was usually allowed only to the privileged groups named above. For the average man it was not a question of fifty blows with the light stick or five *chin* of copper.

Surrender of office, using it to replace punishment, did not, however, reduce an official to the level of a commoner. He was still exempted from taxes and labor services.[43] And after one year he could resume office with a reduction of only one grade in rank. If, during this interval, he committed further offenses punished by life exile or less, he could redeem them by payment of copper.

Deprivation of office could also be a punishment in itself. Certain offenses, in particular those committed within an official's area of jurisdiction, would require that he resign his active-duty office.[44] As in the case of using office to replace punishment, after a year's interval the official could resume office with a reduction of one grade in rank. More

[41] Article 17.

[42] Ibid.

[43] Article 21.

[44] Such as illicit sexual intercourse, robbery, and kidnapping. See Article 19.

serious offenses required resignation from all offices. In such cases the offender was deprived of office for three years, and at the end of this period his rank would be reduced two degrees.

But the severest form of this punishment was disenrollment. The offender was stripped of all offices and any noble titles that he might have. This was for a period of six years. After that time, he might return to office, but his rank would be drastically reduced, in some cases by as much as sixteen grades.[45]

Moreover, the two kinds of resignation from office, as well as disenrollment, could be supplemented by beating, penal servitude, or life exile. In some cases, the official could cancel these latter punishments by using his office to replace them or by payment of copper. In other cases, he would be punished like any other criminal.

The joint prosecution of officials who were involved in errors connected with their duties was parallel to the collective prosecution of families of persons who rebelled, destroyed imperial tombs, and so on.[46] If one official made a mistake in assigning a punishment, others who were also involved in that case, both above and below him in the bureaucracy, would also be punished. However, their sentences would be lessened in relation to their distance from the original error. And should any of them discover and bring out the error before the mistaken punishment had been administered, all of the officials involved would be exempted from punishment.

Officials could also be punished for the offenses of their family members. For example, if within the area under an official's control one of his family members committed extortion or accepted bribes, the official would be punished, even though he knew nothing of the crime.[47]

Or, if an official and two or more commoners jointly committed an offense within that official's area of jurisdiction, the official would be held to be the principal in the crime. The commoners would be prosecuted as accessories and receive a reduced punishment, even though one of them had been the ringleader.[48]

With these various legal privileges granted the members of the bureaucracy, it was almost impossible for them to suffer the usual punishments provided by the *Code* for the less privileged. Their position did not afford them any protection if they violated one of the ten abominations, however, and in some circumstances they had a heavier liability for

[45]Niida, *Statutes*, pp. 299–300.

[46]Articles 40 and 41. See Bünger, "Uber die Verantwortlichkeit der Beamten nach klassischem chinesischem Recht."

[47]Article 146.

[48]Article 42.

punishment than did ordinary persons. This heavier liability for punishment was certainly due to the feeling that those in high position had more of an obligation to obey the law than did their inferiors. We shall see this concept reflected again in the section on the family.

The Inferior Classes (*chien-min* 賤民)

From the standpoint of the *Code*, the population of T'ang China consisted of three kinds of persons: those with privilege, the commoners, and the inferior classes.[49] These last are treated the most severely. With regard to crimes against the person, if they offended against those of higher status, their punishment would be heavier than that of other classes. If those of higher status offended against members of the inferior classes, their punishment would be reduced.

Three such groups are mentioned in the *Code*: personal retainers, bondsmen, and slaves.[50] The least disadvantaged of these mean persons were the personal retainers and the bondsmen. In general, offenses by commoners against personal retainers and bondsmen were punished one degree less than were offenses against another commoner. Conversely, offenses by personal retainers or bondsmen against commoners were punished one degree more heavily than had the offense been committed by another commoner.[51] The law was particularly severe with regard to offenses committed by personal retainers against their masters. Thus a plot to kill their master was punished by decapitation.[52] Even a plot against the life of one of their master's first-degree mourning relatives brought strangulation. However, male personal retainers were allowed to marry commoners as well as members of the bondsmen and slave classes.[53]

Lowest in status were the slaves, who could be owned both by private persons and the government. Offenses against them by commoners were generally punished two degrees less than were the offense against another commoner. And offenses by the slave classes were punished two degrees heavier than had the offender been a commoner. Moreover, if a

[49] On these groups, see Edwin Pulleyblank, "The Origins and Nature of Chattel Slavery in China"; Yi-t'ung Wang, "Slaves and Other Comparable Groups during the Northern and Southern Dynasties"; and Chung-i Yang, "Evolution of the Status of 'Dependants.'"

[50] It should be noted that there were more types of bondsmen during the T'ang dynasty than those mentioned in the *Code*, and that they differed from each other in types and times of services rendered to the government. However, there was no distinction made between them insofar as liability for punishment was concerned.

[51] Article 320.

[52] Article 254; Deloustal 417.

[53] Article 47.

slave struck a commoner so as to break a limb or put out an eye, the punishment was strangulation.[54] But if a master killed a slave who had committed some offense, without asking permission of the government, the penalty was only one hundred blows with the heavy stick, and if the slave had done nothing at all, the master's punishment was no more than one year of penal servitude.[55]

Furthermore, bondsmen and slaves were each required to marry persons of their own class.[56] If a slave took a commoner as his wife, the punishment was one and one-half years of penal servitude.[57] And if the slave's master then listed the woman on his household register as a slave, the master was exiled for life to 3,000 *li*. A general bondsman was punished somewhat less for marriage with a commoner, one hundred blows with the heavy stick, the same as for an official bondsman who married a female commoner.[58] But a commoner who took an official bondsman to wife was sentenced to one and one-half years of penal servitude.

However, most of the laws that placed the inferior classes at a disadvantage are concerned with crimes against the person. And Article 47 states that if the law covering an offense does not specifically provide for a heavier punishment where the offender is one of the inferior classes, the regular punishment is to be sentenced.

Thus the favorable treatment given to officials and nobles in the *Code* is balanced by the increased punishment meted out to the inferior classes. Indeed, the attitude expressed in the *Code* toward these mean persons is bluntly stated in the subcommentary of Article 92, which equates slaves with property and goods. That is, they are not the same as people.

Age, Sex, and Physical and Mental Disabilities

The generally heavy punishments prescribed in the *Code* for all but the privileged classes are somewhat mitigated by the lessened liability for punishment afforded the young, the aged, women, the maimed or crippled, and the mentally ill.

For persons seven years of age or less, even the death penalty was not applicable.[59] The same was true for those ninety years of age or more, though both of these groups were still subject to collective prosecution.

[54] Article 320.
[55] Article 321; Deloustal 489.
[56] Niida, *Statutes*, pp. 258–259.
[57] Article 191.
[58] Article 192.
[59] Article 30.

Persons ten years of age or less, or eighty years of age or more, were allowed the right of petition in cases of rebellion, sedition, or killing someone. If they committed robbery or wounded someone, they could redeem the punishment. Other offenses were not prosecuted. Those who were fifteen years of age or less, or seventy years of age or more could redeem all crimes punished by life exile or less, save the particularly serious ones.

The subcommentary to Article 30 states that the reasoning behind this lessened liability for punishment is that the young and the aged have less knowledge than do ordinary adults, and need to be loved and cherished. This argument is further developed in a clause in that article covering cases where such persons are ordered to commit a crime by someone else. In such circumstances they are not liable at all; rather the person who made them commit the crime is punished.

Neither could persons seventy years of age or more, or fifteen years of age or less, as well as the incapacitated (who are dealt with below) be tortured to obtain a confession if they were accused of an offense. Like the privileged classes discussed above, the evidence of at least three witnesses was needed to convict them.

Women were also generally punished less. Except for cases involving collective prosecution, they could not be exiled for life.[60] Rather they remained at home and were beaten a set number of blows according to the distance of the exile, as a substitute for that punishment. In addition, they did forced labor for three years, two more than the usual length of time. The age limits that would protect women from collective prosecution for rebellion or great sedition were also lower than for men: sixty years of age instead of eighty for men.[61]

In cases of collective prosecution, except for rebellion or sedition, sons fifteen years of age or less and wives could redeem their sentences by payment of copper.[62] Wives who were pregnant were also protected. If they had committed a capital crime, execution had to wait until a hundred days after the child was born.[63] The same period was applicable for administering blows with the light or heavy stick or for questioning in connection with an offense.[64] If the pregnant woman was executed before she had given birth, the magistrate would be punished by two years of penal servitude—one year if a full hundred days had not passed

[60] Article 28.

[61] Article 248; Deloustal 410.

[62] Article 251; Deloustal 411.

[63] Article 494; Deloustal 679. Except for crimes involving the ten abominations, women were not executed in public, following the statute referred to in note 35 above.

[64] Article 495.

since the woman gave birth. One hundred blows with the heavy stick was his punishment for beating her before she gave birth, lessened to ninety if a hundred days had not passed since the birth.

Physical and mental disabilities also acted to lessen liability for punishment. Three types of disabilities are mentioned in the *Code*. In ascending order of severity, they are the maimed, the disabled, and the incapacitated. The first of these groups includes persons who were blind in one eye, or deaf, or had tumors, or less serious malfunctions. The second category brings in somewhat more crippled persons—the dwarfed, the dumb, and those with deformed backs. And the last type is made up of the really helpless members of society, the totally blind and those deprived of the use of two limbs.[65]

The latter two categories, the disabled and the incapacitated, also include persons with mental disorders.[66] Unfortunately, the descriptions given of these two kinds of mental illness are in terms of too much *yin* or *yang*. No symptoms are given, and we do not know how the courts distinguished between persons who were merely feebleminded and those who were perhaps criminally insane.

But such a decision could make considerable difference in a person's liability for punishment. The disabled were classified with those seventy years of age or more, or fifteen years of age or less, but the incapacitated with persons eighty years or older, or ten years or younger.

The Family

The provisions of the *Code* that deal with intrafamily offenses are concerned with the preservation of family status according to a strict hierarchy of generation and age.[67] This is further reinforced by including what are regarded as the most important crimes against elders within the ten abominations.

The *Code* expresses generational differences in terms of the five mourning relationships. The closer the descent from any common male ancestor, the closer the mourning relationship of any two people. And the closer the mourning relationship, the more punishment for the junior offender and the less for a senior offender with regard to crimes against the person, such as hitting, wounding, or even cursing. Where offender and victim were of the same generation, any difference in age would decide the advantage. Few greater crimes were possible in T'ang

[65]Niida, *Statutes*, p. 228.

[66]A general discussion can be found in Bünger, "The Punishment of Lunatics and Negligents According to Classical Chinese Law."

[67]See the survey of this subject in Ch'ü, *Law and Society*, pp. 1-78.

China than for a son to strike his father, while a father who beat his son was not committing any crime at all.

This emphasis on status is also found within the bureaucratic structure, and even within the organization of Taoist and Buddhist monasteries. Within the bureaucracy, official position and rank take the place of generation and age in the family. Hitting someone is an example. This was usually punished by only forty blows with the light stick.[68] But if an official of the fifth rank hit an official of the third rank, the punishment would be sixty blows with the heavy stick.[69] Were the offender of the ninth rank, his punishment would be one year of penal servitude, and were he simply a clerk without any rank at all, the punishment would be two years of penal servitude.

In monasteries, the relationship of teachers to the ordinary priests and nuns was considered to be the second degree of mourning, while the teacher's relationship to his disciples was of the third degree of mourning.[70] The punishment for offenses against these superiors would be that for the same offense as if committed within the family.

In only a few cases was the privilege accorded older family members balanced by increased responsibility. If a family jointly committed a robbery, only the eldest in generation or age would be prosecuted.[71] But this person had to be a male. If the eldest person were a woman, then the responsibility devolved upon the eldest male. Other examples of the punishment falling upon the eldest male in a family could be quoted, but generally the privilege given to the seniors in the family group far outweighed any responsibility placed on them for family offenses.

Just as family relationship increased the ordinary penalties for crimes against the person, it reduced them for robbery. The closer the mourning relationship, the less the punishment. Ordinary robbery of goods worth five *p'i* of silk was punished by one year of penal servitude.[72] But robbery of the same value of goods from fifth or fourth-degree mourning relatives would be punished by one hundred blows with the heavy stick.[73] If the victim were of the third degree of mourning, the punishment would be only ninety blows with the heavy stick, and if of the second degree of mourning, only eighty blows with the heavy stick.

Sons and grandsons in the male line who took goods held in common with their seniors for their private use were not punished at all, unless

[68]Article 381; Deloustal 464.
[69]Article 317; Deloustal 472.
[70]Article 57.
[71]Article 42.
[72]Article 282.
[73]Article 287; Deloustal 438.

the value of the goods was at least ten *p'i* of silk. Even then the penalty was only ten blows with the light stick.[74] The same law was applicable to disciples in monasteries who held goods in common.[75]

Within the family, wives were at a disadvantage vis-à-vis their husbands. A husband who struck his wife or concubine was not punished. But a wife who struck her husband would be sentenced to one year of penal servitude.[76] And a concubine who struck her husband would be punished by one and one-half years of penal servitude; the additional half year reflects her lower status.

The intent of the *Code* is clearly to keep the family together. Sons and grandsons in the male line who divided the family property or set up separate households while their parents or paternal grandparents were still alive were punished by three years of penal servitude.[77] If her husband were sent into life exile, a wife had to follow him, even though she herself had committed no offense.[78] And certain intrafamily offenses did not have to be reported to the authorities; a wife's striking her husband is an example.

In addition, relatives within the third degree of mourning who had goods and property in common, as well as certain of their relatives, were allowed to conceal each others' crimes, except for those against the state.[79] If the offense became known to the authorities and they began a search for the criminal, should any of his third-degree mourning relatives warn him of this, they would not be prosecuted for aiding a criminal. Even fourth-degree mourning relatives who warned a criminal would have their punishment reduced three degrees below that usually given. Outside the family relationships, slaves and personal retainers could conceal their master's offenses.

On the opposite side, if one's parents or paternal grandparents had committed a crime other than rebellion, sedition, or treason, the penalty for accusing them to the court was strangulation.[80] In the case of second-degree mourning relatives, the punishment was two years of penal servitude, even if the accusation proved true.[81]

But seniors who accused junior fifth-degree mourning relatives to the court received only eighty blows with the heavy stick, and the punish-

[74]Article 162; Deloustal 291.
[75]Article 57.
[76]Article 326; Deloustal 480.
[77]Article 155.
[78]Article 24.
[79]Article 46.
[80]Article 345; Deloustal 503.
[81]Article 346.

ment was progressively reduced as the mourning relationship grew closer.[82]

The *Code* also attempted to insure that aged or incapacitated family members would be provided for. If sons or grandsons in the male line were deficient in support of their parents or paternal grandparents. the punishment was two years of penal servitude.[83] And in certain cases, punishment could even be delayed in order to insure that aged family members were cared for. If the parents or paternal grandparents of someone who had committed a capital offense were eighty years of age or more, or incapacitated, petition could be made to the throne to allow the criminal to support the family.[84] But this was not possible when the crime came under the ten abominations. In cases where the crime was punished by life exile, no petition was necessary; permission could be given by the Imperial Secretariat.

Should the only adult in a household have committed a crime punished by penal servitude, it was not necessary that any family member be eighty years of age or incapacitated. Blows with the heavy stick would be substituted for the sentence of penal servitude—one hundred twenty blows for one year and an additional twenty blows for each further half year.[85] Moreover, if the only other adult in the household died, reached old age, or became infirm, and a convict serving penal servitude thus became the sole adult remaining to his family, he would be beaten a prescribed number of blows to make up that part of his sentence that he had not yet served and be released so as to provide for his family.

Through these various provisions, then, the *Code* protected the superior position of seniors in the family and tried to insure that they would be supported during their lifetime. And by allowing family members to conceal each others' offenses (indeed, prohibiting juniors from accusing their seniors to the court in most cases), and by canceling or substituting punishments for the benefit of the family, the *Code* shows its concern to preserve the family.

Confession and Voluntary Surrender

Great efforts were made during the course of a trial to get the accused to confess his guilt to the charges pressed against him. But if an offender would make a confession of his crime before it came to the notice of the court, he might escape punishment altogether.[86]

[82]Article 347.
[83]Article 348; Deloustal 505.
[84]Article 26.
[85]Article 27.

For such a confession to gain a complete pardon of the crime, it was necessary that it be made before a written accusation of the crime had been submitted to the court. If the criminal confessed only upon learning that an accusation would be made, the punishment for his crime would be reduced only two degrees.

It was also necessary that the confession be true and complete. Otherwise, the criminal would still be prosecuted for whatever part of his offense had been concealed, or for whatever circumstances of the crime he had twisted in his confession. But even partial confession prevented a sentence of death. In the case of relatives who were allowed mutual concealment of each others' offenses, a confession to the court by any of these relatives was considered to be the same as if the criminal himself had confessed. Or where the offense would involve collective prosecution, if someone within the group that would be collectively prosecuted arrested the criminal and brought him to the court, this would also be treated as if the criminal himself had confessed.

However, confession of crimes against the person would not gain a pardon for the offense. If during a robbery someone had been wounded, the later confession by the robber could obtain a pardon only for the robbery. He would still be prosecuted for wounding his victim. The *Code* does not have a system of wergeld whereby crimes against the person could be canceled by money payment.

The last clause in Article 37 also makes it clear that the private, unauthorized practice of astronomy could not be pardoned by confession of that crime. The reason for this prohibition was doubtless fear that astronomers might predict the emperor's death or help rebels to make a new calendar.[87]

In cases of robbery or fraud, making a confession to the owner of the goods was considered the same as a confession to the court.[88] But it was necessary that the goods be returned. Even where the return of goods to the owner could not exempt the criminal from prosecution, as in the case of an official who took bribes and subverted the law, he would still get a reduction of three degrees of punishment from the sentence for his offense.

Closely linked with confession, insofar as reduction of punishment or

---

[86]A general discussion on the role of confession in Chinese law and the earliest translation of the relevant articles of the *Code* is given in George Kennedy, *Die Rolle des Geständnisses im chinesischen Gesetz*.

[87]See Joseph Needham, *Science and Civilization in China*, III, 193. He quotes an imperial edict of 840 to the effect that there should be no contact between astronomers and other civil servants.

[88]Article 39.

pardon for the criminal was concerned, was voluntary surrender. If a criminal who had taken flight to avoid punishment should then voluntarily surrender to the authorities, his punishment would be reduced two degrees below that of his original offense. Where several persons took flight together and those whose part in the original crime was less serious seized those whose offense was heavier and brought them to the court, the former would be exempted from punishment.[89] Where the crime was equally serious for all, if some of the criminals were able to seize one-half or more of their fellows, they would be pardoned. However, this was only applicable in cases where the punishment for the offense would be canceled by ordinary amnesty. That is, offenses punished by death or life exile, or disenrollment, could not be pardoned by voluntary surrender.

Sentencing and Review of Cases

When a magistrate pronounced sentence on a case, he had to cite some provision of the *Code*, the *Statutes*, the *Regulations*, or the *Ordinances*.[90] This could be done either directly or through analogy. But failure to cite any applicable provision was punished by thirty blows with the light stick.

It was also important that the correct punishment be sentenced for the crime. The *Code* forsees that magistrates may assign the wrong punishment to a criminal either deliberately or through error. In such cases the magistrate would be punished himself, depending upon the circumstances of his error and whether or not the punishment had already been administered.[91]

Furthermore, if the sentence were penal servitude or more, the magistrate had to inform both the criminal and his family members of it, and try to get the prisoner to accept his punishment.[92] Should the criminal not be willing to do so, the magistrate had to listen to his reasons for not accepting his punishment and examine them at another hearing. A magistrate who failed to do any of these things would be beaten fifty blows with the light stick if the sentence was life exile or less. If the sentence was the death penalty, he would be beaten one hundred blows with the heavy stick.

If two or more articles of the *Code* were applicable in a particular

[89]Article 38.

[90]Article 484; Deloustal 682. The *Statutes* did not carry punishment, but violation of a statute was punished by fifty blows with the light stick. In the case of a special ordinance, the punishment was reduced one degree. See Article 449.

[91]Article 487; Deloustal 685.

[92]Article 490.

case, the one carrying the heaviest punishment was always to be followed in sentencing.[93] However, it was also possible that between the time that the crime took place and the time of sentencing a special regulation might have been issued that amended the *Code* in regard to that particular offense. In such a case, if the regulation called for a lighter punishment, it was to be followed. But if the regulation increased the punishment, the law in force at the time the offense was committed was to be applied.[94]

The articles in the *Code* dealing with the offenses covered are extremely specific. Much attention is given to the circumstances under which an offense took place, the relative official, family, or social positions of offender and victim in crimes against the person, as well as to the injuries done to the victim, or to the amount of goods taken in crimes of theft or fraud.[95] As a result, the compilers of the *Code* foresaw that a great many situations could arise that were not covered by any specific article. In such cases two means were available to a magistrate to allow him to deal with the offense: a catch-all clause and analogy.

The catch-all clause is Article 450, appropriately entitled "Doing What Ought Not To Be Done." The subcommentary to that article states that there are any number of small offenses that cannot be connected by analogy with any specific provision of the *Code*. But by use of this article the magistrate could punish the wrongdoers and to this extent he was able to act on his own initiative. However, the amount of punishment that the magistrate could inflict under this article was severely limited. If the offense were less serious, the penalty was forty blows with the light stick; if more serious, eighty blows with the heavy stick. No other punishments were permitted under this article.

Analogy

Where more flexibility was needed, analogy[96] could be used. Article 50 provides a method whereby analogy could be made between offenses not covered by the *Code* and those that were. The technique for doing so is called "bringing up a lighter offense in order to make clear a heavier punishment," or alternatively "bringing up a heavier offense in order to make clear a lighter punishment." Which of these two means were used depended on how the magistrate viewed the case, and how heavy a sentence he felt would be appropriate.

[93] Article 49.

[94] Niida, *Statutes*, p. 776.

[95] See Bodde and Morris, *Law in Imperial China*, pp. 30–32.

[96] Niida, *Criminal Law*, pp. 265–292, gives a general view of analogy from T'ang through Ch'ing times.

The examples given in the subcommentary to Article 50 will help to make these techniques of analogy clear. As we have seen, the *Code* provides heavier punishment for crimes committed against senior family members by the juniors than for the same crime committed against a person of non-kin status. Thus a plot to kill a second-degree mourning relative is punished by decapitation, while the same plot against a person of non-kin status carries a sentence of only three years of penal servitude.[97] A hypothetical case is put where such a second-degree mourning relative is killed or wounded. These two possible offenses are not covered by the *Code*. The subcommentary states that the analogous article is that providing decapitation for a plot to kill a relative of the second degree of mourning. It then goes on to state that a plot to kill is less serious than actually killing or wounding. Therefore since the punishment for merely plotting to kill is decapitation, it is clear that actually killing or wounding a relative of the second degree of mourning should also be punished by decapitation.

On the other hand, should the magistrate want to sentence a lighter punishment, he would "bring up a heavier offense in order to make clear a lighter punishment." Here the hypothetical case is one where someone has cheated a relative of the fifth degree of mourning, again an offense not covered by the *Code*. However, the *Code* provides that the punishment for stealing goods from a fifth-degree mourning relative be reduced one degree below that for the same offense committed against a person of non-kin status. Hence, by analogy, the crime of cheating a relative of the fifth degree of mourning should also have the punishment reduced one degree below that for the same crime committed against a person of non-kin status.

But whether a case was decided by direct citation of an article or by analogy, the only sentence that a magistrate could carry out without review was beating. All others had to be sent up for review by higher authorities. Sentences of penal servitude had to be approved at the prefectural level, and those of life exile had to be passed on by the Board of Punishments. Death sentences had to be memorialized to the throne, five times if the case were in the capital jurisdiction, three times if in the provinces.[98] Even death sentences for crimes involving the ten abominations had to be brought to the emperor's attention once before the execution could be carried out.

[97]Article 253; Deloustal 415; also Article 256; Deloustal 414.

[98]Niida, *Statutes*, p. 761.

CHAPTER III

The Text of *The T'ang Code*

History of the Text of *The T'ang Code*

The original name for *The T'ang Code* seems to have been the ***Lü-shu*** 律疏, "The Code and the Subcommentary." This is how it is referred to in the bibliographical chapters of the *Old T'ang History* (*Chiu T'ang shu*) and the *Sung History* (*Sung shih*). The present name for the *Code* appears for the first time in the *Yüan History* (*Yüan shih*).

The T'ang Code was based on a code of the Sui dynasty K'ai-huang period (581–600), which was promulgated in 581 and revised in 583 by order of Emperor Wen (reigned 589–604).[1] This code was later replaced by that of the Ta-yeh period (605–616), issued in 607. However, when the T'ang had overthrown the Sui and the Kao-tsu Emperor (reigned 619–626) came to the throne, the 607 code was revoked. In 617 Kao-tsu entered the Han-ku Pass, and thereby gained control of the capital. He then issued a code in twelve articles, which eliminated the death penalty for all crimes except murder, robbery, desertion from the army, and high treason.

In the first year of his reign, Kao-tsu ordered Liu Wen-ching to head a commission for the purpose of revising the code issued during the Sui K'ai-huang period. The resulting code of 53 articles was promulgated in the same year, and a much expanded version containing 500 articles in 624. However, present editions of the *Code* all have 502 articles. I suspect that the number 500 was simply used as a round number, but it is certainly possible that two articles were added later.

In 637, about midway in the great era of administrative reform known as the Cheng-kuan period (627–649), which embraced the reign of the T'ai-tsung Emperor, the well-known scholar Fang Hsüan-ling headed a commission on revision. It is credited with lessening the punishment for ninety-two crimes that had carried the death penalty, and another seventy-one that had been punished by life exile.

During the following Yung-hui period (650–655), there were two further revisions of the *Code*. The first took place in 651, and the second in 653. Ch'ang-sun Wu-chi headed the commission that added the authoritative subcommentary to the edition of 653. This edition of *The T'ang Code* promulgated in 653 is the most celebrated version of the *Code*.

[1]The material presented here on legislation during the Sui and T'ang dynasties is based on the work of Balazs, *Traité juridique*, and Bünger, *Quellen*.

Until the twentieth century, it was assumed that all the extant editions of the *Code* were based on the 653 edition. But in 1931 Makino Tatsumi and Niida Noboru undertook to try to date the *Code* through internal evidence. By comparing the official titles, names of institutions, names of the imperial seals, and so on, in the text with the changes that we know took place in such names during the T'ang dynasty, they were able to demonstrate that all present editions are based on the edition of 737, and not that of 653.[2] We have no evidence, however, that any substantial changes took place in the content of the *Code* between the 653 and 737 versions of it.

No edition of the *Code* printed during the T'ang dynasty is presently extant. Fragments, however, have been found in the substantial manuscript discoveries made in Central Asia during the first part of this century. Some articles differ from those in the *Code* as we have it today, but since the 737 *Code* is complete, I have decided to translate it first. I hope to cover articles from other editions in a separate publication.

The earliest extant edition of the *Code* has been thought to be a Sung manuscript preserved in the nineteenth-century collection of P'an Tsu-yin (1839–1890), known as the P'ang-hsi Chai. This manuscript is the one supposedly reproduced in the Ssu-pu ts'ung-k'an edition published in 1935 by the Commercial Press. All other modern editions, however, derive from Yüan editions based on that of 1332, which contains a preface by Liu Kuan (1270–1342). It was this edition which was included in the eighteenth-century imperial Ssu-k'u ch'üan-shu collection.

Naitō Kenkichi has recently shown that at least one passage in the P'ang-hsi Chai edition is a quote from a Yüan text, and that several substitute characters are used for the tabooed names of Chin dynasty (Jurchen) emperors.[3] Furthermore, the two variorum volumes of the text of the *Code* recently published show different readings for a number of characters between the P'ang-hsi Chai edition and the Ssu-pu ts'ung-k'an edition.[4] Thus it seems that the supposed Sung edition is, in fact, a Yüan edition. Other questions about the relationship between the Ssu-pu ts'ung-k'an edition and the P'ang-hsi Chai edition will most likely remain unresolved until someone can examine the P'ang-hsi Chai edition now in Peking.

[2]Makino Tatsumi and Niida Noboru, "Ko Tōritsusogi seisaku nendai kō" (On the Compilation of the *Ku T'ang-lü shu-yi*, the Official Commentary on the Criminal Code of the T'ang Dynasty).

[3]Naitō Kenkichi, "Bōkisaibon tōritsusogi no kankō nendai" (On the Date of the Edition of *The T'ang Code* in the P'ang-shi Chai).

[4]*Tōritsusogi kokanhyō* (A Variorum to *The T'ang Code*), and *Tōritsusogi kokanhyōho i* (A Supplement to a Variorum to *The T'ang Code*).

After the T'ang period, numerous commentaries were written on the *Code*. As far as I am able to discover, only four of these have survived, and only one is significant. The earliest is the *Lü-yin yi* 律音義 (Rhymes of the Code), by Sun She (962–1033),[5] which is almost entirely concerned with pronunciation, and which I have found of little use in explaining difficult sections. The next two are both by Wang Yüan-liang.[6] One, the *Chuan li* 纂例 (Codification of Standards [for Applying Punishments]), consists of tables on the punishments. The second, the *Shih-wen* 釋文 (Explanation of the Text), is a sometimes very useful commentary on quotations in the *Code* and on the history of certain terms. Last of the four commentaries is a *Shih-wen ting-cheng* 釋文訂正 (Revised Explanation of the Text) by one Shen Ping, on whom I am unable to find any other information. The unique copy is in the imperial collection in Tokyo.[7] It consists entirely of corrections of certain characters that occur in the *Shih-wen*. Through the researches of Niida, Asai Torao,[8] Takigawa Masajirō,[9] and most recently Riko Mitsuo,[10] we know that there were a great many other commentaries on the *Code*. None exist today except in fragmentary form.

Structure of *The T'ang Code*

The *Code* is divided into 12 books, 30 chapters (*chüan* 卷), and 502 articles. The first book is so large and the material that it contains so different from the other parts of the *Code* that I consider it to be a separate section. The other 11 books form the second section containing the specific articles (*pen-t'iao* 本條) on the offenses covered. The names of the books of the *Code*, with the chapters and articles within each chapter, are as follows:[11]

[5]This is included in the SPTK edition of the *Code*.

[6]Wang (fl. ca. 1300) has no biography in the official *Yüan History*. The *Pu Yüan shih yi-wen-chih* (Supplementary Bibliography of the *Yüan History*), 2/9a, states that he was a native of Kaifeng and held office in Kiangsi. As pointed out by Shen, *Bequeathed Writings*, II, 987, the *Shih-wen* was originally written for the *Sung hsing-t'ung* (*The Sung Code*) of 963, and not for *The T'ang Code*.

[7]Here I should like to express my thanks to Miss Naomi Fukuda, who was kind enough to help me obtain a microfilm of this work.

[8]Asai Torao, *Shina ni okeru hōten hensan no enkaku* (Development of Legal Codification in China), p. 171.

[9]Takigawa Masajirō, "Ryō-no-shūge ni mieru tō no hōritsu shiryō" (T'ang Legal Material in the *Ryō-no-shūge*), pp. 95–127.

[10]Riko Mitsuo, "Waga kuni ni hakusai sareta tōritsu no chūshakusho to sono itsubun" (Lost Commentaries on *The T'ang Code* in Japanese Legal Writings).

[11]The names of the 502 articles contained in the Specific Articles section of the *Code* are given in Appendix A.

1. General Principles (*ming-li* 名例)—I/1-7, II/8-18, III/19-28, IV/29-36, V/37-44, VI/45-57.
2. The Imperial Guard and Prohibitions (*wei-chin* 衛禁)—VII/58-75, VIII/76-90.
3. Administrative Regulations (*chih-chih* 職制)—IX/91-113, X/114-132, XI/133-149.
4. The Household and Marriage (*hu-hun* 戶婚)—XII/150-163, XIII/164-181, XIV/182-195.
5. The Public Stables and Granaries (*chiu-k'u* 廄庫)—XV/196-223.
6. Unauthorized Levies (*shan-hsing* 擅興)—XVI/224-247.
7. Violence and Robbery (*tsei-tao* 賊盜)—XVII/248-260, XVIII/261-269, XIX/270-286, XX/287-301.
8. Assaults and Accusations (*tou-sung* 鬬訟)—XXI/302-316, XXII/317-332, XXIII/333-345, XXIV/346-361.
9. Fraud and Counterfeit (*cha-wei* 詐僞)—XXV/362-388.
10. Miscellaneous Articles (*tsa-lü* 雜律)—XXVI/389-422, XXVII/423-450.
11. Arrest and Flight (*pu-wang* 捕亡)—XXVIII/451-468.
12. Judgment and Prison (*tuan-yü* 斷獄)—XXIX/469-482, XXX/483-502.

A more literal translation of the term *ming-li*, which I have translated as General Principles, would be "Names [of the Punishments] and Standards [for their Application]." The following definition is given in chapter 1, page 9b of the text: "*Ming* means the names of the five punishments; *li* refers to the structural standards (*t'i-li* 體例) for their application."

The original meaning of *li*, according to *Shuo-wen*, p. 2603, is to compare (*pi* 比). From this original meaning it came to be a standard of comparison. The earliest reference to the term *ming-li* is in the "Legal Treatise" chapter of *The History of the Chin Dynasty* (*Chin shu*).[12] This passage states that the *ming-li* of a statute cannot be clearly understood from the formal text of the law. There follow several examples that list exceptions to various laws because of age or social position. Then a second statement that, according to the seriousness of the crime, in looking for an applicable law, one uses standards (*li*) in order to find the name (*ming*) of the proper punishment. This fits in very well with the contents of the General Principles section of the *Code*, which begins by listing the various punishments and then goes on to describe the circumstances under which they are to be applied.

In the pre-T'ang codes, various terms were used to designate this in-

[12]*Chin shu* 30/10a.

troductory section. Both in the code attributed to Li K'uei and in the Han code, the section was called "generalities" (*chü* 具). Later it was sometimes divided into two sections, one entitled "names of the punishments" (*hsing-ming* 刑名), and a second called "standards for the laws" (*fa-li* 法例). It was only with the Northern Ch'i code of 564 that these two sections were combined once more, and the telescoped title *ming-li* was given to the resulting single section.[13]

Each individual article of the *Code* has several parts. In addition to the text of the article, which always begins with *chu* 諸 "in all cases," there may also be a commentary (*chu* 註), a subcommentary (*shu-yi* 疏議), and one or more queries and replies (*wen ta* 問答).

The commentaries are usually quite short and are more appendices to the articles than explanations of them. Quite often, essential information is found in the commentary rather than in the article itself. Examples of this are the amounts of copper needed to redeem punishment, the categories of persons included within the eight deliberations, and the specific offenses that come under the ten abominations. Thus it seems probable that the commentary was an integral part of the Sui code rather than an addition made during the T'ang dynasty.

On the other hand, the one or more subcommentaries are often quite lengthy. They, rather than the commentary, serve to explain the meaning of the article. This is done by giving definitions of key terms and phrases, quotes from the classics or other legal material, and references to other relevant articles within the *Code* itself. In many articles, queries and replies serve to give further information on doubtful points, or even to set hypothetical cases not foreseen in the articles of the *Code*. (Where the subcommentary is merely a repetition of material already adequately explained, it has been omitted from the translation. Such omissions are always indicated by ellipses.)

With all of the supplementary apparatus included, reading this translation of the *Code* is not always easy. But it would not have been sufficient to simply translate the text of the articles themselves, while leaving out the commentaries, subcommentaries, and queries and replies. This would have deprived the unsuspecting reader of a great deal of necessary information, as well as of explanations without which the meaning and intent of the articles could not be properly understood.

Previous Studies on *The T'ang Code*

In addition to the work of the late Professor Niida Noboru, which has

[13]A convenient table showing not only the changes of name but also the varying location of this chapter in the pre-T'ang codes is given in Balazs, *Traité juridique*, p. 209.

already been mentioned, several other scholars' research on the *Code* has helped me in making this translation.

Professor Shiga Shuzō of Tokyo University has published a translation into Japanese of the first thirty-six articles of the *Code*.[14] After first finishing my own translation, I carefully read through that of Professor Shiga, and have profited from his work in several better readings.

In Kyoto a group of scholars associated with the Institute of Humanistic Studies of the University of Kyoto has been working on a second Japanese translation of the *Code* for some years. This has not yet appeared, but their two variorum volumes listing the different readings given in the various recensions of the *Code* have been a great help to me.

In Taiwan, Professor Tai Yen-hui of the National Taiwan University has published two volumes on the *Code*, one on the General Principles section and a second dealing with the Specific Articles.[15] Because of his extensive cross-references to articles contained in the *Code*, as well as references to other, supplementary material, his work has been a great help to me. Professor Tai recognized that many articles of the *Code* can be usefully subdivided—thereby making the meaning clearer. I have followed his subdivisions in my own translation.

The earliest work on the *Code* in any Western language was done by Raymond Deloustal in the first quarter of this century. His translation into French of the Annamite Code of 1483 includes many of the articles of *The T'ang Code*, upon which the Annamite Code was based.[16] In 1935, Ou Kouei-hing published a book on the forms and administration of punishment during the T'ang period, which also has valuable information on the relative legal status of social classes.[17] In 1939, the late George Kennedy published a translation and discussion of the articles on confession.[18] Lastly, Dr. Karl Bünger's work on the sources of T'ang legal history appeared in 1946. It contains translations of the treatises on law and punishment from the two T'ang histories as well as from the *Essential Documents of the T'ang Dynasty (T'ang hui-yao)*. In addition, Dr. Bünger has brought many of the basic ideas of the *Code* to light through his articles on Chinese law.

[14]Shiga Shuzō, "Yakuchū tōritsusogi" (*The T'ang Code*, Translated and Annotated).

[15]In addition to his already mentioned volume on General Principles, Tai has also published a book on the Specific Articles section entitled *T'ang-lü ko-lun* (Specific Articles of *The T'ang Code*).

[16]Raymond Deloustal, "La Justice dans l'ancien Annam."

[17]Ou, *La Peine*.

[18]Kennedy, *Die Rolle des Geständnisses*.

[19]Bünger, *Quellen*.

Text Used in This Translation

This translation is based on the text of the *Code* included in Sun Hsing-yen's (1753–1818) Tai-nan-ko ts'ung-shu, which is the best modern edition. Sun based his edition on the Yüan Chih-cheng edition of 1351.

Some years ago, when I began my work on the *Code*, I determined that a concordance would be needed to compare occurrences of technical terms, make cross-references, and establish grammatical usage in the text. My concordance was based on the Kuo-hsüeh chi-pen ts'ung-shu edition, which at that time was the only commonly available edition of the *Code*, since neither the Tai-nan-ko ts'ung-shu nor the Ssu-pu ts'ung-k'an editions had then been reprinted.[20] In order to aid those who may use the concordance to find quotations or technical terminology, the translation also gives volume and page numbers to the Kuo-hsüeh chi-pen ts'ung-shu edition. There is no possibility of confusion, because the pagination for the Tai-nan-ko ts'ung-shu edition upon which the translation is based is always to chapter and then to the verso or recto of a page as indicated by "a" and "b." The pagination for the Kuo-hsüeh chi-pen ts'ung-shu is by volume and page in the Western fashion, so that "a" and "b" are not used.

Following the suggestion of Dr. Bünger, I have numbered the articles of the *Code* consecutively from 1 through 502. All cross-references to articles of the *Code* in my footnotes are made in this way. Through consulting the chart in the second section of this chapter, the reader can immediately establish where a particular article is to be found in whatever edition of the *Code* he may have available to him.

For those who cannot read classical Chinese, I have coupled the cross-references to the specific articles section of the *Code* with Deloustal's translation, if the article was contained in the Annamite Code. However, the reader should be warned that the Annamite Code seems to be a paraphrase rather than an exact reproduction of the articles of *The T'ang Code*. Furthermore, both the criminal behavior described in any particular article of *The T'ang Code* and the punishment given for it may differ in the corresponding article of the Annamite Code.

[20]Chuang Wei-ssu [Wallace Johnson], *T'ang-lü shu-yi yin-te* (A Concordance to *The T'ang Code*).

PART TWO

The T'ang Code: General Principles, Chapters I–VI

CHAPTER I

[1a; I.1] In the beginning,[1] the three powers[2] were established, and only then were the myriad forms divided. Among the creatures endowed with the ethers[3] and possessing consciousness, man may be considered the chief.[4] Never was a prime minister installed without the agreement of the masses, nor were penal laws promulgated except in accord with the moral teachings concerning government.

[1b] However, there were those whose passions were unrestrained and who acted stupidly, those whose knowledge declined and who offended criminally. [2a; 2] If great, then they disrupted the entire world, and if small, they violated the standards for their own group. Thus it would be unheard of not to establish controls for such persons. Hence the statement: "Punishments are used to stop punishments and killing is used to stop killing."[5] Punishments may not be discarded in a country; chastisements may not be dispensed within a home.[6] [2b] Depending upon whether the times are virtuous or unprincipled, the use of punishments is great or small.[7]

Thereupon the knotting of cords to record events was inaugurated and the overflowing channels of watercourses were dredged out.[8] [3] The light punishments of the early rulers were brightly awesome, their

[1]This introduction was not a part of the original Sui dynasty K'ai-huang code, but was written by Ch'ang-sun Wu-chi and added at the same time as the subcommentary.

[2]In this context the three powers represent heaven, earth, and man. *Yi ching*, "Hsi-tz'u," p. 175; Wilhelm, *The I Ching or Book of Changes*, pp. 351–352. "The tao of heaven is in it, the tao of earth is in it, and the tao of man is in it. It combines these three primal powers and doubles them."

[3]The two ethers are the *yin* 陰 and *yang* 陽. Wang Yüan-liang states that heaven, through the two ethers and the five elements, transformed and generated the ten thousand creatures, and that the ethers thereby formed concrete shapes.

[4]This is a paraphrase of a similar statement that occurs at the beginning of the "Treatise on Punishments" chapter of the *History of the Former Han Dynasty*. See *Han shu* 23/1a; Hulsewé, *Han Law*, I 32. The origin of this statement as shown by Hulsewé is in the *Shu ching*, "T'ai shih"; Legge, *The Chinese Classics*, III, 283.

[5]*Shu ching*, "Ta Yü mo"; Legge, *The Chinese Classics*, III, 58. This quotation is not exact. When Legge's translations have been used, I have modernized his transcriptions of Chinese characters.

[6]This statement is based on *Han shu* 23/8b; Hulsewé, *Han Law*, I, 329, and *Lü-shih ch'un-ch'iu* 7/4a; Wilhelm, *Frühling und Herbst des Lü Bu We*, p. 83, both of which insist on the necessity of punishment.

[7]*Shu ching*, "Lü hsing"; Legge, *The Chinese Classics*, III, 607.

[8]Ch'ang-sun Wu-chi also mentions the quipu in his "Treatise on Punishment" chapter in the *Sui History*. See *Sui shu* 25/1b; Balazs, *Traité juridique*, p. 29.

great rules of propriety were exaltedly respectful.[9] [3a] The *Book of Changes* states: "In the heavens are suspended the heavenly bodies. . . . The sages imitated them."[10] They observed the thunder and lightning and so created awe-inspiring punishments;[11] they saw the autumn frost and so had stern executions.[12] They warned those who had not yet offended and so guarded against what had not yet occurred; they laid out the fetters used to bind criminals but maintained their widespread love. [3b] Thus the sage kings used these things only when there was no other recourse.

In antiquity, for the greatest punishment, armor and weapons were used, followed by axes. For the middle punishments, knife and saw were used, followed by auger and chisel. For the smallest punishments, the whip and stick were used.[13] Their origin is indeed ancient. Formerly, there were the white dragon and white cloud officials during the reigns of Fu Hsi and the Yellow Emperor, respectively, [4a; 4] there were the fire official of the west and the water official of the west during the years of Shen Nung and Kung Kung, respectively; the hawk official divined concerning the the visitors for Shao Hao; the administrator of metal held office under Chuan Hsü.[14] All of these held office under the Son of Heaven, and exercised supervision over the penal statutes. [4b] Under the influence of the Great Tao, the people played "hit the tile" and were without offenses.[15]

[5] Coming to the time of Yao and Shun, their influence was per-

[9]A similar phrase appears in *Han shu* 23/1b; Hulsewé, *Han Law*, I, 32/1.

[10]*Yi ching*, "Hsi-tz'u," p. 157; Wilhelm, *I Ching*, p. 320.

[11]*Yi ching*, "Shih-ho," p. 61; Wilhelm, *I Ching*, p. 87.

[12]The commentator here quotes an otherwise unknown apocrypha on the *Spring and Autumn Annals*, the *Ch'un ch'iu fu* 春秋符, "Frost is the sign of Punishment." Several of the apocrypha are quoted in the *Code*; unfortunately they exist only in fragments. See the general discussion on apocrypha in Tjoe Som Tjan, *Po Hu T'ung: The Comprehensive Discussions in the White Tiger Hall*, I, 100 ff., and Fung, *History of Chinese Philosophy*, II, 88–130.

[13]A similar phrase is found in *Han shu* 23/2a; Hulsewé, *Han Law*, I, 322, and *Sui shu* 25/1b; Balazs, *Traité juridique*, p. 29. See in particular Hulsewé's and Balazs' notes on these passages.

[14]This phrase repeats that found in *Sui shu* 25/1a; Balazs, *Traité juridique*, p. 29, quoting the *Tso chuan*, "Chao 17"; Legge, *The Chinese Classics*, V, 667. Dragons, clouds, and so on, represented the omens under which these emperors came to power, hence they were used in the titles of their officials. See Bernhard Karlgren. "Legends and Cults in Ancient China," pp. 218–219.

[15]Alfred Forke, *Lun Heng: Miscellaneous Essays of Wang Ch'ung*, II, 187, translates the phrase *chi-jang* 擊壤 as "beating the earth." However, I believe that the reference here is to a game that the people played, signifying their happy life at this time. Such a game is still played by children in north China today. See Martin C. Yang, *A Chinese Village: Taitou, Shantung Province*, p. 154.

vasive so that offenses were few. [5a] They discussed the punishments in order to fix the penalties and had pictures drawn illustrating them in order to shame the people.[16] The articles and sections of their laws, even though numerous, were simple and concise. However, that period was long ago and we cannot know those laws in detail. [5b] In the time of Yao and Shun, the officer who maintained order was called the *shih* 士. Kao Yao held this office.[17] The general outline of their laws has been preserved and is often in good part visible. This is what the *Treatise on Customs* speaks of when it states: "Kao Yao advised Shun in making the statutes."[18]

[6] A statute is similar to a measure or a model. [6a] The *Book of Changes* states: "Justice means restraining men from wrongdoing by regulation of goods and by rectification of judgments."[19] Therefore the lawmaker must measure the gravity of offenses; he institutes statutes in accordance with justice. The *Great Commentary on the Book of History* speaks of vast heaven's great statute.[20] The commentary explains: "We receive heaven's great law (*lü*)."[21] Thus law is the same as statute. Hence the use of the term statute.

Formerly the sages made treatises which we call classics. The words of the scholars who transmitted these treatises we call commentaries. Such are Tso Ch'iu-ming's and Tzu Hsia's commentaries on the *Spring and Autumn* and the *Book of Rites*, respectively.[22] Coming down to recent times, scholars have combined the classics with the commentaries and have explained them, [6b] calling these later commentaries *yi-shu* 義疏 "explaining the meaning." The character *shu* became established as a technical term for a subcommentary basically because it means to explain widely and deeply. Also, the *Broad Exposition* states: "*Shu* 'to explain' is *shih* 識 'to know.'"[23] It follows that in the writing of a book's *shu* consists the way of recording knowledge. [7] The *Historical Records* states: "What the former rulers considered to be right were written down as statutes. What the latter rulers considered to be right were explained as ordinances."[24] [7a] The *History of the Former Han Dynasty*

[16]This has reference to displaying pictures of the punishments on the palace gates on the first day of the new year, which is described in *Chou li*, "Ta-ssu-k'ou," p. 518; Biot, II, 314. This practice is also mentioned in Article 7.

[17]*Shu ching*, "Yao tien"; Legge, *The Chinese Classics*, III, 44.

[18]*Feng-su t'ung-yi*, p. 101.

[19]*Yi ching*, "Hsi tz'u," p. 166; Wilhelm, *I Ching*, p. 328.

[20]*Shang shu ta chuan* 3/3a.

[21]Ibid.

[22]Tso Ch'iu-ming is supposed to have been a contemporary of Confucius, and Tzu Hsia was one of Confucius' disciples.

[23]*Kuang ya*, p. 72.

states: "They scraped the writing tablets clean so that on them they could make *shu* 'explanations.'"[25] Therefore we call these subcommentaries *shu.*

Formerly the three kings were the first to use corporal punishments,[26] it being difficult to continue having criminals merely wear reddish-brown clothing.[27] With the increasing distance in time from the customs of the sovereigns, simplicity became scattered and sincerity was left behind.[28] Instead there came to be cutting of flesh and breaking of bones as punishments for criminals. [7b] The *Great Commentary on the Book of History* states: "The Hsia dynasty had 3,000 punishments."[29] The *Rites of Chou* states: "The minister of punishments had charge of the five punishments which covered 2,500 crimes."[30] [8] King Mu [1001–947 B.C.] of the Chou dynasty measured the age and accordingly instituted laws. The five punishments covered 3,000 crimes.

As the Chou dynasty declined, the punishments became heavier. The Warring States [403–221 B.C.] had differing systems of laws.[31] [8a] Marquis Wen of Wei [424–387 B.C.] studied under Li K'uei,[32] who brought together the writings on punishments of the various states and wrote the *Canon of Laws* in six chapters.[33] The first dealt with laws on robbery, the second with laws on violence, the third with laws on imprisonment, the fourth with laws on arrest, the fifth with miscellaneous laws, and the sixth with general laws. [8b] Shang Yang transmitted and expounded the *Canon of Laws*, changing laws to statutes.[34]

[9] The Han dynasty [206 B.C.–A.D. 9] chancellor Hsiao Ho added

---

[24]*Shih chi* 122/19a; Burton Watson, *Records of the Grand Historian of China*, II, 449. This is taken from a statement by Tu Chou, one of the so-called "harsh officials" of Han times. He goes on to state: "Anything that suits the present age is right. Why bother with the laws of former times."

[25]*Han shu* 92/14b.

[26]*Sui shu* 25/1b; Balazs, *Traité juridique*, pp. 29–30, identifies these three kings as Yao, Shun, and Yü.

[27]*Hsün-tzu chi-chieh*, "Cheng lun," p. 218; Homer H. Dubs, *The Works of Hsüntze*, p. 193.

[28]This last phrase seems Taoist in flavor. See *Tao te ching*, Chapter 18, Arthur Waley, *The Way and Its Power*, p. 178.

[29]*Shang shu ta chuan* 4/22b.

[30]*Chou li*, "Ssu hsing," p. 539; Biot, II, 354. The last part of this sentence is a paraphrase.

[31]A very good discussion of law in this early period is to be found in the introductory chapters of J. J. L. Duyvendak, tr., *The Book of Lord Shang*.

[32]*Li* 里, should be read *li* 李, following the KHCPTS ed.

[33]See the background section of introduction, Chapter I

[34]I do not understand the significance of this statement. See the discussion in Bodde and Morris, *Law in Imperial China*, pp. 11–15.

three chapters dealing with households, levies, and imperial stables to what Li K'uei had written. This was called the *Statutes in Nine Sections*.[35] The Wei dynasty [A.D. 220–264], basing itself on the Han statutes, made a code in eighteen chapters. It changed the Han chapter on general statutes to one on punishments and their names and put it first. [9a] The Chin dynasty [A.D. 265–313] ordered Chia Ch'ung and others to add to or take from the laws of Han and Wei. They made a law code in twenty chapters, dividing up the section on names of punishments and making a further section on rules of application.

The Sung [A.D. 420–479], Ch'i [A.D. 479–502], Liang [A.D. 502–556], and Latter Wei [A.D. 386–584] dynasties followed the Chin code without change. The Northern Ch'i dynasty [A.D. 550–589] combined the chapters on names of punishments and rules of application, and made from them a single chapter on names of punishment and rules of application. The Latter Chou dynasty [A.D. 557–589] again made a separate chapter on names of punishments. However, the Sui dynasty [A.D. 589–618] followed the Northern Ch'i and again made a chapter on names of punishments and rules of application. The T'ang dynasty [A.D. 619–906] followed Sui and did not change.[36]

[9b; 10] *Ming* "name" means the name of the five punishments. *Li* "application" refers to the structural standards for their application. *Ming* "name" is similar to *ming* "to name." *Li* "application" is similar to *pi* "to compare." *Ming* "naming" is done in the chapter on rules for application. Now names of punishments are established according to crimes, and offenses arise from crimes being committed. Naming the name corresponds to punishment and comparing applications to stating the case. Therefore, the chapter on names of punishments and rules of application is put first. *Ti* 第 "number" is similar to *chü* 居 "place" or *tz'u* 次 "series" and has the meaning of progression. One is the ether of the Supreme Ultimate, which embraces the three and makes them one.[37] As the *huang-chung* 黃鐘 pitchpipe is the one from which the many notes are born,[38] so the chapter on names of punishments and rules for application is at the head of the twelve chapters. Therefore, it is called the first chapter on names of punishments and rules for application.

[10a] The emperor of the Great T'ang Dynasty used the abilities of

[35] On this compilation, see *Han shu* 23/12a; Hulsewé, *Han Law*, I, 333.

[36] See also Balazs, *Traité juridique*, pp. 206 ff., concerning the relationships of these codes to each other, particularly since he also deals with the administrative works and gives tables of the punishments and the legal hierarchy.

[37] On this term, see Fung, *History of Chinese Philosophy*, II, passim.

[38] This was the longest of the pitchpipes, which interestingly enough were also called *lü* 律 . See Bodde, "The Chinese Cosmic Magic Known as Watching for the Ethers," pp. 14–35.

the sages of antiquity to consolidate his plans and his heroic reputation to continue the martial achievements of his ancestors. He showers the spring clouds of his kindness upon all assorted creatures, and he is slow to apply his "Autumn Office" to the people.[39]

[10b] The present statutes follow the pattern of the former sages, whose regulations have not been lost, but both great and small, have all been preserved. [11] Yet there are sharp differences in the way the judicial authorities carry out the law. The Supreme Court can pronounce the death penalty, the Board of Punishments can condemn to life exile, the prefect of a prefecture can sentence a term of penal servitude, a district magistrate can apply the punishment with the heavy stick. If there were no explanation of the law, there would be clashes and mistakes. The emperor cherished a constant law and pitied those who had been cast into the ditch.[40] [11a] Virtue and ritual are the basis of governmental teaching; punishment and chastisements are the instruments of governmental teaching.[41] Like night and day, the *yang* of spring and the *yin* of autumn, they are mutually dependent to bring completeness. Therefore, an edict was sent down to the cabinet ministers and letters were dispatched to eminent[42] officials [11b] which led to the making of a commentary on the laws. It greatly explained both the statutes and the articles, embracing afar the wonderful concepts of the ancient sovereigns and kings, and near at hand the surviving writings of Hsiao Ho and Chia Ch'ung. [12] The commentators "followed up the waves and searched out the source of the river; from the branches they investigated all the leaves."[43] They made clear and illustrated the emperor's wide and great mercy, regulated and completed the laws' conciseness and durability in the same way as the steelyard and balance distinguish light and heavy and the compass and the square distinguish round and square. [12a] They surpassed the [Han] law in three chapters harmonizing and making it a unity.

[39] *Yi ching*, "Ch'ien" and "Chung fu," pp. 10 and 133; Wilhelm, *I Ching*, pp. 4–5 and 236.

[40] This has reference to a story in the *Mencius* about Yi Yin, who was one of the advisors of the legendary emperor T'ang, the supposed founder of the Shang dynasty. Mencius says of Yi Yin that "He thought that among all the people of the kingdom, even the private men and women, if there were any who did not enjoy such benefits as Yao and Shun conferred, it was as if he himself pushed them into a ditch." Legge, *The Chinese Classics*, II, 364–365.

[41] *Li chi*, "Hsiang yin chiu yi"; Couvreur, *Li ki*, II, 664.

[42] *Mao* 旄 , should be read *mao* 髦 , following the KHCPTS edition.

[43] *Wen hsüan*, "Lü shih heng," p. 159.

Article 1

The Five Punishments with the Light Stick

ARTICLE: There are ten, twenty, thirty, [12b] forty, and fifty blows with the light stick (*ch'ih* 笞).[44]

COMMENTARY: Redemption by payment of copper (*shu* 贖) is respectively one, two, three, four, and five *chin*.[45]

SUBCOMMENTARY: *Ch'ih* "light stick" means *chi* 擊 "to beat," and is also glossed as meaning *ch'ih* 恥 "to shame."[46] It means that if a person commits a small offense the law must discipline him. Therefore beating is used to shame him.

During the Han dynasty [206 B.C.–A.D. 220] the light stick was made of bamboo. But at the present time it is made of *ch'u* 楚 wood.[47] Thus the *Book of History* states: "The stick is employed in teaching [persons to

[44]Ratchnevsky, *Un Code des Yuan*, p. 5, points out that this punishment of beating with the light stick was first used in the Han dynasty. It replaced mutilation following the edict of Emperor Wen in 167 B.C. in connection with the case of Shun-yü Yi, which is discussed in note 49 below. The light stick used during the T'ang dynasty was 3.5 *ch'ih* in length and 0.2 *ts'un* and 0.15 *ts'un* in diameter at the large and small ends, respectively. These measurements are given in Article 482, quoting the statute that is found in Niida, *Statutes*, p. 793.

[45]When a punishment could be redeemed by payment of copper because of the criminal's status or other reason, it still had to be paid within a certain length of time, depending on the amount of copper required. Article 493 states that thirty, forty, fifty, sixty, and eighty days will be allowed to pay the quantity of copper needed to redeem beating with the light stick, beating with the heavy stick, penal servitude, life exile, and the death penalty, respectively. If these time limits for payment were exceeded, the first day was punished by ten blows with the light stick, increased by ten blows for each further five days, with a maximum punishment of a hundred blows with the heavy stick. The statute setting these time limits, which is quoted in Article 493, is given in Niida, *Statutes*, p. 788.

The statute also states that if the time limit has been exceeded without a reason, the criminal will not be exempted from punishment even if there is an amnesty. However, this section is not quoted in the *Code*.

The copper paid as redemption usually went to the government. However, where someone had been wounded, or injured, or falsely accused, and the offender had the right to redeem his punishment, the copper was paid to the injured party. See Niida, *Statutes*, p. 792.

[46]This definition comes from the *Shuo-wen chieh-tzu ku-lin*, p. 1971, and its second part rests upon the homophones *ch'ih*, "light stick" and *ch'ih*, "to shame." This kind of definition occurs several times in the *Code*.

[47]*Ch'u* wood is defined in the *Chih-wu-hsüeh ta-tz'u-tien*, p. 1176, as *Vitex negundo*, which has no common rendering in English. See Bodde and Morris, *Law in Imperial China*, p. 80 note 4.

be moral].''[48] This is its meaning here.

In the thirteenth year of Emperor Wen [of the Han dynasty, 167 B.C.], T'i Jung, daughter of Shun-yü Yi, the Superintendant of Granaries, sent up a memorial requesting to be taken as a government slave in order to redeem her father's punishment. The emperor sympathized with [13]
her wish.[49] Thereupon the mutilating punishments were changed so that men condemned to tatooing would have their heads shaved, build walls or fortifications, and stand guard from early dawn. Women would pound rice. Those condemned to amputation of the nose would receive three hundred blows with the light stick.[50] There was not yet any distinction between the light and heavy stick.

The punishment of beating with the light stick is the lightest of punishments. During the changes of successive periods the severity of the punishments has varied. But all dynasties have looked toward a time when there would be no punishments.[51] There would be only righteousness, and punishments would be discarded.

The *Hsiao ching yüan shen ch'i* 孝經援神契 states: "The sages made the five punishments in imitation of the five elements."[52] The *Book of Rites* states: "The punishments (*hsing* 刑) constitute a single body (*hsing* 侀), complete. Once completed they may not be changed. Therefore the superior man exercises the utmost thought concerning them."[53] The *Hsiao ching kou ming chüeh* 孝經鉤命決 states: "The punishments constitute a single body. [The judge] matches the crime [to its punishment] showing that there is an end [to every criminal case]."[54] "All the kings agreed that a murderer should die and that whoever injures another should be punished."[55] The origin of this idea is ancient.

The light stick has five degrees, from ten to fifty blows. Therefore it

[48]*Shu ching*, "Shun tien"; Legge, *The Chinese Classics*, III, 38–39. Translation slightly modified.

[49]As a result of this case, which is found in *Han shu* 23/12b; Hulsewé, *Han Law*, I, 334, the stick was substituted for the punishment of mutilation for everyone. Previously, members of the nobility as well as commoners over seventy and under ten years of age had already been exempted from mutilation by a decree of Emperor Hui in 195 B.C., which is translated in Dubs, *History of the Former Han Dynasty*, I, 176–177.

[50]*Han shu* 23/13b; Hulsewé, *Han Law*, I, 335. In addition, those who had previously been condemned to amputation of the left foot were to be beaten five hundred blows instead.

[51]*Shu ching*, "Ta Yü mo"; Legge, *The Chinese Classics*, III, 59: "through punishment there may come to be no punishment."

[52]Tjan, *Po Hu T'ung*, I, 50 ff., discusses this apocryphal text of Han date on the *Book of Filial Piety*.

[53]*Li chi*, "Wang chih"; Couvreur, *Li ki*, I, 307.

[54]Also an apocryphal text on the *Book of Filial Piety*. See Tjan, *Po Hu T'ung*, I, 103.

[55]*Hsün-tzu*, "Cheng lun," p. 219; Dubs, *Works of Hsüntze*, p. 195.

is stated that the punishments with the light stick are five. The degrees of penal servitude and of beating with the heavy stick also conform to the same standard.

Article 2

The Five Punishments with the Heavy Stick

[13a] ARTICLE: There are sixty, seventy, eighty, ninety, and one hundred blows with the heavy stick (*chang* 杖).[56]

COMMENTARY: Redemption by payment of copper is, respectively, six, seven, eight, nine, and ten *chin*.

SUBCOMMENTARY: The *Analytical Dictionary of Characters* states: "*Chang* 'heavy stick' means *ch'ih* 持 'to grasp.'"[57] It is something that may be used to beat people.

The School Sayings of Confucius states that in Shun's serving of his father, if he were beaten with the small stick he would submit, but if with the large stick he would flee.[58] The *Discourses of the States* states: "Light punishments use the whip and the stick."[59] The *Book of History* states: "The whip is to be employed in magistrates' courts."[60] This latter punishment is like the present punishment with the heavy stick. Further, when Ch'ih Yu made the five oppressive punishments, the whip and the stick were also used.[61] Looking for their origin, we find it to be ancient.

The Han Emperor Ching [reigned 156–141 B.C.] stated that those beaten with the stick were often dead before the blows were finished. He had punishments of three hundred blows changed to two hundred and those of two hundred to one hundred.[62] Later dynasties followed

[56]*Sui shu* 25/4b; Balazs, *Traité juridique*, pp. 39, 210, states that blows with the heavy stick were one of the punishments provided in the Liang dynasty (502–556) code of 503. This is apparently the first time that blows with the heavy stick were used.

[57]*Shuo-wen chieh-tzu ku-lin*, p. 2574.

[58]*K'ung-tzu chia-yü*, p. 37. This is a paraphrase rather than a quotation.

[59]*Kuo-yü*, "Lu yü" (Taipei, 1950), p. 114.

[60]*Shu ching*, "Shun tien"; Legge, *The Chinese Classics*, III, 38. Translation slightly modified.

[61]The basis for this statement is Ying Shao's (fl. ca. A.D. 178) commentary on the *Shu ching*, "Lü hsing"; Legge, *The Chinese Classics*, IV, 590–591, under the passage that refers to Ch'ih Yu as a rebel, and accuses the Miao of inventing the oppressive punishments.

[62]*Han shu* 23/14b; Hulsewé, *Han Law*, I, 336–337. The Emperor Ching actually issued not one but two edicts reducing the number of blows inflicted. In 156 B.C., an edict lessened the number of blows from 500 to 300 and from 300 to 200. Then in 151 B.C., a second edict further reduced the number of blows from 300 to 200 and from 200 to 100.

with little change until, coming to the House of Sui[63] [A.D. 589–618] the heavy stick replaced the whip.[64] The law of the present day states that accumulated sentences of the light and heavy stick may not exceed two hundred blows.[65] Thus it conforms to the Han rule.

Article 3

The Five Punishments of Penal Servitude

ARTICLE: The five punishments of penal servitude (*t'u* 徒)[66] have a duration of one, one and one-half, two, two and one-half, and three years, respectively.

COMMENTARY: Redemption by payment of copper is, respectively, twenty, thirty, forty, fifty, and sixty *chin*.

SUBCOMMENTARY: *T'u* "penal servitude" means *nu* 奴 "slavery," for such slavery shames one. The *Rites of Chou* states: "The male slaves are put to the labor assigned to criminals." Again, [13b] ". . .put them to labor, keep them in jail, and teach them. . . . The highest category of criminals are released after three years, the middle category after two years, and the lowest category after one year."[67] These are the punishments of penal servitude which began in the Chou dynasty [1122?–221 B.C.]

The second edict is not given in *Han shu* 23, but rather in Emperor Ching's annals, for which see Dubs, *History of the Former Han Dynasty*, I, 325.

[63] *Sui* 隨 should be read *sui* 隋, following the KHCPTS edition.

[64] From the time that the heavy stick was first instituted in the Liang code of 503, it was used together with the whip. Then with the Sui code of 581 beating with the whip was dropped as a punishment.

[65] This limitation on blows is specified in Article 29.

[66] Following Ratchnevsky, *Un Code des Yuan*, pp. 6–7, and Ch'ü, *Local Government in China under the Ch'ing*, p. 205 note 33, I have translated the term *t'u* as penal servitude rather than temporary exile as given by Guy Boulais, *Manuel du code chinois*, p. 3. The sentence was not banishment, but rather to forced labor in a fixed place (*chü-tso* 居作). My translation of this term follows Balazs; see the discussion in *Traité juridique*, p. 118 note 103.

From the statute of penal servitude quoted in Article 492 and brought together in Niida, *Statutes*, p. 773, it can be seen that the punishment had changed little since Han times; see Hulsewé, *Han Law*, I, 128–132. It still involved standing watch, repairing city walls and government buildings, or working as a clerk. Women worked at weaving or pounding rice.

[67] *Chou li*, "Ssu li," p. 543; Biot, II, 363, 366.

[14] Article 4

The Three Punishments of Life Exile

ARTICLE: The three punishments of life exile (*liu* 流)[68] are, respectively, for distances of 2,000, 2,500, and 3,000 *li*.[69]

COMMENTARY: Redemption by payment of copper is respectively eighty, ninety, and one hundred *chin*.

SUBCOMMENTARY: The *Book of History* states: "[Shun enacted] life exile as a mitigation of the five [standard] punishments."[70] This means that Shun could not bear to inflict the death penalty, and so reduced it to life exile in a distant place.

It is also stated: "The five banishments have their places of detention, five in number, for which three localities are assigned."[71] The greatest criminals are sent to the four frontier areas or exiled beyond the seas. The next are exiled for life outside the Nine Territories[72] and the next outside the Central States.[73] Thus life exile began in the time of Yao and Shun and was the same in meaning as the present three punishments of life exile.

Article 5

The Two Death Penalties

ARTICLE: The two death penalties are strangulation (*chiao* 絞) and decapitation (*chan* 斬).[74]

[68]These three degrees of life exile each also carry one year of labor. However, another form of life exile described in Articles 11 and 24 and termed life exile with added labor carried three years of labor. But even the heaviest accumulation of sentences could not exceed four years of labor, the limit set by Article 29.

[69]These distances are approximately 700, 850, and 1,000 English miles.

[70]*Shu ching*, "Shun tien"; Legge, *The Chinese Classics*, III, 38. Translation slightly altered.

[71]*Shu ching*, "Shun tien", Legge, *The Chinese Classics*, III, 45. Translation slightly altered.

[72]*Chiu-chou* 九州 , "nine territories," is a metaphorical name for China found in the "Tribute of Yü" chapter of the *Book of History*; Legge, *The Chinese Classics*, III, 141.

[73]This reference to the Central States may indicate that these lesser criminals were exiled for life to the southern part of China. Certainly a great many political exiles were sent to the island of Hainan and other equally unhealthy places during the course of the dynasty. See Schafer, *The Vermillion Bird, T'ang Images of the South*, pp. 31–44.

[74]Decapitation was considered to be the more severe of the two death penalties be-

COMMENTARY: Redemption by payment of copper is 120 *chin*.

SUBCOMMENTARY: Anciently, the former wise kings imitated the models suspended in the heavens, using them to aid in government and to help transform the people, to check violence, and to prevent licentiousness.[75] This was rooted in a desire to benefit the people with the idea of a time when killing would cease.

A sentence of strangulation or decapitation is the most extreme of punishments. Upon death, "the vital force (*hun* 魂) returns to heaven whereas the corporeal force (*p'o* 魄) returns to earth."[76] They merge with the myriad transformations of the universe. Therefore Cheng's commentary on the *Book of Rites* states: "Death is exhaustion. To melt away and become used up constitutes such exhaustion."[77]

The *Ch'un ch'iu yüan ming pao* 春秋元命包 [14a] states: "The Yellow Emperor decapitated Ch'ih Yu in the wilderness of Cho-lu."[78] The *Book of Rites* states: "If one of the relatives of the prince commits a capital crime, the inspector of fields is charged with strangling him."[79] Thus we know that decapitation began in the time of the Yellow Emperor, and that strangulation began in the Chou dynasty.

The death penalties being two in number is in imitation of the numbers of the *yin* principle, which exercises jurisdiction over the death penalties. Accordingly it is taken as a model.[80]

---

cause it damaged the body. According to the tenets of filial piety, the body should be kept whole because it came from one's parents. It should be noted that in case of a reduction of sentence, decapitation was reduced to life exile to 3,000 *li*, and not to strangulation. Similarly, a reduction of sentence of any of the three distances of life exile was to three years of penal servitude. This is provided in Article 56.

As already discussed in Chapter II, all death sentences had to be memorialized to the emperor, five times if within the capital jurisdiction, three times if in the provinces. The only exceptions were cases that came within the ten abominations, where one memorial was sufficient. See Niida, *Statutes*, p. 761.

[75]This is a paraphrase of *Yi-ching*, "Hsi tz'u shang," p. 157; Wilhelm, *I Ching*, p. 320, which states: "In the heavens hang images. . . . The sages imitated them." The same phrase has also been quoted by Ch'ang-sun Wu-chi in his preliminary remarks. See p. 47 above.

[76]*Li chi*, "Chiao t'e sheng"; Couvreur, *Li ki*, I, 613. Translation slightly modified. The *hun* was the spiritual soul that left the body at death, while the *p'o*, or animal soul, remained with the body in the grave for three years. See *Tso chuan*, "Chao 7"; Legge, *The Chinese Classics*, V, 618.

[77]Cheng is, of course, the famous Han commentator Cheng Hsüan (A.D. 127–200). This quotation is a paraphrase of *Li chi*, "T'an kung," p. 126.

[78]This is also an apocryphal text dealing with the *Spring and Autumn Annals*. See Tjan, *Po Hu T'ung*, I, 32 ff.

[79]*Li chi*, "Wen wang shih tzu"; Couvreur, *Li ki*, I, 484. This quotation is not exact.

QUERY: The punishments from beating with the light stick to the death penalties all have rules on redemption by payment of copper. But it remains unknown in which period the redemption of punishment by payment of copper began.

REPLY: The *Book of History* states: "Metal is received for redeemable crimes."[81] The commentary states: "In cases where crimes are committed through mistake the criminal may give metal in order to redeem the punishment."[82]

The Marquis of Fu,[83] in explaining the Hsia dynasty's rules for the redemption of punishment, stated: "When in a doubtful case the infliction of branding is forborne, the fine laid on instead must be one hundred *yuan* 鍰 [of copper]. . . . When the case has reference to the cutting off of the nose, the fine must be double this. . . . Where the penalty would be cutting off the feet, the fine must be double. . . . Where the penalty would be castration, the fine must be six hundred *yuan*. . . . Where the punishment would be death, the fine would be one thousand *yuan*."[84] The commentary states: "Six *liang* 兩 (ounces) are one *yuan*. *Yuan* means 'yellow iron.'"[85]

Under the code of the Chin dynasty [A.D. 265–316] those entitled to one of the eight deliberations and above could all retain their offices (*liu-kuan* 留官) and make redemption by payment of copper without having their heads shaven or being beaten. The present regulations on the amount of copper paid for redemption of punishment are different from those of antiquity. There are differentiated classifications, all covered by regulations; there is no need to give all the details.

Article 6

The Ten Abominations

[15] SUBCOMMENTARY: The ten abominations (*shih-o* 十惡) are the most

[80] *Yang* numbers are odd, *yin* numbers are even. See *Po-hu t'ung*, 9/1a; Tjan, *Po Hu T'ung*, I, 245. Since the *yin* is dark, cold, etc., it exercises jurisdiction over death.

[81] *Shu ching*, "Shun tien"; Legge, *The Chinese Classics*, III, 38. Translation slightly modified.

[82] The commentator here is K'ung An-kuo (2nd century B.C.).

[83] *Fu-hou* 甫候 is another name for the Marquis of Lü. See *Shu ching*, "Lü hsing"; Legge, *The Chinese Classics*, III, 588.

[84] *Shu ching*, "Lü hsing"; Legge, *The Chinese Classics*, III, 605. Translation slightly modified.

[85] This definition of copper in terms of iron by K'ung An-kuo is a curious anachronism, since copper was known in China long before iron.

serious of those offenses that come within the five punishments.[86] They injure morality and destroy ceremony.[87] They are specially placed near the head of this chapter [14b] in order to serve as a clear warning. The number of extreme abominations being classified as ten is the reason why they are called the ten abominations.

Although the Han regulations in nine sections[88] are no longer extant, the headings on *pu-tao* "depravity" and *pu-ching* "irreverence" are still in existence. Thus the origin of these seems to be in the Han dynasty. However, we find that previous to the Liang [A.D. 502–557] and Ch'en [A.D. 557–587] dynasties these sections were listed only sketchily. Even though the Northern Chou [A.D. 557–581] and the Northern Ch'i [A.D. 550–557] dynasties had all ten of them named, they still had no heading of the ten abominations.[89]

This clause was provided for the first time in the regulations instituted during the K'ai-huang period [A.D. 581–600]. The number of abominations was kept at ten in accordance with older statutes. During the Ta-yeh period [A.D. 605–616] excisions again were made so that of the ten sections only eight were retained. From the Wu-te period [A.D. 618–626] onward, however, the number has conformed to the K'ai-huang code without change.

ARTICLE: The first is called plotting rebellion (*mou-fan* 謀反).[90]

SUBCOMMENTARY: The *Kung-yang Commentary* states: "The ruler or parent has no harborers [of plots]. If he does have such harborers, he must put them to death."[91] This means that if there are those who harbor

[86]Elements of this article appeared as early as the Han dynasty. But they were not grouped under a single heading as here. See Hulsewé, *Han Law*, I, 156–204, which gives an exhaustive treatment of the sources. From Hulsewé's evidence, the use of *pu-tao* 不道 and *ta pu-ching* 大不敬 to distinguish certain types of particularly heinous crimes did not begin until the reign of Emperor Wu (140–87 B.C.), and had not been codified as late as 15 B.C.

Ratchnevsky, *Un Code des Yuan*, p. 13, points out that the *K'ung-tzu chia-yü*, "Wu hsing," p. 71, is the earliest source for the classification of such offenses. However, it puts only five crimes in this category.

[87]The translation of *ming-chiao* 名教 as morality follows Balazs, *Traité juridique*, p. 127 note 134.

[88]See note 35 above.

[89]See Balazs, *Traité juridique*, pp. 142–145 note 184.

[90]The ten sections of this article have been translated by Ou, *La Peine*, pp. 99–102; Ratchnevsky, *Un Code des Yuan*, pp. 13–16; Balazs, *Traité juridique*, p. 142 note 184; and Deloustal 2. See my discussion of the ten abominations in the third part of Chapter II of the introduction.

[91]*Kung-yang chuan*, "Chuang 32," p. 112.

rebellious hearts which would harm the ruler or father, he must then put them to death. The *Tso Commentary* states: "When the seasons of heaven are reversed, we have calamities, . . . when the virtues of men are reversed, we have disorders."[92]

The king occupies the most honorable position and receives heaven's precious decrees.[93] Like heaven and earth,[94] he acts to shelter and support, thus serving as the father and mother of the masses. As his children, as his subjects, they must be loyal and filial. However, should they dare to cherish wickedness and have rebellious hearts, they will run counter to heaven's constancy and violate human principle. Therefore this is called plotting rebellion.

COMMENTARY: Plotting rebellion means to plot to endanger the Altars of Soil and Grain (*she chi* 社稷, that is, the ruler and the state which he rules).

[15a] SUBCOMMENTARY: *She* is the spirit of the five colors of soil.[95] *Chi* is the regulator of the fields, which uses the spirits' earthly virtue to control the harvest.[96] The ruler is the lord of these spirits of agriculture. The food which they ensure is as heaven to the people. When their lord is in peace, these spirits are at rest. When the spirits are in repose, the seasons give a plentiful harvest.

However, ministers and subjects may plot and scheme to rebel against morality and have minds which would discard their ruler. If the ruler's position is endangered, what will the spirits rely upon? Not daring to make direct allusion to the honored name of the ruler, we therefore use the phrase, "Altars of Soil and Grain" to designate him. The *Rites of Chou* states: "On the left the Temple of the Ancestors, on the right the Altar of the Soil."[97] These are what the ruler honors.

ARTICLE: The second is called plotting great sedition (*mou ta-ni* 謀大逆).[98]

[92]*Tso chuan*, "Hsüan 16"; Legge, *The Chinese Classics*, v, 328.

[93]The Tai-nan-ko edition here leaves a blank where the Chih-cheng edition has *ta* 大.

[94]A paraphrase of *Li chi*, "Chung yung"; Couvreur, *Li ki*, II, 475.

[95]Soil of five colors was used to make the Altar of the Soil, corresponding to the five elements. See Edouard Chavannes, *Le T'ai Chan*, p. 452.

[96]My translation is questionable. The text seems to be a garbled version of *Li chi*, "Chiao t'e sheng"; Couvreur, *Li ki*, I, 587.

[97]*Chou li*, "Chiang jen," p. 643; Biot, II, 556. The same idea is expressed in *Li chi*, "Chi yi"; Couvreur, *Li ki*, II, 316.

[98]If great sedition was actually committed, the penalty was the same as for plotting rebellion: everyone was decapitated. However, if there was only a plot to commit great

SUBCOMMENTARY: This type of person breaks laws and destroys order, is against morality, and goes contrary to virtue. There can be no greater sedition. Therefore it is called great sedition.

COMMENTARY: Plotting great sedition means to plot to destroy the ancestral temples, tombs, or palaces of the reigning house.

SUBCOMMENTARY: There are persons who "offend against heaven,"[99] "who do not know where to stop,"[100] and who secretly think of letting loose their hatred. Planning recklessness, they conceive evil thoughts and plot destruction of the ancestral temples, tombs, or palaces of the reigning house.

Tsung 宗 "ancestral" means *tsun* 尊 "to respect." *Miao* 廟 "temple" [16] refers to *mao* 貌 "to delineate the ancestors." Wood is carved into ancestral tablets so as to respect the ancestors' image and honor their likeness. These tablets are placed in a palace chamber wherein they are sacrificed to seasonally. Therefore it is called the ancestral temple.

As to tombs, the former kings of antiquity were buried in mountains. The Yellow Emperor's being buried in Mount Ch'iao is an example.[101] It is also stated that the emperor's tomb is like a mountain or a tumulus. Therefore there is reference here to mountains and tumuli. In regard to palaces, in heaven there is the *Tzu-wei* 紫微 Palace.[102] The ruler of mankind models himself on this in the place where he lives. Therefore it is called a palace.

[15b] As to towers, the chapter on "Explaining Palaces" in the *Literary Expositor* states: "To observe (*kuan* 觀) has reference to towers (*chüeh* 闕)."[103] Kuo P'o[104] states that the palace gates have two towers.[105] The "Autumn Office" chapter of the *Rites of Chou* states that on the first

---

sedition and no act was yet underway, the principals would be strangled instead of being decapitated, and the accessories exiled for life to 3,000 *li*. See Article 248; Deloustal 410. On principals and accessories see Article 42.

[99]*Lun yü*, III, 13; Legge, *The Chinese Classics*, I, 159. "He who offends against Heaven has none to whom he can pray."

[100]*Tso chuan*, "Wan 18"; Legge, *The Chinese Classics*, V, 283.

[101]*Shih chi* 1/7b; Chavannes, *Les Mémoires historiques de Se-ma Ts'ien*, I, 36.

[102]This "Purple Palace" is mentioned in *Shih chi* 27/1b. See the discussion in Chavannes, *Mémoires historiques*, III, 340, where it is identified as the north star.

[103]*Erh-ya*, p. 74. This is a play on the meanings of the character *kuan*, which can mean both to observe and a structure from which observations of the stars could be made. Hence the definition here.

[104]Kuo P'o (A.D. 276–324) was a well-known scholar who wrote commentaries on the *Erh-ya* and other ancient works. His style of composition was much admired, and he also supposedly invented geomancy, the "science" of finding the best site for a grave.

[105]*Erh-ya*, p. 74.

day of the first month, illustrations of the punishments are suspended on the palace doors and the people are ordered to observe them.[106] Therefore there is reference to *kuan* "to observe."

ARTICLE: The third is called plotting treason (*mou-p'an* 謀叛).[107]

COMMENTARY: Plotting treason means to plot to betray the country or to serve rebels.

SUBCOMMENTARY: There are persons who would betray the reigning house or go over to a foreign country, or who would betray a city and serve rebels, or who would want to flee the country. "Mou-yi of Chü came as a fugitive [to Lu] giving over to it [the city of] Mou-lou,"[108] or "Kung-shan Fu-jao was holding Pi in rebellion,"[109] exemplify such kinds of treason.

ARTICLE: The fourth is called contumacy (*o-ni* 惡逆).[110]

SUBCOMMENTARY: The kindness of father and mother is like "great heaven, illimitable."[111] "Entering into the inheritance of our ancestors,"[112] we may not be frivolous. Let one's heart be like the *hsiao* 梟 bird or the *ching* 獍 beast,[113] and then love and respect both cease.

[106]*Chou-li*, "Ta-ssu-k'ou," p. 518. This is a paraphrase rather than a quotation.

[107]This offense is covered in Article 251; Deloustal 411. The punishment was the same as for plotting great sedition: decapitation if the act had already begun and strangulation if it had not. If treason was already underway, no distinction would be made between principals and accessories. However, unlike plotting rebellion—where a plot that was not yet underway still brought decapitation to all the plotters and involved the relatives in collective prosecution—if no act of treason or great sedition was underway, the families of the plotters were not collectively prosecuted. Moreover, only the principals in the plot would be decapitated; the accessories to the plot would be exiled for life to 3,000 *li*.

[108]*Tso chuan*, "Chao 5"; Legge, *The Chinese Classics*, v, 603.

[109]*Lun yü*, xvii, 5; Legge, *The Chinese Classics*, i, 319. Translation slightly altered.

[110]See the discussion in the fifth part of Chapter II of the introduction. In general, junior members of the family who committed a crime against the person of a senior member were punished more heavily than if the same crime were committed against a person of non-kin status. However, the opposite was true of crimes involving goods. See Article 287; Deloustal 438, and Article 162; Deloustal 291.

[111]*Shih ching* 202; Legge, *The Chinese Classics*, iv, 352.

[112]*Shih ching* 189; Legge, *The Chinese Classics*, iv, 303. Translation slightly altered.

[113]*Shuo-wen chieh-tzu*, p. 2645, describes the *hsiao* as an unfilial bird that eats its mother, coupling it with the *ching*, an unfilial beast that eats its father. *Wei shu* 59/28b, speaks of "turning one's back on mercy and forgetting righteousness, having a heart like the *hsiao* bird and the *ching* beast."

Those whose relationship is within the five degrees of mourning are of the closest kin. For them to kill each other is the extreme abomination and the utmost in rebellion, destroying and casting aside human principles. Therefore this is called contumacy.

COMMENTARY: Contumacy means to beat[114] or plot to kill[115] (without actually killing) one's paternal grandparents or parents; or to kill one's paternal uncles or their wives, or one's elder brothers or sisters, or one's maternal grandparents, or one's husband, or one's husband's paternal grandparents, or his parents.

SUBCOMMENTARY: Beat (*ou* 毆) means to beat or strike. Plot (*mou*) means to form a plan. When the relationship is that of paternal uncle through to husband's parents [on the list above], if the person has already been killed [the offense then comes under this section on contumacy]. But if there is only a plan to kill, [16a] which has not yet been carried out, the offense comes under the section on discord.[116]

Cases of contumacy are not exempted from punishment under ordinary amnesties (*ch'ang-she* 常赦) and sentences are not delayed. Cases of discord, however, are eligible for pardon under amnesties, and such criminals if officials are only disenrolled (*ch'u-ming* 除名).[117] This distinguishes the two, and therefore the rules established for the two categories of cases differ.

The husband's great- and great-great-grandparents in the male line are considered the same as his paternal great-grandparents. According to the mourning regulations, a wife wears fifth (*ssu-ma* 緦麻) degree of mourning for her husband's great- and great-great-grandparents in the male line. But if her husband is the eldest son of an eldest son whose father is dead, then the wife has the same period of mourning for her husband's grandparents, great-grandparents, and great-great-grandparents in the male line as for the husband's parents. Therefore we know that reference to the husband's grandparents, great-grandparents, and great-great-grandparents in the male line places them in the same category.

[114]Article 329; Deloustal 474 punishes the beating or cursing of paternal grandparents or parents by strangulation. The penalty lessens as the relationship becomes more distant.

[115]Article 253; Deloustal 415 ·ovides for decapitation for plotting to kill all the persons mentioned here.

[116]See the section of this article entitled "Discord," the eighth of the ten abominations.

[117]See the subsection on official privilege and responsibility under the third part of Chapter II for a discussion of levels of punishment for officials. Disenrollment is treated in detail under Article 21.

QUERY: As to the maternal grandparents and the husband, according to the *Book of Ceremonies and Rites*, the degrees of mourning for each of these are not the same but rather are differentiated.[118]

[17] REPLY: In regard to maternal grandparents, if they are those of the mother who has borne one, no matter whether one's mother has been divorced or not, they are still maternal grandparents and should be mourned as such. As to the cause of this, the article states: "The reason is not due to the mourning relationship being raised or lowered."[119] With regard to a mother who has not borne one,[120] if one mourns her parents, the degree of mourning is the same as for the maternal grandparents of one's own mother. If one does not mourn her, they are considered the same as persons of non-kin status (*fan-jen* 凡人).

According to the *Book of Rites*, the son of the legitimate wife may or may not act as his father's heir. But in neither case does he mourn for the clan of a divorced wife, but rather for the clan of his step-mother.[121] Yet in both of these clans he has maternal grandparents. If his own mother has died in the house [that is, has not been divorced], then the son mourns for the clan of his mother and not for the clan of his step-mother. The step-mother's clan has no mourning relationship for him and is considered the same as persons of non-kin status.

A concubine's son may or may not act as his father's heir. But if the legitimate wife is still alive, he mourns for her [16b] clan. If the legitimate wife is dead, he does not mourn her clan. The *Book of Rites* states: "When the person dies, then [the obligation to mourn for their clan] is ended."[122] The mourning relationship is dependent on the legitimate wife. Therefore when she dies it is ended.

As for husbands, according to the *Book of Rites*, "In the third month of marriage [the wife] is presented in the ancestral temple. . . [or it may happen that the wife] is not presented in the ancestral temple."[123] Or the

[118]This is a paraphrase of *Yi li*, "Sang-fu," p. 394.

[119]See Article 52.

[120]Traditional Chinese law recognized eight degrees of motherhood: principal or secondary wife of one's father, step-mother, mother by whom one was adopted, mother by whom one was cared for after death of actual mother, remarried mother, repudiated mother, and nursing mother. See Boulais, *Manuel du code chinois*, p. 17 note 2.

[121]*Li chi*, "Sang fu hsiao chi"; Couvreur, *Li ki*, I, 744.

[122]*Li chi*, "Sang fu hsiao chi"; Couvreur, *Li ki*, I, 748.

[123]*Li chi*, "Tseng tzu wen"; Couvreur, *Li ki*, I, 429. The meaning here is that for a marriage to become legally binding, the wife must have been presented in the ancestral temple of the husband's clan in the third month after the marriage ceremony had taken place. Should the husband die before the wife had been presented in the ancestral temple of his clan, however, she must still mourn his death. These are two of the three types of husband.

husband may go to the wife's house.[124] The rules for mourning these three types of husband are the same.

There are also those cases where the wedding date has been selected and where there has been an engagement. The wife's family may not break the contract and marry her to someone else.[125] Interfamily offenses other than these are considered the same as if between persons of non-kin status.

ARTICLE: The fifth is called depravity (*pu-tao*).[126]

SUBCOMMENTARY: This article describes those who are cruel and malicious and who turn their backs on morality.[127] Therefore it is called depravity.

COMMENTARY: Depravity means to kill three members of a single household (*chia* 家) who have not committed a capital crime, or to dismember someone.[128]

SUBCOMMENTARY: This means that of the three persons from a single household that are killed none has committed a capital crime. If of the

[124]Wang Yüan-liang comments here that *chiu-hun* 就婚 refers to a marriage in which the husband goes to live with the wife's family. This is the third type of husband.

[125]Article 175; Deloustal 314. Violation of this law was punished by sixty blows with the heavy stick.

[126]This category existed already in Han times. See Hulsewé, *Han Law*, I, 156 ff. Two cases in the Han period in which three innocent members of one family were killed are known as having been classified as depraved. Sorcery was also included. But during the Han dynasty, depravity also served as a catch-all clause for many crimes that are variously classified in the *Code*.

[127]Wang Yüan-liang states here that the acts covered under this heading are those that no man should allow to be done.

[128]See the discussion under the third part of Chapter II. The definition of a single household is given in the subcommentary to Article 259; Deloustal 419, which covers this crime. A single household consists of persons whose names are included in the same *chi* 籍 "household register," or any persons within the second (*chi-ch'in* 期親) degree of mourning relationship. The categories did not have to overlap. That is, those listed on the same household register did not have to be kin, while persons within the second degree of mourning relationship did not have to be on the same household register. However, as previously stated, all the victims had to be at least of the same status as the killer. If the killer were a commoner and one of the victims a female retainer, the crime would not come under the ten abominations.

Dismemberment refers either to killing someone and then dismembering the body, or to dismemberment followed by killing. But both acts were necessary, and had to occur at the same time. If dismemberment took place only some time after the killing, the crime would not come under the ten abominations. Burning the body was considered to be dismemberment.

three persons, one has been condemned to death, or if in each of several households two persons are killed, this only provides for the death penalty and the crime does not come under the ten abominations. Or if one kills three members of one household and the specific article does not provide for death, this again does not come under the ten abominations.[129] To dismember someone means to kill him and to dismember the body. This comes under the same article as killing three members of one household and also deserves death.

COMMENTARY: The offense also includes the making or keeping of *ku* 蠱 poison, or sorcery.[130]

[17a] SUBCOMMENTARY: This means to prepare the poison oneself, or to keep it, or to give it to others in order to harm people. But if the preparation of the poison has not yet been completed, this offense does not come under the ten abominations. As to sorcery, there are a great many methods not all of which can be described. All, however, comprise evil customs and secret practices which are illegal and whose intent is to cause the victim pain and death.

ARTICLE: The sixth is called great irreverence (*ta pu-ching*).[131]

[18] SUBCOMMENTARY: Ritual is the basis of respect; respect is the vehicle of ritual. Therefore "The Changes in Ritual" chapter of the *Book of Rites* states: "Ritual is the instrument of the ruler whereby he can clear up doubts, cast light on what is difficult to perceive, . . . test the

[129]That is, if one of them were of inferior status.

[130]Crimes involving *ku* poison are covered in Article 262; Deloustal 423. The subcommentary to Article 262 states that making or keeping *ku* poison is considered to be *tso-tao* 左道, "ways of the left," that is, black magic. See Han-yi Feng and John Shryock, "The Black Magic in China Known as *Ku*," *Journal of the American Oriental Society*, 55 (1935), 1-30.

Wang Yüan-liang states that this article also includes within its scope the use of people's names in order to call demons to harm them, as well as other magical ways of harming people. See Edward Williams, "Witchcraft in the Chinese Penal Code," *Journal of the North China Branch of the Royal Asiatic Society*, New Series 38 (1907), 61-95, particularly pp. 74-75.

[131]Crimes classified under irreverence seem to have been much the same in both the Han and T'ang dynasties. That is, they were concerned with irreverence toward the emperor, the state sacrifices, imperial decrees, and imperial messengers. See Hulsewé, *Han Law*, I, 156 ff. However, one difference is found in a Han pronouncement about sumptuary laws, which states that their continual violation will lead to irreverence. See Hulsewé, *Han Law*, I, 182. There is no mention of sumptuary laws in this article of the *Code*.

institutions and regulations and specify benevolence and right conduct."[132] The responsibility of those who offend against ritual is great and their hearts lack reverence and respect. Therefore it is called great irreverence.

COMMENTARY: Great irreverence means to steal the objects of the great sacrifices to the spirits, or the carriage or possessions of the emperor.[133]

SUBCOMMENTARY: As to the great sacrifices, the statute on sacrifices [states: "The country has great sacrifices, medium sacrifices, and small sacrifices. These are] to the Lord on High of Great Heaven, the Lord on High of the Five Directions, the Spirit of Sovereign Earth, the Spiritual Continent, and the Ancestral Temple. [These comprise the great sacrifices.]"[134] Further, the Articles on Administrative Regulations state: "In all references to sacrifice, *chi* 祭 and *hsiang* 享 are equally applicable."[135] Thus the great *chi* and great *hsiang* sacrifices are both considered to be great sacrifices.

As to the objects of the spirits, this means the objects which have been presented to the spirits. The commentary on the specific article states: "This means the things presented to the spirits [17b] such as hangings, tables, and staffs."[136] If the objects have been made but are stolen before they have been presented, this also is considered to be great irreverence. If liquor, food containers, and *pien-tou* 籩豆 and *fu-kuei* 簠簋 sacrificial vessels are in front of the spirits and are stolen, this also is considered to be great irreverence. But if they are not in the place where the spirits

[132]*Li chi*, "Li yün"; Couvreur, *Li ki*, I, 511–512.

[133]Article 270 punishes the stealing of objects belonging to the great state sacrifices by life exile to 2,000 *li*. Stealing objects belonging to the carriage of the emperor or his possessions is covered under Article 271; Deloustal 429, and is punished by life exile to 2,500 *li*. The subcommentary to Article 271 states that stealing any of the objects pertaining to the carriage or possessions of the emperor's wife, mother, or paternal grandmother is considered to be the same as stealing those of the emperor. However, such theft from the crown prince will have the punishment reduced one degree. Other reductions in punishment depended upon whether the objects had been used by the emperor, had already been discarded, and so on. See also Article 51.

[134]See Niida, *Statutes*, pp. 159–161. Though both medium and small sacrifices are also included in the statute, they are not mentioned in this article.

[135]The quotation is from the subcommentary rather than the text of the article itself. See Article 98; Deloustal 104. The subcommentary goes on to state that the article covers the medium and small sacrifices, which are not mentioned under Great Irreverence. Thus theft of the objects belonging to these lesser sacrifices was punished, but the crime did not come under the ten abominations.

[136]This definition is from the commentary to Article 270.

are, it is not so considered.

The imperial possessions mean the things used by the emperor. The ruler's home is the empire and in his chariot he makes tours. We do not dare refer to the honored name of the ruler and therefore rely on the term "chariot" to designate him. The commentary on the specific article states: "Possessions include such things as quilts and cushions, things which are actually worn, and supplementary things, all of which must be submitted to the inspecting officials. Those things which have been selected for presentation to the emperor are also imperial objects."[137]

COMMENTARY: The offense also includes stealing or forging the imperial seals.[138]

SUBCOMMENTARY: The *Analytical Dictionary of Characters* states: "*Hsi* 璽 means seal."[139] Anciently both high and low had seals. The *Tso Commentary* states: "At the time when Duke Hsiang was returning from Ch'u and had reached Fang-ch'eng, Chi Wu-tzu had taken Pien [and appropriated it for himself]. He sent, however, Kung-ye to [meet the duke and] inquire after his welfare, sending a messenger after him, who overtook him with a sealed (*hsi*) letter [for the duke]."[140] This is the meaning.

Since the time of the Ch'in [221–210 B.C.] and Han dynasties, the seal of the emperor has been called *hsi* and those of the nobles, *yin* 印. During the K'ai-yüan period [A.D. 718–741] the name of the imperial seal was changed from *hsi* to *pao* 寶. When the specific article speaks of "those who forge the emperor's eight seals,"[141] this means the imperial seals. To take the seals of the three empresses [that is, the emperor's wife, mother, and paternal grandmother] also comes under the ten abominations.

COMMENTARY: This section also includes failure to follow the correct

[137]This definition is from the commentary to Article 271; Deloustal 429.

[138]Stealing the imperial seal was punished by strangulation. See Article 271; Deloustal 429. However, Article 362; Deloustal 514, punishes actual forgery of it by decapitation.

[139]*Shuo-wen chieh-tzu*, p. 6127.

[140]*Tso chuan*, "Hsiang 29"; Legge, *The Chinese Classics*, v, 548.

[141]Article 362; Deloustal 514. See the discussion in des Rotours, *Fonctionnaires*, I, 165 note 1. The penalty for stealing or forging the seals of the three empresses was life exile to 3,000 *li* and strangulation, respectively. The distinction between the emperor and other personages is reflected in the fact that the emperor's seal was made of jade and the others' seals were made of gold.

prescription when preparing medicine for the emperor, or making a mistake in attaching the label.[142]

SUBCOMMENTARY: When mixing medicine for the emperor, to commit an error despite reliance on the correct prescription is to violate the correct prescription[143] by mistake. Making a mistake in attaching the label means [18a] to follow the prescription in compounding but then to make a mistake in the label such as to designate pills as powder, or to speak of the medicine as being hot in nature when it is cold.

COMMENTARY: This section also includes making a mistake in preparing the emperor's food by violating the dietary proscriptions.[144]

[19] SUBCOMMENTARY: The *Rites of Chou* states: "The food-doctors are in charge of the eight flavors of the king's [food]."[145] They must be especially careful and reverent in managing the imperial food and must follow the standard cookbook. If they mistakenly do not follow the cookbook, this comes under irreverence.

COMMENTARY: This section also includes making mistakes in constructing boats for imperial use so that they are not sturdy.[146]

[142]Both of these mistakes were punished by strangulation. See Article 102; Deloustal 110. If the ingredients were impure, the punishment was one year of penal servitude, reduced to a hundred blows with the heavy stick if the medicine had not yet been presented to the emperor. This would also reduce the sentences for failure to follow the correct prescription or making a mistake in attaching the label to life exile to 3,000 *li*.

[143]*Fa* 法 should be read *fang* 方, following the KHCPTS edition.

[144]Mistakes of this kind were punished by strangulation. See Article 103; Deloustal 111. If it was a case of dirt in the emperor's food or drink, the penalty was reduced to two years of penal servitude. Where the ingredients were impure or the food was served at the wrong time, the punishment was one year of penal servitude. If the flavors were not right or what should have been tasted had not been, the penalty was one hundred blows with the heavy stick.

Violating the dietary proscriptions means to mix dried meat with millet or rice, or to serve spinach with tortoise, according to the same article. Such errors in cuisine were also punished by strangulation. I wish to thank Rex Niswander for pointing out that the *Hsi yüan lu* 3/48a; Herbert A. Giles, "The 'Hsi Yüan Lu' or Instructions to Coroners," *Proceedings of the Royal Society of Medicine*, 17 (1924), 97, states not only that spinach eaten with tortoise is poisonous, but that this combination will produce tortoises in the stomach of the person who eats them together.

[145]*Chou li*, "Shih yi," p. 72; Biot, I, 93.

[146]Article 104; Deloustal 112, also punishes those responsible for the work being wrongly done with strangulation. Were the boats not kept in repair or not fully equipped, the penalty was two years of penal servitude for those responsible.

SUBCOMMENTARY: Everywhere the emperor goes there is happiness and rejoicing. Boats that are offered to the emperor are called imperial. The workmen who make them must use their minds and strength to the utmost. If by mistake the boats are not sturdy, then the crime comes under this section.

Now crimes involving the imperial boats and the preceeding three clauses are all crimes committed by mistake. Even if these items have not yet been presented to the emperor, the crime still comes under the ten abominations. If such crimes are intentional, then the sentence is for plotting rebellion. The inspecting officials [who fail to note the mistake], however, according to the law have their sentences reduced and are not accounted as irreverent.

COMMENTARY: This section further includes criticizing the emperor where the circumstances are completely reprehensible (*ch'ieh-hai* 切害).[147]

SUBCOMMENTARY: This refers to being disappointed in some circumstance and to issue slanders, thereby criticizing the emperor, and the circumstances are completely reprehensible. If it is not a matter of complaining against the emperor [literally, "heaven"], but only of someone wishing falsely to accuse others of crime, then the case is decided according to the law on reciprocal punishment [for false accusation] ([*wu-kao*] *fan-tso* 誣告反坐),[148] and does not come under the section on the ten abominations [18b]. . . . The reason for this is that the emperor desires to seek out the basic circumstances, spread wide his mercy, and to be cautious in punishing.

COMMENTARY: This section finally includes resisting or driving away messengers carrying imperial decrees (*chih* 制), or lacking the proper behavior that a subject owes to his emperor.[149]

SUBCOMMENTARY: Messengers receive the imperial decrees and are sent

[147]Such lèse majesté was punished by decapitation. See Article 122; Deloustal 132. "Completely reprehensible" is used in reference to such serious offenses as robbery by force, as allowing a faster hearing of the case than was usually permitted. See Niida, *Statutes*, p. 776. That may also be the intent here, though lèse majesté is not specifically mentioned in the statute. However, those who mentioned the emperor's name while discussing governmental affairs or laws would be allowed to petition for mercy. And where such mention was not intended in a harmful way, the sentence was two years of penal servitude.

[148]Article 342; Deloustal 501. See the discussion in the second part of Chapter II.

[149]Article 122; Deloustal 132, punishes this crime by strangulation.

out to announce them to the four corners of the empire. If there are those who resist or drive them away and do not respect the imperial decrees, such persons lack the proper behavior that a subject owes to his emperor. A messenger who carries the imperial decree means one who receives the imperial decree and is ordered to carry it to the provinces.

ARTICLE: The seventh is called lack of filial piety (*pu-hsiao* 不孝).[150]

SUBCOMMENTARY: Serving one's parents well is called filial piety. Disobeying them is called lack of filial piety.

COMMENTARY: This has reference to accusing to the court,[151] or cursing one's paternal grandparents or parents.[152]

SUBCOMMENTARY: The specific article simply speaks of *kao* 告 "accusing" one's paternal grandparents or parents, whereas the present commentary speaks in an extended manner of *kao-yen* 告言 "accusingly speaking."[153] Though the texts are different, the meaning is the same. *Tsu* 詛 is like *chu* 咒 [and means to curse by spells]. *Li* 詈 is like *ma* 罵 [and means to curse with bad language].

According to the specific article, [20] those who use spells desiring to cause death or illness are sentenced for plotting to kill, which is considered to be contumacy. Only if the spell was made to gain the doting love of the parents does it come under the present article.

[19a] QUERY: According to the Articles on Violence and Robbery: "A son or grandson who, seeking the doting love of his parents or paternal

[150] Lack of filial piety is a catch-all clause with several articles grouped under this one heading. That informing on one's father was termed lack of filial piety during the Han dynasty is attested by a case quoted in Ch'eng, *Research on Law*, p. 117. Lack of filial piety does not appear in the list given in the *K'ung-tzu chia-yü*, but is given in the codes of the Northern Ch'i and the Sui. With regard to this crime, the *Hsiao ching*, "Wu hsing," p. 49; Legge, *Hsiao King*, p. 481, states: "Of the three thousand crimes covered by the five punishments, none is greater than the lack of filial piety."

[151] Accusing parents or paternal grandparents to the court was punished by strangulation. See Article 345; Deloustal 503. It should be noted here that Article 52 provides that any reference in the *Code* to paternal grandparents includes great- and great-great-grandparents in the male line as well. Similarly, references to grandsons in the male line include great- and great-great-grandsons in the male line as well.

[152] There are really two articles involved here. Cursing one's parents or paternal grandparents by means of spells was punished by decapitation. See Article 264; Deloustal 422. However, cursing with bad language was punished by strangulation. See Article 329.

[153] This refers to the use of *kao* in Article 345, while the present article uses *kao-yen*.

grandparents, uses either sorcery or spells will be exiled to a distance of 2,000 *li*."[154] Thus there is no distinction here as to penalty between the crimes of sorcery and making spells. Yet making spells is now accounted as lack of filial piety in the present article, whereas it remains unknown under what section to enter sorcery.

REPLY: Even though sorcery and making spells are found together in that text, it is reasonable that making spells be considered the lighter and sorcery the heavier of the two crimes. Thus one might suppose that if only the use of sorcery against persons of non-kin status comes under depravity, making spells would then not come under the ten abominations. However, in the General Principles it is stated: "If the punishment should be increased, a lighter offense is brought up in order to make clear a heavier punishment (*chü-ch'ing yi ming-chung* 舉輕以明重)."[155] Thus since the use of spells, which is accounted the lighter crime, comes under lack of filial piety, it is clear that sorcery, being the heavier of the two crimes, reasonably ought to come under this same section.

COMMENTARY: This section further includes having a separate household register (*pieh-chi* 別籍) or separate goods (*yi-ts'ai* 異財)[156] while the paternal grandparents or parents are still living.

SUBCOMMENTARY: While the paternal grandparents or parents are alive, the sons and grandsons must put no limit on supporting them.[157] When going out, sons and grandsons state where they are going, and when returning report to their parents[158] without following their own wishes.

However, if they have separate goods or have a separate household register, then the circumstance is one in which they lack hearts of utmost filial piety. Reputation and honor are thereby both lost, and parental affection and appropriateness are both thrown aside. If we search through the canons of morality, this crime is the most difficult to forgive. These two crimes [that is, separate goods and separate household registers] need not be combined. Cases of violation of either are considered to be one of the ten abominations.

[154]This statement comes from the subcommentary on Article 264; Deloustal 422.

[155]See the discussion in part seven of Chapter II. The techniques of analogy are explained in Article 50.

[156]Article 155 punishes either of these offenses with three years of penal servitude. A good general discussion of household registers can be found in On Ikeda, "T'ang Household Registers and Related Documents."

[157]This is a paraphrase of *Li chi*, "T'an kung"; Couvreur, *Li ki*, I, 109.

COMMENTARY: This section also includes being deficient in support of one's elders.[159]

SUBCOMMENTARY: The *Book of Rites* states: "A filial son in taking care of his parents, seeks to please them. He does not oppose their desires . . . and loyally supports them with food and drink."[160] In cases where the sons have the ability to support their elders and yet are deficient, if the paternal grandparents or parents accuse them to the courts, then they will be prosecuted.

[19b] COMMENTARY: Further offenses under this section are during the period of mourning for one's parents to arrange for one's own marriage, to make music, or to take off mourning garments and put on ordinary clothing [suitable for happy occasions].[161]

SUBCOMMENTARY: To arrange for one's own marriage during the period of mourning for one's parents means that everyone, principal and accessories alike, is guilty of breaking the law. If, however, it is only the master of the marriage (*chu-hun* 主婚)[162] who is prosecuted, then the bridegroom and bride are not deemed unfilial. The reason given here, referring to arranging for one's own marriage, is in order to make clear that the law regarding the master of the marriage is not the same as this one, which is included in the ten abominations.

If a man during mourning for his wife takes a concubine [rather than another wife], he may be permitted to resign from one occupied office [in place of other punishment].[163] If a woman during mourning for her

[158]*Li chi*, "Ch'ü li"; Couvreur, *Li ki*, I, 12.

[159]Being deficient in support of parents and grandparents is linked with not obeying their orders in Article 348; Deloustal 505. Both of these offenses are punished by two years of penal servitude.

[160]*Li chi*, "Nei tse"; Couvreur, *Li ki*, I, 653.

[161]During the period of mourning for parents, the children were expected to refrain from various kinds of pleasurable activities as well as ceremonies of a happy nature, such as marriages. Article 179; Deloustal 316 punishes marriage during the period of mourning for parents or husband by three years of penal servitude. But taking a concubine during this period brought only one and one-half years of penal servitude. Those who made music or took off mourning and put on ordinary clothing during the period of mourning were also punished by three years of penal servitude. See Article 120; Deloustal 131.

[162]This refers to the person actually responsible for the marriage arrangements. See Article 181, also Pierre Hoang, *Le Mariage chinois au point de vue légal*.

[163]See Article 20 on *mien-so-chü chih kuan* 免所居之官 , "resignation from occupied office." See also the discussion in the subsection official privilege and responsibility in the fourth part of Chapter II.

husband becomes a concubine, her punishment is three degrees less than that for becoming a wife.[164] In neither case does the offense come under lack of filial piety.

As to making music, this includes both the mourner himself or herself making music, and having others to do so for him or her. Music means beating bells or drums; playing stringed instruments, gourds, or chimes; blowing wind instruments; singing, dancing; variety shows; and so on.

Taking off mourning garments and putting on ordinary clothing means that when the mourning period is not yet over, that is, within twenty-seven months, one takes off the mourning garments and puts on ordinary clothing.

[21] COMMENTARY: Still other offenses under this section are on hearing of the death of one's paternal grandparents or parents to conceal and not mourn their death;[165] also to state falsely that one's paternal grandparents or parents have died.[166]

SUBCOMMENTARY: According to the *Book of Rites*, "Hearing of the death of a parent, one responds to the messenger with crying, giving oneself over to sorrow. One asks the cause. . . ."[167] The death of a parent is the greatest of all pain. On hearing that news, one should collapse utterly, beat the breast, stamp the floor, and cry to heaven. However, if one conceals and does not mourn their death, or selects a particular day to begin mourning, both are considered to be lack of filial piety.

Falsely to state that one's paternal grandparents or parents have died means that while they are still alive one falsely states that they are dead. If, however, when they have previously died,[168] and one falsely states that they have only just died, this is not accounted as lack of filial piety.[169]

[164]Like the case of the husband who took a concubine during the period of mourning, a wife who became another's concubine during the period of mourning for her husband was punished by one and one-half years of penal servitude. See Article 179; Deloustal 316.

[165]Article 120; Deloustal 131, punishes such greatly unfilial behavior by life exile to 2,000 *li*.

[166]Officials retired from office during the period of mourning for certain relatives. Article 383; Deloustal 542, states that a false announcement of the death of parents or paternal grandparents made for such reasons as seeking a vacation is punished by three years of penal servitude.

[167]*Li chi*, "Pen sang"; Couvreur, *Li ki*, II, 534.

[168]*Ch'i* 其 should be read *erh* 而, following the SPTK edition.

[169]Article 383; Deloustal 542, reduces this penalty three degrees below the three years of penal servitude given those who falsely announce the death of parents or paternal grandparents, to one and one-half years of penal servitude.

[20a] ARTICLE: The eighth is called discord (*pu-mu* 不睦).[170]

SUBCOMMENTARY: The *Book of Rites* speaks of "striving after sincerity and cultivating concord."[171] The *Book of Filial Piety* states: "The people were in a state of harmony and concord."[172] Concord refers to relatives. The contents of this section all concern offenses by kin and the failure to achieve concord within the nine degrees of kinship.[173] Therefore it is called discord.

COMMENTARY: Discord means to plot to kill or also to sell relatives who are of the fifth or closer degree of mourning.[174]

SUBCOMMENTARY: All the cases of plotting to kill or of selling relatives who are of the fifth or closer degree of mourning, irrespective of whether they are of a higher or lower generation or are older or younger than oneself,[175] come under this section. If one plots to kill a relative of a higher generation, or of the same generation but older than oneself within the second degree of mourning, and actually carries out the murder, this comes under the section on contumacy.

Here, plot to kill is stated, not intentional killing or killing in an affray. But killing which is intentional or done in an affray also comes under this section on discord. Plotting to kill but failing to wound is brought up as being a lighter offense in order to make clear that the crime of killing by intent or in an affray which results in death is

[170]This section deals with relationships outside the one-year mourning system, with the exception of the wife-husband relationship. Offenses within this looser group of relatives are not considered to constitute lack of filial piety, but rather to indicate discord. Therefore the penalties are somewhat lighter.

[171]*Li chi*, "Li yün"; Couvreur, *Li ki*, I, 517.

[172]*Hsiao ching*, "K'ai tsung ming yi," p. 10; Legge, *Hsiao King*, p. 465.

[173]This means a range of relatives, including the male descendants and their wives and children of one's great-great-grandfather in the male line, down to one's own fourth cousins in the male line. Below one's own generation the group lessens until it ends with one's own great-great-grandson(s) in the male line. See the chart in Feng, "The Chinese Kinship System," p. 26.

[174]Article 253; Deloustal 415, punishes a plot to kill relatives of the fifth degree of mourning who are of a higher generation or of the same generation but older than oneself by life exile to 2,000 *li*. Where the plotter was older than the intended victim in either generation or age, the punishment was reduced two degrees. Selling such relatives was punished by strangulation, the same punishment as for intentional killing or killing in an affray. If the person agreed to be sold, the punishment was reduced one degree to life exile to 3,000 *li*. See Article 294; Deloustal 452.

[175]According to Hoang, *Mariage chinois*, p. 2, *tsun* 尊 indicates relatives of a higher generation, irrespective of whether they are older than oneself. *Chang* 長 refers to relatives of the same generation who are older than oneself.

punished more heavily. In this way the lighter and the heavier are mutually made clear, so that it is reasonable that they both are considered among the ten abominations.

As to selling a relative of the fifth or closer degree of mourning, it comes under this section on discord, whether it is done by force or by consent. This is not so, however, if the sale has not yet been completed.

COMMENTARY: This section further includes beating or accusing to the court one's husband or relatives, whether of a higher generation or of the same generation but older than oneself, of the third (*ta-kung* 大功) or closer degree of mourning, or relatives of an older generation of the fourth (*hsiao-kung* 小功) degree of mourning.[176]

SUBCOMMENTARY: According to the *Book of Ceremonies and Rites*, "The husband is as heaven to the wife."[177] It is also stated: "*ch'i* 妻 'wife' means *ch'i* 齊 'whole.'"[178] The husband is separately mentioned, as his relationship to his wife does not involve generation or age.

As to reference to relatives of the third degree of mourning of a higher generation or older than oneself, according to the *Book of Ceremonies and Rites*, a man has no relatives of the third degree of mourning of a higher generation.[179] They exist only in the case of the wife for her husband's paternal grandparents [20b], and accordingly for her husband's paternal uncles and their wives. These are all relatives of the third degree of mourning of an older generation. Relatives of the third degree of mourning of the same generation but older than oneself refer to one's male and female second cousins in the paternal line who are older than oneself.

"Or closer" refers to such relatives as one's paternal uncles and their wives, one's paternal aunts, and brothers and sisters who are older than oneself. Relatives of the fourth degree of mourning of a higher

[176]Article 326; Deloustal 480, punishes a wife who beats her husband with one year of penal servitude. If she wounded him severely, the penalty would be increased. Accusing her husband to the court brought two years of penal servitude. See Article 346; Deloustal 503.

Article 327; Deloustal 482, punishes those who beat relatives of the third degree of mourning with two years of penal servitude, reduced to one and one-half years if the relationship is that of the fourth degree of mourning. Accusing relatives of the fourth degree of mourning to the court was punished by eighty blows with the heavy stick, increased to ninety blows for relatives of the third degree of mourning. See Article 347; Deloustal 503.

[177]*Yi li*, "Sang fu"; Couvreur, *I li, Cérémonial*, p. 400.

[178]*Po-hu t'ung* 9/15a; Tjan, *Po Hu T'ung*, I, 261. The text goes on to state that the wife and husband form one body.

[179]*Yi li*, "Sang fu," p. 377. This is a summary of this material rather than a quotation.

generation than oneself include persons such as one's paternal uncles, their wives, and paternal aunts once removed, one's paternal great-uncles, their wives, and paternal great-aunts once removed, one's maternal grandparents, and one's maternal uncles and aunts.

ARTICLE: The ninth is called unrighteousness (*pu-yi* 不義).[180]

[22] SUBCOMMENTARY: *Li* 禮 [that is, morality, rules of propriety, good manners] honors righteousness. This section originally did not include blood relatives because, basically, righteousness is exercised only toward associates. It is concerned with turning one's back on righteousness and violating benevolence. Therefore it is called unrighteousness.

COMMENTARY: Unrighteousness means to kill one's department head, prefect, or magistrate, or the teacher from whom one has received one's education.[181]

SUBCOMMENTARY: As to department head, according to the statute, active-duty officials of the fifth rank and above and honorary officials of the third rank and above have both bodyguards and houseguards.[182] According to where they serve they are called department heads. Persons acting in like capacity for princes and nobility are in the same position.

Governors and prefects are appointed by dated imperial decrees, but officials of the sixth rank or less are appointed only after signatures by the officials in charge of such appointments.[183]

The term "teacher from whom one has received one's education" refers to the fact that one receives one's Confucian heritage from another and does not acquire it through private study. If such a person is killed, the crime comes under unrighteousness. [21a] If the killing is plotted but has not yet been carried out, this is a different offense.[184]

COMMENTARY: This section also includes an employee or a soldier who

[180]This section covers crimes against superiors. See the subsection offenses against superiors in the third part of Chapter II.

[181]The penalty for killing any of these persons is decapitation. See Article 252; Deloustal 417, and Article 333; Deloustal 487.

[182]See Niida, *Statutes*, pp. 382–384, where the numbers of these guards are given for each rank.

[183]The process of appointing officials is discussed in des Rotours, *Fonctionnaires*, I, 33–34.

[184]That is, while it is serious it does not come under the ten abominations.

kills the chief or commander of his own section who is of the fifth rank or above.[185]

SUBCOMMENTARY: Employee refers to those who have no official rank (*liu-wai* 流外) and other, lower-ranked personnel.[186] Soldier means such categories as militia or guard soldiers. There are many categories of these types of people [so that they may not all be specified]. The crime of killing the chief or commander of their own section who is of the fifth rank or above comes under unrighteousness. As to *kuan-chang* 官長 "chief, commander," according to the statute: "All chief officers in departments are *kuan-chang*. It is the same as *chang-kuan* "senior officer."[187]

COMMENTARY: This section also includes concealing and not mourning the death of one's husband, or making music, or taking off mourning and putting on ordinary clothing, or remarrying during the period of mourning.[188]

SUBCOMMENTARY: The husband is the wife's heaven. Having changed from mourning for her father, she mourns her husband. Mourning for the husband is the first degree of mourning (*chan-ts'ui* 斬衰). This tie of love and righteousness being the highest, the wife on hearing of the death of her husband must cry out and grieve.

If, however, she conceals and does not mourn his death, or if during the period of mourning she makes music or takes off mourning and puts on ordinary clothing, or if again she forgets her sorrow and remarries, all these acts mean turning one's back on morality and violating righteousness. Therefore all come under the ten abominations. If, however, the wife remarries as a concubine, it is not considered to be one of the ten abominations.

[185]Article 252; Deloustal 417, punishes this crime by decapitation.

[186]Personnel having no official rank refers to those who have not taken the examinations and who occupy a low position in the bureaucracy. See the discussion in des Rotours, *Traité des examens*, pp. 218 ff.

[187]See Niida, *Statutes*, p. 774.

[188]The punishment for a wife who conceals and does not mourn her husband's death is the same as that for a man who conceals and does not mourn his parents' or paternal grandparents' death, life exile to 2,000 *li*. If she makes music or puts on ordinary clothing during the period of mourning for her husband, the punishment is three years of penal servitude. See Article 120; Deloustal 130. If she marries during this period, the punishment is also three years of penal servitude, reduced to one and one-half years of penal servitude if she becomes another person's concubine. See Article 179; Deloustal 316.

ARTICLE: The tenth is called incest (*nei-luan* 內亂).[189]

SUBCOMMENTARY: The *Tso Commentary* states: "The woman has her husband's house; the man has his wife's chamber; and there must be no defilement on either side."[190] If this is changed, then there is incest. If one behaves like the birds and beasts,[191] and introduces licentious associates into one's family, the rules of morality are confused. Therefore this is called incest.

[21b] COMMENTARY: This section includes having illicit sexual intercourse (*chien* 姦) with relatives who are of the fourth degree of mourning or closer.[192]

SUBCOMMENTARY: To have illicit sexual intercourse with relatives who are of the fourth degree of mourning or closer means for a man to have illicit sexual intercourse with a woman for whom, according to the *Book of Ceremonies and Rites*, he must wear the fourth degree of mourning.[193] If the woman must wear the fourth degree of mourning for the man, but the man [23] only fifth degree of mourning for the woman in return, then illicit sexual intercourse is not accounted incest. This has reference to such relationships as that of a daughter's daughter with one's maternal grandfather, or a sister's daughter with one's maternal uncle.

COMMENTARY: This section also includes illicit sexual intercourse with one's father's or paternal grandfather's concubines, including those who give their consent.

SUBCOMMENTARY: As to the father's or paternal grandfather's *ch'ieh* 妾 concubines, the case is the same regardless of whether they have had children. To have intercourse with *ying* 媵 concubines is also

[189]This term literally means "[sexual] disorder within [the family]." It seems strange that relatives of the fifth degree of mourning are not included, while some persons are who have no mourning relationship to each other at all.

[190]*Tso chuan*, "Huan 18"; Legge, *The Chinese Classics*, v, 69.

[191]This refers to the passage in the *Li chi*, "Ch'ü li"; Couvreur, *Li ki*, I, 7, where it is stated that animals have no morality; the stag and his male offspring both couple with the same doe.

[192]Illicit sexual intercourse with relatives is covered under Articles 411, 412, and 413. Article 411 does punish illicit sexual intercourse between relatives of the fifth degree of mourning. But apparently this crime does not come under the ten abominations. The punishment for such illicit sexual activity ranges from three years of penal servitude in the case of fifth degree and other distant relatives, to strangulation in the case of illicit sexual intercourse with one's father's concubine.

[193]*Yi li*, "Sang fu"; Couvreur, *I Li*, pp. 421–426.

considered to be incest.[194] Including those who give their consent[195] means that if the woman consents to have illicit sexual intercourse with the man, then both are guilty of incest. If she is forced but later gives her consent, this is also incest.[196]

Article 7

The Eight Deliberations (pa-yi 八議 *)*[197]

SUBCOMMENTARY: The *Rites of Chou* states: "The eight rules are attached to the country's laws."[198] The eight rules of the Chou dynasty are the same as the present eight deliberations. The *Book of Rites* states: "Punishments do not extend up to the great officers."[199] "If they commit offenses, they are judged under the eight deliberations, and the weight of the sentence is not governed by the books of punishment."[200] Persons gain deliberation because of relationship—either direct or indirect—to the emperor, or for long service, or for having many abilities and many arts, or for services and merits, which are recorded in the emperor's heart and written down in the emperor's archives.[201]

If those deserving of one of the eight deliberations commit a capital crime, a memorial is sent up requesting authorization to consider and fix a penalty. The officials do not dare decide the case themselves. [22a] This means that weight is given to relationship to the imperial family and moral worth, that long service is esteemed, that guests of the state and those in high position are honored, and that great abilities and merits are respected. Therefore, when one who deserves the eight

[194]*Ying* concubines have somewhat higher status than do *ch'ieh* concubines. See Article 326. In pre-Han times the *ying* was a bridesmaid who accompanied the proper bride into the house of the groom. As such she had a higher status than later concubines taken by the husband. See *Yi li*, "Shih hun li"; Couvreur, *I Li*, pp. 33 ff. In the T'ang period such *ying* concubines could apparently be possessed only by officials of the fifth rank and higher. See Niida, *Statutes*, p. 251; des Rotours, *Traité des fonctionnaires*, I, 49.

[195]*Che* 者 should be added after *ho* 和, following the KHCPTS edition.

[196]This sentence does not occur in the specific articles dealing with illicit sexual intercourse within the family. Thus it serves to augment the conditions under which both parties who engaged in illicit sexual intercourse would be punished.

[197]Hulsewé, *Han Law*, I, 285 ff., discusses the early history of the eight deliberations. The first time that they formally appear in a code is apparently in the Wei dynasty (A.D. 220–264). See Ch'eng, *Research on Law*, p. 245; Balazs, *Traité juridique*, p. 145 note 185.

[198]*Chou li*, "Hsiao ssu k'ou," p. 524; Biot, II, 320–322.

[199]*Li chi*, "Ch'ü li"; Couvreur, *Li ki*, I, 53.

[200]This is Cheng Hsüan's commentary on the above quotation, *Li chi*, "Ch'ü li," p. 55.

[201]These last two phrases are paraphrases of *Shu ching*, "Chün ya"; Legge, *The Chinese Classics*, III, 578–579, and *Tso chuan*, "Hsi 5"; Legge, *The Chinese Classics*, V, 145.

deliberations commits a capital crime, a memorial is first sent up requesting authorization to deliberate on what has been violated. Therefore this is called the eight deliberations.

ARTICLE: The first is called deliberation for relatives of the emperor.

COMMENTARY: Included are relatives of the emperor of the sixth (*t'an-wen* 袒免) degree of mourning and closer.

SUBCOMMENTARY: Righteousness is: within the family to be in harmony with the nine degrees of family relationship, and outside the family to bring the ten thousand countries into concord, to spread mercy like rain and dew, and to establish the principle of loving one's relatives. Therefore this is called deliberation for relatives of the emperor.

The sixth degree of mourning, according to the rules of propriety, includes five kinds of relatives, namely, the brothers of the paternal great-great-grandfather of the emperor, his paternal great-grandfather's male first cousins in the male line, his grandfather's male second cousins in the male line, his father's male third cousins in the male line, and his own male fourth cousins in the male line.

COMMENTARY: Included also are the emperor's paternal grandmother's and his mother's relatives in the fifth degree of morning and closer.

SUBCOMMENTARY: *T'ai-huang t'ai-hou* 太皇太后 is the title of the emperor's paternal grandmother. *Huang t'ai-hou* 皇太后 is the title of the emperor's mother. *T'ai* 太 is added to their titles to indicate greatness. When the *Book of Changes* speaks of the *t'ai-chi* 太極 , Great Primal Beginning, it takes the word *t'ai* for its idea of exalted greatness.[202] As for *huang* 皇 , according to the son's rank one can understand the mother's rank.

The protection (*yin* 蔭) of the two empresses extends to their relatives in the fifth degree of morning and closer.[203] These are four: the brothers of the paternal great-grandfather of the empresses, their paternal grandfather's male first cousins in the male line, their father's male second cousins in the male line, and their own male third cousins in the male line.

[24] COMMENTARY: Also included are the empress' relatives in the fourth degree of mourning and closer.

[202] *Yi ching*, "T'ai shih," p. 156; Wilhelm, *The I Ching*, p. 318.

[203] See Article 9, which treats this system of protection.

[22b] SUBCOMMENTARY: The protection of the empress extends to her relatives in the fourth degree of mourning and closer. The reason is to lessen the number of relatives who receive leniency. Three groups of relatives come within the fourth degree of mourning: the brothers of the paternal grandfather of the empress, her father's male first cousins in the male line, and her male second cousins in the male line. Aside from this enumeration, according to the rules of propriety, all other relatives, whether or not they are inside the clan, whose mourning relationship is the same as that of the relatives specified here are considered to come under this section.

ARTICLE: The second is called deliberation for old retainers of the emperor.

COMMENTARY: This means persons who have been in the emperor's service for a long period of time.

SUBCOMMENTARY: Those who have been in service for a long period of time thereby merit this favor.

ARTICLE: The third is called deliberation for the morally worthy.

COMMENTARY: This means those whose conduct is greatly virtuous.

SUBCOMMENTARY: This means worthy men (*hsien-jen* 賢人) and superior men (*chün-tzu* 君子) whose speech and conduct may be taken as a model for the country.

ARTICLE: The fourth is called deliberation for ability.

COMMENTARY: This means those of great talent.

SUBCOMMENTARY: This means those who are able to lead armies, manage the affairs of government, correct the course of the emperor, and serve as a model for human relationships.

ARTICLE: The fifth is called deliberation for achievement.

COMMENTARY: This means those of great achievement and glory.

SUBCOMMENTARY: This means those who are able to kill enemy generals and carry off their flags; who are able to lead armies ten thousand *li*, or cause multitudes to render allegiance and become civilized; who are able to bring peace to the entire age and to straighten out all difficulties. The achievements of such are recorded on a grand banner.[204]

[23a] ARTICLE: The sixth is called deliberation for high position.

COMMENTARY: This means active duty officials of the third rank and above, titular officials of the second rank and above, and persons with noble titles of the first rank.

SUBCOMMENTARY: According to the statute, "Those who manage affairs are active duty officials, whereas those who do not manage affairs are titular officials."[205] Noble titles refer to dukes and higher grades of noble titles.

ARTICLE: The seventh is called deliberation for diligence.

COMMENTARY: This means those who have great diligence in their work.

SUBCOMMENTARY: This means military and civil officials who reverently hold office day and night occupied with public affairs, or who, when serving in distant regions, experience dangers and difficulties.

ARTICLE: The eighth is called deliberation for guests of the state.

COMMENTARY: This means treating the descendants of previous dynasties as guests of the state.

[25] SUBCOMMENTARY: The *Book of History* states: "The guest of Yü (Shun) is in his place and all the nobles show their virtue by giving place to one another."[206] The *Book of Poetry* states: "The noble visitor! The noble visitor! Drawn like his ancestors by white horses."[207] The *Book of Rites* states: "The emperor keeps the descendants of the two preceding dynasties [in high positions], in order to honor the virtues [of their ancestors]."[208]

[204] This reference is to two people whose merits in the service of the rulers of the Chou dynasty were recorded on such a grand banner. See *Shu ching*, "Chüan ya"; Legge, *The Chinese Classics*, III, 578–579.

[205] Niida, *Statutes*, p. 590.

[206] *Shu ching*, "Yi chi"; Legge, *The Chinese Classics*, III, 87.

[207] *Shih ching* 284; Legge, *The Chinese Classics* IV. 592

[208] *Li chi*, "Chiao t'e sheng"; Couvreur, *Li ki*, I, 583.

Anciently, when King Wu overthrew the Shang dynasty, he enfeoffed the descendant of the Hsia in Ch'i and the descendant of the Yin (Shang) in Sung. At present, the descendant of the Northern Chou dynasty is Duke of Chieh and the descendant of the Sui dynasty is Duke of Hsi. Both are guests of the state.

[1a]

Article 8

Those Having the Eight Deliberations

ARTICLE: 8.1a—For all cases in which those having the eight deliberations commit a capital crime a memorial must first be sent up setting out the circumstances of the accusation, why the person merits deliberation, and requesting permission to deliberate.[1] Having deliberated, another memorial is sent up requesting the emperor to fix the punishment.

SUBCOMMENTARY: This is called the clause on the right of deliberation. When those having one of the eight deliberations commit a capital crime, the circumstances of the accusation, why it requires the death penalty, and whether the person merits deliberation by virtue of relationship to the emperor, of having been an old retainer of the emperor, of being morally worthy, of having ability, achievement, diligence, of being a guest of the state, or being of high position are first memorialized and permission is requested to deliberate.

According to the statute,[2] those concerned gather and deliberate in the Hall of State.[3] Having deliberated, another memorial is sent up requesting the emperor to fix the punishment.

COMMENTARY: Those who deliberate investigate the circumstances of the case and deliberate on the punishment. The article under which the accused will be punished is decided, but there is no formal passing of sentence.

SUBCOMMENTARY: Those who deliberate investigate the circumstances of the case and deliberate on the punishment means that they investigate the original circumstances of the case and deliberate on the crime that was committed. The article under which the accused will be punished is decided, but there is no formal passing of sentence means that the

[1]The name of this privilege thus comes from the deliberation that takes place when persons who have this privilege commit a crime.

[2]Niida, *Statutes*, p. 782. The crime is discussed by officials of the Board of Punishments who are of the seventh rank or higher.

[3]This Hall of State was where representatives of the three branches of government met to decide policy. A short history of it is given in Ch'ien Mu, *Chung-kuo li-tai cheng-chih te-shih* (A History of the Merits and Deficiencies of Chinese Governments), pp. 29–32.

circumstances of the case are memorialized, stating that the article dealing with the crime that was committed provides for the death penalty, but that those who have deliberated do not dare formally [1b] to decide on strangulation or decapitation. Therefore it is stated that there is no formal passing of sentence.

ARTICLE: 8.1b—Crimes punishable by life exile or less have the punishment reduced (*chien* 減) one degree.

8.2—This article is not applicable to cases involving violation of the ten abominations.

SUBCOMMENTARY: The circumstances of crimes punishable by life exile or less being relatively light, the punishment is reduced in accordance with the usual procedure for sentencing. However, if the case involves violation of the ten abominations, capital crimes may not be memorialized requesting permission to deliberate, and reduction of punishment for crimes punished by life exile or less will not be permitted. Therefore it is stated that this article is not applicable.

Article 9

The Wife of the Crown Prince

ARTICLE: 9.1a—For all cases in which relatives of the third or closer degree of mourning of the wife of the crown prince,

SUBCOMMENTARY: This is called the clause on the right of petition (*ch'ing* 請).[4] The empress' protection[5] extends to her relatives of the fourth or closer degree of mourning, who come under the clause in deliberation.

[4]For cases involving the right of deliberation, the emperor decided the penalty, whereas in cases in which the accused had the right of petition, the Board of Punishments stated in a memorial to the emperor whether the crime was to be punished by decapitation or strangulation. The important differences lay elsewhere. The right of petition was allowed to many more persons. But at the same time, there were a greater number of offenses in which it could not be claimed. Deliberation was allowable in all cases except those that came under the ten abominations. But killing , involvement in collective prosecution for rebellion or sedition, and various offenses committed by officials within their areas of jurisdiction also were outside the right of petition.

[5]Protection is the name for the right granted those who have the eight deliberations, members of the imperial family, and officials of the seventh rank and above. By means of this protection, certain of their relatives also shared their own rights to deliberation, petition, reduction of punishment, and redemption of punishment by payment of copper. See also the discussion in the fourth part of introduction Chapter I.

The wife of the crown prince's protection extends to her relatives of the third or closer degree of mourning, who come under the clause on petition. Thus high and low position are distinguished.

ARTICLE: relatives within the second or closer degree of mourning and grandsons in the male line of those entitled to deliberation,

[26] SUBCOMMENTARY: The protection of those who have the eight deliberations extends to their relatives within the second or closer degree of mourning and to grandsons in the male line, who come under the clause on petition. Relatives within the second degree of mourning include one's paternal uncles and their wives, one's father's sisters, one's own brothers and sisters, one's wife, one's sons, and one's nephews in the male line.

Another of the general principles states in enumerating relatives within the second degree of mourning that one's great- and great-great-grandparents in the paternal line, as well as one's grandsons in the male line are included.[6] This means grandsons born of the legitimate wife and others, and includes males of the third and fourth descending generations in the male line.

As for the wives of sons and grandsons in the male line, even though the mourning relationship is slight, [2a] yet the principle is important and they are also included among the relatives within the second degree of mourning. However, wives of the males in the third and fourth descending generations in the male line are not included.

ARTICLE: or officials and nobles of the fifth rank or higher commit a capital crime, a petition is sent up.

SUBCOMMENTARY: Officials and nobles of the fifth rank or higher means active duty civil and military officials of the fourth and fifth ranks; titular officials of the third rank down through the fifth rank; and honorary officials and nobles of the second through fifth ranks. When these classes of persons commit a capital crime, petition may be made for them.

COMMENTARY: Petition means to set forth the crime, the reasons for claiming petition, and to establish the sentence in a special memorial petitioning the imperial decision.

SUBCOMMENTARY: To set forth the crime means to record why the

[6]See Article 52.

petitioner's crime merits the death penalty. The reasons for claiming petition refers to indicating whether the reason for petition is that of being a relative of the third or closer degree of mourning of the wife of the crown prince, a relative in the second or closer degree of mourning or a grandson in the male line of those entitled to deliberation, or being an official or noble of the fifth rank or above.

To establish the sentence means to specify whether the article violated by the petitioner calls for strangulation or decapitation. Special memorial means that the memorial does not go through the Imperial Chancellery[7] but is a special memorial directly petitioning the imperial decision.

ARTICLE: 9.1b—Crimes punishable by life exile or less have their punishment reduced by one degree.

9.2—However, this law is not applicable to cases involving violation of one of the ten abominations; collective prosecution for rebellion or sedition (*fan-ni yuan-tso* 反逆緣坐);[8] killing (*sha-jen* 殺人); or to those who within their areas of jurisdiction (*chien-[lin] chu-[shou] nei* 監臨主守內)[9] [2b] commit illicit sexual intercourse,[10] robbery (*tao* 盜),[11] or kidnapping (*lüeh-jen* 略人);[12] or to those who take bribes and subvert the law (*shou-ts'ai erh wang-fa* 受財而枉法).[13]

SUBCOMMENTARY: Cases involving crimes punishable by life exile or less

[7]Ordinary memorials were sent through the Imperial Chancellery for comment before reaching the emperor. I have not found out how these special memorials came to the throne.

[8]See the discussion under the subsection on collective prosecution in the third part of introduction Chapter II. See also Articles 18, 248, 249; Deloustal 410.

[9]This term refers to the areas under the direction of either supervisory or custodial officials. See Article 54 for definitions of these two types of officials.

[10]The punishment for illicit sexual intercourse by an official within his area of jurisdiction varied with the status of the victim. The least degree of punishment was two years of penal servitude, a half year more than that given ordinary persons who committed this crime. See Articles 416 and 18.

[11]Officials who committed robbery within their areas of jurisdiction were punished two degrees more than ordinary thieves. Punishment started at eighty blows with the heavy stick and progressed to strangulation. See Articles 283; Deloustal 436, and 18.

[12]Article 292; Deloustal 452, provides no heavier penalty for officials who commit this crime. The punishment varied from strangulation to three years of penal servitude. Hence the loss of the right of petition is the only aggravating factor. See also Article 18.

[13]An official who took bribes and subverted the law within his area of jurisdiction was punished according to the amount of the bribe, the punishment ranging from one hundred blows with the heavy stick to strangulation. See Articles 138; Deloustal 138, and 18.

have their punishments reduced by one degree according to the relevant law. In cases involving violation of one of the ten abominations, collective prosecution for rebellion or sedition, or killing, the latter includes intentional killing (*ku-sha* 故殺), killing in an affray (*tou-sha* 鬭殺),[14] and plotting to kill (*mou-sha* 謀殺).[15] Where death has occurred, no distinction is to be made between principals (*shou* 首) and accessories (*ts'ung* 從).[16] For those who commit illicit sexual intercourse, robbery or kidnapping within their areas of jurisdiction, or those who take bribes and subvert the law, if in so doing the accused has committed a capital crime, petition is not permitted.

Where the crime is punished by life exile or less, reduction of punishment is not permitted. Therefore it is stated that this law is not applicable. However, in cases of robbery where nothing has been taken, or in cases of illicit sexual intercourse or kidnapping where the victim has not yet been seized, the law regarding reduction of punishment is followed.

Article 10

Officials of the Seventh Rank and Above

ARTICLE: All cases in which officials of the seventh rank and above, as well as the paternal grandparents, parents, brothers, sisters, wives, sons, and grandsons in the male line of those officials and nobles permitted petition, commit a crime punishable by life exile or less shall follow this principle allowing reduction of punishment by one degree.

SUBCOMMENTARY: This is called the clause on the right of reduction of punishment. Seventh rank and above refers to active-duty civil and

[14]Article 306; Deloustal 466, punishes killing in an affray by strangulation and intentional killing by decapitation. However, if a knife is used to kill someone in an affray, the punishment is increased to decapitation.

[15]A plot to kill someone of non-kin status is punished by three years of penal servitude. If the plot results in injury, the sentence is strangulation; if the result is death for the victim, the plotter is decapitated. The punishment for plotting to kill relatives is increased with the closeness of the relationship, so that a plot to kill a parent or husband is punished by decapitation even if no harm to them resulted from the plot. See Articles 256 and 253; Deloustal 414 and 415.

[16]For many offenses committed jointly by groups, the *Code* allows accessories to the crime one degree less punishment than the principal(s). Thus even in a crime punished by decapitation, the accessories would be sentenced to life exile to 3,000 *li*, since that is one degree reduction of punishment from either death penalty. See Article 42.

military officials, titular officials, guard officials, and honorary officials of the sixth and seventh ranks. Officials and nobles permitted petition refers to officials and nobles of the fifth rank and above, [27] whose protection extends to their paternal grandparents, parents, brothers, sisters, wives, sons, and grandsons in the male line. If any of these commit a crime punishable by life exile or less, they are allowed reduction of punishment by one degree.

If a person is allowed reduction of punishment under the above clause [3a] on petition, then he may also be allowed reduction of punishment under this clause. If the petitioner is not allowed reduction of punishment under the above clause, he may not get reduction of punishment under this clause. Therefore it is stated that each case follows this principle on reduction of punishment by one degree.

Article 11

Those Entitled to Deliberation, Petition, or Reduction of Punishment

ARTICLE: 11.1a—All cases in which those having the right of deliberation, petition, or reduction of punishment, extending to officials of the ninth rank and above, and including the paternal grandparents, parents, wives, sons or grandsons in the male line of those whose official rank permits them reduction of punishment, commit crimes punishable by life exile or less, permit redemption by payment of copper.

SUBCOMMENTARY: This is called the clause on redemption by payment of copper. Those entitled to deliberation, petition, or reduction of punishment means those who come under the three clauses on deliberation, petition, and reduction of punishment. There are also those who do not hold office and who yet come under these clauses; therefore the word "official" is not used.

Extending to officials of the ninth rank and above means officials of the eighth and ninth ranks. Those whose official rank permits them reduction of punishment means that the protection of officials of the seventh rank and above extends to their paternal grandparents, parents, wives, sons, and grandsons in the male line. If any of these persons commits a crime punishable by life exile or less, they are permitted redemption by payment of copper.

ARTICLE: 11.1b—Cases that require the use of office to replace punishment (*kuan-tang* 官當) follow the law on using office to replace punishment.[17]

Subcommentary: Persons below those entitled to deliberation, petition, or reduction of punishment but who have offices follow the laws on using office to replace punishment, or disenrollment, or resignation from office (*mien-[kuan]* 免官).[18] They may not retain such offices, use protection, or redemption by payment of copper.

[3b] Article: 11.2—Those sentenced to life exile with added labor (*chia-yi liu* 加役流),

Subcommentary: Crimes now punished by life exile with added labor, anciently were punished by death. During the Wu-te period (618–626) this was changed to amputation of the toes. The emperor had pity for the punished, his mercy was great, and his love all pervasive, considering that those punished with amputation could not return to wholeness. He devoted his attention to preserving the life of those sentenced to death. "His feelings were sorrowful for him who faced the corner."[19] "His mercy was great as he prayed [and cut] the net."[20] In the sixth year of the Cheng-kuan period (A.D. 632), there was an imperial decree, changing the punishment of amputation of the toes to that of life exile with added labor.[21]

Article: life exile for collective prosecution for rebellion or sedition,

Subcommentary: In cases of life exile for those who are collectively prosecuted for rebellion or sedition, where the wife has an office, such position is considered to be equal to four years of penal servitude [and may replace it].[22] However, according to this law on using office to replace punishment, she still is disenrolled. If she has no office, she is

[17]See Article 17 and the subsection on official privilege and responsibility in the fourth part of introduction Chapter II.

[18]See Article 19.

[19]This seems to be a quotation from some now lost source. A similar phrase occurs in *Han shu* 23/20b; Hulsewé, *Han Law*, I, 345. The text there goes on to state that the true ruler cannot be happy while even one person does not obtain justice.

[20]Here the reference is probably to the legendary Emperor Yao, as he prayed and cut the hunting net so that some of the trapped animals might escape. See *Shih chi* 3/3b; Chavannes, *Mémoires historiques*, I, 180.

[21]*T'ang hui-yao* (Essential Documents of the T'ang Dynasty), p. 707; Bünger, *Quellen*, p. 191, states that this punishment was ended still earlier in the first year of the Cheng-kuan period, that is, 627.

[22]Article 17 states that life exile is equal to four years of penal servitude. However, this clause is in direct opposition to certain provisions of Article 248; Deloustal 410. In

beaten with the heavy stick and sent to forced labor (*p'ei-yi* 配役) in accordance with the law on remaining and dwelling at home (*liu-chu* 留住).[23]

ARTICLE: Life exile for sons and grandsons in the male line for accidental (*kuo-shih* 過失) killing of their paternal grandparents or parents,

SUBCOMMENTARY: This refers to cases of killing the paternal grandparents or parents, "wherein eyes and ears could not have perceived such a result, and where thought and planning could not have prevented it" (*erh-mu so-pu-chi ssu-lü so-pu-tao* 耳目所不及思慮所不到).[24]

[28] ARTICLE: life exile for lack of filial piety,

SUBCOMMENTARY: Life exile for lack of filial piety means life exile for concealing the fact that one has heard of the death of one's parents, and not mourning; life exile for being an accessory in accusing one's paternal grandparents or parents to the court, [4a] the person who actually does so being strangled; life exile for having used bad language or spells towards one's paternal grandparents or parents; or life exile for having used sorcery to gain their doting love.

QUERY: To arrange for one's own marriage during the period of mourning for one's parents is punishable by three years of penal servitude.[25] If threats of force are used, the punishment is increased to life exile. Does this come under life exile for lack of filial piety?

REPLY: Marriage induced by the fear of threats or force basically is not considered to be lack of filial piety. Punishment increased in this manner to life exile is not an official punishment. The article concerning marriage during mourning emphasizes the original circumstances of the crime which, according to reason, does not accord with the crime of lack of filial piety.

---

cases of such conflict between a general principle and a specific article, Article 49 states that the provisions of the specific article shall be followed.

[23]See Article 28. In such case, however, she does three years of labor instead of the one year that accompanies life exile.

[24]Article 339; Deloustal 498, permits most cases of accidental killing to be redeemed by payment of copper. But Article 329; Deloustal 474, punishes even the killing by accident of parents or paternal grandparents by life exile to 3,000 *li*.

[25]See Section 7 of Article 6 above.

ARTICLE: or life exile despite amnesty,

SUBCOMMENTARY: The Articles on Violence and Robbery state: "In cases of making or keeping *ku* poison, even though there be an amnesty, those who dwell together (*t'ung-chü* 同居) with the criminal as well as those who ordered the making of the poison will be exiled for life to 3,000 *li*."[26]

The Articles on Judgment and Prison state: "Those who kill relatives in the fourth degree of mourning of a higher generation or paternal first cousins older than themselves, or who plot rebellion or great sedition, even though there be an amnesty will still be exiled for life to 2,000 *li*."[27] Such cases will all be exiled for life despite amnesty.

In cases concerning the making and keeping of *ku* poison, whether or not the wives have official position, they under the text below[28] will be sent into life exile in accordance with the law. Wives who have offices will be disenrolled also, but at the place of exile they will be exempted from forced labor in a fixed place.

ARTICLE: in none of the above cases will reduction of punishment or redemption by payment of copper be allowed. Such criminals are disenrolled and sent into life exile (*p'ei-liu* 配役) in accordance with the law.

[4b] SUBCOMMENTARY: Men who commit these crimes punishable by the five kinds of life exile, no matter whether they are officials of the first rank or less, or whether they may receive protection, will not be allowed reduction of punishment or redemption by payment of copper.[29] They will be disenrolled and sent into exile for life in accordance with the law.

The three forms of life exile all include one year of labor. However, life exile with added labor includes three years of labor. Where the family has no other adults, in accordance with the section below, the criminal is beaten with the heavy stick but is exempted from labor.[30] Therefore this is stated to be in accordance with the law.

COMMENTARY: Those who are disenrolled are exempted from forced

[26]Article 262; Deloustal 423.

[27]Article 489.

[28]The reference here is to Article 28, but actually women who made or kept *ku* poison were strangled. See Article 262; Deloustal 423.

[29]Thus official privilege may not benefit anyone who commits crimes punished by these five kinds of life exile. This article then serves as a supplement to Article 6.

[30]See Article 27.

labor in a fixed place. Further, in cases in which the original crime did not require life exile, but where life exile is imposed for special circumstances, even though the criminal has no official rank, he also is exempted from forced labor in a fixed place.

SUBCOMMENTARY: In cases where those who have official or noble rank commit crimes punishable by the five kinds of life exile, they are disenrolled and sent into life exile but are exempted from forced labor in a fixed place.

In cases where the original crime did not require life exile, but where life exile is imposed for special circumstances, even though the criminal has no official rank he also is exempted from forced labor in a fixed place. This has reference to a person whose crime originally provided for punishment of penal servitude or less, or a person who has protection and for whom the relevant law did not provide for life exile, yet who, upon investigation of the circumstances, is specially sentenced to life exile. Even though he has no official rank, he too is exempted from forced labor in a fixed place.[31]

ARTICLE: 11.3a—In no cases requiring penal servitude because of the accidental killing or wounding of relatives of a higher generation, or of the same generation but older than oneself within the second or closer degree of mourning, or one's maternal grandparents, one's husband, and one's husband's paternal grandparents, as well as those cases for which life exile is required because of intentional beating causing disablement, or because of men who commit robbery [29] or wives [5a] who commit illicit sexual intercourse—for none of these cases will reduction of punishment or redemption by payment of copper be permitted.

SUBCOMMENTARY: Accidentally killing one's paternal grandparents or parents already comes under the five crimes punishable by life exile, and wounding them provides for penal servitude.[32] Therefore the article speaks of relatives of the second or closer degree of mourning. Penal servitude is required for the accidental killing or wounding of relatives of a higher generation, or of the same generation but older than oneself within the second or closer degree of mourning, as well as of one's maternal grandparents, one's husband, and one's husband's paternal

[31]The references here are to an increase in punishment beyond that given in a specific article dealing with a particular offense. Article 486 provides for sentencing offenses on the basis of imperial decrees or edicts.

[32]See note 24 of this chapter.

grandparents.[33]

Cases requiring life exile because of intentional beating causing disablement refers in this particular instance to those people who rely on protection to gain redemption by payment of copper and who intentionally beat someone so as to cause disablement. Such cases will be sentenced as comparable to crimes that require life exile.[34] Men who commit robbery punished by penal servitude or more means that calculation of the value of goods obtained in the robbery provides for penal servitude or more. Robbery by force (*ch'iang-tao* 強盜) where nothing has been taken is also considered to be the same.[35]

None of the cases above, including wives who commit illicit sexual intercourse,[36] are permitted reduction of punishment or redemption by payment of copper. Also means that crimes punished by penal servitude like those punished by the five kinds of life exile also do not permit reduction of punishment or redemption by payment of copper.

COMMENTARY: 11.3b—All cases involving those who have official or noble rank follow the laws concerning disenrollment, resignation from office, using office to replace punishment, and redemption by payment of copper.

SUBCOMMENTARY: This means cases of intentionally beating relatives of the fourth degree of mourning of a higher generation so as to cause disablement,[37] or of a man within his area of jurisdiction[38] violating one of the ten abominations or committing robbery, or of a woman who through illicit sexual intercourse comes within the section on incest. All of these provide for disenrollment.[39] If the man has committed a robbery

[33]Article 330 punishes such crimes by the wife against her husband's paternal grandparents by three years of penal servitude. I have not found any specific article *covering the accidental killing or wounding of relatives within the second degree of mourning.*

[34]Article 306 punishes this offense by life exile to 2,000 *li*. The present clause places it among those crimes that require life exile no matter what privileges the offender may have. On comparable sentences, see Article 53.

[35]The lightest punishment for robbery by force is two years of penal servitude. If anyone is wounded, the robber is strangled; and if anyone is killed, he is decapitated. See Article 281.

[36]Article 410 punishes illicit sexual intercourse by wives with two years of penal servitude.

[37]This clause then adds disenrollment to the life exile to 2,000 *li* already provided by Article 306. The reason for this is that crimes against senior relatives are punished more heavily than those against persons of non-kin status.

[38]See Article 54.

[39]See Article 21.

punishable by penal servitude or more, or the wife has committed illicit sexual intercourse, these provide for resignation from office.[40]

Cases requiring penal servitude because of accidentally killing or wounding relatives within the second degree of mourning of a higher generation, or of the same generation but older than oneself, or cases that require life exile because of intentionally beating a person of non-kin status so as to cause disablement provide for using office to replace punishment.[41] In cases where the crime provides for disenrollment, the noble rank is included as well.[42] [5b] In cases providing for resignation from office, resignation from occupied office, or using office to replace punishment, the noble title is retained and redemption by payment of copper is permitted.

Even if holders of official or noble rank would otherwise be allowed reduction of punishment, in these cases such reduction of punishment is not permitted. Therefore, it is stated that each case follows the laws on disenrollment, resignation from office, using office to replace punishment, and redemption.

Query: In cases involving the five kinds of life exile neither reduction of punishment nor redemption by payment of copper is permitted. Should there be a decrease of sentences (*chiang* 降), is either reduction of punishment or redemption by payment of copper allowed?

Reply: In cases involving the five kinds of life exile, the criminal is disenrolled and sent into life exile. If a decrease of sentences would reduce these punishments to penal servitude or less, there is no other text on those having protection and meriting redemption by payment of copper being sent to forced labor. Thus there are cases in which redemption by payment of copper is permitted and others where it is not permitted.

In cases of life exile with added labor, life exile for collective prosecution for rebellion or sedition, and life exile for lack of filial piety—in these three cases, when a decrease of sentences has been promulgated, redemption by payment of copper is permitted. However, in cases of life exile of sons and grandsons in the male line for accidental killing of their paternal grandparents or parents, even though a decrease of sentences is promulgated, redemption by payment of copper will not be permitted. Why is this? The text[43] of the article states

[40]See Article 19.
[41]See Article 17.
[42]See Article 21.
[43]*Yu* 又 should be read *wen* 文 , following the KHCPTS edition.

that in no cases requiring penal servitude because of the accidental killing or wounding of relatives of a higher generation, or of the same generation but older than oneself within the second or closer degree of mourning will reduction of punishment or redemption by payment of copper be permitted. These cases, like accidental killing or wounding, even though a decrease of sentences is promulgated, still require penal servitude, and, therefore, redemption by payment of copper is not permitted.

Cases involving those having office are sentenced in accordance with the principles on disenrollment, resignation from office, using office to replace punishment, and redemption. Where the relevant law does not permit reduction of punishment, neither will such reduction of punishment be permitted after a decrease of sentences is promulgated. As for life exile despite amnesty, it is clear that a decrease of sentences does not allow exemption from punishment for those sentenced under this article.

Article 12

Women Who Have Official Rank or Fief-titles

ARTICLE: 12.1—All cases in which women who have official rank or fief-titles commit offenses follow, depending on their rank, the articles on deliberation, petition, reduction of punishment, redemption by payment of copper, [6a] the use of office to replace punishment, or resignation from office. They are not permitted to protect their relatives.

[30] SUBCOMMENTARY: According to the statute,[44] women who have official rank include those of the rank of *fei* 妃 as well as dames of commanderies, counties, and subdistricts.[45] Fief-titles refer to the name of the principality, commandery, county, or subdistrict. Women of the sixth rank and below do not have fief-titles but only official rank, e.g., *ying* concubines.[46] According to the *Book of Rites*, "A wife's position follows that of her husband"[47] The commentary states: "Etiquette

[44]Niida, *Statutes*, p. 316.

[45]There were two categories of titled women: those who were secondary wives of the emperor or of the crown prince, and those whose title was either due to some family relationship with the emperor or to their husbands' official titles. The statute covers this second category. The title *fei* was borne by the mothers and principal wives of princes.

[46]See translation Chapter I, note 194.

[47]*Li chi*, "Tsa chi"; Couvreur, *Li ki*, II, 139. The Shih-san ching chu-shu edition reads

during life and mourning at death are in accordance with the husband's position."[48]

Where a crime has been committed, the right of deliberation, petition, reduction of punishment, and redemption by payment of copper, depending on the husband's rank, follow the laws on deliberation, petition, reduction of punishment, and redemption by payment of copper. If the offense provides for disenrollment, resignation from office, or the use of office to replace punishment, this also is in accordance with the principles for men.

Therefore it is stated that each case follows the articles concerned with deliberation, petition, reduction of punishment, redemption by payment of copper, the use of office to replace punishment, or resignation from office. However, since women's rank is due to husband or son, they may not protect their relatives.

ARTICLE: 12.2—Fief-titles that are specially conferred and are not due to the husband's or son's position are considered the same as those of men under the principle covering enfeoffment with noble titles.[49]

SUBCOMMENTARY: Cases involving crimes committed by those whose fief-titles are especially conferred are considered the same as those of men who have been enfeoffed with noble titles. In cases punished by disenrollment, the noble title is included as well.[50] Where the punishment is resignation from office or less, the principles on deliberation, petition, reduction of punishment, and redemption by payment of copper are followed. Office is retained and redemption by payment of copper is permitted.

Article 13

Crimes Committed by ch'ieh Concubines Belonging to Officials of the Fifth Rank and Above[51]

ARTICLE: All cases in which *ch'ieh* concubines belonging to officials of the

---

wei 位 for *ming* 命

[48]This is Cheng Hsüan's commentary on this passage from the *Li chi*.

[49]This includes mothers of the secondary wives of the emperor or crown prince, as well. Their rank is given in the *Ta T'ang liu-tien* (The T'ang Institutes), p. 41.

[50]Article 21 states that persons who are disenrolled lose their titles of nobility as well.

[51]*Ch'ieh* concubines were of a lower status than *ying* concubines. See translation Chapter I, note 194.

fifth rank and above commit crimes other than the ten abominations, punished by life exile or less permit redemption by payment of copper.

[6b] SUBCOMMENTARY: Officials of the fifth rank and above are comprehensively honorable (*t'ung-kuei* 通貴).[52] If their concubines commit a crime, they may not be sent into penal servitude or life exile or have beatings with the light or heavy stick administered. If the crime is not one of the ten abominations and is punished by life exile or less, redemption by payment of copper is permitted. However, if the article on redemption by payment of copper does not allow redemption by payment of copper [for the crime that the concubine has committed], the crime does not come within this article either.

In cases where a *ch'ieh* concubine has a son or grandson in the male line or receives protection from other relatives, if she commits a crime other than one of the ten abominations, sentencing follows the principle on redemption by payment of copper.

Article 14

A Person Having the Rights of Deliberation, Petition, and Reduction of Punishment

ARTICLE: 14.1—All cases involving a person having the rights of deliberation, petition, and reduction of punishment, each of which permits reduction of punishment, allow only the highest of them to be used to reduce punishment. Cumulative reduction of punishment (*lei-chien* 累減) is not permitted.

SUBCOMMENTARY: If a person is a relative of the empress within the fourth degree of mourning, reduction of punishment by deliberation for kinship with the imperial family is allowed.[53] If, furthermore, the father is an official of the third rank, reduction of punishment by petition is allowed.[54] Further, if the person is an official of the seventh rank, the principle on reduction of punishment is allowed.[55] Even though all three

[52]Comprehensively honorable is a collective term for officials of the fourth and fifth ranks. This class enjoyed more privileges than lower ranks, but fewer than the highest group of officials—those of the third rank and higher—who were designated *yi-kuei* 議貴, "worthy of deliberation."

[53]See the first subsection under Article 8. The empress' protection extended no further than her fourth-degree mourning relatives.

[54]See Article 9.

[55]See Article 10.

of these allow reduction of punishment, only the highest [deliberation for kinship with the imperial family] will be permitted. Cumulative reduction of punishment is not permitted.

ARTICLE: 14.2—In cases of reduction of punishment for accessories, confession (*tzu-shou* 自首), intentional (*ku* 故) or mistaken (*shih* 失) sentences, or mutual involvement in public offenses (*kung-tso* 公坐), where the criminal is of the class having the right of deliberation, petition, or reduction or punishment, cumulative reduction is permitted.

SUBCOMMENTARY: Reduction of punishment for accessories refers to cases where persons commit a crime together. The one who formulates the plan is the principal. The followers or accessories have their punishment reduced one degree below that of the principal.[56] [7a] Reduction of punishment for confession refers to someone who has broken the law knowing that another person will accuse him to the court and making a confession. Punishment is reduced two degrees below the usual penalty for the offense.[57]

Reduction for intentional or mistaken sentencing refers to the executive officer intentionally decreasing a person's sentence (*ku ch'u jen tsui* 故出人罪). Where the criminal has been released, but has been rearrested, a reduction of one degree of punishment is allowed.[58] In cases where the second officer did not know the circumstances, he is sentenced to mistaken reduction of sentence; that is, a further reduction of five degrees of punishment beyond that of the executive officer.[59]

Further, the Articles on Judgment and Prison state:[60] "Where it is

[56]This reduction of punishment for accessories is specified by Article 42. There are two important exceptions to this statement that the person who formulates the plan is considered to be the principal. If family members commit an offense together, only the oldest male in either generation or age is prosecuted. The others are not punished at all. Second, if an official together with other persons commits a crime within his area of jurisdiction, the official is prosecuted as the principal and the others as accessories, no matter who formulated the plan.

[57]This reduction of two degrees of punishment follows Article 37. Even flight does not preclude a reduction of sentence, providing the criminal returns.

[58]Intentional or mistaken increase or decrease in a criminal's sentence by a magistrate results in the magistrate himself being punished. See Article 487; Deloustal 685. The extent of his punishment depends upon such factors as whether or not the punishment has already been administered, and whether or not the criminal has already been released.

[59]See Article 40, which sets out the conditions for the joint prosecution (*lien-tso* 連坐) of officials. This concept has been treated at length by Bünger, "Verantvortlichkeit der Beamten."

required for the criminal to be sent into penal servitude or life exile,[61] yet redemption by payment of copper is permitted; or where redemption by payment of copper is required, yet the criminal is sent into penal servitude or life exile, each such case allows [the responsible official to receive] one degree of reduction of punishment beyond that for intentional or mistaken sentencing." That is, where the sentencing is intentional the penalty is one degree less than for intentional sentencing, and where mistaken the penalty is one degree less than for mistaken sentencing. [31] This is called reduction of punishment for intentional or mistaken sentencing.

Reduction of punishment for mutual involvement in a public offense refers to officials who are working together committing a public offense.[62] If an executive officer mistakenly lessens the sentence for a crime, a reduction of five degrees of punishment is permitted. Where the criminal has been released, but has been rearrested, a further reduction of one degree of punishment is allowed. The second officer is permitted reduction of seven degrees of punishment, the senior officer reduction of eight degrees of punishment, and the chief clerk nine degrees. If these persons are in the categories of those having the rights of deliberation, petition, or reduction of punishment, each of these allows yet another degree. This is called permitting cumulative reduction of punishment.

Article 15

Leaving Office for Reason

ARTICLE: 15.1a—All cases involving those who leave office for reason allow them the same rights as present office holders.

SUBCOMMENTARY: This means resignation which is not due to the commission of a crime but to such reasons as retirement, promotion, being released due to a reduction of staff, or the elimination of a prefecture or county. If these persons have had the rights of deliberation, petition, reduction of punishment, redemption by payment of copper, and protection of relatives, they still have the same rights as present office holders.

---

[60] Article 498.

[61] *Ying chüeh-p'ei* 應決配 refers to those who have neither office nor protection, and who are not too old, too young, or too disabled to come within the limits set by Article 30.

[62] See Article 40.

[7b] COMMENTARY: 15.1b—Even though retirement is not for reason, if the certificate of appointment (*kao-shen* 告身) is retained,[63] the person has the same rights as present office holders.

SUBCOMMENTARY: Even though retirement is not for reason means that retirement is because of the circumstances of an official's acts or[64] a low rating in the examination of merits,[65] or because office has been used to replace punishment or has been resigned. But if the certificates of appointment have been retained for offices not reached by the demotion (*chiang-so-pu-chih* 降所不至), the person has the same rights as those who hold office.

ARTICLE: 15.2a—Posthumously awarded offices as well as comparable-rank offices have the same rights as regular offices.

SUBCOMMENTARY: Posthumously awarded offices refer to those conferred after death. The statute states:[66] "'Living simply in the countryside,'[67] though sought and invited, he would not take office. His sons and grandsons in the male line may use this solicitation to him to take office as protection and thus have the same rights as regular officials."

As for comparable-rank offices, according to the statute on official rank,[68] both the *sa-pao* 薩寶 and the *hsien-cheng* 祆正 [69] of the *sa-pao* bureau have ranks comparable to those who have official rank (*liu-nei* 流內).[70] If comparable-rank offices are used to replace punishment, or

[63]Office holders were issued a certificate of appointment by the Board of Civil Office. When they were revoked, a time limit was set within which they had to be surrendered and if the time limit were violated the official would be beaten. See Article 493.

[64]*Nai* 乃 should be read *chi* 及 , following the KHCPTS edition.

[65]The examination of merit was an important administrative technique used in T'ang China. See the discussion in des Rotours, *Examens*, pp. 27 ff. Each year a report was made on the achievements of subordinate officials by their superiors. On the basis of these reports officials could be promoted, demoted, or forced to resign from office, and the certificate of appointment revoked.

[66]Niida, *Statutes*, p. 302.

[67]This quotation comes from the *Pei-shih* 64/31a, which gives the biographies of Liu Ch'iu (A.D. 501–554) and his family, who held office for several generations.

[68]Niida, *Statutes*, p. 302. On comparable-rank offices, see also des Rotours, *Fonctionnaires*, I, 45 note 3.

[69]Both of these offices have been linked with the worship of Zoroaster. See Albert Dien, "The Sa-pao Problem Re-examined," for a history and bibliography of the problem. Des Rotours, *Fonctionnaires*, I, 90 note 1, points out that there is no *sa-pao* bureau mentioned in the *Ta T'ang liu-tien*.

[70]Having official rank refers to the officials of the first through ninth ranks of the regular civil service, comprising in all thirty ranks. The first three ranks were divided into superior (*cheng* 正) and inferior (*ts'ung* 從). The fourth through ninth ranks were

to qualify the offender for reduction of punishment or redemption by payment of copper, they are equal to regular offices.

COMMENTARY: 15.2b—Comparable-rank offices of the sixth rank and below do not come within the principle on protection of relatives.

SUBCOMMENTARY: There is some difference between comparable-rank offices and regular offices. Therefore the former are not permitted to protect relatives. However, *sa-pao*, being comparable-rank offices of the fifth rank, are allowed protection of relatives.

ARTICLE: 15.3—It is the same whether the protector is alive or dead.

SUBCOMMENTARY: Cases involving those who are entitled to seek deliberation, petition, reduction of punishment,[71] or protection of relatives, even though the person himself may be dead, are considered the same as if he were alive. Therefore it is stated that it is the same whether the protector is alive [8a] or dead.

ARTICLE: 15.4—If relying on the protection of a relative of a higher generation, or of the same generation but older than oneself, one commits an offense against such a person,

SUBCOMMENTARY: Relatives of a higher generation, or of the same generation but older than oneself refers to paternal grandparents, parents, paternal uncles and aunts, father's sisters, or one's older brothers or sisters.

[32] ARTICLE: or if relying on the protection of a relative one commits an offense against that relative's paternal grandparents or parents, protection will not be allowed.

SUBCOMMENTARY: Relative refers to collateral relatives and not to one's own paternal grandparents, parents, sons, or grandsons in the male line. All collateral relatives who can protect one are included, whether of a higher generation, or of the same generation but older than oneself; or of a lower generation, or of the same generation but younger than oneself. If one relies on a paternal aunt's protection and commits an offense against that paternal aunt's paternal grandparents or parents, or

---

further subdivided into upper (*shang* 上) and lower (*hsia* 下).

[71]Redemption by payment of copper should presumably also be mentioned here, since it was included in the right of protection. See Article 11.

if one relies on the protection of one's nephew in the male line and commits an offense against someone such as that nephew's father and mother, in neither case will protection be allowed.

The text states: "[For cases where a wife] has committed an offense against her husband and is divorced (*yi-chüeh* 義絕),[72] she may still use her son's protection."[73] If a wife who commits an offense against her husband may still use her son's protection, it is clearly evident that a husband who commits an offense against his wife may also use his son's protection. The gaining of protection by means of sons and grandsons in the male line being set out in other texts, they are not included among the collateral relatives.[74]

Thus one who relies on protection from a son or grandson in the male line and who violates his own father's or paternal grandfather's commands, or has been deficient in support of them may still use the sections on protection or redemption of punishment. If one has offended against his paternal grandfather and would use his father's protection, it will not be permitted; whereas if one offends against his father, he may be permitted to use his paternal grandfather's protection.

ARTICLE: 15.5—For cases involving the beating or accusing to the court of one's relatives in the third degree of mourning, whether of a higher generation, or of the same generation but older than oneself, or of a relative in the fourth degree of mourning of a higher generation than oneself, the clause on protection may not be used.[75]

[8b] SUBCOMMENTARY: . . . Neither is redemption by payment of copper permitted.

ARTICLE: 15.6—For cases where a wife has committed an offense against her husband and is divorced, she may still use her son's protection.

SUBCOMMENTARY: No matter whether the wife commits an offense

[72]This type of divorce is due to crimes committed against the other spouse, and is to be distinguished from the seven conditions for repudiation of the wife. See note 76.

[73]See Article 15.6 below.

[74]Here and below an important principle of the *Code* is set forth. Where someone has committed an offense against a senior member of the family, he may not use the protection of another relative who is also junior to the offended person but senior to the offender. On the other hand, one may use the protection of junior members to exempt oneself from punishment for an offense against someone who is senior to both. Furthermore, a superior's protection may prevent punishment for an offense against someone who is that superior's junior.

[75]This is because such crimes come under discord, the eighth of the ten abominations.

against the husband and is divorced or she is repudiated by the husband,[76] she may still use her son's protection. This is because the tie of mother and son may not be broken.

ARTICLE: 15.7—If temporary officials (*chia-pan kuan* 假版官) commit crimes punishable by life exile or less, redemption by payment of copper is permitted.[77]

SUBCOMMENTARY: Temporary offices are not referred to in the statutes or ordinances. Services in such offices is due to the emperor's grace. Even though not aged,[78] such persons are permitted redemption by payment of copper, but the use of office to replace punishment is not permitted. In cases where redemption by payment of copper is not permitted and the punishment is penal servitude or more, the temporary office is also taken away.

Article 16

Crimes Committed while Not Holding Office

ARTICLE: 16.1a—All cases involving those who have committed crimes while not holding office yet who do hold office when the offense is discovered permit redemption by payment of copper if the crime is punishable by life exile or less.

COMMENTARY: This refers to persons who were formerly lesser officials

[76]There were seven conditions (*ch'i-ch'u* 七出) under which the wife could be repudiated and the marriage dissolved. These were: disobedience to the husband's parents, barrenness, adultery, jealousy, incurable disease, loquacity, and theft. However, if the wife had no close relatives to take her in, or had worn three years's mourning for her husband's parents, or if the husband's family, being poor at the time of marriage, had become wealthy, she could not be put aside except for incurable disease or adultery. See Article 189; Deloustal 59–60 (of the section on repudiation and divorce). See also Ch'ü, *Law and Society*, pp. 118–123.

[77]I have not obtained much information on the term *chia-pan*, "temporary commission." Tai, *General Principles*, p. 233, quotes the Sung encyclopedia *Yün-lu man-ch'ao* 雲麓漫鈔 that titles given to barbarians who came to the imperial court were considered to be substitute (*pan-shou* 版授). In the T'ang dynasty, *pan* was the name of a commission that could be given to lower officials without first seeking the emperor's permission, and such a temporary (*chia*) commission seems to be what is referred to here. See des Rotours, *Examens*, p. 272.

[78]*Chi-nien* 耆年 refers to those persons seventy years of age or older. They were allowed to redeem crimes punished by life exile or less by payment of copper. See Article 30.

without official rank or commoners who have been appointed to an office with official rank. They do not use office to replace punishment, are not disenrolled, and do not resign from office. 16.1b—This law is not applicable to cases involving the violation of the ten abominations or the five kinds of life exile.[79]

SUBCOMMENTARY: . . .[9a] Those who have been disenrolled, have used office to replace punishment, or resigned from appointment carrying official rank also come under this principle on crimes committed while not holding office. But where the clause on redemption by payment of copper provides for disenrollment, resignation from office, or using office to replace punishment, redemption by payment of copper is also permitted.[80] Therefore it is stated [here] that they do not use office to replace punishment, are not disenrolled, and do not resign from office.

If there is a violation of the ten abominations [33] or of crimes punished by the five kinds of life exile, each offender in accordance with the original crime is disenrolled and sent into life exile. Such cases are not the same as those specified in this law, which allows redemption by payment of copper. Therefore it is stated that this article is not applicable.

QUERY: All cases involving those who have committed crimes while not holding office yet who do hold office when the offense is discovered permit redemption by payment of copper if the crime is punishable by life exile or less. Although redemption by payment of copper is referred to, if the office is of the seventh rank or above is reduction of punishment permitted or not?

REPLY: It has already been stated that redemption by payment of copper is permitted for crimes punishable by life exile or less. If, according to the section on redemption by payment of copper, reduction of punishment is not permitted, then neither does this section allow reduction of punishment. Those having the right of reduction of punishment for other miscellaneous crimes are sentenced in accordance with the principle on reduction of punishment. In the text below,[81] those who have committed crimes while having no protection, which are discovered when they have protection also follow the law on official protection. Therefore it is known that the principle on reduction of punishment may be used.

[79]See Articles 6 and 11.
[80]See Article 11.
[81]See Article 16.3 below.

ARTICLE: 16.2a—Cases involving public offenses punishable by life exile or less committed while a person is in a low office and the offense is discovered after they have been transferred, or involving crimes committed while a person is in office and the offense is discovered after they have left office, or who leave office when the offense is discovered, will not be prosecuted.[82]

16.2b—Other offenses will be prosecuted in accordance with the relevant laws.

SUBCOMMENTARY: Those who commit crimes while in a low office and the offense is discovered after they have been transferred refers to such cases as committing a crime when one is holding a ninth-rank office and the offense is discovered after getting an eighth-rank office [9b] or above. . . . Or who leave office when the offense is discovered means that when the offense is discovered the criminal is arrested and interrogated but leaves office before he has been sentenced. . . .

Transfer of office refers to changes of office and not only to advancement in official rank. Other offenses will be prosecuted in accordance with the relevant laws refers to private offenses as well as public offenses. Crimes punishable by death are all sentenced in accordance with the relevant laws. Even though the criminal has been transferred or has left office, there is no exemption from punishment.

QUERY: According to the statute, "Officials in the capital and in the provinces who are ordered by imperial edict (*ch'ih* 勅) to fill another position are called provisional officials. If in charge of offices, they are called acting executive officials."[83] It has not yet been discerned whether if these types of officials commit public offenses and leave office, they will be exempt from punishment or not.

REPLY: . . .Provisional and acting executive officials are both supervisory officials (*chien-lin* 監臨),[84] so that if they commit offenses there is no reduction of punishment. But temporary officials who are sent out to the provinces with the imperial edict and tally (*fu* 符)[85] or those acting executive officials who are in charge of an office, are considered to be the same as regular officials.

[82]Article 17 makes the distinction between public and private offenses by officials.

[83]Niida, *Statutes*, p. 594.

[84]See Article 54.

[85]The different types of decrees and tallies are discussed in des Rotours, *Fonctionnaires*, I, 166, 180. See also des Rotours, "Les Insignes en deux parties (*fou*) sous la dynastie des T'ang."

The principle involved is that completion of the assignment is considered to be leaving office, so that public offenses punished by life exile in accordance with this law are exempted from punishment. However, in offenses involving the imperial guard, the circumstances are more serious, and a memorial is sent up awaiting the imperial decision.

Officials such as imperial court assistants or county personnel assistants really are not from other offices. If they temporarily act as administrative officials, the circumstances are not the same as under this principle on leaving office. All offices, in accordance with the statute, [10a] have officials who stand night duty in turns.[86] They are not of the class of acting executive officials and do not come within this section on leaving office.

ARTICLE: 16.3—Cases involving those who commit crimes while holding office which are discovered when they hold no office, or who commit crimes while having protection which are discovered when they do not have protection, or who commit crimes while having no protection which are discovered when they have protection, all follow the law on official protection.

SUBCOMMENTARY: Those who commit crimes while holding office which are discovered when they hold no office refers to the holder of a ninth-rank office committing a crime punishable by life exile which provides for disenrollment. But before the offense is discovered, he commits another crime punishable by one year of penal servitude, which also provides for disenrollment. [34] The ninth-rank office is used to replace the sentence of one year of penal servitude, and the offender is disenrolled.

Later the crime punishable by life exile is discovered. In using office to replace life exile, life exile is considered to be equal to four years of penal servitude.[87] The former office having already been used to replace one year, three years of penal servitude still remain. Therefore the sentence follows the article on official protection. Through payment of sixty *chin* of copper the criminal is released and is exempted from punishment.[88] Those whose office is higher and who have the right to deliberation, petition, or reduction of punishment are also sentenced in accordance with this article.

[86]Standing duty in turns (*tang-chih chih kuan* 當直之官) refers to officials being required to take turns at night duty in their offices. See Tai, *General Principles*, p. 240 note 11.

[87]This equivalence is made in Article 17.

[88]This is in accordance with Article 11. Article 3 makes three years of penal servitude redeemable by sixty *chin* of copper.

Those who commit crimes while having protection which are discovered after there is no protection refers to a son or grandson in the male line committing a crime at the time when his father or paternal grandfather held a seventh-rank office. After the father or paternal grandfather has been disenrolled, the offense is discovered. The son is still permitted redemption by payment of copper because of the seventh-rank office.[89]

If the father or paternal grandfather had been an official of the fifth rank or higher at the time of the offense, deliberation, petition, and reduction of punishment would have been allowed. If the offense were discovered after the father or paternal grandfather had been disenrolled or had resigned from office, sentence would still be in accordance with the laws on deliberation, petition, and reduction of punishment.

Those who commit crimes while not having protection which are discovered when they have protection refers to a son or grandson in the male line committing a crime at the time when his father or paternal grandfather held no office. If, when the offense is discovered, the father or paternal grandfather holds a seventh-rank office, redemption by payment of copper will be allowed. If a fifth-rank office is held, the son or grandson will be allowed reduction of punishment. If the father or paternal grandfather holds an active-duty office of the third rank, [10b] petition will be allowed. If protection is still higher, deliberation will be permitted. In these four cases leniency is allowed. Therefore it is stated that they follow the law on official protection.

Article 17

Using Office to Replace Penal Servitude

ARTICLE: 17.1a—All cases involving those who commit private offenses (*ssu-tsui* 私罪) use office to replace penal servitude.[90]

COMMENTARY: Private offenses mean those committed in a private capacity, including such matters as falsifying and not reporting the true circumstances in replying to imperial edicts,[91] or such

[89]See Article 10.

[90]*Tang* 當, "replacement," does not seem to have the same meaning in the *Code* that Hulsewé believes it to have possessed in Han times. See Hulsewé, *Han Law*, I, 80–81. In the *Code* it is not used in the sense of restoring the proper balance of nature, which was upset by a crime. Rather it is simply a technical term lacking philosophical overtones.

[91]This is punished by two years of penal servitude. See Article 367; Deloustal 519. Should the document concern secret affairs of state, the penalty is increased by one degree. The specific article is broader than just replying to imperial decrees, and also

offenses as subverting the law in receiving requests (*shou-ch'ing wang-fa* 受請枉法).[92]

SUBCOMMENTARY: Private offenses mean those committed in a private capacity which have no connection with public affairs. Even though connected with public affairs, if the motive is prejudiced or partial, it is considered to be a private offense. As to falsifying and not reporting the true circumstances in replying to imperial decrees: although replying to imperial decrees is in itself connected with public affairs, when advantage for the self is involved in not disclosing the true circumstances and the mind harbors secret deceit, the act then becomes the same as a private offense.

Such offenses as subverting the law in receiving requests refers to twisting the law in accepting people's requests for favors. Even though no goods are accepted, there is a subversion of the law. Since these categories of offenses are numerous, therefore, the phrase "such offenses" is used.

ARTICLE: One office of the fifth rank and above replaces two years of penal servitude. One office of the ninth rank and above replaces one year of penal servitude.

SUBCOMMENTARY: Offices of the ninth rank and above are humble. Therefore one office replaces one year of penal servitude. Offices of the fifth rank and above are honorable. Therefore one office replaces two years of penal servitude.

ARTICLE: 17.1b—In cases involving those who commit public offenses (*kung-tsui* 公罪), office replaces an additional year of penal servitude.

COMMENTARY: Public offenses refer to those connected with public affairs which do not involve secret crookedness.

SUBCOMMENTARY: Both secrecy and crookedness are necessary. Where public affairs are involved, if the circumstances lack secret crookedness, then even though the laws and regulations have been violated, it is a public offense [11a] and each office replaces an additional year of penal

---

includes memorials on affairs and sending up memorials.

[92]Article 135; Deloustal 138, punishes such behavior by fifty blows with the light stick. Should the violation of the law actually have been carried out, the penalty is increased to one hundred blows with the heavy stick.

servitude. Thus one office of the fifth rank and above replaces three years of penal servitude, and one office of the ninth rank and above replaces two years of penal servitude.

QUERY: Are cases of infraction in carrying out an imperial edict or decree also public offenses or not?

REPLY: If in carrying out an imperial decree or edict, unknowingly there is an infraction of the meaning, this is breaking an imperial edict. Even though the meaning of an imperial edict has been violated, if the circumstances do not involve secrecy, it is a public offense.[93]

[35] ARTICLE: 17.2—In using office to replace life exile, the three kinds of life exile[94] are the same and are considered to be equal to four years of penal servitude.

SUBCOMMENTARY: When a ranked official commits a crime punishable by life exile, he is not actually sent into life exile but rather uses office to replace punishment and makes redemption by payment of copper to equal four years of penal servitude. If an eighth or ninth-rank official commits a private offense punishable by life exile, four offices are needed to replace punishment.[95] Those without four offices, according to the number of years of penal servitude, use office to replace punishment and make redemption by payment of copper. Therefore it is stated that the three kinds of life exile are the same and are equal to four years of penal servitude.

ARTICLE: 17.3—If there are two offices,

COMMENTARY: Active-duty office, titular office, and guard office are all considered to be one office.[96] Honorary office is also considered to be an office.

SUBCOMMENTARY: This means that the grades within ranks of active-duty

[93]Though not mentioned here, the applicable specific article makes a distinction as to whether the error is intentional, or a misunderstanding of the meaning of the decree (*shih-ts'o chih-yi* 失錯旨意). The respective penalties were two years of penal servitude and one hundred blows with the heavy stick. See Article 112; Deloustal 122.

[94]This refers to the distances of 2,000, 2,500, and 3,000 *li* set out in Article 4.

[95]Offices which had been held previously could also be used to replace punishment if the certificates of appointment had not been revoked. See the fifth section of this article.

[96]See the discussion in the subsection on official privilege and responsibility in the fourth part of introduction Chapter II.

offices, titular offices, and guard offices are all counted in the same order. Because such ranks are acquired on similar bases, therefore they are all considered to be one office. Honorary office is conferred because of merit, and therefore is another office. These are two offices. If active-duty office is used to replace penal servitude, [11b] each grade is considered to be an office, whereas only the superior and inferior grades of honorary offices are considered to be one office [in the resulting demotion].[97]

ARTICLE: first, the higher office is used to replace punishment.

COMMENTARY: Cases involving those who have left office and not yet resumed office (*hsü* 敘) also follow this principle.[98]

SUBCOMMENTARY: First, the higher office is used to replace punishment means that from among the three offices consisting of active-duty office and the others, the highest is used to replace punishment. Cases involving those who have left office and not yet resumed office refer to leaving office for reason, or if the office has not been left for reason that the certificate of appointment has not been revoked. Such cases also follow the above principle in that the highest office is first used to replace punishment.

QUERY: This article states: "Cases involving those who have left office and not yet resumed office also follow this principle." Suppose there is a person who has left office and not yet resumed office, and some offense is discovered; perhaps the crime requires the use of office to replace punishment or more, or perhaps it does not extend to the use of office to replace punishment. However, if a special imperial edict orders resignation from office to replace punishment, under the law on resumption of office, what is to be the punishment?

REPLY: If the original punishment is to use office to replace punishment or more, another article states: "Those who leave office for reason are allowed the same rights as present office holders."[99] Thus, following this law on using office to replace penal servitude, if the office is not entirely canceled, office may be resumed after one year (*nien*)[100] with a

[97]This refers to there being four grades within active-duty, titular, and guard offices from ranks four through nine, while honorary offices had only two grades within each rank.

[98]The rules on resumption of office are given in Article 21.

[99]Article 15.

reduction of one degree from the original rank. If office is entirely canceled, office may be resumed after three years (*tsai*) with a reduction of two degrees from the original rank. If the punishment for the crime does not extend to the use of office to replace punishment, so that the certificate of appointment is not revoked, resumption of office follows the principle on resignation in the Statutes on the Examination of Merits.[101] That is, after one year (*chi-nien*) office is resumed with no reduction in rank. For those who resign from a presently held office, the law on resumption of office is in accordance with the Statutes on Prison Officials.[102]

[12a] Where the criminal has already left office, the original offense not extending to resignation from office but office being resigned upon reception of an imperial edict, in accordance with the Ordinances of the Board of Punishments,[103] the limits for resumption of office are the same as under the principle on resignation in the Statutes on the Examination of Merits. If the original crime requires the use of office to replace punishment, the certificate of appointment is also revoked.

ARTICLE: Second, honorary office is used to replace punishment.

[36] SUBCOMMENTARY: If an active-duty official of the sixth rank who concurrently holds the honorary office of Pillar of the State or above commits a private offense punishable by life exile, following the principle, punishment is reduced one degree to three years of penal servitude.[104] A sixth-rank active-duty office may replace one year of penal servitude. Second, the honorary office of Pillar of the State replaces two years of penal servitude.

QUERY: If a man holds both a third and a fourth-rank active-duty office and also holds an honorary office of the sixth rank or below, and

---

[100]The *Code* distinguishes between *nien* 年, *tsai* 載, and *chi-nien* 期年, all of which, in different ways, mean year. According to the definitions given in Article 21, the period *nien* is 360 days, representing six of the sexagenary cycles. *Tsai*, on the other hand, does not indicate a given number of days, and so includes the intercalary months that were needed periodically to "fill in" the lunar year and keep it in approximate correlation with the solar year. An intercalary month was needed about once in every three years, so for the three or six-year periods without office, *tsai* is used. *Chi-nien* is defined as a round of the four seasons and thus probably means a solar year.

[101]See Niida, *Statutes*, p. 344.

[102]See Niida, *Statutes*, p. 771. Varying lengths of time are given before office may be resumed, depending upon the type of offense.

[103]See Twitchett, "The Fragment of the T'ang Ordinances."

[104]One degree of reduction of punishment lessens all sentences of life exile to three years of penal servitude. See Article 56.

commits a crime requiring the use of office to replace punishment, after the third-rank office has been canceled, what office is next used to replace punishment?

REPLY: The article states: "First, the higher office is used to replace punishment." That is, from among the active-duty, the titular, and the guard offices, the highest rank is first used. Second, the honorary office is used, that is, the sixth-rank honorary office must be used to replace punishment. It is not permitted to make further use of the fourth-rank active-duty office to replace punishment.

ARTICLE: 17.4—Those holding temporary offices in each case use their original rank to replace punishment. Moreover, in each case they resign from the presently held office.

[12b] SUBCOMMENTARY: If an inferior lower fifth-rank official temporarily administers an upper sixth-rank office and commits a private offense punishable by two and one-half years of penal servitude, he is permitted reduction of one degree of punishment. The remaining two years of penal servitude are replaced by the original lower fifth-rank office. Moreover, he resigns from the presently held sixth-rank office. If a sixth-rank titular official temporarily holds a fifth-rank active-duty office and also commits a private offense punishable by two and one-half years of penal servitude, the original rank replaces one year of penal servitude and the remaining penal servitude is redeemed by payment of copper. He resigns from the fifth-rank active-duty office.

QUERY: If a former superior upper sixth-rank titular official moves up so as temporarily to hold an active-duty fifth-rank office, or a lower fifth-rank official moves down so as temporarily to administer an upper sixth-rank office,[105] and either one commits a crime punished by penal servitude for which office is used to replace punishment, is the certificate of appointment revoked?

REPLY: The article states: "Those holding temporary office use their original rank to replace punishment." Moreover, in each case they resign the presently held office.[106] If a superior upper sixth-rank titular official temporarily holds a fifth-rank office, no additional certificate of

[105]The Tai-nan-ko and Chih-cheng editions have a blank here. The SPTK edition reads *shang* 上, and the KHCPTS edition reads *kuan* 官. I have followed the latter reading.

[106]*Shih* 仕 should be read *jen* 任, following the Chih-cheng edition.

appointment is issued. Since the sixth-rank office is used to replace punishment, both the sixth-rank office and the temporary office are canceled. If a fifth-rank official administers a sixth-rank office, the fifth-rank office is used to replace punishment, but he resigns from only the sixth-rank active-duty office. If the certificate of appointment is of the same rank as the office required to be used to replace punishment, both are revoked.

ARTICLE: 17.5—If there is additional punishment, or a further crime, previously held offices may be used to replace punishment.

COMMENTARY: Previously held office refers to those not reached by the reduction in rank.

SUBCOMMENTARY: If there is additional punishment means that after the two offices are used to replace punishment, there is remaining penal servitude; or though replacing punishment has canceled office, [13a] there is then a further violation of the law which has not yet been sentenced—in such cases previously held certificates of appointment not reached by the reduction in rank may successively replace punishment.

[37] ARTICLE: 17.6—Those who hold an office carrying official rank who commit a crime while holding an active-duty office that does not carry official rank use their office that carries official rank to replace punishment, and they may redeem one year of penal servitude. In each case they resign from the office without official rank.

SUBCOMMENTARY: If an honorary official commits a crime punishable by penal servitude or more while holding an active-duty office carrying official rank, the honorary office is used to replace punishment. Or, in a crime punishable by penal servitude, where the honorary office does not cancel the punishment,[107] one or more years of penal servitude may be redeemed by payment of copper. In each case the office that has no official rank is resigned.

[107]For the blank in the Tai-nan-ko edition, the P'ang-hsi chai and SPTK editions have *che* 者 . This does not affect the meaning.

Article 18

The Ten Abominations and Collective Prosecution for Rebellion or Sedition

ARTICLE: 18.1—All cases involving violation of the ten abominations, intentional killing, and collective prosecution for rebellion or sedition,

SUBCOMMENTARY: . . . Intentional killing refers to intentional killing not done in an affray. Plotting to kill if the victim has already been killed is considered the same as intentional killing. Other articles that refer to sentencing for plotting to kill or intentional killing, or which state that they follow the laws on plotting to kill or intentional killing when a killing has taken place, all follow this law.

Personal retainers and slaves do not come under this law.[108] It is submitted that under the Articles on Violence and Robbery on the killing of three persons of a single family who have not committed a capital offense, the commentary states that personal retainers and slaves do not come within this law.[109] However, the intentional killing of a *ch'ieh* concubine,[110] or of a former personal retainer [13b] or slave who has been manumitted (*fang* 放) and become a commoner,[111] even though in the specific article the punishment does not go so far as death, equally comes under this principle on intentional killing.

Collective prosecution for rebellion or sedition refers to those punished by life exile or more for involvement in plotting rebellion or great sedition.[112]

COMMENTARY: Cases which basically require collective prosecution, but

[108]See the discussion on the inferior classes in that subsection of the fourth part of introduction Chapter II.

[109]Article 259; Deloustal 419. The three persons killed had to be at least of the same status as the slayer for the crime to come under the ten abominations. Thus, if a personal retainer or slave were to kill three members of his own or a higher class of the same family, the crime would so be classified. For the definition of family or household, see translation Chapter I, note 128.

[110]Article 325; Deloustal 481, punishes the killing of a concubine by two degrees less penalty than the killing of a wife, that is, three years of penal servitude. This clause adds disenrollment to that punishment when such a killing is done deliberately.

[111]A former master who killed a manumitted personal retainer would be punished by three years of penal servitude, and by two years of penal servitude if he killed a manumitted slave. See Article 336. The translation of a document of manumission is given in Mark Elvin, *The Pattern of the Chinese Past*, p. 74.

[112]These two crimes are the first two of the ten abominations. See Articles 6 and 248; Deloustal 410.

where the criminals are aged or disabled and exempted from punishment, are considered the same [as other cases insofar as disenrollment is concerned. This is specified in the text below].

SUBCOMMENTARY: This means that among those collectively prosecuted, if there are men who are eighty years of age or are incapacitated (*tu-chi* 篤疾),[113] or women who are sixty years of age or are disabled (*fei-chi* 廢疾), even though they are exempted from collective prosecution, will all be disenrolled if they have official rank.

QUERY: If a person who had office and would have been included in collective prosecution has already died and a son or grandson in the male line later commits rebellion, is the dead person also disenrolled or not?

REPLY: The law on collective prosecution is only applicable to the living. Neither will those who have been adopted by other families or who have been ordained as Buddhist or Taoist priests or nuns be collectively prosecuted. How can persons already dead have their certificates of appointment revoked or be disenrolled? This principle must have wide application. Certificates of appointment are not revoked, but even though not revoked they may not be used as protection.

ARTICLE: if the case has been completed, even though there be an amnesty, the criminal will still be disenrolled.

COMMENTARY: A case being completed means that the illicit goods (*tsang* 贓) and the circumstances of the crime have been exposed and investigated and the Imperial Secretariat has already passed judgment without, however, the submission of a memorial to the throne.

SUBCOMMENTARY: In cases involving the ten abominations, if the case has been completed, even though there should be a great amnesty,[114] the criminal will still be disenrolled. If the case has not yet [14a] been completed, then in accordance with the amnesty there is exemption

[113]Disablement and incapacitation are defined and their effect on liability for punishment discussed in the subsection on age, sex, and physical and mental disabilities in the fourth part of introduction Chapter II. See Niida, *Statutes*, p. 228.

[114]During the T'ang period there were several kinds of amnesties: ordinary amnesty (*ch'ang-she*), great amnesty (*ta-she* 大赦), amnesties for the whole country (*p'u-she* 普赦), and amnesties for particular sections of the country (*ch'ü-she* 曲赦). See the discussion in the second part of introduction Chapter II, and in Tai, *General Principles*, pp. 330 ff.

from punishment. The commentary states: "The illicit goods and the circumstances of the crime have been exposed and investigated." Illicit goods [38] mean the illicit goods involved in the offense. Circumstances refers to such crimes as killing. . . .

The Imperial Secretariat having already passed judgment, without, however, the submission of a memorial to the throne means that the Board of Punishments has already reviewed the sentence.[115] Even though the case has not been memorialized to the throne, it is completed. In these cases then, the criminal is disenrolled after an amnesty because he may not be exempted by ordinary amnesty.

ARTICLE: 18.2a—Supervisory and custodial (*chu-shou* 主守) officials[116] who commit illicit sexual intercourse,[117] robbery,[118] and kidnapping,[119] or who take bribes and subvert the law within their areas of jurisdiction, are also disenrolled.

18.2b—If the case is completed, even though there be an amnesty, the criminal resigns from occupied office.

COMMENTARY: If there is a decrease of sentences, the case is treated the same as under the law on resignation from office.

SUBCOMMENTARY: Illicit sexual intercourse within the area of jurisdiction refers to illicit sexual intercourse by officials with commoners. Robbery and taking bribes and subverting the law refer to illicit goods worth one *p'i* of silk or more. By kidnapping is meant kidnapping done without the victim's consent. If the victim is ten years of age or less, the act, even if done with the victim's consent, is considered the same as kidnapping. The text of the article in reference to kidnapping makes no distinction between commoners and the inferior classes.

Where cases have already been completed, they are treated the same as under the above law and the criminal is disenrolled. If there should be an amnesty, the criminal resigns from occupied office. In these cases

[115] All punishments other than beating had to be passed on by authorities higher than the magistrate. See the discussion in the seventh part of introduction Chapter II. The statute providing this review of sentences is in Niida, *Statutes*, p. 757.

[116] Supervisory officials had a general administrative responsibility for any geographical unit, from a prefecture down to a garrison town. Custodial officials, on the other hand, were in charge of particular activities or things, such as a warehouse. Offenses committed by such officials within their areas of jurisdiction were punished more heavily than the same crimes committed by ordinary persons. See Article 54.

[117] See note 10 of this chapter.

[118] See note 11 of this chapter.

[119] See note 12 of this chapter.

then, the criminal resigns from one occupied office after an amnesty because he may not be exempted by ordinary amnesty.

QUERY: Kidnapping within the area of jurisdiction is of the class of crimes covered by disenrollment. The section on slaves does not include slaves within the limits of commoners. If a personal retainer is kidnapped within the sphere of jurisdiction, [14b] does this call for disenrollment or not?

REPLY: According to the law in which the killing of three persons of one family who have not committed a capital crime comes under depravity, personal retainers and slaves are not considered to be the same as commoners.[120] However, in cases of robbery by force, if one of the property owner's personal retainers is wounded, it is considered to be the same as if he were a commoner. Each case is considered under the appropriate article; there is no fixed principle for prosecuting such cases.

Now the kidnapping of commoners and slaves both call for disenrollment. The kidnapping of a slave is brought up as a lighter offense wherein calculation of the value of the illicit goods [that is, the value of the slave] brings it under the law on disenrollment in order to make it clear that the kidnapping of a personal retainer is punished more heavily. Thus it is clear that the kidnapping of personal retainers also calls for disenrollment. Further, the Articles on Assaults and Accusations state that the punishment for beating or wounding a personal retainer is reduced one degree below that for beating or wounding commoners, and for beating or wounding a slave, it is reduced still another degree.[121]

Further, the statute states: "If one transfers a personal retainer to serve another person, the value of their food and clothing is calculated and repaid."[122] The value of this food and clothing must, however, be one *p'i* of silk or more in order to be accounted illicit goods. Thus, on all these counts, the kidnapping of a personal retainer is sentenced the same as that of a slave; further, the punishment is reduced below that for kidnapping a commoner. Thus from several articles it follows that disenrollment would be proper [for an official who kidnapped a

[120]See note 109 of this chapter.

[121]See Article 320.

[122]See Niida, *Statutes*, p. 262. Since personal retainers were not slaves, they were not supposed to be sold. But the repayment of their former master for their food and clothing was simply a way around this. See Niida, *Shina Mibunhō Shi* (A History of Personal Status in Chinese Law), pp. 899 ff.

personal retainer within his area of jurisdiction].

FURTHER QUERY: According to the article, those who collectively commit robbery are sentenced for the total value of the illicit goods.[123] In the case of those who subvert the law by collectively receiving illicit goods, are they sentenced according to the total value of the illicit goods or not?

REPLY: In the section on taking bribes and subverting the law, there is no mention of the total value of the illicit goods. It only states that where an official takes bribes and further takes the bribes received and divides them among other officials, the original receiver is sentenced for the total value of the illicit goods.[124] The others are each sentenced according to the law for their individual shares of the illicit goods. The case of those who collectively plot to take bribes does not [15a] come under the same principle as does that of original receivers and does not call for punishment on the basis of the total value of the illicit goods. Rather, each criminal is sentenced as principal or accessory according to his individual share.

[39] COMMENTARY: 18.2c—If there is a decrease of sentences, the case is treated the same as under the law on resignation from office.[125]

SUBCOMMENTARY: A decrease of sentences reduces the degree of punishment but is not a complete pardon. Therefore, a decrease of sentences in the case of disenrollment is sentenced according to the law on resignation from office. If the punishment is completely canceled, the principle on resignation from office is still followed. Thus, if after the decrease of sentences there is a second sentencing, but before this latter can be memorialized and signed by the emperor there is a further amnesty or decrease of sentences, the criminal still resigns from occupied office.

ARTICLE: 18.3a—Those who commit miscellaneous capital crimes and then die in prison, or who are exempted from the death penalty by being specially sent into life exile, or who escape the death penalty by taking flight, are all disenrolled.

[123]This is specified in Article 297.

[124]Article 136. This article is concerned with the general crime of bribery rather than the specific crime of an official who takes bribes and subverts the law within his area of jurisdiction. Thus, the effect of this clause is to add disenrollment to his punishment.

[125]See Article 21.

SUBCOMMENTARY: Miscellaneous capital crimes refers to capital crimes other than those set out above, that is, other than the ten abominations, intentionally killing persons, collective prosecution for rebellion or sedition, or within one's area of jurisdiction having illicit sexual intercourse, committing robbery, kidnapping, or taking bribes and subverting the law.

Those who are exempted from the death penalty by being specially sent into life exile refers to those whose crime originally was capital but who because of imperial grace have been specially exiled or sent into penal servitude. Those who escape the death penalty by taking flight refers to those who, having committed a capital crime, break out of prison and take flight.

These four categories of cases all follow the article on disenrollment when the case has been completed. . . .[15b] As to those who escape the death penalty by taking flight upon being sentenced to death and disenrollment, in accordance with the law[126] the case is memorialized and signed by the emperor. Such sentencing does not need the criminal's presence. In the text below,[127] cases of those who have committed crimes punishable by life exile or penal servitude and who take flight after the case has been completed also follow this article.

ARTICLE: 18.3b—Should there be a decrease of sentences, the laws on using office to replace punishment and redemption by payment of copper are followed.

SUBCOMMENTARY: Where miscellaneous crimes punished by the death penalty or less have been committed and a decrease of sentence occurs before the sentence has been memorialized and signed by the emperor, cases involving those who have office allow office to be used to replace punishment; cases involving those who have protection follow the law on redemption by payment of copper. Where the relevant law does not permit protection and redemption by payment of copper, however, this article does not place the offense within the limits of the law on redemption by payment of copper. Should there be an amnesty, in accordance with the statute, presently held offices are resigned.[128]

QUERY: In the above text, it is stated that those who violate one of the ten abominations, intentionally kill persons, or are collectively prosecuted for rebellion or sedition are disenrolled despite amnesty. How-

[126]This follows the statute concerning memorials. See Niida, *Statutes*, p. 546.
[127]See Article 19.
[128]Niida, *Statutes*, p. 768.

ever, cases involving those who commit miscellaneous capital crimes follow the laws on using office to replace punishment and redemption by payment of copper if there is a decrease of sentences. If the criminal is released by an edict of special mercy or his punishment is reduced because of a revision of sentences (*lü* 慮), is this considered to be the same as an amnesty and decrease of sentences or not?

REPLY: If a general grace is conferred which is unconnected with particular favors, the distribution of grace and favor [literally, rain and dew] should be equal and follow the ordinary rules. But if there is a special granting of great mercy or a general pardon and an exemption from punishment and release of criminals, such extraordinary decisions are the right of the ruler of men and ranks are restored as before the crime was committed. Such actions are not the same in scope as amnesties or decreases of sentences.

Where there is a revision of sentences and reduction of punishment, the amount of punishment does not differ from that under a decrease of sentences. The use of office to replace punishment or resignation from office must be the same as under the law on a decrease of sentences. But if a revision of sentences gives complete exemption from punishment, the principle on the special release of prisoners is followed.

[16a; 40] FURTHER QUERY: Those who commit crimes punishable by life exile with added labor or less or by the five kinds of life exile are disenrolled and sent into life exile in accordance with the law. It is not yet known what their sentence will be if there is an amnesty or a decrease of sentences.

REPLY: Criminals punished by life exile despite amnesty may not be exempted by ordinary amnesty. Even though there is an amnesty or a decrease of sentences, the criminal as before is disenrolled and sent into life exile. The criminal is also disenrolled despite amnesty for life exile for lack of filial piety, or for collective prosecution for rebellion or sedition. Sons and grandsons in the male line exiled for accidental killing of their paternal grandparents or parents are exempted from punishment if there is an amnesty.

If there is a decrease of sentences, cases involving those who have office follow the laws on using office to replace punishment and redemption by payment of copper. Those who violate the different categories of crimes punished by life exile with added labor or one of the ten abominations are disenrolled even though there be an amnesty or a decrease of sentences. Those sentenced by reference to taking bribes and subverting the law or for robbery within the sphere of jurisdiction resign from occupied office if there is an amnesty.[129]

Punishment under a decrease of sentences is the same as under the law on resignation from office. Other miscellaneous crimes are pardoned if there is an amnesty. If there is a decrease of sentences, the laws on using office to replace punishment and redemption by payment of copper are followed. For all cases sentenced in which the principle of reduction of punishment is merited, the punishment first is reduced and then the sentence is pronounced. For cases involving the five kinds of life exile for which reduction of punishment is not initially permitted, reduction of punishment also is not permitted later even though there be a decrease of sentences.

[129]For sentencing by reference to a particular offense, see Article 53.

[1a]

Article 19

Illicit Sexual Intercourse, Robbery, Kidnapping, and Taking Bribes

ARTICLE: All cases involving illicit sexual intercourse, robbery, kidnapping, and taking bribes without subverting the law (*shou-ts'ai erh pu-wang fa* 受財而不枉法),

COMMENTARY: All of these offenses are punished by penal servitude or more.

SUBCOMMENTARY: Illicit sexual intercourse, robbery, and kidnapping all refer to crimes committed outside the area of jurisdiction. Taking bribes without subverting the law refers to taking bribes because of some matter without any twisting of the law. . . .[1]

ARTICLE: or crimes punished by life exile or penal servitude, where the criminal takes flight after the case is completed,

SUBCOMMENTARY: Crimes punished by life exile or penal servitude refer to those so punished which are outside the categories of doubtful or accidental offenses.[2] The criminal takes flight after the case is completed refers to there still being penal servitude remaining after the reduction of punishment is completed [and the criminal has taken flight to avoid punishment].

If in accordance with the statute,[3] a guarantor is required while the criminal replies to questioning (*tse-pao ts'an-tui* 責保參對), or if the

[1]This offense is defined as obtaining illicit goods through malfeasance (*tso-tsang* 坐贓), for which the punishment is twenty blows with the light stick for goods to the value of one *ch'ih* of silk, rising with each additional *p'i* to a maximum of three years of penal servitude. See Article 137; Deloustal 138. However, since the law was not subverted, the punishment is two degrees less in each case.

[2]Article 502; Deloustal 707, covers the category of doubtful (*yi* 疑) offenses; and Article 339; Deloustal 498, those which are accidental. In both cases, redemption by payment of copper is permitted. A doubtful offense is one in which the evidence and witnesses on both sides of the question are equal. An accidental crime is one in which eyes and ears could not have perceived such a result, and thought and planning could not have prevented it. Such accidental killing of parents or paternal grandparents would, however, still be punished by life exile. See Article 11.

punishment is penal servitude and the criminal is not in prison [when he takes flight, the offense is considered in either case] the same. This article does not specify any limitation of time; if upon investigation and examination the flight is verified, prosecution follows.

QUERY: According to the article,[4] resignation from occupied office is equal to one year of penal servitude. Under this present article, one who has committed a crime punished by penal servitude or life exile and takes flight [1b] is sentenced to resignation from office when caught. It is not yet known whether or not a person who has been sentenced to resignation from occupied office and who takes flight also comes under this article on committing a crime punished by penal servitude and then taking flight being sentenced to resignation from office.

REPLY: The category of resignation from occupied office also includes crimes whose punishment does not extend to penal servitude. If the original crime was punished by penal servitude and the criminal took flight, then the sentence is to resignation from office. If the crime was punished by beating with the heavy stick and the criminal took flight, it differs from this article on crimes punished by penal servitude [41] or life exile. This is because the crime was originally punished by beating with the heavy stick and such offenses do not come within the law on resignation from office.

ARTICLE: or those who while their paternal grandparents or parents have committed a capital crime and are in prison, themselves make music or marry—in all these cases the criminal resigns from office.[5]

SUBCOMMENTARY: If a son or grandson makes music while someone in his male line, extending from his great-great-grandparents down to his parents, has committed a capital crime and is in prison, it is considered the same whether the son or grandson plays the music himself or has someone else do so for him. As the article above did not distinguish

---

[3]Niida, *Statutes*, pp. 776, 783. In cases of lesser importance or where the accused had legal privilege, he might be allowed to put up a guarantor while the case was being heard instead of being held in prison.

[4]See Article 23.

[5]Both of these offenses are punished by one and one-half years of penal servitude. Making music is covered by Article 121; Deloustal 131, while Article 180; Deloustal 317 is concerned with marriage during the period of mourning. The latter article also includes women who take husbands during the period of mourning, an offense specifically excluded from the present article.

between having someone else make music or doing it oneself,[6] it is reasonable that this article should not either.

As to marriage, this article limits itself to men taking wives and does not speak of women being given in marriage, thus making it clear that women do not come under these provisions. Illicit sexual intercourse, robbery, and so on, are all punished by resignation from office.

COMMENTARY: Resignation from office means that two offices are both resigned. Noble titles and offices not reached by the reduction may be retained.

SUBCOMMENTARY: Two offices refers[7] to active-duty office, titular office, and guard office constituting one category of office. Honorary office is yet another[8] category of office. These two [2a] offices are both resigned. After three years offices are resumed with a reduction of two grades from their former rank.[9] Offices not reached by the reduction may be retained. Noble titles are those of prince, duke, marquis, earl, viscount, and baron. Offices not reached by the reduction refers to additional previously held offices of these two categories. If there is a decrease of sentences, any remaining punishment is dealt with following the laws on using office to replace punishment, reduction of punishment, and redemption by payment of copper.

Article 20

Administrative Designations and Official Titles

ARTICLE: All cases involving those who hold posts whose administrative designations or official titles violate their paternal ancestors' name taboos,[10]

SUBCOMMENTARY: Administrative designations refers to the names of departments, tribunals, superior prefectures, courts, and the like. Official titles refer to such titles as president of a board, general, president of a court, or director. Thus if the name of a paternal ancestor was *ch'ang* 常, one may not occupy a post in the office of *t'ai-ch'ang* 太常 [president of a ministry]. Or if the name of a paternal ancestor was *ch'ing* 卿,

[6]See Article 6, section 7.
[7]*Wei* 爲 should be read *wei* 謂, following the KHCPTS edition.
[8]*Yu* 又 should be inserted before *wei* 爲, following the KHCPTS edition.
[9]The rules on reduction of rank are given in Article 21.
[10]Article 121 punishes this offense by one year of penal servitude.

one may not occupy a post in the office of *ch'ing* 卿 [president of a court].

If one accepts such posts, this is called holding posts that violate paternal ancestors' name taboos. In accepting office one is responsible for only three generations. If the name of a paternal great-great-grandfather in the male line is violated, it does not come under this article.

ARTICLE: or those whose paternal grandparents or parents are aged or infirm and are not cared for, or those who leave them with other relatives and take office,

SUBCOMMENTARY: Aged means eighty years of age and above. Infirm means incapacitated. Both of these conditions, according to the statute, need care.[11] If one does not do so, and leaves them to take office, [then the criminal will be sentenced to resignation from occupied office]. However, those whose talent is brilliant and who are forced to remain in office, or are ordered to carry their parents to the place of office and care for them there are not included within this article[12]

[2b] QUERY: When parents are aged or infirm, they need care. Now, if one gets office through the examination system and carries his parents to the place of service, is this the same as leaving parents to take office? Further, if parents become aged or infirm only after one has obtained office and one does not request permission to resign from office and care for them, what [42] is the punishment?

REPLY: Leaving parents to take office is, according to this law, a crime. But taking them to the place of service is in principle different from leaving them. If one is already serving in an office and one's parents then become aged or infirm and one does not request permission to resign from office and care for them, both of these offenses are sentenced to the punishment for violation of a statute.[13]

ARTICLE: or those who have a child[14] or take a concubine[15] during the

[11]Niida, *Statutes*, p. 231.

[12]Niida, *Statutes*, p. 293.

[13]Article 449 punishes the violation of a statute by fifty blows with the light stick.

[14]Article 156 punishes giving birth to a child within the period of mourning by one year of penal servitude. But if the parents confess before anyone else knows of the pregnancy or birth and report it to the court, they will be pardoned.

[15]One and one-half years of penal servitude is the punishment for taking a concubine during the mourning period. See Article 179. This is not as serious as taking a wife, which would come under the ten abominations.

period of mourning for parents,

SUBCOMMENTARY: To have a child during the period of mourning for parents refers to becoming pregnant within the twenty-seven-month period of mourning.[16] If the pregnancy takes place before the parents have died, even though a child is born during the period of mourning, there will be no prosecution. However, if a child is born after the end of the mourning period, and, in calculating the months of pregnancy,[17] conception took place within the mourning period, according to this article it is a crime. The twenty-seven-month limit also applies to taking concubines.

ARTICLE: or brothers who have separate household registers or separate goods, or who violate mourning by seeking office during the period of mourning for parents,[18]

SUBCOMMENTARY: It is not permitted for brothers to have separate household registers or separate goods before the full twenty-seven months of mourning are completed. To violate mourning by seeking office refers to the time when the *t'an* 禫 ceremony has not yet been completed, or the time that lies within the "heart mourning" period.[19] Both of these offenses call for resignation [3a] of one occupied office. Intercalary months are not counted in determining either of these periods.

ARTICLE: or officials who have illicit sexual intercourse with female general bondsmen (*tsa-hu* 雜戶), official bondsmen (*kuan-hu* 官戶), personal retainers (*pu-ch'ü* 部曲), or slaves (*nu-pei* 奴婢) within

[16]The mourning period is often referred to as three years. This is because the twenty-seven months extend into the third year. A table of the various mourning periods and the clothing worn is given in Ou, *La Peine*, pp. 105–111.

[17]I have not been able to find out what the term of pregnancy was reckoned to be during the T'ang period. The *So-yin* commentary on *Shih-chi* 85/4a, states that it should be ten months. See also Bodde, *Statesman, Patriot, and General in Ancient China*, p. 4 note 12.

[18]One year of penal servitude was the punishment for any of these offenses. See Articles 156 and 121. However, Article 155 would punish either of the first two offenses by three years of penal servitude, if they were committed while the parents were still alive.

[19]Though the period of mourning for the parents lasted twenty-seven months, the period of formal mourning, also known as "heart mourning," was only twenty-five months. Two months later the *t'an* ceremony—an offering made to the dead while wearing black outer and yellow inner clothing—was performed, and the period of mourning came to an end. See Couvreur, *Li ki*, I, 761 and the subcommentary to Article 121.

their area of supervision are punished by resignation from occupied office.[20]

SUBCOMMENTARY: General bondsmen refers to those who in earlier dynasties have had their status reduced to that of bondsmen and have been attached to various government offices. Their rendering of taxes and labor services is not the same as commoners.[21] According to the statute, they will be exempted from tax on reaching old age, and be granted lands on becoming adults in the same way as commoners.[22] Each is sent in turn to render services by their own office.

Official bondsmen are also those who in earlier dynasties have had their status reduced to that of bondsmen, their descendants, as well as those whom the present dynasty has enslaved. Their registers of ancestry (*kuan* 貫)[23] are not kept in the county or prefectural offices but in their own offices. A personal retainer may take the daughter of a commoner as a wife.

Slaves refer to both government and private slaves. Illicit sexual intercourse within the sphere of jurisdiction is the same whether by force (*ch'iang* 強) or by consent (*ho* 和). Those who commit any of these offenses from that concerned with administrative designations and official titles on down must resign from occupied office.

COMMENTARY: This means to resign from one occupied office. If one concurrently holds an honorary office, then the active-duty office is resigned.

SUBCOMMENTARY: Reference to resignation from occupied office means that all active-duty offices, titular offices, or guard offices in which a person holds the same rank are considered to be one category of office. If there are several offices, the highest is revoked first. If an honorary office is held concurrently, the active-duty office is resigned. If there is no active-duty[24] office, then the highest honorary office is resigned.

[3b; 43] COMMENTARY: If transfer in office has violated a name taboo, the

[20]This causes the official to give up office for one year and costs him a reduction of one degree of rank upon return to office. See Article 21.

[21]My translation of economic terms in the *Code* follows that used in Twitchett, *Financial Administration*.

[22]Niida, *Statutes*, p. 639; Twitchett, *Financial Administration*, p. 131. The statute goes on to state that official bondsmen are allocated only one-half as much land as a commoner.

[23]Des Rotours, *Fonctionnaires*, I, 119 note 1, quotes sources indicating that the government offices kept lists showing people's ancestry for three generations.

[24]*Chih* 執 should be read *chih* 職 , following the SPTK edition.

certificate of apointment is revoked.

SUBCOMMENTARY: If one's father's or paternal grandfather's name was *ch'ang*, and one violates his name taboo by occupying a post in the office of *t'ai-ch'ang*, and the offense is discovered only after one has completed his term of office and been transferred to a higher office, in sentencing punishment, first the higher rank occupied office is resigned. The certificate of appointment for the previous office which violated the name taboo is also revoked.

Article 21

Disenrollment

ARTICLE: 21.1a—In all cases of disenrollment, both official and noble titles are revoked. Taxes and labor services follow the offender's original status.

SUBCOMMENTARY: Cases of disenrollment refer to official and noble titles acquired since qualification to hold office[25] being revoked. Taxes and labor services follow the offender's original status means that those who have no protection are treated the same as commoners, whereas those who do have protection are treated in accordance with the principle on protection.[26] Therefore it is stated that taxes and labor services follow the offender's original status.

Further, according to the statute, "Those who have been disenrolled and have not yet resumed office are exempted from labor service and from paying the corvée exemption tax. They are not within the scope of liability for miscellaneous labor service."[27]

ARTICLE: After six years (*tsai*), office may be resumed in accordance with the law on qualification to hold office.

SUBCOMMENTARY: In reference to after six years office may be resumed, the term *tsai* is used instead of the term *nien* for the period of a year because different time sequences require different designations. Suppose one commits a crime in a given year, then, after a period of six

[25]This is discussed below.

[26]Niida, *Statutes*, p. 686; Twitchett, *Financial Administration*, p. 146, gives these categories of persons.

[27]Niida, *Statutes*, p. 689; Twitchett, *Financial Administration*, p. 146. My translation differs somewhat from that of Twitchett.

years (*nien*), that is, in the first month of the seventh year, office may be resumed. Inasmuch as intercalary months occur during this period, the term *tsai* is used instead of the term *nien* because this latter is restricted to periods of 360 days.[28] Thus, according to the law on qualification to hold office, one who has committed a crime punished by disenrollment [4a] resumes office after the term of years has been completed.

According to the Statutes on Examination and Selection: "For officials of the third rank and higher, a memorial is sent up [and the period of time before resumption of office] follows the imperial edict. Superior fourth-rank offices are resumed at the inferior lower seventh rank, and inferior fourth-rank offices at the superior upper eighth rank. Superior fifth-rank offices are resumed at the superior lower eighth rank, and inferior fifth-rank offices at the inferior upper eighth rank. Sixth and seventh-rank offices are both resumed at the inferior upper ninth rank. Eighth and ninth-rank offices are both resumed at the inferior lower ninth rank.

Where the degree of qualification to hold office is higher than in this law, sentencing is in accord with such higher degree of qualification. Qualification to hold office refers to those who have protection, or who hold such degrees as that of Cultivated Talent or Understanding the Classics."[29]

According to the text of this statute, where the qualification to hold office is higher than for ordinary resumption of office, the law on qualification to hold office is followed. Where the qualification to hold office is lower than for ordinary resumption of office, it is according to ordinary resumption of office. Therefore, it is stated that for higher degrees of qualification to hold office, the sentence follows such higher degree of qualification.

Further, according to the Statutes on the Army: "Officials with honorary titles who commit crimes punished by disenrollment resume office after the time limit is completed as follows: the second rank resumes office as Captain of Courageous Cavalry [a superior sixth rank], the third rank as Captain of Flying Cavalry [an inferior sixth rank], the fourth rank as Captain of Cavalry Rapid as Clouds [a superior seventh rank], and the fifth rank and below as Captains of War Cavalry

[28]See translation Chapter II, note 100.

[29]Niida, *Statutes*, pp. 299–300. A detailed discussion of the examination system and the degrees gained can be found in des Rotours, *Examens*. The *Code* mentions the degree of Cultivated Talent as if it were still available in 737. However, this degree lasted only from 618–651, according to des Rotours, *Examens*, p. 31. But persons who passed this examination with the highest marks possible were awarded a superior upper eighth rank. This passage seems to mean that such persons could not be demoted below this rank.

[an inferior seventh rank]."[30]

ARTICLE: 21.1b—If the original crime does not extend to resignation from office and yet the criminal is specially disenrolled, the law on resumption of office is the same as that in the principle on resignation from office.[31]

[44] SUBCOMMENTARY: In cases where the original crime does not extend to resignation from office, but the circumstances are so reprehensible that the criminal is specially disenrolled, there is regret because the punishment for the offense originally was light. Therefore, resumption of office is permitted to follow the same principle as that for resignation from office.

[4b] QUERY: Even though the original crime is not punished by resignation from office, office is canceled in replacing penal servitude. According to this article, if office is canceled in replacing penal servitude, the time limit for resumption of office is the same as that for resignation from office. But if office is not canceled in replacing penal servitude and, as in the present case, the criminal is specially disenrolled, it is not yet known whether or not the law on resumption of office is the same as that for resignation from office.

REPLY: References to disenrollment and the use of office to replace punishment[32] are not related to the amount of punishment for the original offense. Disenrollment and resignation from office are in accordance with the principle; the number of years of penal servitude are not calculated. Where the punishment does not extend to penal servitude and there is special disenrollment, the sentence is as for a formal crime under the law on resignation from office. Office being canceled in replacing penal servitude does not come within this section.

21.1c—COMMENTARY: Women whose fief-titles are due to their husband or son and who commit crimes punished by disenrollment are permitted, after the term of years has been completed and in accordance with the ordinance, to resume title according to the office or noble title presently held by the husband or son.

[30] Niida, *Statutes*, p. 377.

[31] That is, only three years instead of six.

[32] I believe that the text here should read resignation from office (*mien-kuan* 免官), rather than using office to replace punishment (*kuan-tang* 官當), since this latter is directly related to the amount of punishment sentenced. Shiga raises the same point.

SUBCOMMENTARY: Women whose fief-titles are due to their husband or son[33] . . . and who commit crimes punished by disenrollment have their resumption of title, after the term of years has been completed, calculated according to the office or noble title presently held by the husband or son. . . . However, they receive their title as previously conferred without reduction in rank. If the husband or son is reduced in office, it is in accordance with this law on conferring and reduction in office. If the husband or son has advanced in office, resumption of office follows the higher office.

As for the law on women's resumption of title, the text of the statute makes it clear that women's rank is in [5a] accordance with their husband's or son's official or noble title. Therefore it does not follow this principle on reduction in rank.[34]

QUERY: Are women whose fief-titles are specially conferred and are not due to husband or son permitted, when disenrolled, to resume such titles or not?

REPLY: The article states that fief-titles that are specially conferred and are not due to husband or son are considered the same as under the section on enfeoffment with noble titles. Since there is no law for the ordinary resumption of noble titles, if the woman is disenrolled, the noble title may not be resumed.

ARTICLE: 21.2—Those who resign from office resume office after three years(*tsai*) with a reduction of two degrees from the former rank.

SUBCOMMENTARY: . . .In a reduction of two degrees from the former rank, for the superior fourth rank and below each grade counts as a degree.[35] For the inferior third rank and above as well as for honorary office, only superior and inferior grades count as a degree. If a superior upper fourth rank is resigned, office is resumed after three years (*tsai*) at the inferior upper fourth rank. If the honorary office of Grand Pillar of State [a superior second-rank office] is resigned, office is resumed after three years as Grand Military Protector [a superior third-rank office]. This is resumption of office after three years with a reduction of two degrees from the former rank.

ARTICLE: 21.3a—Those who resign from occupied office or use office to

[33]Niida, *Statutes*, p. 316, gives certain titles to the wives and mothers of members of the bureaucracy and those who have noble titles.

[34]*Chien* 減 does not mean reduction of punishment in this context. Rather it is linked with the character *chiang* 降 immediately preceeding, both of which here refer to reduction in rank.

[35]See translation Chapter II, note 70.

replace punishment resume office after one year (*chi-nien*) with a reduction of one degree from the former rank.

[45] SUBCOMMENTARY: Those crimes are relatively light for which one resigns from occupied office or uses office to replace punishment. Therefore office is resumed after one year. *Chi* refers to a round [5b] of the four seasons. . . . The space of time is from the day when the imperial edict is issued to resign office until a year later—a full 360 days. . . .

ARTICLE: 21.3b—If the original crime does not extend to resignation from occupied office or the use of office to replace punishment and the criminal is required to specially resign from office, the law on resumption of office is the same as for resignation from occupied office.

SUBCOMMENTARY: The original crime does not extend to resignation from occupied office means that the crime was not of the type in which administrative designations and official titles violate the father's or paternal grandfather's name taboos[36] or the other offenses listed below. The original crime does not extend to the use of office to replace punishment means that the punishment for a crime committed by an official of the ninth rank or above does not extend to one year of penal servitude for a private offense nor does it extend to two years of penal servitude for a public offense. Where the official is of the fifth rank or above, the crime does not extend to two years of penal servitude for a private[37] offense nor does it extend to three years of penal servitude for a public offense.[38]

For those who are specially ordered by imperial edict to resign from office the law on resumption of office is the same as for resignation from occupied office. Office is resumed after one year with a reduction of one degree from the former rank. Therefore, it is stated that the law on resumption of office is the same as for resignation from occupied office.

ARTICLE: 21.4—If those who resign from office hold two offices, each is resumed with a reduction in rank.

COMMENTARY: If an honorary office is reduced one degree, such offices as Grand Pillar of the State would be reduced to Pillar of the State, and if two degrees, to Grand Military Protector. However, where reduction in rank would be to an office lower than Captain of Mil-

[36]See Article 20.

[37]*Fan* 犯 should be inserted before *ssu* 私, following the KHCPTS edition.

[38]The length of penal servitude replaced by office in connection with public and private offenses is given in Article 17.

itary Cavalry, office is resumed as Captain of Military Cavalry.

SUBCOMMENTARY: Two offices refer to active-duty office, and so on, and honorary office as previously explained.[39] If a crime is punished by resignation from office, then both active-duty office and honorary [6a] office are resigned. If resignation is from a superior upper sixth-rank active-duty office, this is reduced to an inferior upper sixth-rank upon resumption of office. If, further, one has the honorary office of Grand Pillar of the State [a superior second rank], it is also resigned and resumption of office is as Grand Military Protector [a superior third rank]. This is resumption of each office according to a reduction in rank.

ARTICLE: 21.5a—For those who have resigned from office, or resigned from occupied office, or have used office to replace punishment and commit a further offense, other previously held offices may be used in accordance with the laws on the use of office to replace punishment and resignation from office.

SUBCOMMENTARY: If a man commits a crime punished by resignation from office or resignation from occupied office, or if he uses office to replace penal servitude, in each instance he uses one or two offices to replace punishment or he resigns from office. If he commits a further crime punished by penal servitude or life exile, or by resignation from office, or resignation from occupied office, or the use of office to replace punishment, and has other certificates of appointment for previously held offices, they may be used in accordance with the above law. Where the use of office to replace punishment or resignation from office has not yet been sentenced and a further crime is committed, rank not reached by the reduction may be used to replace punishment.

COMMENTARY: Those who concurrently hold two offices use the higher to replace punishment.

SUBCOMMENTARY: This refers to one who has committed a second crime. It makes clear that it is not necessarily the presently held active-duty office that is used first to replace punishment. If there are two offices, an honorary office and an active-duty office, [6b] the higher is used first to replace punishment. Thus if one has previously held a sixth-rank active-duty office and a fifth-rank [46] honorary office, the honorary office is used first to replace punishment. If this does not completely replace the punishment, then the next highest office is used. Thus the use of office to replace punishment is not limited either to honorary office or to active-duty office.

[39]The different kinds of office are described in Article 17.

ARTICLE: 21.5b—However, cumulative reductions in rank (*lei-chiang* 累降), even though there be several reductions in rank, may not exceed four degrees for each office.

SUBCOMMENTARY: If there has been a previous offense punished by resignation from office for which there has already been a reduction of two degrees in rank, and then a further offense is punished by resignation from office or the use of office to replace penal servitude, office is canceled. This reduces rank another two degrees. Therefore it is stated that there may be cumulative reduction in rank. Even though the further offenses committed after sentencing may reach a number of three or more, the day for resumption of office follows this article.

In regard to this law on repeated reduction in rank to four degrees, if in resignation from occupied office or in using office to replace penal servitude office is not exhausted, and if after sentencing there is a further offense, the later resumptions of office then each reduce rank by one degree until four have been reached, making, with repeated offenses, an overall reduction of four degrees in rank. Even though there be several subsequent offenses, the limit of reduction in rank is four degrees.

Or if, following repeated offenses punished by resignation from office, there should be further offenses punishable by resignation from occupied office, each is calculated as an offense and office is resumed with a reduction of four degrees in rank. Therefore, it is stated that even though there are several reductions in rank they may not exceed four degrees for each office.

COMMENTARY: Each means that each of the two offices may be reduced in rank. Such reduction in rank is not limited to an overall total of four degrees for both of them.

SUBCOMMENTARY: Active-duty offices, titular offices, and military offices constitute one category of office, and reduction in rank may not exceed four degrees. Honorary office is another category of office in which reduction in rank also may not exceed four degrees. If those who have two offices commit offenses, each office may be reduced in rank by four degrees. Reduction in rank is not limited to an overall [7a] total of four degrees for both of them.

ARTICLE: 21.6—When office has been canceled and not yet resumed, if further crimes are committed punished by life exile or less, redemption by payment of copper is permitted.

SUBCOMMENTARY: This means that if office has been canceled either through being used to replace punishment or in resignation from office, and before the day that office is resumed a further offense is committed punished by life exile or less, redemption by payment of copper is permitted. In such cases even though the term of years is not yet completed, the laws governing resumption of office must be followed. Therefore, the criminal is exempted from being sent into life exile and redemption by payment of copper is permitted. However, where the original crime does not permit redemption by payment of copper, neither is it permitted here.

QUERY: Within this article, if one beats or accuses to the court a relative of the third degree of mourning of a higher generation, or of the same generation but older than oneself, or a relative of the fourth degree of mourning of a higher generation, is redemption by payment of copper permitted or not?[40]

REPLY: In the above article, if one beats or accuses to the court a relative of the third degree of mourning of a higher generation, or of the same generation but older than oneself, or a relative in the fourth degree of mourning of a higher generation than oneself, one may not use their protection.[41] The present case, where one's own office is canceled and redemption by payment of copper is allowed, though it is not of the type that allows protection, is considered the same as cases that fall under the law on redemption by payment of copper.

COMMENTARY: The time limit for resumption of office in each instance depends upon the number of years imposed by the later crime.

SUBCOMMENTARY: Where an offense is punished by resignation from office or by resignation from occupied office, and when, prior to office having been resumed, a second offense is committed punished by resignation from office, or resignation from occupied office, or by the use of office to replace punishment, the calculation of years after which office may be resumed in each case is based upon the later crime. Where office is completely used up and there is a further offense, sentencing is in accord with the [47] article on redemption by payment of copper.

If the offense is punished by the use of office to replace punishment or resignation from office, there is a further three years (*tsai*) before office

[40] *Yi* 以 should be inserted before *fou* 否, following the KHCPTS edition.

[41] See translation Chapter II, note 72. These crimes come under discord, the seventh of the ten abominations.

may be resumed. Where the offense is punished by resignation from occupied office, there is one further year (*chi-nien*) before office can be resumed.

Where the offense is punished by penal servitude or life exile [7b] and redemption by payment of copper is not allowed, so that the criminal is really sent into life exile or penal servitude; for life exile, according to the statute, six years (*tsai*) must intervene before office is resumed; for penal servitude, office is resumed when the term of labor is completed. And if, although the term of labor has been completed, something still remains of the time limit imposed by resignation from office, the principle on resumption of office after resignation from office is followed.

ARTICLE: 21.7a—Officials who have not yet resumed office do not come within the sphere of liability for taxes and labor services.

21.7b—Even though they have previously held offices, they may not attend the imperial audiences.[42]

SUBCOMMENTARY: Do not come within the sphere of liability for taxes and labor services means that persons within the limits of those allowed resumption of office are therefore exempted from taxes and labor services. Even though they have previously held offices refers to an active-duty official of the first rank who has committed a crime punished by the use of office to replace punishment or resignation from office, but who has previously held offices of the second rank and below.

During the period when office has not yet been resumed, they may not attend the imperial audiences. Those who have resigned from occupied office, or who have used office to replace penal servitude, and whose office has not yet been resumed, are to follow this same rule.

Article 22

Office Not Being Canceled in Replacing Penal Servitude

ARTICLE: 22.1a—For all cases in which office is used to replace penal servitude, where the punishment is light and does not cancel the office, office is retained and redemption by payment of copper is allowed.

22.1b—Where office is insufficient and does not fully replace the punishment, the remaining punishment is redeemed by payment of

[42]The classes of officials who attend imperial audiences and the times when they do so are set forth in Niida, *Statutes*, pp. 473–474. See also des Rotours, *Fonctionnaires*, I, 83.

copper.

SUBCOMMENTARY: If an official of the fifth rank or above commits a private offense punished by two years of penal servitude,[43] following the principle, punishment is reduced by one degree.[44] This punishment being light, so that office is not canceled, he may retain such office and use redemption by payment of copper. Where office is insufficient and does not fully replace the punishment refers to such cases as an official of the eighth rank committing a private [8a] offense punished by one and one-half years of penal servitude. Office is used to replace one year of penal servitude, and the remaining half year may be redeemed by payment of copper.[45]

ARTICLE: 22.2a—Those who commit offenses punished by disenrollment or resignation from office, even though the punishment may be light, are sentenced in accordance with the principles on disenrollment and resignation from office.[46]

SUBCOMMENTARY: If a fifth-rank or above active-duty official who also has honorary rank commits a robbery of goods worth one *p'i* of silk within his sphere of jurisdiction, the basic sentence is eighty blows with the heavy stick.[47] Furthermore, in accordance with the principle, the criminal is disenrolled.

If he takes a bribe worth six *p'i* and one *ch'ih* of silk without subverting the law, the basic sentence is one and one-half years of penal servitude.[48] In accordance with the principle, he also resigns from office.

If an official has illicit sexual intercourse with a slave within his sphere of jurisdiction, this is punished by ninety blows with the heavy stick. In accordance with the principle, he also resigns from occupied

[43]Article 17 gives the definitions of public and private offenses.

[44]The categories of persons allowed reduction of punishment and the types of crimes for which reduction was not permitted are given in Article 10.

[45]There is no provision made in Article 3 for the redemption of one-half year of penal servitude. Presumably it would be one-half the cost of a full year or ten *chin* of copper.

[46]In the specific articles of the *Code*, only the punishments are given. Thus in order to find out what other provisions may affect an official, it is necessary to check all applicable articles in this general principles section.

[47]See Article 282. Because the crime was committed within the official's sphere of jurisdiction, Article 283 adds two degrees of punishment. Article 18 provides for disenrollment in such cases.

[48]Article 138. Article 19 forces resignation from office when this offense is committed outside the sphere of jurisdiction.

office.[49]

ARTICLE: 22.2b—If punishment is heavy, however, the laws on using office to replace punishment and redemption by payment of copper are followed.

SUBCOMMENTARY: All cases requiring disenrollment or resignation from office even though the basic punishment is light, follow the principles on disenrollment and resignation from office. Where the punishment is heavy, each case, according to the offense, follows the laws on using office to replace penal servitude and life exile or redemption by payment of copper.

If a superior upper seventh-rank official who also has a previously held inferior lower seventh-rank office commits a crime punished by life exile and disenrollment, the principle on reduction of punishment is not allowed.[50] Life exile is equal to four years of penal servitude.[51] The superior upper seventh-rank office replaces one year of penal servitude, and the inferior lower seventh-rank office replaces another year of penal servitude.

If there are no further previously held active-duty offices or honorary offices, then the criminal pays forty *chin* of copper to redeem the remaining two years of penal servitude.[52] The sentence, in accordance with the principle, requires disenrollment. If the punishment is replacement by office and resignation from office, this [8b] also follows the laws on using office to replace punishment and redemption by payment of copper. However, in accordance with the principle, the criminal resigns from office. This is the meaning of the statement if punishment is heavy; however, the laws on using office to replace punishment and redemption by payment of copper are followed.

[48] ARTICLE: 22.3—In cases where the title of nobility is revoked, remaining punishment may not be redeemed by payment of copper.

SUBCOMMENTARY: Noble titles being passed down to sons and grandsons

[49]Article 410. Because the victim was a member of the inferior classes and not a commoner, the crime comes under Article 20, which punishes the crime by only resignation from occupied office. Had she been a commoner, Article 18 would have forced the criminal's disenrollment.

[50]See Article 10.

[51]This equivalent is made in Article 23.

[52]Article 3 gives the amounts of copper necessary to redeem penal servitude.

in the male line is the same in concept [as is the saying: "Until the Yellow River becomes] a rivulet, and [Mount T'ai] a pebble."[53] So if now, nevertheless, the title is taken away, this is already a very grave degree of culpability. The fief is revoked; therefore remaining punishment may not be redeemed by payment of copper.

Article 23

Disenrollment Is Equal to Three Years of Penal Servitude

ARTICLE: 23.1a—In all cases disenrollment is equal to three years of penal servitude, resignation from office is equal to two years of penal servitude, and resignation from occupied office is equal to one year of penal servitude.
23.1b—This article is not applicable to offices that do not carry official rank.[54]

SUBCOMMENTARY: Disenrollment, resignation from office, and resignation from occupied office have differing reductions in rank.[55] Therefore they are counted differently in making equivalents to penal servitude. Service that does not carry official rank is low in grade and in cases of reciprocal punishment for false accusation[56] such officials are not treated differently from adult males of commoner status. Therefore it is stated that this article is not applicable.

COMMENTARY: This refers to such crimes as falsely accusing someone of a less serious crime or of decreasing or increasing punishment.[57] Therefore these equations of disenrollment, and so on, to penal servitude have been instituted.

SUBCOMMENTARY: If someone accuses an official of the fifth rank or

[53] *Shih chi* 18/1a; Chavannes, *Mémoires historiques*, III, 121; *Han shu* 16/1a–b. Han Kao-tsu is supposed to have said this when enfeoffing a noble. The meaning is that the title would pass down from generation to generation until the impossible occurred.

[54] This is because false accusations cannot deprive persons who hold these offices of rank.

[55] See the statute quoted in Article 21.

[56] This is one of the main principles of the *Code*. See the discussion in the second part of introduction Chapter II. The accuser is usually punished by the penalty for the crime of which he falsely accused someone else. See Article 342; Deloustal 501. The present article spells out the equivalent punishments for disenrollment, and so on, which would be applicable to officials.

[57] See Article 487, which establishes the conditions for punishment of this crime.

higher to the court of committing robbery of goods worth one *p'i* of silk within his area of jurisdiction and there really was such a crime, the punishment is eighty blows with the heavy stick and also disenrollment.[58] If, however, the accusation proves empty or false, the accuser cannot then only receive the punishment of beating with the heavy stick. Therefore [9a] there is reciprocal punishment for the accuser equivalent to three years of penal servitude.

As to resignation from office, if someone accuses a fifth-rank official to the court of committing robbery of goods worth five *p'i* of silk outside his area of jurisdiction, the punishment is one year of penal servitude and also resignation from office.[59] If, however, the accusation proves empty, the reciprocal punishment cannot be only one year of penal servitude. Therefore, there is punishment for the accuser equivalent to two years of penal servitude.

As to resignation from occupied office, if someone accuses an official to the court of illicit sexual intercourse with a slave within his area of jurisdiction, the official is punished by ninety blows with the heavy stick and also resigns from occupied office.[60] If, however, the accusation proves empty, reciprocal punishment cannot be limited to blows with the heavy stick. Therefore there is punishment for the accuser equivalent to one year of penal servitude.

Such crimes as decreasing or increasing punishment means that though there has been no robbery of articles within the official's area of jurisdiction, yet the official is wrongly sentenced for having committed robbery of things over which he had jurisdiction. Or there really having been robbery of articles within the official's area of jurisdiction, yet the official is not sentenced for robbery. These are cases in which the official in charge has decreased or increased punishment. Where in such cases[61] punishment has been decreased or increased, disenrollment is equivalent to three years of penal servitude, resignation from office is equivalent to two years of penal servitude, and resignation from occupied office is equivalent to one year of penal servitude.

As to those who hide criminals or give aid to fugitives,[62] or those who

[58]Articles 282 and 283; Deloustal 436 sets the punishment, and Article 18 forces disenrollment.

[59]Article 282 is the only one applicable here, hence the lighter basic punishment. Article 19 stipulates that robbery committed outside the area of jurisdiction requires resignation from office.

[60]Article 410 provides ninety blows with the heavy stick, and Article 21 forces resignation from occupied office.

[61]*Fa* 法 should be read *lei* 類, following the KHCPTS edition.

[62]If someone knowingly gives aid to a fugitive, his punishment is only one degree less than that of the criminal. See Article 468.

act as guarantors (*pao-cheng* 保證)[63] and deliberately connive (*ku-tsung* 故縱) to violate their guarantee, and so on, whenever disenrollment or resignation from office applies, this section on making equivalents for penal servitude is always followed. Therefore, "such crimes" is stated.

COMMENTARY: Where the law that is subverted carries a heavier punishment, the law with such heavier punishment is followed.

SUBCOMMENTARY: This means that where the punishment for false accusation or for decreasing or increasing punishment is heavier than that under this article concerning equivalents for penal servitude, sentencing is then made in accordance with the law providing heavier punishment for reciprocal punishment and other such offenses. Such cases need not follow this article on equivalents for penal servitude.

ARTICLE: 23.2a—If someone falsely accuses a Taoist or Buddhist priest or nun to the court of an offense that would require that they return to lay life, reciprocal punishment must be equivalent to one year of penal servitude. For those who must undergo chastisement (*k'u shih* 苦使) ten [9b] days of chastisement is equivalent to ten blows with the light stick.

23.2b—The punishment of officials in charge who decrease or increase punishment for a priest or nun is also like this.

[49] SUBCOMMENTARY: According to the *Regulations*[64] on priests and nuns, those who freely put on ordinary clothing must return to lay life. If someone accuses priests or nuns to the court of having freely put on ordinary clothing and the accusation proves true, then they must return to lay life. If, however, the accusation proves empty, the reciprocal punishment for the accuser is equivalent to one year of penal servitude. For those who must undergo chastisement, ten days are equivalent to ten blows with the light stick.

According to the *Regulations*, priests or nuns who proselytize from door to door are to receive one hundred days of chastisement. If, in reality, however, there has been no proselytizing but rather they have been wrongfully or falsely accused, there must be reciprocal punishment for such false accusation. Ten days of chastisement are equivalent

[63]See Article 386.

[64]Some of these regulations on religious groups have been brought together by Akitsuki Kanei. On chastisement, see his "Tō-dai shūkyō keihō ni kansuru kanken," p. 149, where chastisement is defined as being chained in an empty courtyard and being forced to copy five pages of sūtras a day.

to ten blows with the light stick, and one hundred days are equivalent to one hundred blows with the heavy stick.

Officials in charge who decrease or increase punishment has reference to cases in which the priest or nun should have been sentenced to return to lay life, or chastisement, but the official has released him or her, or where the priest or nun should not have been required to return to lay life or chastisement, but the official has wrongfully increased the punishment.

Each of these is punished in accordance with this law on reciprocal punishment for penal servitude and beating with the heavy stick. Therefore, it is stated that cases of decreasing or increasing punishment are also treated like this. Where such decreasing or increasing of punishment occurs by mistake, the relevant law is followed in each instance.

Article 24

Crimes Punishable by Life Exile Which Require Life Exile

ARTICLE: 24.1—All cases of crimes punished by life exile which require life exile carry one year of labor for each of the three types of life exile.

COMMENTARY: Where the specific article refers to life exile with added labor, it means life exile to 3,000 *li*, carrying three years of labor.

SUBCOMMENTARY: Where the crime is punished by life exile and the criminal is not of the class that may use office to replace punishment or redemption by payment of copper and is not aged or infirm,[65] life exile is required. Even though the three types of life exile have [10a] differing distances, each carries one year of labor. In the case of life exile with added labor, the basic law provides heavier punishment than for ordinary life exile, and the principle is different. Therefore this type of life exile is to a distance of 3,000 *li* and carries three years of labor.

COMMENTARY: When labor is completed or there is an amnesty and exemption from labor, the same principles are applicable to those in life exile as to the general population.

[65]Infirm refers to those who are either disabled or incapacitated. See the discussion in the subsection on age, sex, and physical and mental disabilities in the fourth part of introduction Chapter II. See also Article 30.

SUBCOMMENTARY: If the one to three years of labor have been completed or if, not completed, there is an amnesty, the same principles are applicable to those in exile as to the general population. Taxes and labor service are the same for them as for the ordinary population.

Those who have been selected as officials must complete six years of life exile before they can resume office. Therefore the statute states: "A man sent into life exile must stay at the place of exile for six years (*tsai*), after which he is allowed to take up an official post. Those who are exiled for life because of collective prosecution for rebellion or sedition, or because of being in rebellion or committing sedition but who have escaped the death penalty and have been sent into life exile, do not come within this principle. Those whose original crime did not require life exile but who were specially sent into life exile may return to office after three years. . . ."[66]

ARTICLE: 24.2a—Wives and concubines follow their husbands into life exile.[67]

SUBCOMMENTARY: Wives and concubines whose marriages have already taken place follow their husbands into life exile. According to the statute: "Crimes punished by life exile and which have already been sentenced . . . do not allow the criminal to end the marriage by repudiating his wife and concubines."[68]

QUERY: In circumstances where the wife comes under the seven causes for repudiation[69] or has committed offenses against her husband, is she to be repudiated or not?

REPLY: In cases of the seven causes for repudiation, if the husband does not repudiate his wife, he is not punished. If when he committed a crime punished by life exile he were permitted repudiation of his wife, many such cases would be fabricated.

[10b] According to the statute, it is fully reasonable not to repudiate [the wife and concubines]. Should the husband and wife commit crimes against each other, the government separates and divorces [50] them. If such laws are violated and they do not divorce, the punishment is penal

[66] Niida, *Statutes*, p. 771.

[67] Since the wife must share her husband's exile even though she is innocent of any crime herself, this clause resembles the laws in which the wife is collectively prosecuted. Here, however, she would not be forced to do any labor at the place of exile.

[68] Niida, *Statutes*, p. 769.

[69] These are given in translation Chapter II, note 76.

servitude.[70] For crimes committed against each other, husband and wife are divorced, but none of the seven causes allow repudiation of the wife to avoid her being sent into exile.

ARTICLE: Father, paternal grandfathers, sons, and grandsons in the male line who wish to follow the criminal into life exile are permitted to do so.

SUBCOMMENTARY: From great-great-grandfathers in the male line through great-great-grandsons in the male line, those who wish to follow the criminal into life exile are permitted to do so.

ARTICLE: 24.2b—The households of persons removed from the community (*yi-hsiang jen* 移鄉人) also follow this article.[71]

SUBCOMMENTARY: When a person is removed from the community, his wife and concubines accompany him. Fathers, paternal grandfathers, sons, and grandsons in the male line who wish to follow him are permitted to do so. The criminal may not end his marriage by repudiating his wife and concubines. All of them follow him into life exile. Therefore, it is stated that the rulings on who must accompany the criminal and who are allowed to do so are decided according to this article.

ARTICLE: 24.3a—If the person exiled or removed from the community dies, even though his household members may have been put on a household register [at the place of exile], if within three years they wish to return, they are permitted to return to their original home.

SUBCOMMENTARY: Household registry takes place once every three years and the resulting census is sent up to the Department of State.[72] A person in exile, if he has been at the place of exile for three years, must by then

[70]Article 189 requires divorce for such reasons as beating parents-in-law or illicit sexual intercourse with relatives by marriage. If the husband and wife do not divorce after such offenses, the punishment is one year of penal servitude.

[71]If someone who has been sentenced to death for a killing is later pardoned by an amnesty, he must still move 1,000 *li* away from where the crime took place if the victim has a living relative within the one-year mourning group. The purpose of this clause is to avoid private revenge by the victim's relatives. See the discussion on blood revenge in Ch'ü, *Law and Society*, pp. 78–87.

[72]Niida, *Statutes*, p. 240; Twitchett, *Financial Administration*, pp. 330–331. See also Ikeda, "T'ang Household Registers," pp. 121–150, for a general discussion. Three copies were made, one for the county, one for the prefecture, and one for the Board of Finance.

already have been registered. Therefore, it is stated that even though his household members have been put on a household register if within three years they wish to return, they are permitted to return to their original home. If, however, they do not wish to return, they are allowed to remain in the place of exile.

ARTICLE: 24.3b—The households of those who make or keep *ku* poison do not come within this principle on permission to return to their original home.

[11a] SUBCOMMENTARY: According to the specific article, those who make or keep *ku* poison, together with those who dwell together with the criminal are exiled despite amnesty.[73] Still more so then should they be required to remain once they have already arrived at the place of exile. Therefore, it is stated that they do not come within this principle on permission to return to their original home.

COMMENTARY: Articles below follow this principle.

SUBCOMMENTARY: This means that where articles below refer to persons in exile who die while taking flight, the household members who have accompanied them to the place of exile are permitted to return to their original homes in accordance with the above law. The language above that articles below follow this principle indicates that where in texts below it is stated that in accordance with the above law, householders are or are not to be permitted to return to their original homes, such decisions are all in accordance with the meaning of the law given above.

Article 25

Amnesties While Persons Being Sent into Life Exile Are on Their Journey[74]

ARTICLE: 25.1a—All cases of amnesty while persons being sent into life exile are on their journey, where it is calculated that they have exceeded the time limits of their journey will not permit pardon under the amnesty.

[73]Article 262; Deloustal 423. See translation Chapter I, note 81.
[74]*Hui she* 會赦 should be added after *tao* 道, following the KHCPTS edition.

SUBCOMMENTARY: According to the statute: "Regarding the time limits for a journey, a horse travels seventy *li* in a day, a mule or a man on foot fifty *li*, and a cart thirty *li*. . . ."[75] For journeys by water, on the Yangtze, the Yellow River, and other rivers, the downstream and upstream stages are all different. For carts, horses, and men on foot who are traveling together, although their speeds are not the same, the time limits for the slowest are followed.

[11b; 51] COMMENTARY: The general calculation of whether the time limit for a journey has been violated begins with the day that the criminal sets out on the road.

SUBCOMMENTARY: If a criminal is sent into life exile of 2,000 *li*, the time limit for the journey on foot is forty days. Should there be an amnesty before the forty days have been completed, irrespective of the distance already covered, the criminal is pardoned under the amnesty. However, if the general calculation of the time limit for the journey has been violated, then the criminal does not come within the limits of the amnesty.

ARTICLE: 25.1b—Where there is cause, this article is not applicable.

SUBCOMMENTARY: Cause refers to being ill, or a relative's death, or requesting provisions and so being delayed on the road. According to the statute: "Those who should temporarily be given delays, or who because of difficulties ahead are not able to proceed, may subtract the delay."[76] Therefore, they do not come within the time limits for the journey and, therefore, it is stated that this article is not applicable.

ARTICLE: 25.2—If within the time limit for the journey, the criminal arrives at the place of exile, he is pardoned in accordance with the amnesty.

SUBCOMMENTARY: If a person is exiled to 2,000 *li* for which the time limit is forty days and if within the forty days he has already reached the place of exile, if because of imperial grace there should be an amnesty, he is exempted from punishment.

[75]Niida, *Statutes*, pp. 602–603. The different distances to be traveled by boat according to the river are also given here.

[76]Niida, *Statutes*, p. 752.

ARTICLE: 25.3a—Those who take flight, even though an amnesty occurs within the time limit for the journey, do not come within the limits of those who are exempted from punishment.

25.3b—However, should the one who takes flight die, the household members who have accompanied him into exile are still permitted, in accordance with the above section, to return to their original home.

[12a] SUBCOMMENTARY: If within the time limit for the journey the criminal takes flight, even though because of imperial grace there is an amnesty, he is not released and exempted from punishment. However, if the one who takes flight dies, the household members who have accompanied him, even though they have already been put on a household register at the place of exile, if within three years they wish to return, are permitted, in accordance with the above section, to return to their original home.

Article 26

Crimes Punished by Death Other Than the Ten Abominations

ARTICLE: 26.1—All cases involving those who commit crimes punished by death other than the ten abominations, where their paternal grandparents or parents are aged or infirm and require service and the family has no adult relative within the second degree of mourning, may send up a petition.

SUBCOMMENTARY: This refers[77] to capital crimes other than those within the group of plotting rebellion and incest [that is, are not within the ten abominations]. Paternal grandparents and parents include both the great-grandparents and the great-great-grandparents in the male line whose age is eighty or above or who are incapacitated.[78]

According to the statute: "They must be served. If within the household there is no relative within the second degree of mourning between the ages of twenty-one and fifty-nine, petition may be sent up to the Board of Punishments setting forth the circumstances and requesting decision by an imperial edict. If the imperial edict permits the criminal to fulfill his service, then when a relative of the second degree of mourning reaches adulthood, or the relatives being served die, another

[77]*Fei wei* 非謂 should be read *wei fei* 謂非, following the SPTK edition.
[78]See Article 30.

memorial is sent up, unless the original decree specified what should be done in the case."[79]

[With respect to the clause] the family has no adult relative within the second degree of mourning, the article here has reference to relatives within the second degree of mourning of someone who is aged or infirm. If, from four higher through four lower generations in the male line there is no relative within the second degree of mourning living other than the criminal, then a petition may be sent up. However, if one among those in the third or fourth lower generation in the male line commits a capital crime, petition will not be allowed.[80]

[12b; 52] ARTICLE: 26.2a—Those who commit crimes punished by life exile and whose family circumstances are as described above are given temporary permission to remain at home and support their relatives.

SUBCOMMENTARY: Those who commit crimes punished by life exile, even though one of the five kinds of life exile,[81] or who violate one of the ten abominations, also are given temporary permission to remain at home and support their relatives. However, crimes punished by life exile despite amnesty do not come within this principle on giving temporary permission to remain at home. The decision giving temporary permission to remain at home is made by an office of the Imperial Secretariat. A petition need not be sent up to the emperor.

ARTICLE: They do not come within the principle of amnesty.

SUBCOMMENTARY: Those who have temporary permission to remain at home to support their relatives very often stay there for many years. Thus if because of imperial grace there should be an amnesty, they are not included in it. According to the statute, "[All] those going into life exile are sent together season by season."[82] If an amnesty occurs before the exiles of the same season have started their journey, they are pardoned in accordance with the amnesty.

ARTICLE: *K'o* 課 [83] and *tiao* 調 taxes are paid as before the crime was committed.

[79]Niida, *Statutes*, p. 232.

[80]This is because great-great-grandsons in the male line do not come within the second degree of mourning.

[81]See Article 11 for the five kinds of life exile.

[82]Niida, *Statutes*, p. 770.

SUBCOMMENTARY: "An adult who serves his relatives is exempted from labor service, according to the statute,[84] and only pays *tiao* and *tsu* 租 taxes."[85] Since he has not yet been exiled, therefore, it is stated that *k'o* and *tiao* taxes are paid as before the crime was committed.

QUERY: When there are no relatives in the second degree of mourning within the household of a prisoner sentenced to death, a memorial is sent up. If the imperial edict then allows the criminal to carry out his service at home and if because of imperial grace there is an amnesty, is the criminal exempted from the death sentence or not?

REPLY: Temporary permission to remain at home to support relatives does not come within the principle of amnesty. The absence of the word "each" with reference to amnesty means that the denial of amnesty applies only to persons who would be sent into exile.[86]

In the case of the death penalty, however, a memorial is sent up. If the resulting imperial edict allows the criminal to remain at home and serve his relatives, it is reasonable that, following an amnesty, there should be no death sentence. How much more then, should this article contain no ruling preventing exemption from the death penalty. This means that in the event of an amnesty [13a] the criminal is pardoned.

Further, a criminal who has been condemned to death in accordance with this principle need not pay *k'o* taxes. Even when allowed to remain at home and serve his parents, he need not pay *k'o* taxes. Such exemption from *k'o* taxes being a bestowal of the imperial grace, there is every reason that it should be granted.

FURTHER QUERY: The death penalty is heavy, whereas the penalty of life exile is lighter. Yet one who has committed a crime punished by life exile and is allowed to remain at home to support his relatives is not exempted from his sentence by an amnesty, whereas those who have committed a capital crime and who by imperial edict are permitted to remain at home and serve their relatives are allowed the imperial grace. How is it that the death penalty is thus treated leniently, whereas the penalty of life exile on the contrary is treated more seriously? If light

---

[83]*K'o* was the general name for taxes, but is used here simply as a synonym for *tsu* taxes. See Twitchett, *Financial Administration*, p. 247.

[84]Niida, *Statutes*, p. 688; Twitchett, *Financial Administration*, p. 146.

[85]*Tiao* was a tax paid in cloth and *tsu* a tax paid in grain. The other two basic taxes consisted of labor services.

[86]That is, the sentence "They do not come within the principle of amnesty" applies only to Article 26.2a, and not to Article 26.1.

and heavy punishments are not properly categorized, there will be doubts concerning their meaning.

REPLY: Those under a death sentence send up a memorial and permission is by imperial edict. But those under a sentence of life exile remain at home because of this article. Remaining at home thus necessarily follows the ordinary principle, whereas the imperial edict is an expression of special grace. How then is this grace allowed to a person condemned to death to be equated with the judgment made by an official? In view of this difference, the applicability or nonapplicability of the amnesty is not due to the punishment being heavy or light.

ARTICLE: 26.2b—If someone in the household reaches adulthood or the relatives die, then within a year the criminal is sent into exile for life.

26.2c—The calculation of the time limit for his journey and the occurrence of amnesties follow the ordinary principle.

[53] SUBCOMMENTARY: Basically it was because his household had no other adults that the criminal was permitted to remain at home and serve his relatives. So if someone in the household within the second degree of mourning reaches adulthood, or if the parents die, in both cases, within a year the criminal will be sent into exile for life in accordance with the law.[87] Calculation of the time limit for his journey and the occurrence of amnesties follow the ordinary principle for those sent into exile for life.

ARTICLE: 26.2d—Those at the place of exile who must serve their relatives and who had done forced labor in a fixed place,[88] again do forced labor in a fixed place one year after the relatives' death.

SUBCOMMENTARY: If an exiled person is at the place of exile and his relatives become aged or infirm and must be served, this follows the law on serving relatives. Those who had done forced labor in a fixed place [13b] again do forced labor in a fixed place one year after the relatives' death.

QUERY: Those who have committed a capital crime may by imperial decree be permitted to serve their relatives and those under sentence of

[87]See Article 27.

[88]Forced labor in a fixed place refers to the labor done by those sent into life exile.

life exile may be given temporary permission to remain at home and support their relatives. In such cases, if the criminal commits a crime punished by the death penalty or less, what is to be the sentence?

REPLY: According to the text below, if someone, after his crime has been discovered and he has been sent into life exile, then commits further crimes, each of these increases his punishment.[89] Thus if a criminal condemned to death commits an additional crime punished by the death penalty, the sentence is the same as under the law on substituting blows with the heavy stick.[90] If the original sentence was strangulation and the additional crime is punished by decapitation, then the original sentence must be changed to decapitation. If the second crime is punished by strangulation, the principle on substituting blows with the heavy stick is followed.

If, according to the previous sentence, the criminal is required to serve relatives and he commits a second crime, then a petition is sent up. If the second crime is punished by life exile or penal servitude, each sentence is in accordance with the laws on life exile and penal servitude.

If the crime is punished by the heavy stick or less, the number of blows is administered. If someone sentenced to exile for life serves relatives and commits a crime punished by death, a petition is sent up. If they commit a crime punished by life exile, in accordance with the law on remaining and dwelling at home, blows with the heavy stick are substituted. When the relatives served die at the place of exile, the accumulated term of labor is served. Crimes punished by penal servitude which require labor also follow this law. Cases of those who have the rights of protection or redemption by payment of copper, each follow the relevant law.

Article 27

Crimes Punished by Penal Servitude Which Require Labor and There are No Other Adults in the Household Except the Criminal

ARTICLE: 27.1—All cases of crimes punished by penal servitude which require labor and there are no other adults in the household except the criminal,

COMMENTARY: Wives twenty-one years of age or more are considered to

[89]See Article 29.
[90]See Article 27.

be adults. Unmarried women are considered to be adults if there are no men in the household.

Subcommentary: Those who are required to labor are persons who do not have the rights of redemption by payment of copper or more.[91] The law requires that they perform bodily labor. There are no other adults in the household [14a] means that within the household there are no other adults whatsoever. A wife is considered to be an adult. Unmarried women are not considered to be adults but, according to ritual, the wife and husband are a whole.[92] Therefore, if the wife is twenty-one years of age or over she is considered to be an adult. If an unmarried woman commits a crime punished by penal servitude and the household has no males over twenty-one, such cases are treated the same as under this principle on having no other adults in the household except the criminal.

The term "over" refers to those fifty-nine years of age or less. Those who are maimed (*ts'an-chi* 殘疾)[93] are exempted from the labor services required of adults,[94] and thus are not classified as adults.

Query: If there are two adults within a household and both commit crimes punished by penal servitude, or if, while one has previously gone to serve as a soldier, or to hold office, or taken flight, or been put in prison, the other commits a crime punishable by penal servitude, is this to be considered as there being no other adults in the household or not?

Reply: In cases where the household has no other adults, the criminal is exempted from penal servitude and additional beating with the heavy stick is substituted. This is due to pity that the criminal's household may have their food supply cut off, and the further fear that there may be difficulties and poverty within the household.

If one household has only two adults and both are serving sentences of penal servitude and labor, it is reasonable that such cases be considered the same as under this law on a household having no other adults. Thus, it is required that one should be released. Cases involving persons who were rendering military service, distant service in a frontier outpost, or who had committed a crime punished by penal servitude or more, where the case has been completed and the criminal is in prison—these cases

[91]These rights are given in Articles 8–11.

[92]See translation Chapter I, note 178.

[93]These maimed persons do not, however, have any of the lessened liability for punishment afforded those who were disabled or incapacitated.

[94]On these labor services, see Niida, *Statutes*, p. 668; Twitchett, *Financial Administration*, p. 141, and pp. 25 ff.

are all considered to be the same as under this principle on a household having no other adults. It is reasonable that this principle should be widely inclusive.

[54] Those who hold office, even though they are not of the class of ordinary adults,[95] yet inasmuch as they are receiving honor and salary, such cases are not considered the same as those in which the household has no other adults.

If an adult takes flight before an offense is discovered, inasmuch as it was then not yet known, such cases are permitted to be treated the same as those where the household has no other adults. However, where persons of the household commit a crime punished by penal servitude and the adult takes flight only after the crime is discovered, were the situation then treated the same as that of a household having no other adults, this would serve to encourage such unlawful behavior. [14b] Thus such cases are considered the same as if the household had other adults and the criminal does bodily labor in accordance with the law.

FURTHER QUERY: Where two men both commit crimes punished by penal servitude, it is permitted to release one. If three men all commit offenses punished by penal servitude, and there are no other adults in the household, how many are to be released?

REPLY: Where the article states that the household has no other adults, this basically means that there are no other adults whatsoever. But if one of the three is released, the household will then have an adult, who will be sufficient to sustain their food supply. Thus a second may not be released.

However, if four members of a single household commit crimes punished by penal servitude and labor, two are released. Where the length of penal servitude is not the same, or the generations are different, the one with the shortest term of remaining labor is released first. Where the length of labor service is the same, the criminal who is of a higher generation or is the elder of the same generation is released. If a husband and wife both commit crimes punished by penal servitude, and the household has no other adults, the woman is released.

ARTICLE: substitute one hundred twenty blows with the heavy stick for a single year of penal servitude, and the criminal does not do forced labor in a fixed place. For each further degree of penal servitude, twenty blows with the heavy stick are substituted.

[95] In addition to their legal privileges, officials were not liable for taxes and labor services. See Niida, *Statutes*, p. 687; Twitchett, *Financial Administration*, p. 146.

COMMENTARY: Cases of those already at the place of exile who are required to labor also follow this article.

SUBCOMMENTARY: . . . For each further degree of penal servitude, twenty blows with the heavy stick are substituted means twenty blows for each additional half year. The criminal does not do forced labor in a fixed place refers to the fact that beating with the heavy stick having already been substituted, the criminal is, therefore, exempted from forced labor in a fixed place. Cases of those already at the place of exile who are required to labor refers to the exile being required to do labor in a fixed place and the household later having no adults. The number of blows substituted also follows this article.

ARTICLE: 27.2—If during the years of penal servitude, the household comes to have no other adults, blows with the heavy stick are substituted according to a general calculation of the required labor remaining. The remaining sentence is thus canceled by the administration of blows with the heavy stick and the criminal [15a] is released.

SUBCOMMENTARY: . . . Where the number of days of labor is not yet replaced, those remaining are made up by ten blows with the heavy stick. The article states: "In substituting, the number of blows must complete the sentence."[96] Where the sentence is incomplete, ten are added, and it is reasonable then that the criminal be released.

[55] ARTICLE: 27.3a—This article is not applicable to cases of robbery and wounding people.

27.3b—COMMENTARY: If, however, relatives are old or infirm and require service, this law on substituting blows with the heavy stick is followed.

[15b] SUBCOMMENTARY: In cases of robbery and wounding punished by penal servitude or more, the criminal is sent into penal servitude. Such cases do not come within this principle on substituting blows with the heavy stick. In all those articles which have reference to sentencing for robbery, or intentionally killing or wounding, or killing or wounding in an affray, in each instance the case is considered the same as if under the laws on actually robbing, killing, or wounding.[97]

[96]Article 56.

Relatives are old or infirm and require service means that the paternal grandparents or parents are eighty years of age or older, or that they are incapacitated and require service, and the household has no other adults. In such cases, even though the criminal has committed robbery or has wounded someone, the preceding law on substituting blows with the heavy stick is followed.[98]

Article 28

Artisan Bondsmen, Musician Bondsmen, and General Bondsmen

ARTICLE: 28.1—All cases of artisan bondsmen (*kung* 工), musician bondsmen (*yüeh* 樂), general bondsmen, and Musicians of the Court of Imperial Sacrifices (*t'ai-ch'ang yin-sheng jen* 太常音聲人),

SUBCOMMENTARY: Artisan bondsmen are attached to government offices and musician bondsmen to the Court of Imperial Sacrifices. Their registers of ancestry are not kept in prefectural or county offices. General bondsmen are scattered among various government offices and give service in turn, as explained previously.[99] Musicians of the Court of Imperial Sacrifices refers to those who make music in the Court of Imperial Sacrifices. They were originally no different from artisan bondsmen or musician bondsmen, all being of the class that had been enslaved.

However, unlike these others, Musicians of the Court of Imperial Sacrifices were not attached to prefectures and counties but only to the Court of Imperial Sacrifices. Since the Yi-ning period (A.D. 617) they have had their registers of ancestry kept in prefectural and county offices. But in accordance with old tradition, they are sent up in turn to serve in the Court of Imperial Sacrifices, where they are separately designated Musicians of the Court of Imperial Sacrifices.

ARTICLE: who commit crimes punished by life exile to 2,000 *li* have one

---

[97]Several articles in the *Code* state that when they are violated, the punishment is the same as that given in another article. This identity of punishment is stated in two ways. The first is that crime "A" *yi* 以, crime "B" *lun* 論. That is, crime "A" is sentenced the same as crime "B." The second is that crime "A" *chün* 准, crime "B" *lun* 論. That is, crime "A" is sentenced as comparable to crime "B." In such cases, the maximum punishment is life exile to 3,000 *li*. Article 53 states that crimes sentenced as comparable to another crime may not be punished by death.

[98]Thus this article is applicable even in certain crimes punished by life exile or death.

[99]See Article 20.

hundred blows of the heavy stick administered instead. Each further degree of life exile adds thirty blows with the heavy stick. They remain and dwell at home and labor for three years.

COMMENTARY: Those who commit crimes punishable by life exile with added labor, labor for four years.

[16a] SUBCOMMENTARY: These classes of persons are not the same as ordinary people. They perform duties only in the Court of Imperial Sacrifices and in various government offices. Therefore, if they commit crimes punished by life exile, they do not come under the same principles as ordinary people. Those who would be sent into life exile to 2,000 *li* have one hundred blows with the heavy stick administered instead. For 2,500 *li* it would be one hundred thirty blows, and for 3,000 *li* it would be one hundred sixty blows. They all remain and dwell at home and labor for three years. . . .

The general principle states: "Combined penal servitude or life exile requiring labor may not exceed four years."[100] Therefore, beyond three years of penal servitude, only a single year may be added to complete the four years. If the case involves a member of the inferior classes, it follows the laws on official bondsmen and slaves.[101]

ARTICLE: 28.2a—Those who have already learned a skill and are specialized in a particular duty, or have practiced astronomy, or are servants, or servitors have two hundred blows with the heavy stick substituted for life exile.

SUBCOMMENTARY: Artisan bondsmen, musician bondsmen, and Musicians of the Court of Imperial Sacrifices all receive training in a skill at their own government offices. In accordance with the law, each has his own program of training. As to the statements about the skill that they have studied having already been learned and their being specialized in a particular duty, or having practiced astronomical skills—this has reference to student observers in the Astronomical Service[102] and astronomical students who perform duties in astronomy.

According to the statute: "All prefectures have eunuchs who are sent to various government offices. Those sent to the Department of Service within the Palace or to service within the Palace of the Heir Apparent are called servants, whereas those sent to princes and below are called

[100]Article 29.

[101]See Article 47.

[102]See des Rotours, *Fonctionnaires*, I, 212, on the Astronomical Service and its students.

servitors."[103] Most of these eunuchs were originally commoners who have been sent into the palace. Should they, as well as those who have there already learned a skill and are students of astronomy, and so on, commit a crime punished by life exile, they are [16b] not [56] sent into life exile but two hundred blows with the heavy stick are substituted.

ARTICLE: 28.2b—Those who commit crimes punished by penal servitude, in accordance with the principle on a household having no adults, have blows with the heavy stick substituted and are returned to their original status.

SUBCOMMENTARY: . . .[None of those persons mentioned previously] are sent to forced labor if they commit a crime punishable by penal servitude. Instead, following the principle on a household having no adults, blows with the heavy stick are substituted.[104] If, however, their study of a skill is not yet completed, they are then, in accordance with the ordinance, sent to forced labor.

Cases involving those who were originally official bondsmen or slaves follow the relevant law. Are returned to their original status means that artisan bondsmen and musician bondsmen return to their original work, while general bondsmen and Musicians of the Court of Imperial Sacrifices are returned to their original government offices. Those who are studying as students of astronomy are returned to their original service. Servants and servitors are returned to their original places. Therefore it is stated that they are returned to their original status.

Those who have office or protection, in accordance with the relevant laws, use office to replace punishment or redemption by payment of copper.[105] If an office having official rank is used to replace penal servitude or if an office having no official rank is resigned, this is the same as above, there is a return to original status. The time limit on return to office follows the ordinary law.[106]

ARTICLE: 28.3a—Women who commit crimes punished by life exile also remain and dwell at home.

COMMENTARY: Those who make or keep *ku* poison must be exiled and are sent into life exile in accordance with the law.

[103]Niida, *Statutes*, p. 861.
[104]See Article 27.
[105]See Articles 17 and 11.
[106]See Article 21.

SUBCOMMENTARY: The law regarding women sets forth that they may not be sent alone into life exile. Therefore, if they commit a crime punished by life exile, they are not sent into exile but remain and dwell at home. Blows with the heavy stick are administered and they do forced labor in a fixed place.

However, making and keeping *ku* poison falls within what is intolerable and women who do so are expelled to the frontiers of the empire in order to cut off the root of this evil.[107] They, therefore, even though women, are banished. If [they escape] [17a] and marry within China, upon discovery of the crime they are returned to their place of exile.

In accordance with the law on sending into life exile, the three degrees of life exile each carry one year of labor.[108] Even though there be an imperial grace, those who make or keep *ku* poison are not pardoned and are not exempted from further punishment. However, women who order others to make and keep *ku* poison are only sentenced for the order. This is not the same as their making and keeping the poison themselves. Thus they are sentenced to punishment as if for an ordinary crime.[109]

ARTICLE: Sixty blows with the heavy stick are administered for life exile to 2,000 *li*. For each additional degree of life exile, twenty blows are added. However, they all carry three years of labor.

SUBCOMMENTARY: . . . For life exile with added labor, one hundred blows with the heavy stick are administered. . . .

ARTICLE: 28.3b—If a husband or son commits a crime punished by life exile and is sent into life exile, those who accompany him to the place of exile are exempted from forced labor in a fixed place.

SUBCOMMENTARY: Basically women are not sent into life exile. If because of the life exile of husband or son a wife accompanies husband or son into life exile, there is pity for the woman since the relevant law did not exile her.[110] Therefore, they are exempted from forced labor in a fixed place. Neither are women who accompany their husbands or sons into

[107]See Article 262; Deloustal 423. This crime comes under depravity, the fifth of the ten abominations.

[108]See Article 24.

[109]That is, since their crime does not come under the ten abominations, their sentence may be reduced or canceled by an amnesty.

[110]Article 24 requires that wives and concubines follow their husbands into life exile.

exile beaten with the heavy stick, since they do not come within the principle on administrating blows with the heavy stick. If the husband or son dies on the road to the place of exile, the woman does not continue but rather is permitted to return home. Further, she need not do forced labor in a fixed place.

[57] QUERY: First if a woman commits a crime punished by life exile and has office and protection in her own right, or if her husband or son commits a crime punished by life exile and she is to accompany them into life exile, it is not yet [17b] known if office and protection may be used or not.

REPLY: This article only states that at the place of exile women are exempted from forced labor in a fixed place. She is thus allowed exemption from labor, and no further punishments are given. If, however, the case involves violation of one of the ten abominations or of one of the five kinds of life exile, each of these follows the law on disenrollment.[111] If some other crime has been committed punished by life exile or less, the laws on using office to replace punishment, reduction of punishment, and redemption by payment of copper are followed.

FURTHER QUERY: The commentary states that women who make or keep *ku* poison must be exiled and are sent into life exile in accordance with the law. It is not yet known if this commentary is only applicable to women or if it further includes artisan bondsmen, musician bondsmen, [and others] .

REPLY: It is submitted that the Articles on Violence and Robbery state that in cases of making and keeping *ku* poison there is no exemption from further punishment even though there be an amnesty.[112] Those who dwell together with the criminal are also exiled even though they do not know the circumstances. As to these several articles on committing crimes punished by exile or substituting beating with the large stick for sending into penal servitude, if the case involves *ku* poison, the criminal must be sent into life exile. Therefore, this principle has been established following the sections on artisan bondsmen and musician bondsmen, and so on, remaining and dwelling at

[111] Articles 18 and 11 punish violation of any of the ten abominations or the five kinds of life exile by disenrollment.

[112] This is a paraphrase of the provisions of Article 262; Deloustal 423.

home. The commentary states: "Those who make or keep *ku* poison must be exiled for life and are sent into life exile in accordance with the law." This then includes artisan bondsmen, musician bondsmen, and other categories of persons and is not a special text limited to women alone.

[1a; II.1]

Article 29

Crimes That Have Already Been Discovered

ARTICLE: 29.1—For all cases in which crimes have already been discovered and the criminal has been assigned punishment, should he commit further offenses, each of these increases the punishment for the crime.[1]

SUBCOMMENTARY: Already discovered means that there already has been an accusation to the court. According to the statute, three hearings (*shen* 審) are required for each case, but upon the first accusation to the court the crime is already considered to be discovered.[2]

Already been assigned punishment refers to committing an offense punished by penal servitude and the criminal having already been assigned punishment. Should he commit further offenses punished by blows with the light stick or more, each of these later offenses increases the punishment for the crime and they are cumulatively sentenced (*lei-k'o* 累科).

ARTICLE: 29.2a—Cases where the second offense is punished by life exile administer blows with the heavy stick following the law on remaining and dwelling at home.[3] And the criminal does an additional three years of labor at the place of exile.

SUBCOMMENTARY: In cases where an offense punished by life exile has been committed but not yet sentenced, or where the criminal already has been sentenced and assigned punishment but has not yet arrived at the place of exile, should he commit further offenses punished by life

[1]The *Code* distinguishes three types of multiple offenders. Cases in which two or more offenses are discovered at the same time are dealt with in Article 45. If the same crime is committed three times, the case comes under Article 299; Deloustal 428. The third commission of the same crime raises original punishments of penal servitude to life exile and punishments of life exile to strangulation.

[2]Niida, *Statutes*, pp. 776–777. The T'ang criminal process required three hearings before there could be a decision, with the exception of cases involving murder, rape, or such crimes as treason. Written statements (*tz'u* 辭) were given and the hearings had to take place on three separate days unless one of the parties was in transit. In this case, the three hearings could all take place on one day.

[3]See Article 26.

exile, the law regarding artisan bondsmen and musician bondsmen remaining and dwelling at home is followed. For life exile to 2,000 *li*, one hundred blows with the heavy stick are administered; if to 2,500 *li*, one hundred thirty blows with the heavy stick; and if to 3,000 *li*, one hundred sixty blows with the heavy stick.

In addition, each criminal does three years of labor at the place of exile. Combined with the one year of required labor for previously having committed an offense punished by life exile,[4] [1b] there are altogether four years of labor. Should the offense committed previously have been punished by ordinary life exile and that committed later by life exile with added labor,[5] the maximum punishment is still four years of labor altogether.

ARTICLE: 29.2b—Cases where the criminal is already at the place of exile and commits further offenses also follow this article.

SUBCOMMENTARY: . . . If the place of exile to which the criminal has been sent for the first crime be near and the place of exile to which he would be sent for the later crime farther away; should the crime be sentenced and punishment administered at the first place of exile, the criminal may not then be sent into life exile farther away.

ARTICLE: 29.3a—Thus, in cases of cumulative punishment of life exile and penal servitude, the required labor may not exceed four years. 29.3b—Cases of further offenses punished by life exile or penal servitude follow the principle on substituting blows with the heavy stick.[6]

SUBCOMMENTARY: If someone commits a crime punished by penal servitude and when the labor has not yet been completed, he commits a further offense punished by life exile and labor, and when the life exile and labor have not yet been completed, he commits a further offense punished by penal servitude and labor, or, if within the period of labor for penal servitude or life exile, he commits another offense punished by penal servitude or labor, the bodily labor required may in no case exceed four years.

If the original offense is punished by life exile with added labor and the later offense is also punished by life exile with added labor, even

[4]See Article 24.

[5]Since life exile with added labor carries three years of labor with it, the increased punishment would have been seven years of labor without this limitation.

[6]See Article 27.

though the cumulative punishment of penal servitude may be more, labor is limited to four years. If the penal servitude is not finished, further offenses punished by life exile or penal servitude follow the principle on substituting blows with the heavy stick. [2] Even though more offenses are committed, the cumulative administration of blows with the heavy and light stick still may not [2a] exceed two hundred.[7]

QUERY: If someone commits a second offense punished by life exile, blows with the heavy stick are administered following the law on remaining and dwelling at home. And the criminal does an additional three years of labor at the place of exile. It is not yet known whether, concerning these three years of labor, if the household has no other adults, the principle on the household having no other adults is to be followed or not?

REPLY: For persons in life exile, the principle on substituting blows with the heavy stick is not applicable, even though the household has no other adults. Three years of labor basically is meant to take the place of life exile.[8] So even though the household has no other adults, blows with the heavy stick cannot be substituted. Only where the original offense is punished by life exile requiring labor at the place of exile and the household has no other adults is the principle on substituting blows with the heavy stick for penal servitude followed.

ARTICLE: 29.4a—Where there are punishments by blows with the heavy stick or less, each is administered according to the number of blows.

29.4b—However, cumulative blows with the light and heavy stick may not exceed two hundred.

29.5—Cases that substitute blows with the heavy stick are also treated like this.

SUBCOMMENTARY: Cumulative punishments of life exile and penal servitude are limited to four years of labor. If within this period further offenses are committed punished by blows with the heavy and light stick, the number of blows is administered according to the offense that

[7]*T'ang hui-yao*, p. 718; Bünger, *Quellen*, p. 214, quotes imperial edicts expressing concern over deaths brought about by even one hundred blows with the heavy stick and reducing the number of blows for certain crimes that had been punished by a hundred blows with the heavy stick.

[8]Women who are allowed to remain and dwell at home do three years of labor as a substitute for life exile.

has been committed. Thus if the first offense is punished by one hundred blows with the heavy stick, a second with ninety blows with the heavy stick, and the last with a further fifty blows with the light stick, even though there are, from first to last, two hundred forty blows, the cumulative administration of blows with the heavy and light stick may not exceed two hundred.

For offenses punished by penal servitude, substituting blows with the heavy stick is also treated like this. For artisan bondsmen, musician bondsmen, general bondsmen, government or private slaves, and so on, blows with the heavy stick are substituted.[9] But even if they commit a second offense punished by life exile or penal servitude, the cumulative administration [2b] of blows with the heavy and light stick still may not exceed two hundred.

Article 30

Those Who Are Aged, Juvenile, or Disabled

ARTICLE: 30.1a—All cases of those who are seventy years of age or over, or fifteen years of age or less, or disabled, who commit a crime punished by life exile or less allow redemption by payment of copper.

SUBCOMMENTARY: According to the *Rites of Chou*, those who are seventy years of age or over and those who have not yet shed their milk teeth may not be enslaved.[10] Under the present code, if those between the ages of seventy and seventy-nine, or fifteen and eleven, or disabled, commit a crime punished by life exile or less, redemption by payment of copper will be allowed. This is because of pity for those who are aged, juvenile, or infirm.[11]

QUERY: The article above with the clause on redemption by payment of copper states that for offenses punished by life exile or less, redemption by payment of copper is permitted.[12] However, this article and that on using office to replace punishment,[13] speak of redemption by payment of copper being allowed. It is not yet known what the difference is

[9]See Article 28, which substitutes blows with the heavy stick when these persons are sentenced to life exile.

[10]*Chou-li* "Ssu li," p. 543. This is a paraphrase rather than a quotation.

[11]Infirmity includes both those who are disabled and those who are incapacitated.

[12]Article 11.

[13]Article 17.

between "permitted" and "allowed."

Reply: There are cases in the articles above on violation of the ten abominations, and so on, where redemption by payment of copper is not permitted, and cases where it is permitted.[14] Therefore it is stated that redemption by payment of copper is permitted.

Where the offices which are used to replace penal servitude are insufficient and do not cancel the punishment, redemption by payment of copper is allowed for the remaining punishment. There being pity for the aged, the juvenile, and the disabled, even though they violate one of the ten abominations, it is granted that redemption by payment of copper is allowed. "Permit" and "allow" are phrases set up according to the text and are not a special principle.

[3a; 3] Commentary: 30.1b—In cases of life exile with added labor, life exile for collective prosecution for rebellion or sedition, and life exile despite amnesty, this article is not applicable.[15] However, there is exemption from forced labor in a fixed place at the place of exile.

Subcommentary: Life exile with added labor originally was a death penalty and basically does not come under the principle on redemption by payment of copper.[16] Therefore redemption by payment of copper is not granted.

In cases of life exile for collective prosecution for rebellion or sedition, the rebels' closest relatives, who are of the same mind regarding joy and sorrow, are collectively prosecuted. Thus persons will be doubly concerned that members of the family do not commit crimes which may involve the whole group. In such cases as these, even the aged and the infirm are not granted redemption by payment of copper.

In cases of life exile despite amnesty, the harm done is extremely serious, so that even though there be a great granting of imperial grace [that is, an amnesty],[17] the criminals are sent into life exile. These three kinds of life exile in particular are more serious than the ordinary law on

[14]Most violations do not permit it. An exception is made in Article 251; Deloustal 411, where the sons of the plotters are fifteen years of age or less. In such case the wife may redeem her and her sons' punishment by payment of copper. Also if she has no sons, the law on remaining and dwelling at home is applicable in her case.

[15]These are three of the five kinds of life exile covered in Article 11.

[16]See the subcommentary under life exile with added labor in Article 11.

[17]See the discussion of amnesties in the second part of introduction Chapter II.

life exile. Therefore none of them grant that redemption by payment of copper be allowed.

As for exemption from forced labor in a fixed place at the place of exile, there is pity that the aged and the juvenile cannot endure bodily labor. Therefore they are exempted from forced labor in a fixed place.

The law on life exile is not the same for women and men. Even though an aged or juvenile woman commits an offense punished by life exile with added labor, redemption by payment of copper is still allowed by payment of one hundred *chin* of copper.[18] Regarding life exile for collective prosecution for rebellion or sedition, according to the Articles on Violence and Robbery: "Women who are sixty years of age or disabled are exempted from punishment," and do not come under this law.[19]

"In cases of plotting rebellion, even though their speeches do not move groups of people and their charisma is not sufficient to command people, they are all decapitated. Their fathers and sons, mothers and daughters, wives and concubines are all exiled for life to 3,000 *li*."[20] However, their daughters, wives, and concubines who are fifteen years of age or less, or sixty years of age[21] or more, are still exempted from being sent into exile by payment of one hundred *chin* of copper.[22]

If women commit offenses punished by life exile despite amnesty, only those who make and keep *ku* poison as well as those who dwell together with them are sent into exile.[23]

[3b] ARTICLE: 30.2a—Where those who are eighty years of age or more, or ten years of age or less, or incapacitated, commit rebellion or sedition, or kill people, if the death penalty is required, they may send up a petition.[24]

SUBCOMMENTARY: In the *Rites of Chou*, there are three rules on amnesty: the first is called youth and weakness; the second is called age and senility; and the third is called feeblemindedness.[25] At present, those

[18]The amount of copper required to redeem sentences of life exile to 3,000 *li* is one hundred *chin*, according to Article 4.

[19]See Article 248; Deloustal 410. In order for men to be exempted from collective prosecution for rebellion or sedition, they had to be eighty years of age or incapacitated.

[20]This is a continuation of the above quote from Article 248.

[21]*Shih-yi* 十一 should be read *liu-shih* 六十, following the KHCPTS edition.

[22]In fact, the article as now constituted makes no provision for redemption by payment of copper. All these persons are exiled for life to 3,000 *li*.

[23]See Article 262; Deloustal 423.

[24]This brings their offense to the emperor's attention for his decision on their punishment. See Article 9.

aged ten and under are considered to be young and weak, those eighty years of age or more are considered to be aged and senile, and those who are incapacitated are considered the same as those who are feeble-minded. Such persons fit the three rules on amnesty.

There are cases which may not be amnestied, even though the offender is aged or juvenile, because the circumstances of the crime are difficult to pardon. Therefore in cases of rebellion or sedition, or killing people, if, according to the article, the death penalty is required, the officials do not sentence the offense, but send up a petition in accordance with the ordinance.[26] A memorial is sent up to await the imperial decision.

ARTICLE: 30.2b—Those who rob or wound people are still allowed redemption by payment of copper.

COMMENTARY: Cases involving those who have office or noble title follow the laws on using office to replace punishment, disenrollment, and resignation from office.

SUBCOMMENTARY: Robbers whether aged, juvenile, or incapacitated are all motivated by desire for wealth. Cases of wounding people whether the offender be aged, juvenile, or infirm are rarely unrelated to hatred. Therefore, for these two crimes, encroachment upon and injury to people, complete exemption from punishment is not granted.

If they are allowed redemption by payment of copper and have office or noble title, then the laws on using office to replace punishment, disenrollment, and resignation from office must be followed; they may not remain in office and make redemption by payment of copper. This means that those who commit such crimes as beating paternal first cousins older than themselves are disenrolled. Those who commit robbery of goods worth five *p'i* of silk or more resign from office. Those who beat a person of non-kin status and break a limb use office to replace punishment.

QUERY: It has already been stated that those who rob or wound people are still allowed redemption by payment of copper. But in cases of robbery by force, which is punished by death, or of wounding a relative

---

[25]*Chou-li*, "Ch'iu kuan," p. 540. This is a paraphrase rather than a quotation.

[26]As mentioned previously, very little is known today about the ordinances. It is particularly felt here where the ordinance would have given us information about how such petitions reached the emperor. According to Article 9, they did not go through the Imperial Chancellery, as did other memorials.

within the five degrees of mourning, [4a] which is also punished by death, it is not yet known if redemption by payment of copper is allowed or not.

[4] Reply: Those who rob and wound people are still allowed redemption by payment of copper. However, there is no reference as to whether robbery is by force or stealth (*ch'ieh-tao* 竊盜),[27] and the reference to wounding people does not make it clear whether the relationship is close or distant. It is only stated that redemption by payment of copper is allowed; the gravity of the offense is not discussed. This means that there is special sympathy and pity for the aged and the juvenile. Even if they commit robbery by force or wound a relative, both of which crimes are punished by death, following this text, in both cases it will be granted that redemption by payment of copper be allowed.

Further Query: It has already been stated that those who wound people will be allowed redemption by payment of copper. Thus it would seem that if they are not wounded, there is no crime. But in cases of beating or killing another person's personal retainer or slave, or of beating their own father or mother without wounding them, what is to be the sentence?

Reply: Slaves are an inferior class. Only when their household is being robbed are they referred to as ordinary people.[28] Aside from this, all other articles on killing and wounding do not consider them to be the same as commoners.

If someone is aged, juvenile, or incapacitated, the *Code* grants them sympathy and pity. They are not sentenced to punishment for miscellaneous offenses punished by the death penalty.[29] Should they wound people or commit robbery, for both of these crimes they are allowed redemption of punishment by payment of copper.

The principle states that killing three persons of one household is considered depravity.[30] The commentary states that killing a personal

[27]These are the two divisions of the crime of robbery and are covered in Articles 281 and 282; Deloustal 427 and 426. The least punishment for robbery by stealth was fifty blows with the light stick. However, for robbery by force, it was two years of penal servitude. Furthermore, if anyone, no matter whether commoner or member of the inferior classes, were wounded, the punishment was strangulation.

[28]That is, wounding them as mentioned in the above note is treated the same as wounding a commoner. See also Article 47.

[29]These crimes are negatively defined in Article 18.

[30]This is the fifth of the ten abominations.

retainer or slave is not so considered.[31] This shows that they are not considered to be the same as commoners, with the exception of cases of wounding or killing as the result of robbery.

In cases where punishment should be decreased, a heavier offense is brought up in order to make clear a lighter punishment.[32] Thus if miscellaneous offenses punished by the death penalty are not punished, it is clear that there is no punishment for killing or wounding a personal retainer or slave.

As for those who beat parents, even though they are juvenile or infirm and may be pitied, yet if they dare to beat their parents, they are contumaceous.[33] Whether they commit the offense because of being simpleminded [4b] or deliberately because of feelings of hatred, despite not being punished, according to morality they are unfilial. In cases of those who are aged or juvenile or seriously infirm, a petition is sent up and they await the imperial decision.

FURTHER QUERY: If those who are eighty years of age or more, or ten years of age or less . . . rob or wound people, they are still allowed redemption by payment of copper. The commentary states that those who have office or noble title follow the laws on disenrollment, resignation, using office to replace punishment, and redemption by payment of copper. It is not yet known whether, if the original punishment reaches the death penalty, the use of office to replace punishment and redemption by payment of copper will be permitted or not.

REPLY: The text of this article allows redemption by payment of copper and the commentary establishes the law on disenrollment and resignation from office only because of pity for the aged and infirm. This does not mean to deliberately lighten their punishment. But for miscellaneous offenses punishable by the death penalty, the principle does not permit the use of office to replace punishment and redemption by payment of copper.[34] So that if they have office and noble title, they are disenrolled. There is no text giving an equivalent in penal servitude for the death penalty.[35] The principle on using office to replace penal servitude makes it clear that the laws on disenrollment, resignation

[31]This statement does not come from the commentary on depravity, but rather from the subcommentary on Article 259; Deloustal 419.

[32]See the discussion on analogy in the seventh part of introduction Chapter II. See also Article 50.

[33]Contumacy is the fourth of the ten abominations.

[34]See Article 18.

[35]In Article 17, which does give equivalents for the punishments, life exile is made equal to four years of penal servitude, but the death penalty is not covered.

from office, and using office to replace punishment only apply to punishments of life exile or less.

If it were desirable to use office to cancel the death penalty, that would be a special text not in this *Code.* According to the law such criminals must be disenrolled, while the death penalty follows the principle on redemption by payment of copper.[36]

ARTICLE: 30.2c—Other crimes are not punished.

SUBCOMMENTARY: Aside from rebellion or sedition and killing someone, which require the death penalty, and robbing and wounding someone, all other crimes are not prosecuted. Therefore it is stated that other crimes are not punished.

ARTICLE: 30.3a—If those who are ninety years of age or more or seven years of age or less commit a capital crime, the death penalty is not applicable.

COMMENTARY: 30.3b—In cases of collective prosecution which require sending into slavery, this article is not applicable.

[5a; 5] SUBCOMMENTARY: The *Book of Rites* states that those who are ninety years of age are called ancients and those who are seven years of age are called minors.[37] Penalties are not applied to ancients and minors even though they commit a capital crime. The meaning is that the young are loved and the old cherished.

Cases of collective prosecution which require sending into slavery refer to a father or paternal grandfather committing rebellion or sedition and the plot has already been completed. Their sons and grandsons in the male line who are seven years of age or less are still sent into slavery.[38] Therefore it is stated that this law is not applicable.

ARTICLE: 30.3c—If someone orders them to commit a crime, the person who gives the order is prosecuted.

30.3d—If there are illicit goods that require repayment, the one who receives the illicit goods repays them.

SUBCOMMENTARY: Those who are ancients or minors have little intel-

[36]Article 5 makes both strangulation and decapitation redeemable by one hundred twenty *chin* of copper.

[37]*Li chi,* "Tien li," p. 17. This is a paraphrase rather than a quotation.

[38]Article 248; Deloustal 410.

ligence or strength. If someone orders them to commit a crime, only the person who gives the order is prosecuted. Or if there are goods and articles which have been robbed and received by another person who takes and uses them, then that person repays them and makes reparation. The person who receives and uses the goods repays them. If the aged or juvenile use the goods themselves, then repayment falls on the aged or juvenile. Therefore, it is stated that if there are illicit goods which require repayment, the one who receives the illicit goods repays them.

QUERY: If ancients and minors are ordered by others, only the person who gives the order is prosecuted. It is not yet known whether the crimes which are ordered to be committed are arranged in classes or not.

REPLY: If someone orders a crime to be committed, the person who gives the order is prosecuted for the crime that is committed. Should someone order a seven-year-old boy to beat and strike his father or mother or order a ninety-year-old ancient to slash and kill a son or grandson in the male line, it is considered the same as if the person who gave the order had himself beat and struck or killed a person of non-kin status. The punishment for committing an offense against a relative may not be added to that applicable for offenses against a person of non-kin status.

Article 31

[5b] *Offenses Committed before Becoming Aged or Infirm*

ARTICLE: All cases in which an offense has been committed before a person is aged or infirm, yet the person is aged or infirm at the time that the crime is discovered, are sentenced according to the article on age and infirmity.

SUBCOMMENTARY: If an offense is committed when a person is sixty-nine years of age or less, and the crime is discovered when the person is seventy years of age, or if an offense is committed when a person is not infirm, and the crime is discovered after the person has become disabled, both of these cases follow the law on allowing redemption by payment of copper which has been explained above.[39]

Should a person seventy-nine years of age or less commit an offense

[39]See Articles 30 and 11.

requiring the death penalty such as rebellion or sedition or killing someone, and the crime is discovered when the person is eighty years of age, or if an offense is committed when a person is disabled and the crime is discovered when the person has become incapacitated, cases such as these come within the article on sending up a petition.[40]

Should a person eighty-nine years of age commit a capital offense and the crime is discovered when the person is ninety years of age, this comes within the class of crimes that are not punished. Therefore it is stated that sentence is according to the article on age and infirmity.

QUERY: This article states that cases in which an offense has been committed before a person is aged or infirm, yet the person is aged or infirm at the time that the crime is discovered, are sentenced according to the article on age and infirmity. Should the person become aged or infirm after the crime has been discovered but not yet sentenced and punishment administered, how is such a case to be sentenced?

REPLY: This article considers that the aged and infirm cannot endure punishment. Therefore its divisions and grades are differentiated. Those seventy years of age are old and feeble and not able to do penal servitude and labor. And so they are permitted redemption by payment of copper. Even though the crime was discovered when they were sixty-nine years of age, it is all one with regard to age and feebleness if they are seventy years of age when sentenced, and they may not be sent to do bodily labor. Sentence follows the section on age and infirmity regarding penal servitude and labor for the aged and infirm.

If a person seventy-nine years of age commits an offense punished by life exile with added labor and the crime is discovered and sentenced when the person is eighty years of age, exemption from punishment is gained on account of age and the person may not be sent into penal servitude or life exile.

Further, according to the Statutes on Prison [6a] Officials: "If a person commits an offense and a regulation is promulgated changing the punishment, should the regulation provide for a lighter punishment, then sentencing follows such lighter punishment."[41] The articles and the statutes must be applied to follow such laws providing lighter punishment. When a person has become aged [6] or infirm, how can they be sent into exile?

[40]See Article 9.

[41]Niida, *Statutes*, p. 776. The statute goes on to state that if a new regulation provides a heavier punishment than that in force at the time of the offense, the punishment shall be that given in the earlier law. This statute then, insured that there would be no *ex post facto* increase in penalties for any given crime.

For a person eighty years of age, the discovery of the crime and the sentencing are linked together. The principle is to follow the lighter rule[42] and sentencing is according to the law at the time of discovery.

However, the principle is different for the infirm and the aged. In many cases infirmity appears only after the crime has been discovered. Thus the sentence is only provisional and the basic circumstances must be looked into. If the person was already suffering before the time of discovery and has become infirm at the time of sentencing, then the same law on infirmity is followed.

But if at the time of discovery, the person was not infirm but has become infirm by the day of sentencing, there is an investigation. If the infirmity was caused deliberately, the sentence is according to the time that the offense was committed. But if there was real suffering, the decision follows the principle on infirmity.

ARTICLE: If within the term of years of penal servitude, a person becomes aged or infirm, such cases are also treated as in this article.

SUBCOMMENTARY: If a person sixty-nine years of age or less is sent into penal servitude and labor and in two or three years reaches age seventy without the term of labor being complete, or if a person was not infirm at the time of being sent into labor, but becomes disabled during the term of labor, both cases follow the law stated above and redemption by payment of copper is allowed. Therefore, it is stated that if within the term of penal servitude a person becomes aged or infirm, such cases are also treated as in this article.

Further, a year of penal servitude is calculated as three hundred sixty days.[43] Where redemption by payment of copper is required, it is twenty *chin* of copper. Thus one *chin* of copper cancels eighteen days. If the calculation of the remaining labor is not a full eighteen days, this is not a full *chin*. If the amount to be paid is not complete, in such cases it is proper that the criminal be exempted from punishment and released.

[6b] ARTICLE: If a person was a youth at the time when the offense was committed and has become older when the crime is discovered, the sentence is according to the article on youth.

SUBCOMMENTARY: If a person commits a capital offense when seven years of age and the crime is discovered when the person is eight years of age, the death penalty is not sentenced. If someone kills a person when ten

[42]*Ch'ü* 曲 should be read *tien* 典, following the SPTK edition.
[43]See translation Chapter II, note 100.

years of age and the crime is discovered when he is eleven years of age, then he is permitted to send up a memorial. If a person pilfers or robs when fifteen years of age and the crime is discovered when the person is sixteen years of age, the section on redemption by payment of copper is followed. This is called sentencing according to the article on youth if a person has committed an offense while a youth and the crime is discovered when the person has become older.

Article 32

Illicit Goods that Involve Both Parties in Offenses

ARTICLE: 32.1a—All cases of illicit goods that involve both parties in offenses,

COMMENTARY: The calculation of the value of the illicit goods determines the punishment.

SUBCOMMENTARY: Officials who take bribes, no matter whether they subvert the law or do not subvert the law, or take goods and articles in the area under their supervision (*shou so-chien-lin ts'ai-wu* 受所監臨財物)[44] are [sentenced][45] for illicit goods gained through malfeasance. According to the law, the offense includes the giver of the goods, and each is punished. This is called illicit goods that involve both parties in offenses, and means that the calculation of the value of the illicit goods determines the punishment.

ARTICLE: and forbidden articles which it is an offense to possess, will have such goods and articles confiscated by the state.

[44]Here again the general principle differs from the provisions of the specific articles involved. Article 138; Deloustal 140, punishes officials who take bribes, no matter whether or not they subvert the law, more heavily than Article 389, which covers illicit goods gained through malfeasance. Article 140, which deals with officials who take goods and articles in the area under their supervision also makes no mention of the lighter penalties given in Article 389. Hence Article 389 is not applicable here for two reasons. The first is that the heavier punishment prescribed in the *Code* is always applicable when two articles cover any offense. The second is because where the general principles section and the specific article differ, the specific article takes precedence. See Article 49.

[45]The Tai-nan-ko edition has a blank here. The SPTK edition reads *tsui* 罪, which does not make sense. *Lun* 論 "to sentence" would be the most likely reading here, but no edition gives it.

SUBCOMMENTARY: This refers to such things as armor, crossbows, spears, halberds, banners, ensigns, pennons, and flags,[46] as well as forbidden books[47] and imperial and official seals, which private households are required not to possess.[48] These are called forbidden articles that it is an offense to possess. Illicit goods that involve both parties in offenses and such articles mentioned subsequently will all be confiscated by the state.

[7] COMMENTARY: 32.1b—If there is a robbery of articles that were obtained by robbery, the doubled amount of illicit goods repaid is confiscated by the state.

[7a] SUBCOMMENTARY: If B robs A of articles which are then in turn robbed by C, both parties are required to return double the amount of the illicit goods to the owner. Thus A gets a double repayment from B but he does not also get C's repayment. B, however, was the original robber and robbers may not benefit from illicit goods. Therefore, the doubled amount of illicit goods repaid is confiscated by the state. If there is an informer who should be rewarded, the reward given is according to the statute.[49]

QUERY: If there is private casting of coins and the crime is discovered, the tools, copper, and coins are seized;[50] or if there is a violation of the law in the slaughter of horses, oxen, or other meat animals,[51] for crimes such as these neither the *Code* or the *Statutes* states whether confiscation

[46]Those who had private possession of weapons were punished with a minimum of one and one-half years of penal servitude. Depending upon the number and type of weapons, the sentence could reach strangulation. See Article 243.

[47]Article 110; Deloustal 117, defines forbidden books as those dealing with astronomy, prognostication, and military strategy. Possession of any of these was punished by two years of penal servitude. Article 37 expands the category of forbidden books to include official books and papers, from which I infer that the *Code* was not allowed to be in general circulation.

[48]The penalties for possession of these seals ranged from life exile to decapitation, depending upon their being imperial or official, stolen or forged. See Articles 362-364; Deloustal 514-516.

[49]Niida, *Statutes*, p. 729. The reward depended upon how much of the goods were recovered.

[50]All of the crimes mentioned here are, in fact, covered in the specific articles section of the *Code*. The private casting of coins is particularly interesting, since we have both the original edict and what seems to be a quote from the regulation of 737 on this subject. See Twitchett, "Tunhuang Fragments of the T'ang Regulations," pp. 377-378. For a general discussion on the casting of coin in T'ang times, see Penelope A. Herbert, "A Debate in T'ang China on the State Monopoly on Casting Coin." Article 391 punishes the private casting of coins by life exile to 3,000 *li*, with lesser penalties where the tools for such casting had not yet been used or not yet made.

by the state is provided for or not.

REPLY: Private households may possess meat and coins. The *Code* and the *Statutes* do not provide for confiscation by the state. However, such tools and coins may not be used. They are destroyed, returned to the owner, and the crime is sentenced according to the law.

As for casting of coins, there is a separate regulation and sentencing should follow the regulation.[52] Cases of other articles where there are separate regulations currently to be followed which counteract the *Code* also follow this ruling.

ARTICLE: 32.2—In cases of taking or giving without consent,

COMMENTARY: Giving with consent, however, is not punished.

SUBCOMMENTARY: Taking or giving without consent refers to such crimes as threats,[53] fraud,[54] forcing purchase, gaining excessive profits through forcing the market,[55] and forcing demands [for taxes, and so on].[56] Giving with consent, however, is not punished refers to leaving office and receiving food and gifts [through donations, and so on] from the literati and common people within the jurisdiction of the old office, or supervisory officials getting excessive profits within their sphere of jurisdiction by fair trading practices, or to hiring a person to make a true accusation to the court of another person's crime. These are all cases where the taker has not required goods [7b] but they have been given. None of these is punished.

ARTICLE: the illicit goods that have been extorted are all returned to the

[51]On the theory that horses were needed for warfare and oxen for tilling, the *Code* punishes their intentional killing by one and one-half years of penal servitude. See Article 203.

[52]The regulation broadens the group to be punished if they have knowledge of the crime to include the family head, members of the *pao* 保 group, and local headmen.

[53]Obtaining goods by threats is punished as comparable to robbery, with the punishment increased one degree. Thus the punishment was sixty blows with the heavy stick for goods worth one *p'i* of silk. See Article 285; Deloustal 435.

[54]Fraud is also sentenced as comparable to robbery. See Article 373.

[55]Article 142 States that forcing the market is using fear or force to cause selling. This is punished by fifty blows with the light stick. If this results in excess profits, such profits are sentenced according to the section on subverting the law in Article 138; Deloustal 138. The penalty is severe, one hundred blows with the heavy stick for goods worth one *ch'ih* of silk, increasing to strangulation for goods worth fifteen *p'i* of silk. See also the discussion in Twitchett, "The T'ang Market System," particularly the appendix where other articles and statutes dealing with the markets are translated.

owner.

SUBCOMMENTARY: Though the punishments for extortion by force and extortion without the use of force are different, the illicit goods are returned to the owner in both cases.

Reference to all means that the illicit goods that are taken or given without consent, or are mentioned below, are all returned to the owner.

ARTICLE: 32.3a—In cases where the articles have been registered to be collected, even though punishment should have already been administered, upon the arrival of an amnesty, if the goods have not yet come into the hands of the authorities, such goods will not be confiscated in accordance with the amnesty.

SUBCOMMENTARY: Articles that have been registered to be collected refer to confiscation by the state of the household and wealth of persons who have plotted rebellion or great sedition.[57] After the arrival of an amnesty, even though punishment should already have been administered, if the criminal's articles have not yet come into the hands of the authorities, such goods will not be confiscated, in accordance with the amnesty.

If such articles have already come into the hands of the authorities in that area and are under their control, they will not be released and exempted from confiscation.

ARTICLE: 32.3b—If the offense has not yet been sentenced and punishment administered, even though the articles have been sent to the government office, if they have not yet been disposed of, they will not be considered to have come into the hands of the authorities.

SUBCOMMENTARY: If the crimes of rebellion or sedition have not yet been sentenced and punishment administered, or if the criminal has already been sentenced but is still alive, even though the articles have already been sent to the government office, if they have not yet been disposed of, such goods will not be confiscated in accordance with the amnesty.

---

[56]Article 145 sentences forced demands under the provisions of Article 140; Deloustal 140, concerning supervisory officials who take goods and articles in the area under their supervision. The penalties range from forty blows with the light stick for goods worth one *ch'ih* of silk to life exile to 2,000 *li* for goods worth fifty *p'i* of silk.

[57]Certain of the relatives of persons who commit these crimes are enslaved and their goods and real property are confiscated by the state. See the discussion in the third part of introduction Chapter II and part 1 of Article 6.

[8a; 8] ARTICLE: 32.4—Cases in which household members have been collectively prosecuted, even though they have already been sent into slavery, if the criminal is permitted exemption from punishment, they will also be exempted from punishment.

SUBCOMMENTARY: This refers to the households of those who commit rebellion or sedition being collectively prosecuted and enslaved by the state. Should the criminal later because of imperial grace be permitted exemption from punishment, those who have been collectively prosecuted, even though already sent into slavery, will also be released and exempted from punishment.

The criminal's slaves are considered the same as wealth and goods and the law on persons collectively prosecuted being exempted from punishment is not followed.

QUERY: Now those collectively prosecuted being allowed imperial grace is because the criminal has been permitted exemption from punishment. If the grace does not exempt the criminal from punishment, is the law on those collectively prosecuted also having exemption from punishment applicable or not?

REPLY: Plotting rebellion and great sedition are criminal to the utmost degree of censure and extermination. Such crimes defile the whole family and property and the eradication of evil must reach to the roots. Thus the criminal may not be amnestied and neither will those who are collectively prosecuted be pardoned. The fitness of rejecting or allowing pardon for those who are collectively prosecuted always takes the criminal as a measure.

Where plotting treason is already under way,[58] or three members of one household who have not committed a capital crime have been killed, or someone has been dismembered,[59] even though collective prosecution extends to the members of the criminal's household, the abomination is not considered the same as committing rebellion or sedition. Further, the text of the article is especially clear that those who are collectively prosecuted for rebellion or sedition are sentenced the same as those who violated the ten abominations, and are not permitted petition, reduction of punishment, or redemption by payment of copper.[60] They are considered to be the same as those who commit crimes

[58]See Article 248; Deloustal 410.

[59]See Article 259; Deloustal 419. Fewer persons are involved in collective prosecution.

[60]The rights of petition, reduction of punishment, and redemption by payment of copper are covered in Articles 9, 10, and 11; all of which specify that they are not applicable in cases involving violation of one of the ten abomiantions.

punished by the five kinds of life exile and are disenrolled and sent into exile according to the law. Those collectively prosecuted and exiled for life for other offenses are permitted reduction of punishment and redemption by payment of copper and are not disenrolled.

Even though it is stated that cases punished by life exile permit reduction of punishment and redemption by payment of copper, it is clear that those involving collective prosecution for rebellion and sedition are not the same, and an amnesty does not pardon cases of violation of the ten abominations. If those who have been collectively prosecuted for crimes other than rebellion or sedition are allowed imperial grace, they are exempted from punishment. The reason is that they themselves have not committed one of the ten abominations, nor are they members of a household which has been involved in rebellion or sedition.

Article 33

[8b] *Offenses Involving Illicit Goods*

ARTICLE: 33.1a—All cases of offenses involving illicit goods in which the original illicit goods are still in existence[61] return them to the government or owner.

COMMENTARY: If there has been an exchange for other goods or natural increase, the illicit goods are still considered to be in existence.

SUBCOMMENTARY: There are six types of original illicit goods mentioned in the *Code*. These are: 1) robbery by force, 2) robbery by stealth, 3) taking bribes and subverting the law, 4) taking bribes without subverting the law, 5) taking goods and articles in the area under one's supervision, and 6) illicit goods gained through malfeasance. All other articles involving illicit goods can be subsumed under these six categories in determining punishments.[62]

Now in cases involving such offenses, if the original illicit goods are in existence and have not yet been expended, they are returned to the

[61]A distinction is to be made between original illicit goods in existence and illicit goods. Original illicit goods are those listed in the subcommentary immediately below. But illicit goods is also the term used for gain resulting from officials using government-owned horses, carts, and so on, for their own purposes, as described later on in this article.

[62]The specific offenses referred to here are covered in Articles 281, 282, 138, 140, and 389; Deloustal 428, and 140. "All other articles involving illicit goods can be subsumed under these six categories. . . ," means that other articles state that they are sentenced as or comparable to one of these six categories.

government or the owner.

Exchanged for other goods refers to such cases as the original illicit goods, a mule, having been traded for a horse. Natural increase refers to such cases as a slave giving birth to a child, or a mare bearing a colt.

QUERY: If a robber takes another's goods and articles and through trade or loan gets a profit, is this considered the same as natural increase or not?

Or, if the illicit goods originally consisted of a person or a domestic animal which passed through many hands, some knowing the circumstances and some not, what is the decision regarding the natural increase?

REPLY: When the commentary on this article speaks of natural increase, it basically refers to such things as natural increase through giving birth. But if there is profit or increase from trade or loans, this is due to the efforts of the later possessor [9] and not the original owner. Since goods do not breed and give birth, [9a] they do not have the same limits as natural increase and the profit obtained goes to the later possessor.

Where those who had temporary possession of a person or a domestic animal knew the circumstances, the natural increase is returned to the owner. If they did not know the circumstances, it goes to the later possessor.

FURTHER QUERY: If a person knows a slave to be illicit goods and yet deliberately buys her for his own pleasure, as a result of which she gives birth to a child, to whom should the child go?[63]

REPLY: If a person knows that a slave is illicit goods, there originally should not have been a trade. Deliberately buying her was a violation of the law and the intent was licentious. Children born of a slave who is illicit goods cannot be commoners, they are only natural increase through birth and according to this article are returned to their owner together with the mother.

ARTICLE: 33.1b—If the illicit goods have already been expended, and the punishment is death or sending into life exile, they need not be repaid.

[63]A certificate was required for the sale of a slave, which had to be drafted in accordance with the official verification from the authorities of her place of origin. Thus it would be likely that a potential buyer would know the status of a slave before he bought her. See Niida, *Statutes*, p. 720; Twitchett, "The T'ang Market System," p. 246.

COMMENTARY: Cases where there has been a separate offense punished by life exile or where the person has died are considered to be the same.

SUBCOMMENTARY: Offenses for which a person is sentenced to death or to be sent into life exile because of illicit goods are very serious. In most cases the family property has been broken up and the illicit goods already expended. There is pity because of the sentence to life exile or death and the illicit goods need not be repaid.

If a case has not yet been memorialized and signed by the emperor and an amnesty gives exemption from punishment, the illicit goods are repaid according to the law.[64] If the emperor has already signed and there is an amnesty through imperial grace, it is considered the same as this principle on exemption from repayment.

The commentary states that cases where there has been a separate offense punished by life exile or where the person has died are considered to be the same. This refers to persons who have committed crimes punished by sending into life exile other than for illicit goods or where the person was not executed but died from other causes. Where the illicit goods from the original offense have been completely expended, such cases also follow this principle on exemption from repayment.

ARTICLE: 33.1c—All other illicit goods are to be repaid.

COMMENTARY: 33.1d—Cases of robbery are doubly repaid.[65]

[9b] SUBCOMMENTARY: Aside from cases of a person's death or of having already been sent into life exile, no matter whether the illicit goods are in existence or already expended, all others come within the limits for repayment. Therefore it is stated that all other illicit goods are to be repaid.

Cases of robbery are to be doubly repaid means that cases of robbery because of desire for goods are more serious. Therefore, it is ordered that there be double repayment, which means that for such a robbery as of goods worth one *ch'ih* of silk, two *ch'ih* are repaid.

ARTICLE: 33.2—In cases where the illicit goods are calculated from use

[64]This refers to a capital case that would have to be memorialized to the emperor. See the discussion of review in the seventh part of introduction Chapter II.

[65]However, crimes sentenced as comparable to robbery by force or by stealth do not require double repayment of goods. See Article 53.

or rent, there need be no repayment.

SUBCOMMENTARY: Use refers to making unauthorized use of labor in the area under one's supervision as well as borrowing such things as carts and horses. The use is calculated as three *ch'ih* of silk for each day and is sentenced under the section on taking goods and articles in the area under one's supervision.[66]

Rent refers to such things as grinding mills, warehouses, wholesale stores, and boats. Sentence is calculated according to the value of the rent. Thus, illicit goods that are calculated[67] from use or rent originally were not real articles, and even though there be no amnesty need not be returned. Other articles regarding use and rent all follow this article.

[10] ARTICLE: 33.3a—In cases of robbery, fraud, and taking bribes and subverting the law, even though there be an amnesty or a decrease of sentences, the original illicit goods must still be repaid.

SUBCOMMENTARY: This means that in three types of cases: robbery, fraud, and taking bribes and subverting the law, even though there be an amnesty or a decrease of sentences, the original illicit goods must still be repaid either to the government or the owner. However, cases of robbery are exempted from double repayment. Therefore it is stated that the original illicit goods must still be repaid. This refers to crimes discovered before the amnesty.

If the crime is discovered after the amnesty, the existent illicit goods are seized and must be repaid according to the Articles on Assaults and Accusations.[68]

[10a] QUERY: In cases of taking bribes and subverting the law, even though there be an amnesty, the original illicit goods must still be repaid. It is not yet known if these illicit goods should be returned to the government or the owner. A clear principle must be established.

REPLY: The principle on illicit goods that involve both parties in offenses provides for confiscation. If later there is a confession and the crime is pardoned, the original illicit goods must still be returned according to the law. Other illicit goods will be taken and confiscated.[69] What

[66]Article 140 punishes this crime by forty blows with the light stick for use calculated worth one *ch'ih* of silk, rising to life exile for use calculated worth fifty *p'i* of silk.

[67]*Hsü* 許 should be read *chi* 計, following the SPTK edition.

[68]This follows Article 353.

[69]Article 32, provides for confiscation of the illicit goods by the state since both parties are involved in the offense.

question is there about the law?

ARTICLE: 33.3b—If other illicit goods that are no longer in existence, as well as copper when redemption is allowed, have not been sent to the government but the time limit for payment has not yet passed, in both cases there is a decrease of sentences or pardon according to the amnesty.

SUBCOMMENTARY: Other illicit goods that are no longer in existence refer to illicit goods that have already been completely expended before the amnesty, or illicit goods that cannot be exchanged for other goods or produce natural increase. These are illicit goods that are no longer in existence.

Copper when redemption is allowed refers to payment of copper for the offense that was committed. According to the statute, the divisions and grades of payment each have a time limit.[70] If the copper has not been sent to the government but the time limit for payment has not yet passed, there is a decrease of sentences or pardon according to the amnesty. But if the copper has not been sent to the government and the time limit for payment has been exceeded, the case does not come within the limits of exemption from punishment.

Exceeding the time limit for payment without sending to the government only refers to copper for redemption of crimes, since there has never been a time limit set for return of other illicit goods. When an amnesty has been promulgated, the criminals in such cases are released and exempted from repayment.

Where a crime has been committed and redemption must be made by payment of copper, the copper must be sent to the government within the time limit for payment. If the time limit is exceeded without the copper being received, the amnesty does not pardon the criminal. Therefore, when it is stated that the time limit has been exceeded without the copper having been sent to the government within the time limit for payment, this text only concerns redemption by payment of copper and does not establish a rule for other illicit goods.

QUERY: If a person who is allowed redemption by payment of copper is away from his native place and is there sentenced to punishment, a dispatch is sent to his original place of registration so that the copper can be paid. It is not yet known whether the time limit for payment is from the date that the dispatch arrives in his native place, or from the date of the sentence.

[70]See translation Chapter I, note 45.

[10b] REPLY: According to the statute: "Those holding office are exempted from taxes and labor service."[71] However, such exemption starts only from the day that the tally of exemption arrives.[72] Where persons who can make payment of copper have been sentenced or are in prison far away from their native place, even though they were released, they would have no copper with which to pay. So a tally is sent to their native place to receive payment. The time limit for payment must be according to the day of the tally's arrival. If it were fixed at the particular place of sentencing, why trouble further to send a dispatch to the criminal's native place?

Article 34

Assessing the Value of Illicit Goods

ARTICLE: 34.1—All cases of assessing the value of illicit goods do so according to the value of the articles at the time and place of the offense in terms of the set price of the highest grade of silk.[73]

SUBCOMMENTARY: Illicit goods refer to illicit goods taken by the criminal. Assessment is always according to the value of the highest grade of silk at the time and place of the offense. In accordance with the statute: "Three grades of prices [are fixed for each commodity] for ten-day periods in every month."[74] The assessment of the value of the articles during the ten-day period in which the offense took place decides the punishment in terms of the price of the highest grade of silk during that ten-day period.

For example, a person commits a robbery of salt in Pu Prefecture and when the crime is discovered in Sui Prefecture, the salt has already been used. In accordance with the statute,[75] an assessment of the value from a

[71]Niida, *Statutes*, p. 680; Twitchett, *Financial Administration*, pp. 144–145. The statute goes on to say that even before the certificate of appointment arrives, an official's credentials may be verified and he be allowed exemption.

[72]The tally was an important means of identification used extensively by the T'ang bureaucracy. It was in two sections that matched, so that the holder of one half was identified by fitting his section together with the other half. See the detailed study by des Rotours, "Les Insignes en deux parties."

[73]This clause has been translated in Twitchett, "The T'ang Market System," p. 246. Historically, commodity money has played an important role in the Chinese currency system. Though copper cash was also popular in the T'ang period, whenever the *Code* requires estimates of value to be made, the standard is silk. See the discussion in Lien-sheng Yang, *Money and Credit in China, A Short History*, pp. 16–19.

[74]Niida, *Statutes*, pp. 716–718; Twitchett, "The T'ang Market System," p. 245.

[75]Ibid.

distance is made taking the average set price of salt in Pu Prefecture [11] in terms of the price of the highest grade of silk, in order to sentence and administer punishment in Sui Prefecture. Even though the buying and selling prices may be higher or lower, that is, not the same as the set price, the set price is still taken as the basis.

QUERY: If illicit goods are still in existence at the place of the offense, they can be compared and assessed. But if they have been expended or damaged, what [11a] is to be taken as a basis in making an assessment of value from a distance?

Further, if the place where the illicit goods are seized is not the seme as the place where the offense took place, should they be sent to that place for assessment, regardless of distance, or not?

REPLY: The assessment of the value of illicit goods from a distance, according to the statute, follows the average set price. If the illicit goods are seized far away from the place of the offense, their value can only be assessed from a distance. If the illicit goods were sent back to the place of the offense in order to get the set price of the articles, then there would be transportation costs and it is to be feared that such illicit goods as animals would become emaciated. Problems would arise from fraudulent substitutions of goods. There would also be no source to pay for food for the men sent to carry the goods. Assessing the value from a distance is reasonable, convenient, and should be applied.

FURTHER QUERY: If an offense is committed abroad which is then sentenced in China, or if there is an offense involving illicit goods in a border prefecture where there are not set prices, what is to be taken as the average in assessing the value of the illicit goods in fixing punishment?

REPLY: Distant foreign countries have different customs and we cannot send dispatches there to assess the value of their set prices. We can only follow the set prices of prefectures and counties close to foreign countries and select a suitable price for use.

In cases of offenses in places where there are no set prices, the price is carefully decided in the prefectural capital.

ARTICLE: 34.2—In cases of assessing the value of labor usage, one man-day is the equivalent of three *ch'ih* of silk,[76] and oxen, horses,

[76]Article 143 states that this is the value of the labor of a man between the ages of sixteen and sixty-nine. Should the man be older, younger, or infirm, the value of his labor would be less.

camels, mules, donkeys, and carts are the same.

SUBCOMMENTARY: In calculating labor as usage in order to punish, one man-day is the equivalent of three *ch'ih* of silk, and oxen, horses, camels, mules, donkeys, and carts are the same.

[11b] ARTICLE: 34.3—Assessment of the value of such things as boats, grinding mills, warehouses, and wholesale stores is also according to the value of the rent at the time of the offense.

SUBCOMMENTARY: Boats, as well as the other things mentioned above, have different sizes and periods of importance.[77] Therefore, the set price is according to the value of rent at the time of the offense and not the ordinary rent.

As for warehouses and wholesale stores: a warehouse is a place where articles are stored, and a wholesale store is where they are sold. There are many classes of shops, stalls, gardens, and houses, so that they have been summarized in general terms, since they cannot be completely detailed. Therefore the phrase "such as" is used.

ARTICLE: 34.4—Punishment may not be for more than the basic value of a particular thing, even though its use or rent produced more than its basic value.

SUBCOMMENTARY: If a donkey is borrowed and used for one hundred days, the usage is calculated at seven *p'i* and two *chang* of silk. However, the set price of a donkey is only five *p'i* of silk. In this case even though the use produced more than the donkey's basic value, the punishment is for five *p'i* of silk. Other cases where the use or rent of a particular thing produces more than its basic value all follow this article.

Article 35

[12] *Kidnapping or Misleading Persons*

ARTICLE: 35.1a—In all cases of kidnapping, misleading persons (*ho-yu* 和誘), or selling by mutual agreement,

SUBCOMMENTARY: Kidnapping being defined as that act done without the victim's consent has already been explained previously.[78] Misleading

[77]This refers to harvest times when storage space would be at a premium, as compared with slack seasons when it would be cheaper.

refers to mutual agreement by both parties to deceive someone, either by causing a member of the inferior classes to become a commoner or a commoner to become a member of the inferior classes. Both of these offenses come under this article if they are concealed beyond the time limits of an amnesty. The rules on the amount of punishment follow the relevant [12a] laws.[79]

Or selling by mutual agreement means that both parties mutually agree and consent, knowing that there is a violation of the law.

ARTICLE: or of kidnapping or misleading a personal retainer or slave, or selling them into marriage where the person who buys them for a wife knows the circumstances,

SUBCOMMENTARY: The texts above all are based on commoners. This section deals with personal retainers, female retainers, and slaves, but the meanings of kidnapping and misleading are the same as in the above section. It is also the same whether the person is kept by the kidnapper or deceiver, sold into marriage, or given to another person.

Where the person who buys them for a wife knows the circumstances means that for kidnapping, misleading, and sections below, there is no distinction made between commoners and members of the inferior classes.[80] If both parties know the basic circumstances and she is either taken as a wife or bought, and the time limits of an amnesty are exceeded without surrender, this also is considered to be concealment.

ARTICLE: or of concealing a fugitive personal retainer or slave,[81]

SUBCOMMENTARY: Concealment has no time limit. This refers to cases where it is known that the personal retainer or slave is fleeing and deliberately concealing them.

ARTICLE: or of exceeding the limit in appointing and creating officials, or of creating officials who are not required,

SUBCOMMENTARY: In the statutes concerned with creating officials, each office has a certain number of personnel. If additional personnel are

---

[78]See Article 18.

[79]See Articles 292–295; Deloustal 426.

[80]That is, for kidnapping, in contradistinction to beating, no lesser penalty is given the offender when the victim is a member of the inferior classes.

[81]The penalty for knowingly concealing a fugitive is only one degree less than that for the crime that the fugitive has committed. See Article 468.

created, this is called exceeding the limit. It is submitted that the Articles on Administrative Regulations state: "Offices have a certain number of personnel and if the limit is exceeded in appointing and creating officials, or officials are created who are not required," and that the commentary states: "This refers to those who have not been memorialized and appointed by the emperor."[82]

Here, even if they have been memorialized and appointed by the emperor, it is still considered the same as concealment. Where officials are created without such personnel being specified in the *Regulations* or the *Statutes*, it is called creating officials who are not required.

[12b] ARTICLE: or of fraudulently creating ficticious office, or of ficticiously giving someone an office, or of accepting a ficticious office,[83]

SUBCOMMENTARY: Fraudulently creating ficticious offices means that one really has no office but ficticiously does administrative duties. Though the offenses are different for those offices having official rank and those which do not have official rank,[84] the idea of fraud and ficticiousness is the same for both.

No matter whether one makes a certificate of appointment oneself, or hires someone to make it, or obtains another person's certificate of appointment and uses it oneself, all such cases are situations where one is not an official but fraudulently takes a certificate of appointment and uses it.

Or ficticiously give someone an office means to ficticiously give office within one's bureau, or to counterfeit a memorial nominating to office, or to make ficticious decisions to fill a vacant post in a bureau.

Or to accept a ficticious office refers to taking an office while knowing it is false.

ARTICLE: or of fraudulently reporting death[85] or of private possession of forbidden articles,[86]

[82]One hundred blows with the heavy stick is the punishment for the first person over the limit, rising to two years of penal servitude for ten such persons. See Article 91; Deloustal 97.

[83]The punishment for all of these is life exile to 2,000 *li*. Criminals who seek to get office are punished by two years of penal servitude under the same law. See Article 370.

[84]I have not been able to find any difference in the punishments for these supposedly different offenses.

[85]Article 380 punishes this offense by two years of penal servitude.

[86]The punishment may be as little as one and one-half years of penal servitude or as much as death, depending upon what articles are possessed and in what amounts. See Articles 243 and 110.

COMMENTARY: This refers to articles that should not be in private possession, such[87] as forbidden books.

[13] SUBCOMMENTARY: Fraudulent report of death has as its basic aim avoidance of punishment, or the intent to escape taxes and labor services, or flight due to an offense, and the like. Therefore there is a fraudulent report of death.

Private possession of forbidden articles, the commentary states, refers to things that should not be in private possession, such as armor, crossbows, spears, and halberds. Forbidden books means those on astronomy, military strategy,[88] the calendar,[89] and so on. These are called forbidden books. Referring to "such as" means astronomical instruments, and so on, which are not books.[90] Therefore "such as" is stated.

ARTICLE: if within one hundred days after the arrival of the amnesty, should the criminal be present and not surrender but deliberately conceal his offense, the offense is treated as it was originally. 35.1b—However, go-betweens and guarantors are not [13a] prosecuted.

SUBCOMMENTARY: The pardoning of offenses by an amnesty is according to the day that the imperial decree appears. On that day before daybreak, there is exemption from punishment in accordance with the amnesty.[91] But this article states regarding concealment: "One hundred days after the arrival of the amnesty." This is based on taking one hundred days after the amnesty reaches a certain place as the time limit.

Should the criminal be present and not surrender but deliberately conceal his offense means that the persons, the articles, the ficticious officials, and so on, are present but the offenses are deliberately concealed and the illicit goods are hidden and the criminals do not come forth and surrender. The offense then is treated as it was originally.

Originally refers to the time when the crime was originally committed. All illicit goods and articles must be repaid or doubly repaid according to the relevant law on the original offense. If a person has moved to another place but is alive and does not surrender, it is considered deliberate concealment.

[87]*Wu* 物 should be read *lei* 類, following the SPTK edition.

[88]Wang Yüan-liang states that this refers to such books as *Sun-tzu on the Art of War (Sun-tzu ping-fa)*.

[89]Because it was a part of the Ch'ing dynasty Ch'ien-lung Emperor's (R. 1736–1795) name, *li* 曆 is written 厤, here and below.

[90]The unauthorized possession of astronomical instruments was punished by one and one-half years of penal servitude. See Article 110.

However, go-betweens and guarantors are not prosecuted refers to there being go-betweens in marriages and guarantors in buying and selling.[92] Should there be an amnesty, they are pardoned whether or not they confess within one hundred days. They are not prosecuted in either case.

ARTICLE: 35.2—If the crime is discovered within the time limit of the amnesty, even though it has not been confessed, this is not considered to be concealment.

SUBCOMMENTARY: . . .

[13b] COMMENTARY: If within the time limits of the amnesty one has undergone questioning without admitting the crime (*ching-wen pu-ch'eng* 經問不承), this is considered to be concealment.[93]

SUBCOMMENTARY: The statement above—if the crime is discovered within the time limit of the amnesty, even though it has not been confessed—this is not considered to be concealment, refers to the crime being discovered within the time limits of the amnesty. Having undergone questioning if there is admission of the crime without any hidden aim, this is not considered to be concealment. But if one has undergone questioning without admitting the crime, even though within the time limit of the amnesty, it is considered the same as under the law on concealment.

ARTICLE: 35.3—Where there are time limits, the last day of the amnesty is calculated in prosecution.

SUBCOMMENTARY: As for time limits, according to the statute: "Matters of least importance have a five-day time limit, matters of medium importance have a ten-day time limit, and matters of greatest importance have a twenty-day time limit."[94] And public envoys have time limits for

[91]Amnesties differed in the degree of reduction of punishment and in the offenses covered. See the discussion in the second part of introduction Chapter II.

[92]See Gernet, "La Vente en Chine," p. 334. A copy of a sale agreement from the T'ang period illustrating the use of guarantors is given on p. 350 and translated on p. 349.

[93]The *Code* permits judicial torture within certain limits as a means of securing a confession. The relevant articles have been translated by Balazs, *Traité juridique*, p. 197 note 1. See also his Appendix IV, which contains a translation of a discussion that took place in the sixth century A.D. on this subject.

[94]Niida, *Statutes*, p. 595. The matters referred to here are documents that had to be processed. Differing periods of time are allowed, according to their complexity or whether they had to be passed through several levels.

their travel. All of these are [14] time limits. An article of the *Code* states: "to go beyond the time limit without arriving at a great gathering for inspection."[95] There are also time limits for annual tax registers, and so on; each of these is given a time limit by the statutes.[96]

For these types of violation of time limits that took place before the amnesty, it is not necessary to wait for a hundred days after the imperial grace arrives at a given place, but only until the last day after the amnesty has been issued. If there is still a violation of the time limit, the days of violation after the amnesty are calculated in prosecution. However, after the amnesty, the time limit should be in accordance with the importance of the matter.

ARTICLE: 35.4—Those who have taken flight because of an offense are exempted from punishment in case of an amnesty. If they go beyond the time limits of the amnesty without surrendering, only the flight is prosecuted, not the original offense.[97]

[14a] SUBCOMMENTARY: . . . Further, if those on military service[98] take flight,[99] an amnesty gives exemption from punishment. But one hundred days is calculated as being the outside time limit of the amnesty, and if those on military service have not yet returned, then the remaining days of military service are calculated as flight in determining punishment. [But if those on military service][100] return within the time limits of the amnesty, it is considered the same as under the law on fleeing from home to avoid various services.[101] Thus, if a soldier goes up to serve a turn of service and takes flight[102] because of an offense, and if during the am-

[95] Article 229. The penalty was one hundred blows with the heavy stick for the first day, increased one degree for each further three days.

[96] Niida, *Statutes*, p. 240; Twitchett, *Financial Administration*, pp. 330–331.

[97] Article 459; Deloustal 649. The punishment for the first day of flight was forty blows with the light stick, increasing to a maximum punishment of life exile to 3,000 *li* for fifty-nine days.

[98] *Cheng* 征 and *fang* 防, which I have translated as military service, are the two types of duty required of males. *Cheng* are armies sent out on expeditions, while *fang* are armies that guard the frontier. This militia system is described in des Rotours, *Fonctionnaires*, I, 1 ff.

[99] See Articles 457 and 458. The punishment for fleeing expedition duty was much heavier than that for fleeing frontier guard duty, being one year of penal servitude, as against eighty blows with the heavy stick for the first day of absence.

[100] Tai, *General Principles*, p. 339, makes an emendation here that must be correct even though it is not given in any extant edition. He changes *liu* 流 and *li* 例 to read *cheng* 征 and *fang* 防.

[101] See Article 461. This is a greatly reduced penalty, being thirty blows with the light stick for the first day, with a maximum punishment of three years of penal servitude.

[102] *Tsou* 走 should be read *wang* 亡, following the KHCPTS edition.

nesty he would have finished his turn of service, this is also considered the same as under the article on ordinary flight.

COMMENTARY: This means that the time limit of the amnesty is calculated to be one hundred days after the arrival of the amnesty.

SUBCOMMENTARY: The section above on concealment takes one hundred days as the time limit for an amnesty. Here, on prosecution for flight, the calculation is also for exceeding the time limit of one hundred days.

Article 36

Amnesty, Correction, and Return of Goods

ARTICLE: All cases in which there is an amnesty require correction of status and return of goods. If a person is responsible for registration documents (*pu-chang* 簿帳)[103] and does not correct the registration and return goods, each case is punished according to the article on the specific crime.

[14b] SUBCOMMENTARY: The previous article took one hundred days as a time limit. But here, after the amnesty if a person is responsible for registration documents, then he must correct them. If there is secrecy or deceit and they are not corrected, all such cases are punished according to the specific crime. Examples where correction of registration and return of goods are required are set forth in the commentaries.

COMMENTARY: This refers to: 1) treating the children of the proper wife as those of a concubine and those of a concubine as the children of the proper wife, or violating the law in adoption of children;

SUBCOMMENTARY: According to the statute: "Princes, dukes, marquises, earls, viscounts, and barons, all pass down their titles through sons and grandsons in the male line by the proper wife. If the eldest son by the proper wife is dead, then his son is made heir. If there is no such grandson, then the second son by the proper wife is made heir. If the second son is dead, then the son of a concubine is made heir. If there is no such concubine's son, then the son of the second son by the proper wife is made heir. If there is no such grandson, then the grandson in the male line by a concubine is made heir, and so on down through great-great-

[103]Registration documents is a general term covering household registers, tax lists, and so on. See the discussion in Twitchett, *Financial Administration*, p. 217.

grandsons in the male line."[104] If the statute is not followed, this is treating the children of the proper wife as those of a concubine and those of a concubine as the children of the proper wife.

[15] Further, according to the statute: "If one has no sons, it is permitted to adopt a son of the proper generation from one's own clan."[105] If one violates the statute in adopting a son, this is called violating the law.[106] Thus artisan bondsmen, musician bondsmen, general bondsmen [and other classes] should adopt children of the same class. Even though there is no formal text, if they have no sons, it is reasonable that they should follow the article on commoners.[107]

COMMENTARY: 2) unauthorized ordainment as a Buddhist or Taoist priest or nun, or fraudulent avoidance of taxes and labor services, or leaving one's basic status;

SUBCOMMENTARY: Unauthorized ordainment refers to those who become Buddhist or Taoist priests or nuns without official authorization.[108] This is called unauthorized [15a] ordainment.

Fraudulent avoidance of taxes and labor services refers to exemption from both taxes and labor services, such as the life exemption given to the original followers [of the Kao-tsu emperor when he began his uprising at] T'ai-yüan. Those who have been captives among the barbarians and return to China, or barbarians who seek to adopt civilization, are given ten years' exemption, and members of the inferior classes who are manumitted to commoner status are given three years' exemption.[109] Cases of those who ought not to be given exemption but who fraudulently claim to be of these classes are called fraudulent avoidance of taxes and labor services.

Leaving one's basic status refers to artisan bondsmen, musician bondsmen, general bondsmen, and Musicians of the Court of Imperial Sacrifices; each have their basic status. If they leave and change to

[104]Niida, *Statutes*, p. 305.

[105]Niida, *Statutes*, p. 233.

[106]In fact, Article 158 of the *Code* covers this point. Violations of the statute in establishing an heir are punished by one year of penal servitude.

[107]See Article 47. Here it is specified that where there is no special ruling on the inferior classes in an article, they are considered the same as commoners.

[108]This offense was punished by one hundred blows with the heavy stick. If the monastery authorities knowingly allowed such unauthorized ordainment, they received the same punishment. See Article 154.

[109]The punishment for either refusing such exemption where it was due or giving it where it was not due was two years of penal servitude. See Article 172. On exemptions afforded for various reasons, see Niida, *Statutes*, p. 682; Twitchett, *Financial Administration*, p. 145.

another status, this is called leaving one's basic status.[110]

COMMENTARY: 3) such offenses as increasing and decreasing age, encroaching upon or secretly cultivating land, omitting to file or leaving household members off of a household register, and such like offenses, must be corrected;

SUBCOMMENTARY: Increasing or decreasing age refers to increasing persons' ages so that they reach old age, or decreasing it so that they are adolescent or juvenile.[111] Where there is such increase or decrease, even if not for the purpose of avoidance of taxes or labor services, it is a crime. . . .[112]

Encroaching upon or secretly cultivating land refers to encroaching on others' land as well as unauthorized exchange of other persons' land.[113]

Such offenses refer to increasing the circumstances of illness,[114] or omitting to file a household register, or leaving off the names of artisan bondsmen, musician bondsmen, or general bondsmen.[115]

After an amnesty, if a person is responsible for registration documents, they must be corrected. If they are not corrected, then the punishment is according to the article on the specific crime.

COMMENTARY: 4) supervisory and custodial officials who borrow such things as goods, articles, and domestic animals for their own unauthorized use or who borrow and lend them to others must return such goods, articles, and domestic animals;

[15b] SUBCOMMENTARY: Supervisory refers to directing what is within one's charge. Custodial refers to places under one's personal protection.[116] In cases of unauthorized personal use of goods, articles, and domestic animals or of taking official goods, articles, and domestic

[110]Article 380 punishes such change of status by two years of penal servitude.

[111]Old age refers to those sixty years of age or more and juvenile means those fifteen years of age or younger. See also Twitchett, *Financial Administration*, p. 248.

[112]Article 150; Deloustal 284 punishes this offense by one year of penal servitude if four persons are involved.

[113]Articles 164–168. The punishment is ten to sixty blows for the first *mou* of land, depending upon the offense.

[114]Article 150 punishes this offense by one year of penal servitude for one person if the purpose is to escape taxes and labor services, increasing one degree for each further two persons, with a maximum sentence of three years of penal servitude.

[115]Article 380 punishes this offense by sixty blows with the heavy stick.

[116]See Article 54.

animals and lending them to other persons,[117] carts and boats are considered to be the same as goods and articles, while falcons and dogs are considered to be the same as domestic animals. Therefore it is stated that things in all these categories must be returned.

QUERY: The previous article took one hundred days after the amnesty as the time limit. The article here takes the submission of registration documents during an amnesty as the time limit. If within the hundred days specified by the previous article a person submits registration documents but conceals illicit goods and has not made the necessary corrections, or if in the article here a person undergoes questioning without admission of the crime, even though he has not yet submitted the registration documents, are such persons to be punished or not?

REPLY: The offenses in the previous article are more serious, therefore, if within one hundred days after an amnesty a person has undergone questioning without admission of the crime, the punishment is the same as for concealment of the crime. Even though a person has submitted registration documents within that time limit, if the crime is never discovered and the person does not come out with the truth, he is not punished.

In this later article [16] the offenses are less serious. If, after the amnesty, a person has submitted registration documents which are not correct, then the relevant punishment is assigned. If the amnesty occurs in a year in which the person does not submit registration documents, then it is reasonable that he is not guilty of any crime. So that even if he again undergoes questioning without admitting his crime, he is not punished for concealment.

FURTHER QUERY: Where crimes are concealed and not confessed within the time limit of the amnesty, or correction of status is required yet the registration documents are not correct, if a person other than the owner of the goods should accuse the criminal to the court, it is not yet known if the accuser will be punished or not.

[16a] REPLY: There is a time limit for any crime that took place before the amnesty, and if the crime is discovered within that time limit, exemption from punishment is allowed. In the end, the criminal must correct registration documents and return any goods. It is reasonable that anyone who accuses him to the court should not be prosecuted.

[117] Articles 208, 212, and 213. The least punishment for such unauthorized personal use of government property was fifty blows with the light stick.

CHAPTER V

[1a] ### Article 37

Confession of Crimes that Have Not Yet Been Discovered

ARTICLE: 37.1a—In all cases where there is confession of crimes that have not yet been discovered the crime will be pardoned.[1]

SUBCOMMENTARY: To have faults and not to correct them, this is indeed a fault.[2] Now if persons are able to correct their faults and come and confess their crimes, they will all gain pardon. But if there is a written accusation accusing them to the officials, and the three hearings have been ordered, even though the accusation may not yet have reached the government office, still the offense is known.[3] Thus even though there is a desire to renew oneself, confession is not allowed.

COMMENTARY: 37.1b—The original illicit goods are still repaid in accordance with the law.

SUBCOMMENTARY: Reference to original illicit goods means that if the robber confesses, he does not doubly repay the illicit goods.

Reference to in accordance with the law refers to being the same as the previous law on not confessing and the illicit goods being returned to the government or the owner.[4] Illicit goods obtained by such means as subverting the law or by offenses involving both parties are still confiscated by the state.[5] Goods taken, or given without consent, or which have been extorted are still returned to the owner.[6]

[1b] ARTICLE: 37.2a—Cases of those who, because of a lesser offense being discovered, confess a heavier offense are exempted from the heavier punishment.

[1]These articles on confession were first translated into German in Kennedy, *Die Rolle des Geständnisses*. See his discussion there of the history of confession as well as my survey in the sixth part of introduction Chapter II.

[2]*Lun yü*, XV, 19; Legge, *The Chinese Classics*, I, 302. This quotation is not exact.

[3]On the criminal process, see translation Chapter IV, note 2.

[4]See Article 33.

[5]See Article 32.

[6]Ibid.

SUBCOMMENTARY: If there is a crime such as robbery of oxen and because of the crime being discovered the criminal confesses to counterfeiting of coins, the offense of counterfeiting is pardoned. But the robbery of oxen is still prosecuted.

ARTICLE: 37.2b—Cases where because of questioning on a crime which is being examined the criminal speaks of other crimes are also treated like this.

SUBCOMMENTARY: Examine is another term for investigate. If someone is already being investigated and because of questioning then speaks of other crimes, he will still obtain exemption from these other punishments. The meaning is the same as confessing a heavier offense because of being questioned for a lesser offense. Therefore it is stated that it is treated like this.

[17] ARTICLE: 37.3a—Cases where a representative is sent to confess and the person who makes the confession is one who is allowed mutual concealment (*hsiang jung-yin* 相容隱) by the law, or where a person who is allowed mutual concealment makes an accusation to the court are each decided according to the law on the criminal himself confessing.

SUBCOMMENTARY: As for cases where a representative is sent to confess, should A commit a crime and send B to represent him and make a confession, B need not be a relative. Sending a representative to confess is the same as confessing oneself.

Cases where the person is allowed mutual concealment by the law refers to, in the sections below, those who dwell together or are relatives of the third or closer degree of mourning.[7]

If a personal retainer or slave confesses for his master or one of those who are allowed mutual concealment makes an accusation to the court, the case is still treated as one where mutual concealment is allowed. Even though the accusation has already gone through to the officials, all such cases are considered the same as under the law on the criminal's confessing in person.

If relatives of the fourth and fifth degrees of mourning mutually conceal each others' crimes, their punishment is reduced three degrees below that for persons of non-kin status. [2a] Or if they make a

[7]See Article 46. Personal retainers and slaves were also allowed to conceal their masters' crimes.

confession for such relatives, the relative will also get a reduction of three degrees of punishment.

COMMENTARY: 37.3b—Should a person be arrested and accused to the court of crimes involving collective prosecution or plotting treason or more by a relative who originally was within the one year degree of mourning, both of these cases are considered the same as under the principle on confession.

SUBCOMMENTARY: Crimes involving collective prosecution refer to plotting rebellion, or plotting great sedition or plotting treason and the plot being under way. All of these involve collective prosecution.[8]

Plotting treason or more where originally there was a one year degree of mourning relationship refers to there not being collective prosecution for such crimes if the treason is not yet under way or if the great sedition has not yet been carried out.

Each of these is according to the original one-year degree of mourning relationship, even though it may have been raised or lowered so that there is no mourning relationship.[9] Thus even though the criminal is arrested and sent to the court, both of these types of offenses are considered the same as under the law on the criminal himself confessing.

ARTICLE: 37.3c—Whoever hears that a confession or accusation to the court has been made and though sought for will not appear at court will not be pardoned.

SUBCOMMENTARY: This refers to a criminal hearing that a representative has made a confession or that a person who is allowed mutual concealment has accused him to the court, and even though pardon is allowed, though sought he will not appear in court. He does not get exemption from punishment. This means that only those who will not appear in court are prosecuted. Cases of those who themselves confess or who are accused to the court by others who would be collectively prosecuted follow the law on confession.[10]

ARTICLE: 37.4a—If a confession is untruthful or incomplete, crimes that

[8]See Articles 248 and 251; Deloustal 410 and 411, and parts 1-3 of Article 6.

[9]Mourning relationships would be changed either by marriage or by adoption.

[10]This, then, broadens the range of persons from those within the third degree of mourning of the plotters plus the plotters' personal retainers or slaves to include anyone who would be collectively prosecuted as a result of the offense.

have not yet been confessed truthfully or completely will be punished. But should the punishment reach the death penalty, it will be reduced one degree.

[2b] SUBCOMMENTARY: A confession being untruthful refers to committing such offenses as obtaining illicit goods through robbery by force and in the confession stating that it was robbery by stealth. Even though the amount of illicit goods has been completely confessed, still the crime of robbery where nothing has been taken is punished.[11]

Or incomplete refers to taking bribes and subverting the law and obtaining goods worth fifteen *p'i* of silk, but only confession to fourteen *p'i*, so that one *p'i* remains. This is a crime that is incompletely confessed.

In reference to punishment, however, it does not come within the principles applying disenrollment, resignation from office, double repayment of goods, added punishment for supervisory and custodial officials, or life exile with added labor.[12]

If a person commits robbery by force and obtains goods worth twenty *p'i* of silk and confesses to ten, ten still remain unconfessed. The relevant law still punishes the crime by the death penalty.[13] But because the criminal himself had a repentant heart and the circumstances of the crime were discovered because of his confession, the death penalty is reduced one degree.

[18] QUERY: If someone plots to kill a person of non-kin status and then states that the plot was against his maternal uncle, or if he plots to kill his maternal uncle and then states that the plot was against a person of non-kin status, the surnames and personal names being the same, but the circumstances of the crime against a maternal uncle and against a person of non-kin status being different, how are cases like this to be sentenced?

REPLY: Plotting to kill a person of non-kin status is a less serious crime, while plotting to kill a maternal uncle is a more serious crime. Confession gets exemption from the heavier punishment and the lighter punishment may not be added.

[11]Article 281 punishes robbery by force with two years of penal servitude, even if no goods have been taken.

[12]See Articles 18–21.

[13]Where robbery was by force, goods worth ten *p'i* of silk brought a sentence of strangulation. Note the sharp contrast with Article 282, covering robbery by stealth, where the penalty when no goods are taken is only fifty blows with the light stick. Even the theft of goods worth fifty *p'i* of silk was punished by only life exile with added labor, which was the maximum penalty.

Since the surnames and personal names that were confessed are the same, the only difference is that one of the persons is a maternal uncle and the other a person of non-kin status. The confession of a plot to kill being complete and only the circumstance of maternal uncle or person of non-kin status being false, the sentence is to the lighter punishment for doing what ought not to be done, that is, forty blows with the light stick.[14] This is for the case of plotting to kill a maternal uncle and then stating that the plot was against a person of non-kin status.

However, a plot to kill a person of non-kin status is at most sentenced to penal servitude, while a plot to kill a maternal uncle is punished by life exile. Even though the plot [3a] to kill has been confessed, that part of the crime which was incompletely confessed must be sentenced. The three kinds of life exile are comparable to four years of penal servitude.[15] Plotting to kill a person of non-kin status is punished by three years of penal servitude. Since it was not stated that the intended victim was a maternal uncle, the confession was not complete and the sentence is to one year of penal servitude.

FURTHER QUERY: If a family omits eighteen persons from its household register who are liable for taxes and labor services and then confesses to nine of them, it is not yet known what the punishment is to be.[16]

REPLY: The *Code* decides punishments that can be found in the appropriate articles. If a household only conceals nine members and the accusation to the court makes reference to eighteen members, and upon investigation nine members prove to be the correct number, the person who made the false accusation is not reciprocally punished. According to the relevant article, the punishment for concealing nine members is the maximum, that is, three years of penal servitude. This is the maximum punishment. Even though the false accusation was for more persons, there is no reciprocal punishment.

Now, aside from those who were confessed, nine members of the household are concealed. The sentence for those who were not included in the confession, according to the appropriate article, is three years of penal servitude.

[14]See Article 450.

[15]This equivalent is made in Article 17.

[16]The head of the household was responsible for all members being listed on the household register. His punishment depended on how many persons were omitted and whether or not those omitted were liable to taxes and labor services. See Article 150; Deloustal 284.

FURTHER QUERY: If B has private possession of armor and a crossbow and confesses only to having one lance, the degree of seriousness for these two crimes is not the same. How is this to be sentenced?

REPLY: The armor and crossbow were not confessed, so that these must be completely punished. In confessing to possession of a lance the criminal was speaking of another crime. The confession for possession of a lance gets exemption from punishment only for that crime. But the crime of possession of armor and a crossbow has not been truthfully confessed. The sentence is to death reduced one degree.[17]

FURTHER QUERY: If a supervisory official takes bribes without subverting the law of illicit goods worth a full thirty *p'i* of silk, this is punished by life exile with added labor.[18] If the person confesses to taking goods and articles in the area under his supervision but the amount of illicit goods are completely confessed, what punishment is to be sentenced?

[3b] REPLY: The article states that crimes which have not been confessed truthfully or completely will be punished. But should the punishment reach the death penalty, it will be reduced one degree. Now, even though taking bribes and subverting the law and taking goods and articles in the area under his supervision are different crimes, yet the amount of illicit goods has been completely confessed so there are no goods to be sentenced. Since only the causes of the affair are different, the sentence is to eighty blows with the heavy stick, the heavier punishment for doing what ought not to be done.

If an official has subverted the law and taken articles and confesses to have taken them in the area under his supervision and the amount of the illicit goods is still completely confessed, there are no goods to be sentenced. But the crime of subversion has not been confessed, and it is proper to sentence the criminal according to the subversion. If the subversion concerned decrease or increase of punishments of penal servitude or life exile, then the punishment is for deliberately decreasing or increasing punishments of penal servitude or life exile.[19] If the subversion concerned decrease or increase of punishment to one hundred blows of the heavy stick or less, the subversion is less serious [19] and

[17]The punishment specified here does not correspond to that provided by Article 243, which penalizes the private possession of three crossbows and armor by life exile to 2,000 *li*, not by death. However, strangulation was provided for possession of three pieces of armor or five crossbows.

[18]Article 138.

[19]See Article 487.

may be prosecuted according to the law on petitions seeking illegal actions that have been carried out.[20]

Basically this is a crime involving illicit goods, and if the illicit goods have already been confessed, the law regarding the death penalty reduced one degree is not applicable.

COMMENTARY: 37.4b—If the confession of the amount of illicit goods is not complete, the sentence may only be for the calculation of the value of the incomplete amount.

SUBCOMMENTARY: If there is a robbery by stealth of goods worth ten *p'i* of silk and the confession is only for five *p'i*, the five *p'i* that were not confessed are punished by one year of penal servitude.[21] This means that the sentence may only be for the calculation of the value of the incomplete amount.

The meaning of sentencing is again like the above section, no different from the meaning of punishing. That is, even though there is a large amount of illicit goods so that punishment reaches the death sentence, it is reduced one degree.

ARTICLE: 37.5a—Cases of those who make a confession: 1) knowing that someone will accuse them to court, 2) after they have fled (either to avoid punishment or various duties),[22] or 3) after treason is already under way,[23] will have their punishment reduced two degrees.

[4a] SUBCOMMENTARY: Where the criminal knows that someone will accuse him to the court or that an investigation will take place and confesses, or where he has taken flight, or where treason is already under way, and when these kinds of offenses are discovered returns and confesses—each such criminal will have the punishment for his offense reduced two degrees.

ARTICLE: 37.5b—If a person who has fled or whose treason is under way returns to his native place, even though he does not confess, it is considered the same.

[20] Article 135.

[21] Article 282.

[22] The various offenses involved are covered in Articles 457–464.

[23] See Article 251; Deloustal 411. The penalties are greatly increased for the plotters if their treason is actually under way.

SUBCOMMENTARY: Even though he does not confess refers to not having confessed to the officials. Returning to his native place refers to returning to the place from which he first fled or committed treason. These cases are still considered the same as under the law on confession and punishment is reduced two degrees. If his native place has changed, return to such a changed place is the same.

ARTICLE: 37.6—Cases involving those who injure or wound people,

SUBCOMMENTARY: Injure means to injure the body. Wound means to shed blood in making a wound. Even though a personal retainer or slave is the one wounded or injured, it is considered the same as the principle on commoners.

COMMENTARY: If a person kills or wounds because of committing a crime and confesses, he is exempted from punishment for the crime which was the cause of the killing or wounding. But the law on intentionally killing or wounding is followed.[24] If the killing or wounding was accidental, the sentence follows the relevant law.

SUBCOMMENTARY: If because of a robbery a criminal intentionally kills or wounds someone, or if the owner of the goods is accidentally killed or wounded and the criminal confesses, [4b] the criminal is exempted from punishment for robbery and sentenced for intentionally killing or wounding. If the killing or wounding was accidental, the relevant law on accidents is followed. Therefore, it is stated that if the killing or wounding was accidental, the sentence follows the relevant law.

ARTICLE: or articles which cannot be returned,

COMMENTARY: Where the original articles are present, confession is the same as under the law on exemption from punishment.

[20] SUBCOMMENTARY: Reference to articles means such things as *pao* and *yin* seals,[25] tallies and ensigns (*chieh* 節),[26] imperial decrees, official documents, armor, crossbows, flags, banners, forbidden military weapons, and proscribed books, which private households may not pos-

[24]Article 281 punishes wounding someone during the course of a robbery by strangulation and killing by decapitation. Confession, however, would get those punishments reduced to life exile to 3,000 *li*.

[25]See translation Chapter I, notes 138 and 141.

[26]See translation Chapter II, note 85.

sess.[27] These types of things cannot be returned.

Confession where the original articles are present refers to such things as cannot be returned. But if the original articles are present, the case is considered the same as under the law on exemption from punishment.

ARTICLE: or those who flee when the affair is discovered,

COMMENTARY: Even though the crime is not confessed, reduction of punishment for flight is allowed.

SUBCOMMENTARY: If there is a robbery, the punishment is penal servitude. If the criminal takes flight after the crime is discovered and then returns after several days and confesses, but the robbery has already been discovered, even though he confesses, he will not be pardoned. But the punishment for taking flight will be reduced two degrees.

ARTICLE: or those who climb over boundary gates,[28] or who have illicit sexual intercourse,[29]

SUBCOMMENTARY: There are three kinds of offenses concerning boundary gates: climbing over the boundary gate, illegally passing through the boundary gate, and falsifying a name and passing through the boundary gate. Illegally passing through the boundary gate and passing over the boundary gate are not pardoned by confession. But confession does get exemption from punishment for falsifying a name and passing through the boundary gate.

Confession does not get pardon for illicit sexual intercourse by members of the inferior classes with commoners.

[5a] ARTICLE: or those who make unauthorized studies of the heavenly patterns do not come within the principle on confession.[30]

[27]See the discussion on forbidden books in translation Chapter IV, note 47.

[28]Articles 82, 83, 87, and 88 cover the various forms of this offense. Simply climbing over a boundary gate without having the proper credentials was punished by one year of penal servitude.

[29]See Articles 410–415. Illicit sexual intercourse could be punished by as little as ninety blows with the heavy stick where the offense involved a commoner and a member of one of the inferior classes. On the other hand, a man who had illicit sexual intercourse with his father's concubine would be strangled.

[30]The word patterns is used here because both astronomy and astrology are included. See the discussion in Needham, *Science and Civilization in China*, III, 193.

SUBCOMMENTARY: The heavenly patterns are mystical and far away, they may not be studied without authorization. From injuring and wounding persons down to the unauthorized study of the heavenly patterns, none of these cases come within the principle on confession.

Article 38

Those Who Commit Crimes and Flee Together

ARTICLE: 38.1a—All cases involving those who commit crimes and flee together where those whose crime is less serious are able to arrest those whose crime is more serious and surrender (*shou*),

SUBCOMMENTARY: Where a crime has been committed and those who are in prison or who are not yet in prison flee together with those who have committed the same or a different offense, and those whose punishment is life exile are able to arrest those who are sentenced to death, or those who are sentenced to penal servitude are able to arrest those punished by life exile and surrender, such are considered to be cases where those whose crime is less serious are able to arrest those whose crime is more serious and surrender.

COMMENTARY: Where the more serious offense requires the death penalty, it is the same if the person is killed by the others who then surrender.

SUBCOMMENTARY: The article refers to the death penalty being required. This does not mean that it must have already been sentenced but that the death penalty is provided for by the crime and that the criminal has fled. If one whose offense is less serious kills him and comes to surrender, it is considered the same as under the law on arrest and surrender.

Where those punished by life exile or less take flight, and those with a lighter punishment are able to arrest those with a heavier punishment, the law on arrest is comparable to that in the Articles on Arrest and Flight on those who flee.[31] But if the prisoner has been sentenced to death, arrest is not necessary. Where it is more convenient to kill him, this is considered the same as arrest.

[5b] ARTICLE: where the crimes are equally serious, if some of the

[31] Article 453. That is, if a criminal is killed while resisting arrest, his slayer will not be punished.

criminals are able to seize one-half or more of their fellows and surrender, they will have their punishment canceled.

[21] SUBCOMMENTARY: If five men, all of whom have committed crimes punishable by one hundred blows with the heavy stick, flee together, and one man has a repentant heart and seizes another two men and surrenders, this is considered to be seizing one-half or more [and surrendering].[32] In this section on fleeing together and below, both the original crime and the crime of flight are pardoned. Therefore it is stated that their punishment will be canceled.

COMMENTARY: 38.1b—Cases not pardoned by ordinary amnesty follow the ordinary law.[33]

SUBCOMMENTARY: Cases not pardoned by ordinary amnesty refer to such sentences as death or life exile, disenrollment, resignation from occupied office, and removal from the community, which are still in effect even though there be a great amnesty. These types of offenses are not pardoned by amnesty. Therefore, even if some of the criminals seize others and surrender, they will not be exempted from punishment.

QUERY: If ten men who are to be punished by one hundred blows with the heavy stick flee together and six return and surrender, having seized two others who fled, is this the same as seizing one-half or more, canceling punishment?

REPLY: The article set forth in the law on mutual arrests is based on a minority being able to arrest a majority, or those whose offense is less serious being able to arrest those whose crime is more serious, or where the offenses are of equal seriousness some of the criminals being able to seize one-half of their fellows.

Now six men together seizing two men is rather a majority arresting a minority, which according to the meaning of the article does not provide for surrender getting pardon. But where those who have fled from punishment surrender, the original punishment for the offense will be reduced two degrees from that sentenced in accordance with the law.

If those whose offense is less serious are able to arrest those whose

[32]Tai, *General Principles*, p. 358, adds here the character *shou* 首, "to surrender," even though no edition gives this reading. I have followed Tai's reading in order to have the passage make sense.

[33]See Articles 11 and 488. In addition to the ten abominations, several other particularly serious crimes were not pardoned by ordinary amnesty.

offense is more serious, even though the latter are a minority, [6a] pardon is given. But where the offenses are of equal seriousness, surrender does not gain pardon in case a majority of the criminals seize a minority, but only if [at least] an equal number are seized.

FURTHER QUERY: If two persons, A and B, whose crimes are of equal seriousness flee together and A seizes B and surrenders, does A get exemption from punishment or not?

REPLY: The article mentions that if some of the criminals seize one-half or more of their fellows and surrender, their punishment will be canceled. If A and B flee together and A seizes B, the crime of flight has been ended, there are no others in flight. If seizure of one-half of the criminals gets exemption from punishment,[34] how much more then should A be pardoned for seizure of all others who took flight? If ten persons under sentence of death flee together and five arrest five, this is a case of one-half surrendering having seized the other one-half. Since the law has opened the way for arrest and surrender,[35] such cases will get complete exemption from punishment.

FURTHER QUERY: If relatives of the fifth or closer degree of mourning commit a crime and flee together, is the same law on arrest and surrender applicable or not?

REPLY: Accusations to the court in cases of crimes committed by relatives of the fifth or closer degree of mourning are not provided for. They may conceal those who flee and still be permitted reduction of punishment. How then can they arrest and send each other to the court? This principle was set forth for persons of non-kin status and is not a text concerned with relatives.

Cases of arrest and surrender involving relatives gain reduction of the sentence for taking flight, but the punishment for the original offense is not pardoned. Thus it still follows the law on wounding, killing, or accusing relatives to the court. But where the crime is plotting treason or more, the article on arrest and surrender is followed.[36]

[22] ARTICLE: 38.2a—Cases of crimes that are the result of a criminal,

[34]*Ku* 辜 should be read *tsui* 罪, following the KHCPTS edition.

[35]*Shou pu* 首捕 should be read *pu shou* 捕首, which is the order in every other occurrence of this phrase in the *Code*.

[36]See Article 46. For such crimes as plotting treason, it is not permissable for relatives to conceal each others' crimes.

and where the criminal dies a natural death, reduce the punishment for the original crime two degrees.

[6b] SUBCOMMENTARY: Crimes that are the result of a criminal refer to such crimes as concealing criminals, or giving them aid,[37] or failing as a guarantor, or giving false evidence.[38] Should the criminal die a natural death rather than being executed, the punishment of those involved because of him is reduced two degrees.

ARTICLE: 38.2b—Cases where the criminal confesses or meets with imperial grace and is pardoned or has his punishment reduced also follow this law on the criminal being pardoned or having his punishment reduced.

SUBCOMMENTARY: This refers to crimes that are the result of a criminal, where later the criminal confesses or meets with imperial grace and is pardoned or has his punishment reduced. Some criminals get a complete pardon, others have their punishments reduced one or two degrees and the like. But all cases follow this law on the criminal gaining complete pardon, reduction of punishment, or a decrease of sentence.

ARTICLE: 38.2c—Cases that require substitution of blows with the heavy stick or redemption by payment of copper, each follow the principles on the heavy stick or redemption by payment of copper.

SUBCOMMENTARY: As for substituting blows with the heavy stick, should an official bondsman or a slave commit a crime punished by life exile and be given aid by someone, when the official bondsman or slave is caught, the punishment of life exile is replaced by two hundred blows with the heavy stick.[39] The person who gave aid has his punishment reduced from that of two hundred blows with the heavy stick and not from the punishment of life exile. Should the criminal himself be allowed redemption by payment of copper, the punishment for those who gave aid also follows the law on redemption by payment of copper. They need not use office to replace punishment or have blows with the

[37]Article 468 punishes this crime if done knowingly with a sentence only one degree less than that of the criminal who was concealed.

[38]Someone who guaranteed that a criminal would not run away would be punished only two degrees less than the sentence given that criminal if flight occurred. If someone gave false evidence, he also would be punished only two degrees less than the sentence given his victim. See Articles 386 and 387.

[39]See Article 28.

heavy stick substituted, or be sent to labor.

QUERY: If an official bondsman, and so forth, commits a crime punished by life exile, two hundred blows with the heavy stick are substituted. But how many degrees of reduction are required for those who give aid?

REPLY: In cases where blows with the heavy stick are substituted for crimes punished by penal servitude, each degree of penal servitude adds twenty blows, with a maximum of two hundred blows replacing three years of penal servitude.[40] If the [7a] punishment extends to life exile, this is also two hundred blows with the heavy stick. Where reduction of punishment is required in cases where blows with the heavy stick are substituted for life exile, the text gives no degree of reduction. By analogy it follows the one degree of reduction for penal servitude—one hundred eighty blows with the heavy stick.

Article 39

Goods and Articles Taken by Robbery or Fraud

ARTICLE: 39.1—In all cases of goods and articles taken by robbery or fraud, confession to the owner of the goods is considered to be the same as confession to the officials.

SUBCOMMENTARY: Robbery refers to robbery by force or by stealth. Fraud refers to taking someone's goods and articles by fraud or cheating.[41] But if the criminal repents his fault and confesses to the owner of the goods, it is considered the same as confession to the officials.

In cases where the criminal confesses to the owner of the goods upon knowing that someone is going to accuse him to the court, he will still get a reduction of two degrees of punishment.

QUERY: If A robs B of goods worth five *p'i* of silk, and confesses to B, who then takes goods worth ten *p'i* of silk from A as the original and doubled illicit goods, what is the proper punishment?

[23] REPLY: According to the article, those who confess only repay the

[40]Article 27.

[41]Article 373 sentences this crime as comparable to robbery.

original illicit goods.[42] If A confesses to B, who, therefore, takes in excess of his original articles, and if B is an official other than a supervisory or custodial official, then he has taken goods because of an affair, and is sentenced to punishment for illicit goods gained through malfeasance.[43]

ARTICLE: 39.2a—In cases of other illicit goods where prosecution is required, if the criminal repents his fault and returns them to the owner, his sentence will be reduced three degrees below the original punishment.

[7b] SUBCOMMENTARY: Other illicit goods refers to those other than from robbery or fraud, but where punishment is required. If the criminal is able to repent his fault and return the goods to their owner, even though he does not make a confession to the officials, his sentence will be reduced three degrees below the original punishment.

If an official has subverted the law and taken bribes worth ten *p'i* of silk, this is punished by life exile. If he then repents his faults and returns them to the owner, he gets a reduction of three degrees of punishment and is sentenced to two years of penal servitude. Thus it is stated that sentencing follows the principle below.[44]

ARTICLE: 39.2b—Cases which require that the owner of the goods be prosecuted also have their punishment reduced in accordance with this principle.

SUBCOMMENTARY: Required prosecution for the owner of the goods refers to cases of officials taking bribes and subverting the law or not subverting the law, or taking goods and articles in the area under their supervision, or of gaining illicit goods through malfeasance. In each of these cases the giver of goods is also punished.[45] If one takes illicit goods from a person and repents his faults and returns them to the owner, he gets a reduction of three degrees of punishment. The owner of the goods' sentence is also reduced three degrees below the original punishment.

QUERY: If someone sells or exchanges government property and later

[42]See Article 37.

[43]Article 389. Depending upon the amount of goods, the punishment could range from twenty blows with the light stick to a maximum of three years of penal servitude.

[44]See Article 53. Crimes sentenced as comparable cannot force an official's resignation from office or disenrollment.

wants to return it but the original articles have already been expended and new articles are substituted, does this kind of repentance of fault get exemption from punishment or not?

REPLY: If a person wants to return the original articles, he gets exemption from calculating the value of the illicit goods in determining punishment and is sentenced for robbery where nothing has been taken.[46] If one no longer has the original government property and uses new goods to replace it, even though there is double payment by one's own goods, the crime of trading government property still remains.

Article 40

Public Offenses by Those Who Work Together[47]

[8a] ARTICLE: 40.1a—All cases of public offenses by those who work together make the positions of senior officer, second officer, executive officer, and chief clerk each one class. Each person is the principal for that which originated with him.

SUBCOMMENTARY: Working together refers to officials who sign documents together. Public offenses refers to there being no secret crookedness. If the Supreme Court of Justice makes a mistake in sentencing a crime, then its president[48] is the senior officer, the vice president and the revisory judges are the second officers, the assistants are the executive officers, and archivists and the secretaries[49] are the chief clerks. These are the four classes.

Each person is the principal for that which originates with him means that if a chief clerk makes a mistake in examination of the petition, then he is the principal. The assistants are the second-degree accessories, the vice president and the two revisory judges are the third-degree accessories, and the president is the fourth-degree accessory. The registrars and scribes are also fourth-degree accessories. If the mistake in sentence originated with an assistant, then he is the principal, the vice president

[45]However, his punishment is reduced five degrees below that of the official who took the bribe. See Article 140.

[46]Article 282 punishes this offense with fifty blows with the light stick.

[47]Articles 40 and 41 have been translated and discussed by Bünger, "Verantwortlichkeit der Beamten." See also Article 14.

[48]Both here and below, *t'ai-ch'ing* 太卿 should be read *ta-ch'ing* 大卿, following the SPTK edition.

[49]*Li* 吏 should be read *shih* 史, following the KHCPTS edition.

and the two revisory judges are second-degree accessories, the president is the third-degree accessory, and the chief[50] clerks are the fourth-degree accessories. The registrar and scribe are also considered to be fourth-degree accessories.

[24] COMMENTARY: In cases where the mistake is due to different sentences by executive officers or higher officials, only such officials are prosecuted.

SUBCOMMENTARY: If one revisory judge makes a mistake because of differing with the sentence given by the assistant, and another revisory judge agrees with him, then both revisory [8b] judges are principals in the crime. If one revisory judge first allows the assistant's sentence, and only then does another revisory judge disagree, the one who disagrees is sentenced as the principal, the one who agreed with the assistant is not punished.

If the sentence given by an assistant is correct, one revisory judge's sentence is mistakenly in disagreement with that sentence, and the later revisory judge only states that he follows the sentence, then his offense is the same as that of the earlier revisory judge. But if he states that he follows the sentence given by the assistant, then the later revisory judge is not at fault. Should the president and vice president disagree, such mistakes also follow this principle. Where there is mistaken reasoning because of disagreements by second officers or higher officials, and where collective responsibility is required, only the senior officer and such officials as examine or recheck the documents are punished. Those officials below them are not prosecuted.

If there is a mistake by a second officer or a lower official, or one is right and the other wrong, but the decision of the senior officer follows the correct formal law, then the other officials are all exempted from punishment. All offices, both in the capital and the provinces, follow this principle.

QUERY: If an executive officer's sentence is contrary or mistaken, and that of the second officer disagrees with him and is correct but the senior officer does not follow the sentence of the second officer, rather agreeing with that given by the executive officer, then what punishment does each of them get?

REPLY: If a case is sent up for review and only the second officer is cor-

[50]*Chu* 主 should precede *tien* 典, following the KHCPTS edition.

rect, then those above and below him are both exempted from punishment. If the sentence was proper but its administration was contrary or mistaken, then those who did so are punished according to the law. But if the second officer and the senior officer were correct, the other officials are not prosecuted.

ARTICLE: 40.1b—Where offices have not been filled, the law on these four classes of officials is still followed. Where there are not four classes of officials, [9a] those classes that exist are punished.

SUBCOMMENTARY: Within the four classes of officials if there are posts that have not been filled, although only one officer makes the decision, should his sentence be contrary or mistaken, four classes of officials are still prosecuted. If the post of president of the Supreme Court of Justice, or of an assistant, or of a revisory judge has been filled, and his decision is contrary or mistaken, he is the principal. The official who rechecks his decision is still to be considered the fourth-degree accessory.

Where there are not four classes of officials refers[51] to such places as customs stations and military outposts where there are no second officers. From the assistants to the commander at the customs barrier, including the chief clerks, there are only three classes. If the chief clerk goes contrary to the law or is mistaken in examining a petition, the assistant is the second-degree accessory and the commander is the third-degree accessory. The scribe is also considered to be a third-degree accessory. In lower-grade prefectures and counties, the market supervisors have only two clerks. Thus only the two classes of offices filled are included in punishment.

ARTICLE: 40.2—If among those who work together there is a private offense,[52] and the officials who are collectively responsible do not know the circumstances, they are sentenced for having made a mistake.

SUBCOMMENTARY: Working together refers to officials and clerks who are jointly involved in a decision. If there is a mistaken or deliberate violation of correct principle, those other officials who are jointly involved in the decision but who did not know of or take part in the circumstances of the private offense, are sentenced for having made a mistake.

[51] *Wei* 爲 should be read *wei* 謂, following the KHCPTS edition.

[52] See the definition of private offense in Article 17.

If someone commits an offense punished by one year of penal servitude, and the executive [25] officer twists principle in sentencing so that the criminal is exempted from punishment, the other officials who are not aware of the circumstances are punished according to the law on mistakenly decreasing punishment.[53] The official who has committed the private offense is the principal; those who were not aware of the circumstances are the accessories. Thus there are four classes of officials sentenced. A mistaken decrease of sentence has the punishment reduced five degrees, a mistaken increase in sentence has the punishment reduced three degrees, and the like. The other officials, as compared with the one who decided the crime, are sentenced for having made a mistake and get a reduction of three [9b] degrees of punishment.[54] And, as stated, they are sentenced for having made a mistake. Each offense follows the specific article.

Query: Should a chief clerk add to or delete from the text of a case and by fraud or cheat obtain illicit goods worth five *p'i* of silk, and the executive officer, not being aware of these circumstances, sentence the case according to the added or deleted circumstances, it is not yet known if the executive officer gets a reduction of punishment for a mistake concerning the illicit goods obtained by fraud or cheat, or a reduction of punishment for a mistake concerning addition to or deletion from the text of an official document.

Reply: In accordance with this article, offenses are all prosecuted according to the sentence. The crime of obtaining illicit goods lies outside the case. The text of the case which was added to or deleted from has been circulated, and the sentence may only follow such additions or deletions, and not the illicit goods.

Further Query: If the executive officer and the chief clerk commit a private offense by deliberately lessening a punishment of life exile, and the second officer and senior officer do not know the circumstances, how is the punishment for principal and accessories to be sentenced?

Reply: Where the chief clerk is the principal, he is sentenced to life exile. The executive officer is the second-degree accessory, and he is sentenced to three years of penal servitude. For those who do not know the circumstances, the law on committing a public offense by mistake is

[53]See Article 487.

[54]That is, three degrees below the proper punishment.

followed. Including those punished for a public offense there would be four classes. The second officer would be the third-degree accessory and his punishment would be reduced two degrees below that of the clerk. There would be a further reduction of five degrees of punishment for a mistaken decrease of sentence, so that the reduction of punishment of seven degrees from life exile would be ninety blows with the heavy stick. The senior officer would get still another degree of reduction of punishment, or eighty blows with the heavy stick. Where the prisoner has been released and seized again or a relevant principle requires reduction of punishment,[55] the relevant law is followed in each case.

ARTICLE: 40.3a—Thus if other officials or higher officials examine the case and are not aware of the circumstances, each gets a further degree of reduction of punishment.

40.3b—If lower officials are not aware of the circumstances, [10a] they also get a further degree of reduction of punishment. Each is still the principal for that which originated with him.

SUBCOMMENTARY: Other officials refers to those of nearby prefectures, counties, or departments as well as those of various superior prefectures, courts, and directorates, which are independent of each other. Higher officials are those of the various offices in the capital vis-à-vis the departments and tribunals, those of the various prefectures vis-à-vis the Department of State, those of the various counties vis-à-vis the prefectures, and the like.

If a prefecture sends up a document to the Department of State that has an error or mistake, and the official of the department is not aware of it, the punishment for the department official's responsibility as principal is reduced one degree below the prefecture's responsibility as principal. Those who work together are the four classes given in the law and their punishment as principal and accessories is progressively reduced. Should other officials not be aware of the error, this principle is also followed.

If a departmental official sends down a document to a prefecture, which has an error or mistake that the prefectural official is not aware of, the punishment for the prefectural official's responsibility as principal is reduced two degrees below the departmental official's responsibility as principal. Those who work together are the four classes and their punishments as principal and accessories are progressively reduced following this law.

[55]See Article 10.

ARTICLE: 40.4—Officials who examine or recheck documents are punished the same as the lowest accessories.

[26] SUBCOMMENTARY: Examine refers to scribes in the various offices who investigate errors at the time when documents are issued. Recheck refers to administrators who sign their names as final approval. All such persons are punished the same as the lowest accessories. If there are four classes of officials they are punished the same as the fourth class of accessories, and it is the same if there be three or two classes of officials involved.

If there are no officials to examine and recheck, then the executive officer approves and rechecks at the time when the document is issued. If there are contradictions or mistakes, the punishment is for the sentence. The rechecking and examination of the document is not prosecuted.

[10b] ARTICLE: 40.5—In matters that must be memorialized, if officials make mistakes in checking and proofreading, or if in the departmental examination of documents the officials do not correct the mistakes, such officials have their punishment reduced one degree below that of the lowest accessories.

SUBCOMMENTARY: Matters that must be memorialized by the Department of State pass through the Imperial Chancellery and the documents are dispatched there. In accordance with the ordinance and following the statute, "[The document is] first checked by the scribe of the Imperial Chancellery, proofread by the grand secretary of the Imperial Chancellery, examined by the vice president of the Imperial Chancellery, and re-examined by the president of the Imperial Chancellery."[56] If there are contradictions or mistakes, in accordance with the law these must be corrected, and the document is sent back to the office of the Department of State. If these inconsistencies are real and not corrected, the scribe and those above him have their punishments reduced one degree below those of the lowest accessories in the Department of State. There is no text on progressive reduction of punishment. Thus the president and those below him have their punishment reduced equally one degree.

This article considers reduction of punishment to below that for the lowest accessories to be the lightest. If there should be progressively further reduction of punishment, others would not be prosecuted at all. The law on correction of mistakes is only for scribes and those above

[56]Niida, *Statutes*, p. 546.

them. Therefore, the article provides no punishment for chief clerks who handled the document.

ARTICLE: 40.6—If the phraseology of a document is obscure so that there is no way to know it through examination, this is not punished.

SUBCOMMENTARY: The phraseology of a document is obscure means that words have been left out, or there are mistakes, or there have been additions or deletions of crimes and circumstances. If the phraseology is obscure and unclear, those who review the case will find it difficult to be aware of such mistakes. Therefore, it is stated[57] that other officials and those below them who review the case without being aware of the mistakes will all be exempted from punishment. Therefore it is stated that there is no prosecution.

Article 41

Mistakes in Public Matters

[11a] ARTICLE: 41.1a—In all cases where there are mistakes in public affairs and one of those involved becomes aware of the mistake himself and brings it out, the offense will be pardoned.

SUBCOMMENTARY: Mistakes in public matters refer to cases of offenses due to public affairs that have no private crookedness. If one of those involved becomes aware of the mistake himself and brings it out before the matter has been discovered, he will be exempted from punishment for the mistake.

The meaning of "to become aware of and bring out" is different from that of confession. If a person confesses[58] knowing that someone will accuse him to the court, there is a reduction of two degrees of punishment. But this article on becoming aware of and bringing out has no such text. If an official speaks of the mistake himself before it is discovered, he will be exempted from punishment.

ARTICLE: 41.1b—Where collective responsibility is required, if one person becomes aware of and brings out the mistake, the others are also pardoned.

[57] *Ku yün* 故云 should be inserted here, following the SPTK edition.
[58] *Tzu* 自 should precede *shou* 首, following the KHCPTS edition.

SUBCOMMENTARY: Where collective responsibility is required refers to senior officers and below and chief clerks and above as well as officials who examine and recheck—all those who together decide and sign the documents on a case. If one of them becomes aware of and brings out the mistake, the others are also pardoned.

Should the officials who examine and recheck bring out [27] the mistake in examination and the affair is connected with private crookedness, the officials are punished according to the law. But if it is a public offense and the circumstances have no private crookedness, even if the mistake is brought out by officials who examine and recheck, none of them is responsible for the offense.

ARTICLE: 41.2—Should the sentence be mistaken and the punishment already have been administered, this article is not applicable.

SUBCOMMENTARY: Should the sentence be mistaken and the punishment already have been administered refers to the death sentence or blows with the light or heavy stick having already been administered, or those sentenced to life exile already being at the place of exile and having finished their labor, or those sentenced to penal servitude having finished their labor. If these types of punishment have already been administered, then even though the officials themselves become aware of and bring out the mistake, the offense does not come within this principle on exemption [11b] from punishment. Rather each official is sentenced according to the law on mistaken increase of punishment. Therefore it is stated that this law is not applicable.

For such cases as a person being wrongly sentenced to two years of penal servitude, and when he has done one year of labor, only then does an official become aware of and bring out the mistake, the official is accordingly exempted from punishment for the one year that was not done and which he became aware of and brought out. The one year that has already been served is punished following the law on mistaken increase of punishment and the punishment is reduced three degrees to eighty blows with the heavy stick.

ARTICLE: 41.3—Where there is a delay in official documents and collective responsibility is required, if one person becomes aware of[59] and brings out the delay, the others will also be pardoned. But the chief clerk will not be exempted from punishment. If the chief

[59]Both here and below *chüeh* 覺 should precede *chü* 舉, following the SPTK edition.

clerk himself becomes aware of and brings out the delay, his punishment will also be reduced two degrees.

SUBCOMMENTARY: Documents refer to official cases. "Matters of least importance have a five-day time limit, matters of medium importance have a ten-day time limit, and matters of greatest importance have a twenty-day time limit."[60] Thirty days is the limit for those involving penal servitude or more after the sentence has been accepted by the criminal.[61] If these limits are exceeded without the case being finished, it is called delay.

Should an official become aware of the delay himself and bring it out, he and the others involved will get a complete pardon. Only the chief clerk will not be exempted from punishment. If the chief clerk becomes aware of the delay himself and brings it out, he will also have his punishment reduced two degrees. Because the officials did not bring it out, the chief officer and those below will all have their punishment reduced [only] two degrees.

If an official and the chief clerk jointly sign and bring out the delay, the official will get exemption from punishment and the chief clerk's sentence will be reduced two degrees. When imperial decrees or edicts are completed and are to be issued, there is a time limit for their being copied. For two hundred pages or less, the time limit is two days. For more than two hundred pages, one day is added for each two hundred pages with a maximum of five days for any number. The Commentary states: "Even though the number of pages of an amnesty is more, the time limit for copying may not [12a] exceed three days."[62]

The time limit for this type of copying is stated to be after the document has been completed. According to the statute, there is no separate time limit for issuing completed imperial decrees and edicts, that is, it must be done on the same day that they are completed. If the statute on time limits is violated, this is delay.

If there is delay and the one who caused it becomes aware of it and brings it out himself, it is considered the same as the law on official documents. Thus it is a public offense with four classes of officials sentenced, each as principal for that which originated with him. If there is any connection with private crookedness and the delay is deliberate,

60Niida, *Statutes*, p. 595.

61The meaning of *pien* 辨 or *fu-pien* 服辨 is for the criminal to accept his sentence. See Yang, "Notes on Maspero's *Les Documents Chinois*," p. 154.

62This commentary does not appear in the *Code*. But from the sentence above, the phrase which begins "For two hundred pages. . ." to the end of this quotation from the commentary is found in the *Statutes*, p. 598.

then it is considered the same as the law on private offenses.

QUERY: Public offenses are collective, and the punishment is according to the divisions and grades of officials involved. If one of them becomes aware of and brings out the delay, the others also are pardoned. Delay of a case then is a public offense and the officials who recheck the documents are also collectively responsible. But if the officials who examine and recheck bring out the delay, for what reason are the other officials punished?

REPLY: As for mistakes that are public offenses, such affairs can be found and corrected. So if one person becomes aware of the mistake and brings it out, the others will also be pardoned.

But as for matters that need to be administered, if they are delayed or held up this is not the same principle as for mistakes. Since the delay has been brought out by the officials who recheck such documents, the responsible officials are not exempted from sentence.

Article 42

[28] *Where Crimes Are Committed Collectively the Person Who Formulates the Plan Is the Principal*

ARTICLE: 42.1—In all cases where crimes are committed collectively the person who formulates the plan (*tsao-yi* 造意) is the principal. The accessories have their sentences reduced one degree.

42.2a—If the members of a household commit a crime collectively, only the person highest in generation, or oldest of the same generation is prosecuted.

SUBCOMMENTARY: Cases where crimes are committed collectively refer to crimes committed collectively by two or more persons. The person who first formulated the plan is the principal, the others are all [12b] accessories.

Cases where the members of a household commit a crime collectively refers to crimes committed collectively by a man together with his paternal grandfather, his father, his sons and grandsons in the male line, his paternal uncles, his younger brothers, and his nephews in the male line. Only the person highest in generation, or oldest of the same generation of those who dwell together is prosecuted. Those younger in generation or age are not punished.

COMMENTARY: In cases involving those who by law cannot be prosecuted, the punishment devolves on the next oldest in generation or age. Highest in generation, or oldest of the same generation refers to males.

SUBCOMMENTARY: Those who by law cannot be prosecuted refers to those who are eighty years of age or more, ten years of age or less, or are incapacitated.[63] In such cases the punishment devolves on the next oldest in generation or age. Highest in generation, or oldest of the same generation refers to males. If a woman who is the highest in generation or the oldest of the same generation commits a crime together with males who are younger, even though the woman formulated the plan, only the males are prosecuted.

ARTICLE: 42.2b—In cases where the members of a household encroach upon or injure people, they are sentenced as principal and accessories following the laws on encroaching upon or wounding persons of commoner status.

SUBCOMMENTARY: Encroach upon means robbery of goods and articles by stealth. Injure refers to such crimes as assault, beating, killing, and wounding.

If a father and sons together with other members of the household commit such crimes together, and persons are encroached upon or injured, the law regarding persons of non-kin status is followed. In such cases prosecution is not limited to the eldest person in generation or age.

ARTICLE: If supervisory or custodial officials collectively commit crimes together with commoners, even though a commoner formulates the plan, the supervisory or custodial official is the principal. The commoners are prosecuted as ordinary accessories.

[13a] SUBCOMMENTARY: Supervisory and custodial officials are explained later.[64] Even suppose an outsider [that is, a non-official] puts forward the plan, if he together with a chief clerk of the Bureau of the Treasury of the Left robs the granary of goods worth five *p'i* of silk, the chief clerk is the principal and is sentenced to two years of penal servitude, even though the outsider formulated the plan.[65] The outsider is sentenced as an ordinary accessory to robbery, which is punished by one hundred

[63]See Article 30.

[64]See Article 54.

[65]See Article 283.

blows with the heavy stick.[66].

Article 43

Where Crimes Are Committed Collectively Yet the Basic Punishments Are Different

ARTICLE: 43.1—All cases where crimes are committed collectively yet the basic punishments are different, even though the principal and accessories have committed the same crime, punish the crime according to the specific articles on principal and accessories.

SUBCOMMENTARY: If relatives within the five degrees of mourning collectively with others beat or accuse their relatives to the court, or encroach upon or rob their goods and articles, even though the crime was collective yet the specific punishments are different.

If A brings in an outsider, B, and they together beat A's [29] older brother, A is the principal and is punished by two and one-half years of penal servitude.[67] B is the accessory to ordinary assault. Since he was not the initiator and did not actually strike the blow (*hsia-shou* 下手), he gets a further degree of reduction of punishment to twenty blows with the light stick.[68]

Further, if a person of a lower generation, or of the same generation but younger than other household members brings in another person and they together rob his own household of goods and articles worth ten *p'i* of silk, the person of a lower generation, or of the same generation but younger than other household members is the principal and is punished by thirty blows with the light stick.[69] The other person is the accessory and is punished by one year of penal servitude.[70] However, this punishment is reduced one degree below that for ordinary robbery to one hundred blows with the heavy stick. . . . This principle encompasses many offenses, which cannot all be recorded. But cases where the principal and accessories have committed the same crime, yet the basic punishments are different, [13b] all follow this law.

[66]Article 282 punishes this offense by one year of penal servitude, which reduced one degree would be one hundred blows with the heavy stick.

[67]See Article 328.

[68]See Article 308. Thus he gets two degrees of reduction of punishment below the forty blows with the light stick for assault.

[69]Article 288.

[70]Article 288 makes Article 282 applicable for the accessory, whose punishment is reduced one degree below the one and one-half years of penal servitude for the crime.

ARTICLE: 43.2—If a specific article refers to "all," then the crime does not distinguish between principal and accessories. If it does not refer to "all," then this law on principal and accessories is followed.

SUBCOMMENTARY: It is submitted that in the Articles on Violence and Robbery: "Those who plot to kill a relative of a higher generation, or of the same generation but older than themselves within the second degree of mourning, or maternal grandparents will all be decapitated."[71] In such cases as this, where the specific article refers to "all," the crime does not distinguish between principal and accessories.

If the specific article does not refer to "all," the sentence follows the law on principal and accessories. Thus the Articles on Violence and Robbery also state: "Those who plot to kill people are punished with three years of penal servitude." If two persons together plot to kill a person but the crime has not yet been carried out, the one who formulated the plan is the principal and is punished by three years of penal servitude. The accessory is punished by two and one-half years of penal servitude. In such cases as this, which do not speak of "all," the law on principal and accessories is followed.

ARTICLE: 43.3—In cases of robbery by force, as well as illicit sexual intercourse, kidnapping persons to be slaves, entering without authorization (*lan-ju* 闌入), taking flight, illegally passing through or climbing over customs barriers, palisades, walls, or hedges, no distinction is made between principal and accessories also.

SUBCOMMENTARY: Those who rob by force use strength and power.[72] Illicit sexual intercourse is committed by the persons themselves,[73] so that there are no principals and accessories. In kidnapping persons to be slaves,[74] the principle is the same as robbery by force.

Entering without authorization refers to entering the palace or other forbidden place without authorization.[75] Each of these crimes is

[71]Article 253; Deloustal 415.

[72]This is the definition of robbery by force given in Article 281.

[73]See note 29 of this chapter.

[74]Kidnapping persons and selling them as slaves was punished by strangulation. If they were sold as personal retainers, the penalty was life exile to 3,000 *li*, and if as a wife, concubine, son, or grandson, the penalty was two years of penal servitude. See Article 292.

[75]This offense is punished by two years of penal servitude or more, depending upon the circumstances and how far into the palace the criminal went. See Articles 58–60; Deloustal 50–52.

committed by the criminal himself so there is also no distinction between principals and accessories.

An example of taking flight is ten men who are all doing military service and all of them neglect their duties.[76] Illegally pass through refers to illegally going through a customs barrier gate without having a passport.[77] Climb over refers to not going through the gate. Customs barrier refers to a place where travelers are investigated. [14a] Palisade refers to a place with ditches and stake fences. Walls refer to the walls of palace and government buildings. Hedges refer to walls that are not made of pounded earth, but which are secured by hedges and the like.

From robbery by force on down, all of these offenses are sentenced as formal crimes. Therefore, it is stated that there is no distinction between principals and accessories.

Article 44

Where Crimes Are Committed Collectively and There Is Flight

ARTICLE: 44.1—All cases in which crimes are committed collectively and the criminals take flight, when the one who is caught states that the other who is still at large is the principal and there are no other witnesses provide for him to be sentenced to the punishment as an accessory.

SUBCOMMENTARY: If two persons, A and B, obtain articles by fraud or cheating, this is punished by one year of penal servitude.[78] A really was the principal and is seized. B originally was the accessory but has taken flight. A, upon being investigated and questioned (*chü-wen* 鞫問), states that B was the principal, and there are no witnesses. A then is sentenced as the accessory to one hundred blows with the heavy stick.[79] This is called sentencing him to punishment as an accessory.

ARTICLE: Later B, who had taken flight, is seized and states that the first person, A, was the principal and upon investigation and questioning this proves to be true. A is then sentenced as the principal.

[76]See Article 457. The minimum punishment was one year of penal servitude for one day of absence from duty.

[77]See note 28 of this chapter.

[78]See Article 373. This crime is sentenced as robbery, so the amount of the fraud here is goods worth five *p'i* of silk.

[79]Article 42 reduces the punishment of accessories by one degree below that of the principal in an offense.

However, the previous punishment is included in the later total.

[30] SUBCOMMENTARY: If the criminal who was seized later, B, states that A was the principal, and upon investigation and questioning A states that this is true, he is then sentenced as the principal to one year of penal servitude. [14b] A is a commoner and the one hundred blows with the heavy stick that have already been administered must have their redemption value deducted from the one year of penal servitude, which can be redeemed by twenty *chin* of copper. The redemption value of one hundred blows with the heavy stick is ten *chin* of copper, which cancels one-half year of penal servitude, so that in accordance with the law, A is sent to labor for one-half year of penal servitude.[80]

If A had been the only adult member of his household, so that one hundred blows with the heavy stick had already been administered, and he were now sentenced to one year of penal servitude, which is equivalent to one hundred and twenty blows with the heavy stick, then twenty more blows are administered.[81] Thus the previous punishment is included in the later total.

QUERY: Two persons, A and B, commit a crime of robbery equivalent to that punished by life exile. A originally formulated the plan and B was an accessory. But when the affair is discovered, B takes flight. Thereupon A states that B was the principal and the officials sentence A as the accessory. He is sentenced to three years of penal servitude and when his labor is finished, B is seized. A admits that he is the principal, further A is a commoner, what is the sentence?

REPLY: The punishment of life exile is equivalent to four years of penal servitude. Further, it is stated: "An increase of penal servitude to life exile is equal to one additional year of penal servitude."[82] Cumulative sentences of penal servitude and life exile that require labor may not exceed four years. Even though this person has fraudulently falsified the circumstances to the officials, he may not be sentenced again to life exile, but only to one year of penal servitude.

If the sentence were life exile with added labor, which itself carries three years of penal servitude, even though the criminal had already been sent to labor and had labored for three years, he still would be sent into life exile at a greater distance. But since the previous punishment would be included, this would cancel forced labor in a fixed place at the

[80] Article 3 gives the equivalents of penal servitude and amounts of copper.

[81] See Article 27.

[82] This quotation from Article 487 is not exact.

place of exile.

ARTICLE: 44.1b—If one has already turned over articles as redemption and their return is later required, they are returned.

[15a] SUBCOMMENTARY: If a ninth-rank official, A, commits a crime punished by one year of penal servitude and fraudulently gets reduced punishment as an accessory, he redeems the sentence of one hundred blows with the heavy stick with ten *chin* of copper. Now, if he is later sentenced as principal to one year of penal servitude, this cancels a single office of the ninth rank in replacing the sentence of penal servitude. The ten *chin* of copper which has been paid previously is returned to him. . . .

ARTICLE: 44.2—Where punishments have been increased or decreased, whether they are light or heavy, this article is still followed.

SUBCOMMENTARY: Suppose a case is of the type in which the supervisory official increases someone's punishment. A person has committed a crime punished by one year of penal servitude and has only one office of the ninth rank. The official increases his punishment and sentences him to two years of penal servitude. His office replaces one year and the remaining penal servitude is redeemed by payment of copper. Later at a further hearing and questioning it is determined that the punishment should have been only one year of penal servitude. The articles for redemption of the previous increase of one year of punishment are returned.

As for reduction of punishment, if a person holds two administrative positions both of which are of the ninth rank or above and commits a crime punished by two years of penal servitude and the official reduces this to one and one-half years, one office replaces one year of penal servitude. The remaining one-half year does not cancel the other office so it is redeemed by ten *chin* of copper. Upon investigation it becomes known that the first sentence was a mistake, so that two offices must be used to replace two years of penal servitude. The articles for redemption that had previously been turned over are returned to the owner.

Further, a commoner commits a crime punished by three years of penal servitude. The official sentences him to one year of penal servitude and after the labor is completed, the matter is discovered. He must again be sentenced to another two years of penal servitude. Since the first [31] year's has been completed, the criminal must later be sent to an additional two years of labor.

[15b] Article: 44.3—In cases where there is subversion of the law in increasing persons' sentences of penal servitude, the penal servitude is calculated in terms of the labor service exemption tax and cancels taxes and labor services, as does the value of copper for redemption of punishment.

Subcommentary: Reference to subversion of the law in increasing persons' sentences of penal servitude is not limited to the innocent, but includes all cases where penal servitude and labor were not required but were nevertheless sentenced. This is what is meant by subversion of the law in increasing penal servitude.

Subversion of the law in increase of sentence for a whole year is made clear in the texts of the commentaries. Where labor is not a full fifty days and the labor imposed by subversion of the law is calculated as twenty days or less, each day cancels one day from the adult service exemption tax. Thirty-five days also cancel the *tiao* taxes. Other days fewer than fifty do not further cancel taxes or services.

As does the value of copper for redemption of punishment refers to where the son of an official of the seventh rank or above is sentenced to one year of penal servitude through subversion of the law. The bodily labor of the labor service exemption tax is canceled by the redemption value of one year of penal servitude. The labor service exemption tax is calculated and set off against the copper. If not completely used up, the excess copper is returned. If the copper is used up without the labor service exemption tax being completely canceled, the remainder is not paid. Taxes and labor services are canceled according to the law above. The offense of the supervisory official follows the law on deliberate or mistaken increase of sentence.

If an adolescent male sixteen years of age or above who has the right of redemption by payment of copper commits a crime punished by one hundred blows with the heavy stick, and the official sentences him to one year of penal servitude, the days of labor are also calculated in terms of the labor service exemption tax and may cancel the full value of the copper to be paid for redemption. Whether taxes are completely replaced or not follows the explanation above.

Commentary: Each year of increase due to subversion of the law cancels two years. If not a full year, but more than fifty days, it replaces one year.

[16a] Subcommentary: One year of penal servitude due to subversion of the law completely cancels two years of taxes and labor services. Three

years cancels six years of taxes and labor services. . . . In accordance with the statute, fifty days of an adult's labor replaces one year and gets exemption from both taxes and labor services.[83]. . . In all cases, a year means three hundred sixty days.

COMMENTARY: If there are no taxes and labor services for the corresponding year, then they are canceled for the following year. Military service is canceled by days.

SUBCOMMENTARY: Where penal servitude is due to subversion of the law and there are no taxes and labor services because of imperial grace or because of flood or drought, they are canceled in the following year. Military service is canceled by the days of the next turn of duty. Where one year of penal servitude is due to subversion of the law, it replaces two years' service duties.

QUERY: The article refers to the following year being canceled. But suppose because of drought or flood or a grant of imperial grace once again there are no taxes or labor services. Are these then canceled in a later year or not?

REPLY: The article states that if there are no taxes and labor services for the corresponding year, then they are canceled for the following year. The article pities those whose increase of penal servitude and labor was due to subversion of the law and allows them cancelation of taxes and labor services for the following year. If in the next year there are no taxes and labor services, this is put off until the following year [32] when both are required. The basic desire is that they be canceled.

Where there has been an imperial grace or frost or drought, according to the statute, there is exemption from both taxes and labor services.[84] How can this be considered as the year [in which taxes and labor services are canceled because of increased sentence]? [16b] If the people have already labored and paid taxes, these are canceled for the following year. If in such a later year there are no taxes and labor services, these must be canceled for a year in which there are such taxes and labor services. The principle is the same, and no other opinions are possible.

ARTICLE: 44.4—In cases where penal servitude was originally required

[83]Niida, *Statutes*, p. 668; Twitchett, *Financial Administration*, p. 141.

[84]Niida, *Statutes*, p. 676; Twitchett, *Financial Administration*, p. 144. The extent of the remission depended upon what percentage of the crop was destroyed.

and where beating with the heavy or light stick has already been carried out, the value of the copper for redemption of beating with the heavy or light stick decreases the years of penal servitude accordingly.

SUBCOMMENTARY: If the original sentence was one year of penal servitude and the officials have already had one hundred blows with the heavy stick administered when the matter is discovered, the criminal is returned and sentenced to penal servitude. The one hundred blows with the heavy stick that have already been administered cannot be withdrawn.

One year of penal servitude is redeemed by payment of twenty *chin* of copper, which is eighteen days of penal servitude for each *chin*, corresponding to ten blows with the light stick. The previously administered one hundred blows with the heavy stick altogether reduce the penal servitude to one hundred eighty days. Thus the ten *chin* of copper cancel one-half year of penal servitude.

If for a punishment of one year of penal servitude the criminal had already been beaten fifty blows with the light stick, then the five *chin* of copper would reduce the penal servitude labor by ninety days. For the remaining penal servitude, aside from that which has been reduced, each criminal is sent into labor in accordance with the ordinance.

CHAPTER VI

[1a]

Article 45

The Heavier of Two Punishments Is Sentenced

ARTICLE: 45.1a-i—In all cases where two or more offenses are discovered together, the heavier punishment is sentenced.[1]

SUBCOMMENTARY: Suppose that A, who holds a ninth-rank office, commits a robbery of goods worth five *p'i* of silk, for which the punishment is one year of penal servitude.[2] Further, he has private possession of a spear, for which the punishment is one and one-half years of penal servitude.[3] Further, he accidentally breaks two limbs of a person, for which the punishment is life exile to 3,000 *li*, which is redeemed by payment of copper.[4] This is a case where two or more crimes are discovered together.

Following the law on private[5] possession of forbidden weapons, the sentence would be to one and one-half years of penal servitude, for which office would be canceled in replacement. Moreover, ten *chin* of copper would have to be paid. Since robbery, however, is punished by penal servitude and resignation from office, this is sentenced as being the heaviest punishment.

COMMENTARY: This means that the punishments may not be combined. The circumstances of each offense are set out, but lighter punishments may not be combined with heavier.

SUBCOMMENTARY: [1b] . . .The reasons that the circumstances of each offense are set out are: 1) to make it clear that there were several crimes, and 2) to provide against amnesties. The reason is that miscellaneous crimes punished by the death penalty may be pardoned by amnesties, but persons sent into life exile for crimes associated with *ku* [33] poison are not exempted from punishment even by a proclamation of imperial grace.[6]

[1]Regarding multiple offenses, see also translation Chapter IV, note 1. The situation described here brings the lightest punishment to the criminal.

[2]The case seen here is robbery by stealth covered in Article 282.

[3]Article 243.

[4]Article 305.

[5]*Ssu* 私 should be inserted following *ts'ung* 從, following the KHCPTS edition.

[6]Article 262; Deloustal 423.

COMMENTARY: If the heaviest punishment may be redeemed by payment of copper but a lighter punishment requires forced labor in a fixed place or the use of office to replace punishment, this latter is considered to be the heavier punishment.

SUBCOMMENTARY: This means that if A accidentally breaks two limbs of a person, which requires life exile, but according to law he is allowed redemption by payment of copper, and he also has private possession of a forbidden weapon, which is punished by penal servitude and the use of office to replace punishment, then the use of office to replace punishment is considered to be the heavier punishment.[7]

If a commoner committed the crime, the one and one-half years of penal servitude for possession of a forbidden weapon, that is, forced labor in a fixed place, would be the heavier punishment. If there were still further crimes, the law providing the heaviest punishment would be followed.

QUERY: If the son of a seventh-rank official breaks someone's limb, he may redeem by payment of copper the one year of penal servitude that is the punishment.[8] Further, if he commits a robbery, this is punished by one year of penal servitude.[9] But his household has aged relatives, so that blows with the heavy stick are substituted for penal servitude.[10] The two offenses are discovered together. Which is the heavier punishment?

REPLY: This article considers the law on redemption by payment of copper to be a lighter punishment and blows with the heavy stick to be a heavier punishment.[11] Therefore, the robber is not allowed to use protection and redemption by payment of copper.

If his household has aged relatives, blows with the heavy stick are substituted and he is released because blows with the heavy stick are considered to be the heavier punishment. But should the redemption by payment of copper have been for one and one-half years of penal servitude, then the payment of redemption would have been sentenced as the heavier punishment, and not the lighter, that of substituting blows

[7]Article 17 allows office to be used to replace punishment and gives the rules governing such replacement.

[8]Article 11 gives the right of redeeming punishment by payment of copper to officials and certain of their relatives.

[9]Article 282. The case here is where goods worth five *p'i* of silk are taken.

[10]Article 27 allows beating with the heavy stick to be substituted for penal servitude where the criminal's parents or paternal grandparents are eighty years of age or more, or infirm, and the criminal is the only other adult member of the family.

with the heavy stick.

[2a] ARTICLE: 45.1a–ii—Punishments that are equal are sentenced as one.

SUBCOMMENTARY: If a commoner commits a robbery of goods worth five *p'i* of silk, the punishment is one year of penal servitude. Further, if he assaults, beats, or breaks a limb and wounds a person so as to cause physical injury, this is also punished by one year of penal servitude. . . .

ARTICLE: 45.1b–i—If one crime is discovered first, and when it has already been sentenced and punishment administered, further crimes are discovered later, those which are less serious or equally serious are not sentenced.

45.b–ii—Those which are more serious are sentenced, but the previous sentence is included in the later total.

SUBCOMMENTARY: If A breaks B's tooth, the punishment is one year of penal servitude. If he breaks C's finger, this is also punished by one year of penal servitude.[12] The crime of the broken tooth is discovered first, so that A would have already been sent to one year of penal servitude. In case there were no other adults in the household save the criminal, or his household had aged relatives, punishment of one hundred twenty blows with the heavy stick would have already been administered.[13]

Later, the crime of breaking a finger is discovered. But since it is of equal seriousness, it is not sentenced. . . .

If A had beaten C so as to break two or more fingers, the punishment would have been one and one-half years of penal servitude. Thus one-half year of penal servitude would have to be added. So if A were the only adult in his household, a further twenty blows with the heavy stick would be added. This is then the law on more serious crimes being subsequently sentenced, but the previous sentence being included in the later total.

ARTICLE: 45.2a–i—In repeated crimes (*p'in-fan* 頻犯) concerned with illicit goods, the value of the illicit goods is combined in sentencing.

[11]Blows with the heavy stick have to be substituted for the one year of penal servitude incurred for the robbery, since Article 11 does not allow robbery to be redeemed by payment of copper.

[12]Article 303.

[13]This is the number of blows needed to replace one year of penal servitude, following Article 27.

[2b] SUBCOMMENTARY: If, in one day, an official takes goods worth eighteen *p'i* of silk from three sources within the area under his supervision, or if three persons together give goods worth eighteen *p'i* of silk and send them to him at the same time; in each case the sentence is for one-half of the value, or nine *p'i*. [34]. . .

ARTICLE: 45.2a-ii—If the punishments are not equal and the laws are not the same, then the illicit goods carrying the heavier punishment are combined with the illicit goods carrying the lighter punishment. 45.2a-iii—In each case the sentence is one-half of the total.

SUBCOMMENTARY: If the punishments are not equal and the laws are not the same, refers[14] to the amount of punishment not being the same for the crimes of robbery by force, taking bribes with or without subverting the law, robbery by stealth, and taking goods and articles in the area under one's supervision.[15] The illicit goods carrying the heavier punishment are combined with the illicit goods carrying the lighter punishment.

If a county magistrate takes a bribe of goods worth six *p'i* of silk and subverts the law, the punishment is three years of penal servitude.[16] If he takes a bribe of goods worth fourteen *p'i* of silk without subverting the law, this is also punished by three years of penal servitude.[17] Further, if outside his area of supervision he commits robbery by stealth of goods worth twenty-nine *p'i* of silk, this is also punished by three years of penal servitude.[18] If he commits robbery by force of goods worth two *p'i* of silk, this is also punished by three years of penal servitude.[19] If he takes goods worth forty-nine *p'i* of silk within the area under his supervision, this is also punished by three years of penal servitude.[20]

The punishment for these five offenses described above is three years of penal servitude for the illicit goods in each case. If the illicit goods are combined under the offenses of taking goods and articles in the area under his supervision, the total is goods worth one hundred *p'i* of silk. This is then halved to fifty *p'i*, which is punished by life exile to 2,000 *li*.[21]

[14]*Wei* 爲 should be read *wei* 謂, following the KHCPTS edition.

[15]In addition to the penalties given below, Article 18 requires disenrollment for all these offenses.

[16]Article 138.

[17]Ibid.

[18]Article 282.

[19]Article 281.

[20]Article 140.

[21]Ibid.

[3a] COMMENTARY: Combine means that only the illicit goods that are present when discovered are combined. Halve means that two *ch'ih* become one *ch'ih*.

SUBCOMMENTARY: An official takes bribes from four persons, A, B, C, and D and subverts the law, each of them having given illicit goods worth eight *p'i* of silk. Two of them, A and B, were discovered first and the value of their illicit goods was sixteen *p'i* of silk. Combining and halving the total, the sentence is for eight *p'i* of silk, which is life exile and disenrollment.

After this has taken place, there is a second discovery of C and D. Their illicit goods being combined and halved, there would be another sentence for eight *p'i* of silk. But since the former and latter discoveries are for the same amount, in principle there is no further sentence. It is not permissible to combine the latter with the former amount of illicit goods to make sixteen *p'i* of silk, for which the sentence would be the death penalty.

QUERY: A person takes bribes of goods worth fifteen *p'i* of silk and subverts the law. Goods worth seven *p'i* of silk are discovered first, and when he has already been sentenced to life exile, goods worth eight *p'i* of silk are discovered later. How is this to be sentenced?

REPLY: If the illicit goods taken as a bribe to subvert the law come from a single person, then even though what was discovered first has already been sentenced, what was discovered later must be combined with it so that the whole crime is sentenced. This is not the same as a repeated crime in which only the illicit goods present are combined.

If the total value of the illicit goods received from a single person is fifteen *p'i* of silk, the sentence is strangulation. However, those officials who have no salary are sentenced following the law on reduction of punishment.[22]

FURTHER QUERY: If ten persons in business together have their capital goods in one place and the thieves take them away at one time, is this the same as a repeated [3b] crime or not?

[35] REPLY: The commentary on this article states that if a supervisory or

[22]That is, following Article 138, their punishment is reduced one degree. Persons working in government offices who had no official rank are not listed in the statute on salaries. See Niida, *Statutes*, p. 321.

custodial official takes bribes because of some matter, or is given goods in connection with the same matter, or if the official repeatedly takes bribes because of one matter, or if he commits repeated robberies within his area of supervision, the illicit goods are combined but not halved. But aside from these three crimes, all others are sentenced for one-half the value of the goods.

If the goods of ten persons are taken together at one time, although this seemingly is not a repeated crime yet the owners of the goods are different persons. The goods are not those of a single person and in principle it is the same as robbery being committed ten times. Thus it is sentenced the same as a repeated crime, and the illicit goods are reduced by half.

But if the goods had been transferred to one person's sole charge and lost, replacement would also be his sole charge. In principle, they would then be the same as one man's goods, and the crime would not be considered as repeated robbery.

COMMENTARY: Not equal refers to the illicit goods obtained through robbery by force and subverting the law being combined with the illicit goods from robbery by stealth or those which were taken within the area under one's supervision.

SUBCOMMENTARY: The calculation of the value of illicit goods obtained through robbery by force or subverting the law is punished more heavily.[23] Those illicit goods obtained through robbery by stealth or which were taken within the area under one's supervision are punished less heavily.[24] Therefore they are called not equal.

To combine the crimes of robbery by force and robbery by stealth refers to a person repeating the crime of robbery by stealth at different places and obtaining goods worth eighty-two *p'i* of silk. The illicit goods are combined and halved, and the sentence is for forty-one *p'i* of silk, the punishment being life exile to 3,000 *li*. Further, if the crime of robbery by force is repeated in different places and goods worth eighteen *p'i* of silk are obtained, the illicit goods being combined and halved make nine *p'i*. This also is punished by life exile to 3,000 *li*. Now if the goods worth nine *p'i* of silk from the robberies by force are

[23]Both of these offenses are punished by strangulation if goods worth ten *p'i* of silk are taken during a robbery by force or if goods worth fifteen *p'i* of silk are taken in the case of subverting the law.

[24]The maximum punishment for robbery by stealth is life exile with added labor, and that for taking goods within the area under one's supervision is three years of penal servitude.

combined with the forty-one *p'i* from the robberies by stealth, the total is fifty *p'i* and the sentence would be to life exile with added labor.

As for [4a] subverting the law being combined with taking goods and articles in the area under one's supervision, if an official repeatedly takes goods and articles within his area of supervision, and these halved are worth twenty-one *p'i* and two *chang* of silk, the punishment is one and one-half years of penal servitude. Further, if he repeatedly takes bribes and subverts the law and the illicit goods halved are worth two *p'i* and two *chang* of silk, this is also punished by one and one-half years of penal servitude. Now if the illicit goods worth two *p'i* and one *chang* of silk from subverting the law are combined with the goods[25] and articles worth twenty-one *p'i* and two *chang* of silk taken within his area of supervision, the total is twenty-four *p'i*, for which the sentence is two years of penal servitude.

Thus for these types of crimes, robbery by force is combined with taking goods and articles in one's area of supervision, and taking bribes and subverting the law is combined with robbery by stealth. Both combine the illicit goods punished more heavily with those punished less heavily and sentence under the same law for the total amount.

COMMENTARY: 45.2b—If a supervisory or custodial official takes bribes because of some matter or is given goods in connection with the same matter, or if the official repeatedly takes bribes because of one matter, or if he commits repeated robberies within his area of supervision, the illicit goods are combined but not halved.

SUBCOMMENTARY: If ten men together cast copper coins and an official takes articles from them, this is taking bribes because of some matter.[26] If ten men together take money to the official to get favors, this is being given goods in connection with the same matter. Repeatedly taking bribes in sentencing one man's crime is repeatedly taking bribes because of one matter. If warehouse men repeatedly rob their warehouse, or a county magistrate repeatedly commits robbery within the area under his control—in these three crimes, the goods received are combined but not halved.

But where there is separate giving for the same matter, or giving together for separate matters, in each [4b] case the goods received are

[25]*Ts'ai* 財 should be inserted before *wu* 物, following the KHCPTS edition.

[26]On the private casting of copper coins, see translation Chapter IV, note 50. The amount of the bribe is sentenced under Article 389, covering illicit goods gained through malfeasance.

halved in sentencing, as in the previous section. These cases are not the same as this principle.

ARTICLE: 45.3a—Where one matter can be separated into two crimes and the punishments are equal and the laws are the same, they will be combined in sentencing.

SUBCOMMENTARY: As to one matter can be separated into two crimes, suppose someone takes a privately owned horse worth five *p'i* of silk and trades it for a government horse worth ten *p'i* of silk. According to the article on exchanging government property, that part which is calculated to be equal in value is sentenced as comparable to robbery.[27] That part which is calculated [36] to be profit is sentenced as robbery.

Thus the crime concerning the government horse worth ten *p'i* of silk must be separated into two crimes with two kinds of punishment. The five *p'i* of silk that is equal is sentenced as comparable to robbery, and is punished by one year of penal servitude. The five *p'i* of silk that is profit is sentenced as robbery and also punished by one year of penal servitude. These combined total ten *p'i* of silk, which is sentenced to one and one-half years of penal servitude. This is the law for commoners where there are other adults in the household.[28]

For officials, sons of ranked officials who have the right of redemption by payment of copper,[29] and for those who are the single adult in a household, there are differences in the law's application. If a ranked official exchanges government property, the five *p'i* of silk that is profit would be punished by resignation from office. If the official were of the eighth or ninth rank and had only one office, he would resign from office. Further, he would also have to pay ten *chin* of copper.

Were he a sixth-rank or lower supervisory official, the offense would be the same as robbing his own office.[30] If the five *p'i* of silk sentenced as robbery were combined with the five *p'i* of silk mentioned above sentenced as comparable to robbery, following the law on comparable to robbery, the sentence would be one and one-half years of penal servitude. This is combining the illicit goods without increasing the seriousness of the offense so that only the heavier punishment is sentenced.

[27]See Article 53.

[28]If there were no other adults in the household except the criminal, and certain other conditions were met, Article 27 would substitute blows with the heavy stick for penal servitude.

[29]See Article 11.

[30]Article 283. Since two degrees are added to the punishment for robbery by stealth under this law, the minimum punishment would be eighty blows with the heavy stick.

But the sentence is only for the five *p'i* considered as robbery, so that two degrees of punishment are added to that for ordinary robbery. The sentence is two years of penal servitude and disenrollment.

For sons of ranked officials who have the right of redemption by payment of copper, only the five *p'i* of profit are considered, for which the one year of actual labor at penal servitude is the [5a] heaviest punishment.

ARTICLE: 45.3b—If the punishments are not equal and the laws are not the same, then the law carrying the heavier punishment is combined with the law carrying the lighter punishment.

SUBCOMMENTARY: If an official has illegally taxed and collected goods worth fifty *p'i* of silk from one household, for the forty-five *p'i* which have been turned over to the government, he is sentenced for illicit goods gained through malfeasance, which is punished by two and one-half years of penal servitude.[31] For the five *p'i* of silk that came into his own hands, he is sentenced for subverting the law, which is also punished by two and one-half years of penal servitude.[32] In such a case, the five *p'i* that came into his own private hands are combined with the forty-five *p'i* that were turned over to the government, making the crime fifty *p'i* of illicit goods gained through malfeasance. The sentence is to three years of penal servitude.

COMMENTARY: Punishments and laws being equal refers to such cases as exchanging government property, where the part that is accounted equal is sentenced as comparable to robbery, and the part that is accounted profit is sentenced as robbery.

SUBCOMMENTARY: . . . The law is subverted in sentencing an offense and afterwards the official receives goods worth ten *p'i* of silk. Five *p'i* are given first [that is, before the sentence] and this is actual subversion of the law. The other five *p'i* were not given first but only sent after the subversion of the law was accomplished. In these types of offenses, the illicit goods should be combined in sentencing. Therefore the commentary states such cases.

[5b] COMMENTARY: The punishments are not equal and the laws are not

[31] Article 389. Article 56 provides that where an amount of illicit goods, for instance, falls between two set figures for punishment, it should be revised downward.

[32] Article 138.

the same refers to such cases as being responsible for government tools and weapons. If some are lost, they are combined with those that are destroyed in sentencing the offense.

SUBCOMMENTARY: This refers to being responsible for government tools and weapons at an army camp. If the offense concerns one thousand of them and two hundred are lost, this is punished by eighty blows with the heavy stick. If four hundred are destroyed, this is also punished by eighty blows with the heavy stick. Therefore the Miscellaneous Articles state: "In being responsible for government tools and weapons, the sentence considers them under ten parts."[33]

If two parts are lost and four parts destroyed, each of these cases is punished by eighty blows with the heavy stick. If three parts are lost and six parts are destroyed, each of these cases is punished by one hundred blows with the heavy stick. Here the two hundred lost are combined with the four hundred that are destroyed, which is the same as six parts being destroyed, and is punished by one hundred blows with the heavy stick.

[37] COMMENTARY: Such cases as making deliberate errors in examinations are combined with errors through mistake.

SUBCOMMENTARY: The Articles on Administrative Regulations state that if the wrong persons are recommended for appointment or promotion, the punishment is one year of penal servitude for the first person, increased one degree for each further two persons,[34] with a maximum punishment of three years of penal servitude. If there is a deliberate error made in examination, the penalty is reduced one degree, and if the error were through mistake, three degrees.

If nine men are examined and there is a deliberate error about two of them, this is punished by one hundred blows with the heavy stick. If there is an error through mistake about seven of them, this is also punished by one hundred blows with the heavy stick. The two men about whom there was a deliberate error must be included with the seven about whom the error was through mistake, making altogether nine men about whom the error was through mistake, which is punished by one year of penal servitude.

Further, the Articles on Household and Marriage state that if persons are omitted from the household register in order to escape taxes and labor services, the punishment is one year of penal servitude for the first

[33]Article 444.

[34]Article 92.

person, increased one degree for each further two persons.[35] The maximum punishment [6a] is three years of penal servitude. If persons are left off the household register who have no tax and labor service obligation, four such persons are equal to one person who does have such obligation.

Thus the omission of two persons who have tax and labor service obligation is punished by one year of penal servitude. If ten persons who have no tax and labor service obligation are left off, this is also punished by one year of penal servitude. In such cases, the two persons who have tax and labor service obligation must be included with the ten persons who have no tax and labor service obligation, making altogether twelve persons who have no tax and labor service obligation, which is punished by one and one-half years of penal servitude.

ARTICLE: 45.4—Combine does not mean to increase but only to sentence the heavier punishment.

SUBCOMMENTARY: If private property worth five *p'i* of silk is exchanged for government property worth nine *p'i* of silk, the five *p'i* that are sentenced as comparable to robbery are punished by one year of penal servitude. The four *p'i* that are accounted as profit are punished by ninety blows with the heavy stick. If the punishments are equal and the laws are the same, then they are combined in sentencing. The four *p'i* are combined with the five *p'i*, which altogether makes nine *p'i*. But a year of penal servitude is not added, rather the sentence is to one year of penal servitude for being comparable to robbery.

If in the previous section on tools and weapons, where the one part that was lost was included with the two parts that were destroyed, this would be punished by sixty blows with the heavy stick. Since these would be only three parts and not a full four parts, there would be no increase in punishment.[36] Rather the sentence would be only for the one part that was lost.

ARTICLE: 45.5— Where a case requires disenrollment, resignation from office, double repayment, confiscation by the state, or replacement, each of these is the maximum punishment provided by the relevant laws.

SUBCOMMENTARY: If an official of the eighth rank takes bribes worth five *p'i* of silk and subverts the law, the punishment is two and one-half years

[35] Article 150.

[36] See note 31 above.

of penal servitude. If he takes bribes worth twelve *p'i* of silk without subverting the law, [6b] the punishment is also two and one-half years of penal servitude. If he commits robbery by stealth of goods worth twenty-four *p'i* of silk, the punishment is also two and one-half years of penal servitude. If he takes bribes worth thirty-nine *p'i* of silk within his area of supervision, punishment is also two and one-half years of penal servitude. Further, if goods worth twenty-four *p'i* of silk are obtained through fraud or cheat, the punishment is also two and one-half years of penal servitude. Illicit goods gained through malfeasance worth forty-nine *p'i* of silk are also punished by two and one-half years of penal servitude. Halved, their value is seventy-six *p'i* and two *chang* of silk. Further, if he is responsible for ten spears and one is lost, this is punished by sixty blows with the heavy stick.

The illicit goods are combined with the illicit goods gained through malfeasance to the extent of fifty *p'i*, which is punished by three years of penal servitude.[37] This is the maximum punishment. The remaining illicit goods may not increase it.

Taking bribes and subverting the law is punished by disenrollment and taking bribes without subverting the law by resignation from office. Robbery must be doubly repaid. Bribes taken with or without subverting the law, and bribes taken within the area of supervision together with the illicit goods gained through malfeasance are all confiscated by the state. The loss of a [38] government spear must be replaced. The illicit goods gained through malfeasance receives the maximum punishment of three years of penal servitude.

Thus if two or more offenses are discovered together, the heaviest punishment is sentenced first. Office is used to replace punishment, and according to the principle, the criminal is either disenrolled or he resigns from office. A second punishment may not be imposed. Only the heaviest punishment is sentenced.

Article 46

Dwelling Together and Mutual Concealment

ARTICLE: 46.1a—All cases involving those who dwell together or relatives of the third or closer degree of mourning, including maternal grandparents, grandsons in the female line, the wives of grandchildren in the male line, and a husband's brothers and their

[37] Article 389.

wives allow mutual concealment should one of them commit a crime.[38]

SUBCOMMENTARY: Dwelling together refers to having goods and dwellings in common, and is not limited by differences in household registration. There may even be no mourning relationship. [7a] Relatives of the third or closer degree of mourning each have a definite mourning relationship. But even though the mourning relationship with maternal grandparents, grandsons in the female line, the wives of grandsons in the male line, and a husband's brothers and their wives is slight, the circumstances of their being relatives are important. Therefore, should there be an offense, they conceal each other's crimes and make no accusations.

In this case, however, maternal grandparents do not include the maternal great- and great-great-grandparents, and grandsons in the female line do not include the great- and great-great-grandsons.[39]

ARTICLE: Personal retainers and slaves who conceal their master's offenses will not be punished.

SUBCOMMENTARY: The master need not conceal his personal retainers' or slaves' offenses, but they do conceal his. If the offense is not plotting treason or more, they will not be punished.

ARTICLE: 46.1b—If a crime becomes known and any of these persons inform the criminal that the authorities are searching for him, they will not be prosecuted.

SUBCOMMENTARY: Where there are crimes such as casting of copper coins or robbery, such crimes must be secretly found out and the criminals arrested. If a crime becomes known and any of these persons inform refers to telling the criminal that his crimes have been secretly found out.

If any of these persons are able to conceal the criminal or help him to

[38]See the discussion on the family in the fifth part of introduction Chapter II. The basis of this article goes back to a supposed saying of Confucius. "Confucius said, 'Among us in our part of the country, those who are upright are different from this. The father conceals the misconduct of the son, and the son conceals the misconduct of the father. Uprightness is to be found in this.'" *Lun-yü*, XIII, 18.2; Legge, *The Chinese Classics*, I, 270.

[39]References in the *Code* to grandparents and grandchildren usually include the four ascending and decending generations. The reason for the limitation here is that the persons excluded do not come within the five degrees of mourning relationship.

flee, this is also mutual concealment. Therefore they will not be prosecuted.

ARTICLE: 46.2—If relatives of the fourth degree of mourning or less mutually conceal each others' offenses, their punishment will be reduced three degrees below that for persons of non-kin status.

SUBCOMMENTARY: Persons unrelated to the criminal who conceal a capital offense have their punishment reduced only one degree below that of the criminal.[40] But relatives of the fourth or fifth degree of mourning have their punishment reduced a further three degrees below that for persons of non-kin status—altogether four degrees or to two years of penal servitude.

[7b] ARTICLE: 46.3—If the crime is plotting treason or more, this article is not applicable.

SUBCOMMENTARY: This refers to plotting rebellion, plotting great sedition, and plotting treason.[41] These three crimes do not permit mutual concealment. Therefore this article on mutual concealment is not applicable. Rather, sentencing follows the specific article in each case.

QUERY: If relatives of the fourth degree of mourning or less mutually conceal each others' crimes, their punishment will be reduced three degrees below that for persons of non-kin status. But if a crime becomes known and they inform, will they also get a reduction of punishment or not?

[39] REPLY: As for a crime becoming known and they inform, the meaning is the same for mutual concealment as in the text above on relatives of the third or closer degree of mourning, and there is no difference in principle. There is fear that the text is unclear, so mutual concealment is brought up as an example. In such cases there will also be a reduction of punishment of three degrees below that for persons of non-kin status.

[40] Article 468.

[41] Thus this article does not bring in all crimes that provided collective prosecution, but only the major ones against the state.

Article 47
Official Bondsmen and Personal Retainers

ARTICLE: 47.1—All cases of crimes committed by official bondsmen, personal retainers, or government or private slaves, where the specific article has no formal text concerning these inferior classes, treat them as commoners.

COMMENTARY: References to personal retainers include their wives as well as female personal retainers.

SUBCOMMENTARY: Official bondsmen are attached to the Court of Administration of Agriculture. Prefectures and counties originally did not have their registers of ancestry. Personal retainers belong to private households, and [8a] their wives can be commoners, female personal retainers, or slaves. If the daughter of a personal retainer commits a crime, it is the same as if committed by an official bondsman or a personal retainer.

If a government or private slave commits a crime where the specific article has a formal text refers to such crimes as those against a master or beating commoners.[42] Each such case follows the specific article.

Where the specific article has no formal text refers to such crimes as unauthorized entry into the palace, climbing over [such things as customs barriers where a passport is required], crimes against the same class of person, or cursing one's paternal grandparents, parents, or elder brothers or sisters. Each such case treats them as commoners.

ARTICLE: Official bondsmen, personal retainers, and slaves who commit crimes punished by life exile or penal servitude have blows with the heavy stick substituted and are exempted from forced labor in a fixed place.

SUBCOMMENTARY: Official bondsmen, personal retainers, and slaves who commit crimes punished by penal servitude will be treated as specified in the principle of there being no adults in the household save the criminal.[43] That is, blows with the heavy stick are substituted. For one

[42]See the discussion on the inferior classes in the fourth part of introduction Chapter II. In cases of petty treason such as a plot to kill their master, execution did not have to wait for a favorable time, but could be carried out as soon as the emperor approved the sentence. Article 321 punishes a master who kills an offending slave by only one hundred blows with the heavy stick. If the slave were blameless, the punishment was only one year of penal servitude.

[43]Article 27.

year of penal servitude one hundred twenty blows with the heavy stick are substituted—with an additional twenty blows for each further degree—to two hundred blows for three years of penal servitude.

They are treated the same for crimes punished by the three degrees of life exile; the maximum punishment being again two hundred blows with the heavy stick. After the punishment is administered, they are returned to the government or their master, and are exempted from forced labor in a fixed place.

ARTICLE: 47.3a—Official bondsmen, personal retainers, or slaves who must repay the original illicit goods or make redemption by payment of copper and have no goods, have ten blows with the heavy stick substituted for each two *chin* of copper. After the punishment is administered, they are returned to the government or their master.

SUBCOMMENTARY: In all cases where a crime has been committed and the original illicit goods must be repaid or redemption by payment of copper made, and the official bondsmen, personal retainers, or slaves have no goods to make repayment, the original offense and the original illicit goods are made equivalent to amounts of copper. Ten blows with the heavy stick are substituted for each two *chin* of copper, and after the punishment is administered, the criminals are returned to the government or their master. Even though the amount of copper required may be more, the beating may not exceed two hundred [8b] blows.[44]

Now only original illicit goods have been spoken of, not doubled illicit goods.[45] If the official bondsmen, personal retainers, or slaves have no goods to repay the original illicit goods, then it is allowed to substitute beating with the heavy stick and release the criminal, exempting him from further punishment. If they have no goods to repay the doubled illicit goods, in principle these are not sentenced. But those who have goods and are able to pay do so according to the ordinary article.

ARTICLE: 47.3b—Where the official bondsmen, personal retainers, or slaves are aged, young, or disabled, blows with the heavy stick are not substituted. Those who have no goods are released and exempted from punishment.

[44]Article 29 imposes this limit of two hundred blows with the heavy stick.

[45]In cases of robbery, Article 33 provides for double repayment of the goods taken.

SUBCOMMENTARY: In the reference above to those who must make repayment or redemption by payment of copper, if they are seventy years of age or more, fifteen years of age or less, or disabled, in accordance with this article, blows with the heavy stick are not substituted.[46] If upon further investigation they have no goods, they are released, exempted from punishment, [40] and do not make repayment.

As for cases where personal retainers and slaves must repay illicit goods or make redemption by payment of copper, this is done by the personal retainers or slaves themselves, and not by their masters.

ARTICLE: 47.4a—If slaves of the same master should kill each other and their master request exemption from the death penalty, it will be reduced one degree.

SUBCOMMENTARY: Slaves are an inferior class; the *Code* considers them to be domestic animals. Should they kill one another, even though this should be atoned for by death, if their master requests exemption from the death penalty, it will be reduced one degree.[47]

If a personal retainer intentionally kills a member of the inferior classes belonging to the same master, this also is punished by death. But if their master requests exemption from the death penalty, this same law on reduction of punishment will be permitted. If a slave killing a slave is a serious crime and the master's request for exemption from the death penalty is still allowed, then a personal retainer killing a slave is less serious and exemption from the death penalty may certainly be allowed if they belong to the same master.[48] This has reference to private ownership. If the slave belongs to the government, this article is not applicable.

[9a] COMMENTARY: 47.4b—Should family members kill each other, the ordinary article is applicable.

SUBCOMMENTARY: This article states that they are treated as commoners. Thus it is known that the law for commoners is used. So for crimes

[46]The aged and the juvenile had a lesser liability for punishment which is set out in Articles 30 and 31. However, the exemption from beating set forth here is not mentioned though Article 30 does provide that crimes punished by life exile or less may be redeemed.

[47]Article 56 establishes that a reduction of one degree of punishment from either of the two death penalties will be to life exile to 3,000 *li* and that a reduction of one degree from any of the three distances of life exile will be three years of penal servitude.

[48]That is, the higher the status of the offender as against that of his victim, the less serious the crime.

against family members, this principle on request for exemption and reduction of punishment is not applicable.

Article 48

Crimes Committed against Each Other by Foreigners[49]

ARTICLE: 48.1—All cases involving foreigners of the same nationality who have committed crimes against each other will be sentenced following their own customary law.

48.2—Cases involving those of different nationalities who have committed crimes against each other will be sentenced following Chinese law.

SUBCOMMENTARY: Foreigners refers to persons of those barbarian countries who have their own rulers and leaders. They each have their own habits and customs and their regulations, and the laws are not alike. In cases involving those of the same nationality who have committed crimes against each other, the court must ask about the regulations in their native country and sentence the offense following their customs and laws.

In all cases involving those of different nationalities who have committed crimes against each other, such as one person from Koryo and another person from Paekche [countries in the Korean peninsula], Chinese law will be used to sentence and decide the punishment.

Article 49

Specific Articles Having Different Regulations

ARTICLE: 49.1—All cases in which a specific article has a different regulation from that in a principle follow the specific article.

[9b] SUBCOMMENTARY: The principle states: "All cases where crimes are

[49]There were large numbers of foreigners resident in China during the T'ang period. See the references to them in Schafer, *Golden Peaches*. A portion of a regulation concerning them is found in Article 88. Unlike the fragments discussed in Twitchett, "Tunhuang Fragments of the T'ang Regulations," p. 373, this regulation quoted in the *Code* does begin with the word *chu* 諸, "in all cases." The translation is as follows: "In all cases where a foreigner (*fan-jen* 蕃人) takes a Chinese woman (*Han fu-nü* 漢婦女) as a wife or concubine, she will not be allowed to return with him to his country."

committed collectively make the person who formulates the plan the principal. The accessories have their sentences reduced one degree."[50] But the Articles on Assaults and Accusations state: "Where persons plot together to beat or wound someone, in each case the one who strikes the blow is the main offender and is given the heaviest punishment. The original plotter's punishment is reduced one degree and that of the accessories one further degree."[51]

Further, the principle states that officials of the ninth rank and above who commit crimes punished by life exile or less will be allowed redemption by payment of copper.[52] The Articles on Judgment and Prison state: "Ranked officials who serve in a position carrying no official rank or in miscellaneous positions within their own office or in the area under their supervision and commit crimes punished by the heavy stick or less have punishment administered in accordance with the relevant article."[53]

Cases such as this, where the specific article is not the same as the principle, are sentenced according to the specific article.

ARTICLE: 49.2—However, where more than one article may be appropriate, whichever has the heaviest punishment will be followed.

SUBCOMMENTARY: According to the Articles on Fraud and Counterfeits, fraudulent avoidance of taxes and labor services is punished by two years of penal servitude.[54] But where several adults have been exempted from taxes and labor services, the law on omitting persons in the Articles on Household and Marriage punishes omission of one person by one year of penal servitude, increasing one degree for each further two persons, and with a maximum [41] punishment of three years of penal servitude.[55]

The Articles on Fraud and Counterfeit also state: "Fraudulent addition of years of merit or subtraction of years of demerit . . . which result in office being obtained is punished by one year of penal servitude."[56] But where profit is fraudulently obtained and there is a large amount of illicit goods, the sentence is comparable to robbery following

[50]Article 42.
[51]Article 308.
[52]Article 11.
[53]Article 498.
[54]Article 380.
[55]Article 150.
[56]Article 370.

the article on obtaining goods and articles by defrauding or cheating the government or private persons.[57] The maximum punishment is life exile to 3,000 *li*.[58]

Article: 49.3a—Cases that are basically more serious but in which the circumstances are not known at the time the crime is committed are sentenced following the ordinary law.
49.3b—However, those cases that are basically less serious are sentenced according to the basic circumstances.

Subcommentary: Suppose a paternal uncle and his nephew in the male line have grown up in different places and are not known to each other. Should the nephew hit his paternal uncle and wound him and the relationship only become known when they are questioned by the officials, [10a] sentencing will follow the law on assault of persons of non-kin status.[59]

Further, cases such as stealing the objects for the great sacrifices to the spirits, but at another place [so that the robber is not aware of their purpose] will all be prosecuted as ordinary theft if the circumstances are not known at the time the crime is committed.[60]

As for those cases that are basically less serious, should a father not recognize his son or a master his slave and beat and hit him, only learning the circumstances afterward, all such cases follow the relevant laws on hitting sons and slaves and are not sentenced for assaulting persons of non-kin status. . . .

Article 50

Sentencing of Crimes That Have No Formal Article

Article: 50.1—All cases involving sentencing of crimes that have no formal article bring up a heavier offense in order to make clear a

[57]Article 373.

[58]Article 53 limits the amount of punishment for crimes sentenced as comparable to other crimes to life exile to 3,000 *li*.

[59]The difference in punishment is considerable. Hitting and wounding a paternal uncle is punished by life exile to 1,000 *li*, while the same crime against someone of non-kin status is punished by only sixty blows with the heavy stick. The relevant articles are 328 and 302.

[60]Here again the punishments differ. Stealing any object belonging to the great spirits was punished by life exile to 2,000 *li*. However, the punishment for robbery depended upon the value of the goods stolen rather than their status. See Articles 270 and 282.

lighter punishment (*chü-chung yi ming-ch'ing* 舉重以明輕) if the punishment should be decreased.

SUBCOMMENTARY: Sentencing of crimes that have no formal article refers to an article not listing the crime that has been committed.

As for the punishment should be decreased, according to the Articles on Violence and Robbery: "[All] cases involving those who enter other people's houses at night without cause [are punished by forty blows with the light stick]. If the master of the house should immediately kill the intruder, he will not be punished."[61] Thus it is clear that there will be no prosecution for breaking a limb or wounding.

Further, for such crimes as robbery of goods from relatives of the fifth or closer degree of mourning, according to the degree of relationship the punishment is reduced below that for the same crime against persons of non-kin status.[62] For crimes such as fraud or cheating, or illicit goods obtained through malfeasance, and the like, even though the article has no text on reduction of punishment, punishment will still be reduced. Thus it is clear that other crimes follow this article on reduction of punishment. For them, a heavier offense is brought up to make clear a lighter punishment.

ARTICLE: 50.2—If the punishment should be increased, then a lighter offense is brought up to make clear a heavier punishment.

[10b] SUBCOMMENTARY: It is submitted that the Articles on Violence and Robbery state: "Those who plot to kill a relative of a higher generation, or of the same generation but older than themselves within the second degree of mourning . . . will all be decapitated."[63] The text is not concerned with their being either already wounded or killed. Thus if they are either killed or wounded, the lighter offense of plotting is brought up as still calling for the death penalty. If someone has been killed or there is a plot and someone has already been wounded, this should be punished more heavily then, and it is clear that they all should be decapitated.

Further, the principle states: "For cases involving the beating or accusing to the court of one's relatives in the third degree of mourning,

[61]Article 261.

[62]Article 287. For fifth-degree mourning relatives, the punishment would be reduced one degree below that for ordinary robbery; for third-degree mourning relatives, the reduction would be two degrees; and three degrees for second-degree mourning relatives.

[63]Article 253.

whether of a higher generation, or of the same generation but older than oneself, or of a relative in the fourth degree of mourning of an older generation than oneself, the clause on protection may not be used."[64] Thus if a relative of a higher generation, or of the same generation but older than the offender within the one year degree of mourning should be beaten or accused to the court, the case of the third-degree mourning relative is brought up as the lighter offense. Since the case involving the relative within the second degree of mourning is punished more heavily, protection also may not be used. This is bringing up a lighter offense to make clear a heavier punishment.

Article 51

The Emperor and the Imperial Cortege

ARTICLE: 51.1—All references to the emperor or to the imperial cortege include his paternal grandmother, his mother, and his empress, and their corteges as well.

SUBCOMMENTARY: In regard to the emperor, it is submitted that the Articles on Violence and Robbery state: "Robbery of the emperor's possessions or goods is punished by life exile to 2,500 *li*."[65] Robbery of the possessions or goods of his paternal grandmother, his mother, and his empress receives [42] the same punishment.

With regard to the imperial cortege, according to the Articles on the Imperial Guard and Prohibitions: "Interference with the imperial cortege is punished by one year of penal servitude."[66] Interference with the cortege of any of the three empresses is also punished by one year of penal servitude.

A further example: to enter the imperial presence without authorization is punished by decapitation.[67] To enter the presence of any of the three empresses is also punished by decapitation. This means that the offenses are considered to be the same.

ARTICLE: 51.2—In reference to imperial decrees and edicts, the punishment for violation of orders of the emperor's paternal grandmother, his mother, his empress, and the crown prince is reduced

[64]Article 15.
[65]Article 270; Deloustal 429.
[66]Article 74.
[67]Article 59; Deloustal 51.

one degree below the punishment for violating imperial decrees and edicts.

[11a] SUBCOMMENTARY: According to the Statutes on Public Standards: "The three empresses and the crown prince issue orders."[68]

The Administrative Regulations state: "Cases of violation of imperial decrees that have been issued are punished by two years of penal servitude."[69] However, the punishment for violation of the orders of the three empresses and the crown prince is reduced one degree.

ARTICLE: 51.3a—Cases that require prosecution either because of a crime or error within the palace of the crown prince, or because of some violation by the palace guard are also considered the same as under this principle on reduction of punishment.

SUBCOMMENTARY: Cases of crimes against the crown prince refer to criticizing the crown prince or resisting or driving away messengers carrying the orders of the crown prince,[70] the accessories of chariots and horses not matching, or the equipment not being in order, as well as entering the palace of the crown prince without authorization, or guards who stand night duty falsifying their names and replacing each other, or guards who put down their arms, suddenly leave their duties and sleep in another place; such are called crimes.

Mistakes refer to such cases as failure to follow the correct prescription when preparing medicine for the crown prince, or making a mistake in attaching the label, as well as guards not being aware that someone has entered the palace of the crown prince without authorization. The sentences for both crimes and mistakes are reduced one degree below sentences for the same crimes and mistakes involving the emperor.

COMMENTARY: 51.3b—However, cases that basically come within the ten abominations follow the relevant law even though there is a reduction of punishment.

SUBCOMMENTARY: This refers to crimes and mistakes affecting the crown prince being comparable to and included in the laws affecting the emperor. Thus crimes that come within the ten abominations [11b] follow

[68]Niida, *Statutes*, p. 548.

[69]Article 112; Deloustal 119.

[70]Article 132 punishes criticism of the emperor with decapitation. The other offenses mentioned below are punished varyingly.

the relevant laws even though there is a reduction of punishment.

Article 52

References to Relatives of the Second Degree of Mourning and Paternal Grandparents

ARTICLE: 52.1—All references to relatives of the second degree of mourning and to paternal grandparents include paternal great- and great-great-grandparents as well.

SUBCOMMENTARY: As for references to relatives of the second degree of mourning, the Articles on the Household and Marriage state: "Those who marry during the period of mourning for a relative of the second degree of mourning are punished by one hundred blows with the heavy stick."[71] Thus marriage during the period of mourning for paternal great- and great-great-grandparents is considered the same as during the period of mourning for a relative of the second degree of mourning.

As for paternal grandparents, the Articles on the Household and Marriage state: "While the paternal grandparents or parents are still living, to have a separate household register or separate goods is punished by three years of penal servitude."[72] Thus, the punishment for having a separate household register or separate goods while the paternal great- or great-great-grandparents are still living is considered to be the same. Therefore, it is stated that references to relatives of the second degree of mourning and to paternal grandparents include paternal great- and great-great-grandparents as well.

ARTICLE: 52.2—References to grandsons in the male line include great- and great-great-grandsons in the male line as well.

[43] SUBCOMMENTARY: The Articles on Assaults and Accusations state: "Sons and grandsons in the male line who violate teachings and commands . . . are punished by two years of penal servitude."[73] Thus great- and great-great-grandsons in the male line who violate teachings and commands are also punished by two years of penal servitude. . . .

ARTICLE: 52.3a—If a grandson in the male line by the proper wife be-

[71]Article 179.

[72]Article 155. This crime also comes under the ten abominations.

[73]Article 348.

comes the heir of his paternal grandparents, they are considered to be the same as his father and mother.

Subcommentary: According to ritual and the statute: "If there is no son by the proper wife, then a grandson of the proper wife is made heir."[74] Thus the grandson in the male line becomes the heir of his paternal grandparents. If hearing of the death of his paternal grandparents [12a] he conceals and does not mourn their death, the punishment is life exile to 2,000 *li*.[75] Therefore it is stated that they are considered to be the same as his father and mother.

Commentary: 52.3b—Cases of collective prosecution each follow this basic law concerning paternal grandparents and grandsons in the male line.

Subcommentary: According to the Articles on Violence and Robbery, in cases of rebellion and sedition the father and sons of the criminal who are sixteen years of age and over are all punished by strangulation. His paternal grandfather and grandsons in the male line are enslaved by the state.[76] But if a grandson in the male line of the proper wife has become the heir of his grandparents, he is enslaved and not killed. Therefore, it is stated that each case follows this basic law concerning paternal grandparents and grandsons in the male line.

Article: 52.4—The proper mother, stepmother, and foster mother as well as adopted parents are considered to be the same as parents.

Subcommentary: . . .As for foster mother, according to ritual, if a concubine has no children, or a concubine's children have no mother and the father orders them to be mother and child, this relationship is that of foster mother. If the father had not ordered it, according to ritual, the relationship would be that of the fourth degree of mourning and not that of mother.

Adopted parents refers to cases where there are no children and a son is adopted from the same clan. Foster mothers and others are all referred to as mother, but adopted parents also include the father. . . .

Article: 52.5a—References to children include both male and female.

[74]Niida, *Statutes*, pp. 305–306.
[75]Article 120.
[76]Article 248; Deloustal 410.

COMMENTARY: 52.5b—In cases of collective prosecution, females are not included.

SUBCOMMENTARY: As for references to children, the Articles on Violence and Robbery state: "Sons and grandsons in the male line who violate teachings and commands . . . are punished by two years of penal servitude."[77] Here both male and female are included.

[12b] Cases of collective prosecution refer to such crimes as killing three members of one family. Collective prosecution extends to wives and sons, but daughters are exempted from punishment. Therefore it is stated that females are not included.

However, collective prosecution does extend to females in the specific articles on rebellion, sedition, or the making or keeping of *ku* poison. Where the specific articles include females in collective prosecution, the relevant law is followed.

ARTICLE: 52.6—In cases that refer to relatives of the sixth degree of mourning or closer, the sentence is according to the original mourning relationship, which may not be lowered because of higher position or reduced by marriage or adoption. Mourning relationship due to affection is considered to be the same as formal mourning relationship.

SUBCOMMENTARY: The emperor's protection extends to his relatives of the sixth or closer degree of mourning. According to the Articles on the Household and Marriage: "Marriage to the former wife of a relative of the sixth degree of mourning is punished by one hundred blows of the heavy stick for both."[78]

If the imperial house severs mourning relations with a collateral relative of the second degree of mourning, or a woman is married, or a man is adopted outside the family, all of these actions lower the mourning relationship by one degree. But if there is a crime and protection is sought, each case is according to the original mourning relationship, which may not be lowered because of higher position or reduced by marriage or adoption. Thus the law regarding the lesser mourning relationships is followed.

Mourning relationships due [44] to affection are those such as that of

[77]Article 348.

[78]Article 183. Marriage between relatives was forbidden in traditional China. In the case of fifth-degree mourning relatives, Article 411 punishes both partners to the marriage by three years of penal servitude. Even persons of the same surname who married were punished by two years of penal servitude. See Article 182.

the wife and concubine for the husband, the concubine for the husband's eldest son, and the wife for her parents-in-law. If such persons commit offenses against each other, the crimes are considered to be the same as for formal mourning relationships.

Article 53

References to Reciprocal Punishment

ARTICLE: 53.1a—All references to reciprocal punishment, both with regard to punishment and sentence, are for the same punishment that the victim would have suffered, and the sentence is limited to that punishment.

COMMENTARY: 53.1b—The death penalty is limited to strangulation.

SUBCOMMENTARY: As for references to reciprocal punishment, the Articles on Assaults and Accusations state: "Those who falsely accuse other persons are reciprocally punished."[79] As for punishment, [13a] the principle states: "If the confession is untruthful or incomplete, crimes that have not been confessed truthfully or completely will be punished."[80]

As for sentence, according to the principle: "In cases of other illicit goods where prosecution is required, if the criminal repents his fault and returns them to the owner, his sentence will be reduced three degrees below the original punishment."[81]

As for the same punishment, the Articles on Fraud and Counterfeits state: "If a translator either through fraud or counterfeit causes an offense to have the punishment either decreased or increased, he is given the same punishment."[82]

As for sentence is limited to that crime, this means that from reciprocal punishment on down in this article, that sentence is limited to that punishment. These offenses are not the same as actual crimes. Therefore the death penalty is limited to strangulation.

If A[83] accuses B to the court of plotting to kill a relative of a higher generation, or of the same generation but older than B within the second

[79]Article 342. See the discussion in the second part of introduction Chapter II.

[80]Article 37.

[81]Article 39.

[82]Article 387.

[83]The following paragraph is given only in the Japanese editions of the *Code*.

degree of mourning, and the accusation proves true, then B's punishment is decapitation. If the accusation proves false, however, A is only strangled. Therefore it is stated that the death penalty is limited to strangulation.

ARTICLE: 53.2—References to cases sentenced as comparable to taking bribes and subverting the law, comparable to robbery, and the like, mean that the punishment is limited to life exile to 3,000 *li* but is otherwise comparable.

SUBCOMMENTARY: As for references to sentences as comparable to taking bribes and subverting the law, the Articles on Administrative Regulations state: "If bribes are not accepted at first, but are taken after the crime, and the law has been subverted in sentencing the crime, the case is sentenced as comparable to subverting the law."[84] Another article states that forcing the market or gaining excessive profits within an official's area of supervision is sentenced as comparable to subverting the law.[85]

As for references to sentences as comparable to robbery, and the like, the Articles on Fraud and Counterfeits state: "Taking goods and articles by fraud or cheating, whether from the government or private persons, is sentenced as comparable to robbery."[86] The Miscellaneous Articles state: "The throwing away or destruction of tallies or ensigns or gate keys is sentenced as comparable to robbery."[87] Crimes such as these, which are sentenced as comparable to subverting the law or comparable to robbery, limit the punishment to life exile to 3,000 *li*. Thus, cases involving comparable punishment limit the punishment. They are not the same as actual crimes.

ARTICLE: 53.3—None of these crimes comes within the principles on disenrollment, resignation from office, double repayment of illicit goods, added punishment for crimes committed by supervisory or custodial officials, or life exile with added labor.

[13b] SUBCOMMENTARY: . . . Even though the relevant laws do not call for reduction of punishment, these crimes are considered the same as under the laws on miscellaneous crimes, and the sentence is reduced.[88]

[84]Article 139.

[85]Article 142. See also the discussion in translation Chapter IV, note 55.

[86]Article 373.

[87]Article 437.

[88]That is, Article 11 is applicable.

ARTICLE: 53.4—Reference to cases sentenced for subverting the law, for robbery, and the like, mean that the punishment is the same as for the actual crime.

SUBCOMMENTARY: As for sentenced for subverting the law, the Articles on the Family and Marriage state: "If the village headman or official in charge fraudulently omit households, leave out individuals, or add to or subtract from persons' ages in order to decrease or increase the amounts of taxes and labor services . . . and a large amount of illicit goods comes to themselves, the case is sentenced as subverting the law."[89] Another article states: "If taxes are collected [45] illegally or arbitrarily . . . going into private hands, the case is sentenced as subverting the law."[90]

As for cases sentenced for robbery and the like, the Articles on Violence and Robbery state that where government property is exchanged, the part that is calculated to be profit is sentenced as robbery.[91] The Articles on the Public Stables and Granaries state: "In cases of supervisory or custodial officials who make unauthorized personal use of government property or lend it to other persons without a written record, both the officials and those who borrow it are sentenced for robbery."[92]

Where the crime is considered to be the same as actual subversion of the law or actual robbery, disenrollment or resignation from office, and double repayment of illicit goods all follow as if for a normal crime. Cases of intentional killing or wounding, killing or wounding by assault, or illicit sexual intercourse, and so on, are sentenced the same as actual crimes. . . .

Article 54

[14a] *Those Who Are in Charge of Offices or Who Investigate Cases Are Supervisory Officials*

ARTICLE: 54.1—All references to supervisory officials mean that those who are in charge of offices or who investigate cases are supervisory officials.

SUBCOMMENTARY: In charge of refers to all offices both in the capital and in the provinces whose senior officers are in charge of the areas under

[89]Article 153.
[90]Article 173.
[91]Article 290.
[92]Article 212.

their control. Investigate cases refers to the executive officials in offices who decide cases and sentence crimes.

COMMENTARY: Those who are executive officers or above in prefectures, counties, garrisons, frontier posts, intrepid militia,[93] and so on, are all supervisory officials.

SUBCOMMENTARY: This means that even though the positions and duties of executive officials and above in prefectures, counties, garrisons, frontier posts, intrepid militia, and so on, are not the same, nevertheless, within the area under their control they all are considered to be supervisory officials under this principle.

Officers in garrisons, frontier posts, and intrepid militia are only in charge of soldiers and not their family members. The meaning is that those living within the area under their control, whether temporarily or to do business, if such persons have the proper documents and their names are registered[94] in the prefecture or county, are considered to be within the area of supervision.

As for commoners, they are within this principle on supervision, even though they are not on a household register and have not submitted an annual tax register ([*chi*]-*chang* 計帳).[95]

COMMENTARY: As for other offices, as long as an official is in charge of an office or an investigation, even if he is only in charge of individuals and not their family members, if he commits illicit sexual intercourse or takes goods, such cases also come within this principle on surveillance.

[14b] SUBCOMMENTARY: Other offices refers to offices other than prefectures, counties, garrisons, frontier posts, and intrepid militia all having supervisory officials. Whoever is appointed to be even nominally in charge of an office, whether in a department, a tribunal, a court, a directory, a guard office, or any other office is a supervisory official. If he then investigates matters, this is a supervisory function.

Even though the Department of State governs the prefectures and superior prefectures, if there are no documents involved, this is not ordinarily a supervisory function. All offices, both in the capital and in the provinces, follow this principle.

[93]On the intrepid militia, see des Rotours, *Fonctionnaires*, II, 548 ff.

[94]*Li* 暦 should be read *li* 歷 , following the KHCPTS edition.

[95]On tax registers, see Twitchett, *Financial Administration*, pp. 27 ff., and Ikeda, "T'ang Household Registers."

As for the imperial guards, if an officer is in command of soldiers and scribes but not their family members and he commits illicit sexual intercourse with one of their family members or takes goods from their households, this also comes within this principle on supervision. An officer of intrepid militia only commands his militiamen, and if he commits illicit sexual intercourse with one of their family members or takes goods from their households, both of these offenses come within this law on supervision.[96] Offices both within the capital and in the provinces, where an official has illicit sexual intercourse or takes goods from households that are not under his control, all follow this principle.

[46] QUERY: If a junior officer robs the households of the guards under his command of goods, is this the same as a supervisory official taking goods or not?

REPLY: A junior officer has only guards under his command. Robbery is not covered under this article and since the goods were not taken [by coercion, or as a bribe], the offense is only ordinary robbery. He is not here considered as a supervisory official.

[15a] ARTICLE: 54.2—References to custodial officials take those whose duties are personal protection to be custodial officials.
54.3—Those who temporarily serve as supervisory or custodial officials are considered as such, even though their regular duties are neither supervisory nor custodial.

SUBCOMMENTARY: Custodial refers to those who issue decisions to clerks and have sole control over matters, as well as those who supervise granaries, jails, miscellaneous articles, and the like. Those whose regular duties are neither supervisory nor custodial refers to those who are sent temporarily to serve as supervisory or custodial officials being considered as such, even though they are officials whose regular duties are neither to govern nor to direct.

Article 55

References to Day as Being One Hundred K'o

ARTICLE: 55.1—All references to day take it to be one hundred *k'o* 刻 .

[96]The effect is to increase the punishment. Article 18 also requires resignation from office.

But dawn to dusk is used in calculating labor.

SUBCOMMENTARY: The Articles on Administrative Regulations state: "Officials who, without a reason, do not take their turn at duty are beaten twenty blows with the light stick for each day."[97] Here the basis for prosecution is a whole day and night, one hundred *k'o*.

As for calculating labor, the Articles on Administrative Regulations state: "Supervisory officials who make unauthorized use of labor within their area of supervision . . . in each case have the labor calculated and are sentenced for taking goods and articles within their area of supervision."[98] Here dawn to dusk is a day. It is not necessary to take one hundred *k'o* as a standard.

COMMENTARY: If there has been much use of labor, even though not a full day, all segments of time are counted.

[15b] SUBCOMMENTARY: As for calculating much use of labor, if two men work from dawn to noon, this is one day's labor. If six men each work for two hours, this is also one day's labor. No matter whether many men each work for a segment of time or one man works many days, segments of time are used to count the total.

ARTICLE: 55.2—References to year consider it to be three hundred sixty days.

SUBCOMMENTARY: In the *Code* there is much reference to "year" as a basis for penal servitude and labor. Years are calculated by days; references to year do not consider it to be twelve months.

ARTICLE: 55.3—References to persons' ages take the household register as a standard.

SUBCOMMENTARY: References to persons' ages then must take the household register as a standard. Some persons' appearance is that of great age while they are young, others appear young when their age is great. All cases follow the household register and not appearance. The household register is compiled once each three years. If the year is not one in which the household register is compiled, then the person's age is calculated from the old household register.

[97] Article 95.
[98] Article 143.

[47] QUERY: The Household Statutes state: "If there is doubt in regard to abuses or deceit, the appearance of those involved is taken as a standard."[99] If a crime is committed and the age and appearance of the accused are greatly different, is the statute's taking appearance as a standard followed in sentencing the crime or not?

REPLY: The *Statutes*' text concerns[100] taxes and labor services, while that of the *Code* determines punishment and sets up regulations. If a person's appearance could gain mitigation of punishment then abuses would flourish. [16a] Taxes and labor services are less serious, therefore appearance may temporarily be taken as a standard. But matters concerning punishment are serious, and may only follow the household register.

If the meanings of the *Code* and the *Statutes* are different, that of the *Code* may not be rejected and that of the *Statutes* followed. If someone who has the appearance of an adult commits a capital crime and the household register gives his age as seven years, he may not be sentenced.[101] Or if someone whom the household register lists as being sixteen[102] years of age or above commits a capital crime and upon investigation he has the appearance of not being over seven years of age, in matters such as this, where the appearance and the age given by the household register are greatly at variance, if the crime is punished by life exile or more, or involves disenrollment, resignation from office, or the use of office to replace punishment, a memorial is sent up to the Department of State for consideration and decision. Where the throne must be memorialized, a provisional memorial is sent up to get the emperor's decision.

ARTICLE: 55.4—References to groups (*chung* 衆) mean three or more persons.
55.5—References to plots mean two or more persons.

SUBCOMMENTARY: As for references to groups, the Articles on Judgment and Prison state that officials of the seventh rank and above who commit crimes may not be tortured [to gain a confession].[103] Rather, conviction depends upon evidence given by a group. The group must be three per-

[99]Niida, *Statutes*, pp. 242–243.

[100]*Yi* 以 should be read *wei* 爲, following the SPTK edition.

[101]See Article 30.

[102]*Liu-shih* 六十 should read *shih-liu* 十六, following the SPTK edition.

[103]Article 474. The same rights are given those seventy years of age or more, or fifteen years of age or less, as well as the disabled.

sons or more; only then can it be considered a group. Other references to groups also follow this text.

As for plots, the Articles on Violence and Robbery state: "Those who plot to kill people are punished by three years of penal servitude."[104] However, the plot must have two or more persons. References to plots in other articles all follow this principle.

COMMENTARY: If the circumstances of the plot are clear and evident, then one person may be considered to be the same as two persons.[105]

SUBCOMMENTARY: If someone enters another person's home carrying a knife or club, and investigation proves them to be enemies who each desire to kill the other, then even though there be only one person, this situation is considered the same as a plot. Therefore it is stated that one person may be considered the same as two persons.

Article 56

[16b] *References to Addition Mean Increase*

ARTICLE: 56.1—All references to addition mean a degree of increase.
56.2a—All references to reduction mean a degree of decrease.

SUBCOMMENTARY: If someone commits a crime punished by one hundred blows with the heavy stick [and some other circumstance] adds one degree of punishment, then the sentence is to one year of penal servitude.[106] If one degree of punishment is added to a required year of penal servitude, the sentence is to one and one-half years of penal servitude. This is called a degree of increase.

Further, if a crime is punished by one year of penal servitude [and some other circumstance] requires that the punishment be reduced one degree, then the sentence is to one hundred blows with the heavy stick.[107] Or, if one hundred blows with the heavy stick and a reduction of one degree is required, then ninety blows with the heavy stick are administered. This is called a degree of decrease.

ARTICLE: 56.2b—The two death penalties and the three degrees of life

[104] Article 256.
[105] The same is true in plotting rebellion. See Article 248; Deloustal 410.
[106] Such a circumstance might be that a slave hit a commoner.
[107] Here the circumstance might be that a commoner hit a slave.

exile are both considered to be one degree of reduction of punishment.

SUBCOMMENTARY: If a crime is committed that is punished by decapitation and the accessories have their punishment reduced one degree, then the sentence is to life exile to 3,000 *li*.[108] Or if a crime is committed that is punished by life exile to 3,000 *li*, and some principle calls for reduction of one degree, then the sentence is to three years of penal servitude. Therefore, it is stated that the two death penalties and the three degrees of life exile are both considered to be one degree of reduction of punishment.

Where reduction of punishment is required for life exile with added labor, it is considered the same as under this law on the three degrees of life exile.

[48] ARTICLE: 56.3a—In adding, the number must be complete to be prosecuted.

56.3b—Further, adding to punishment may not extend to the death penalty. But where the specific article adds punishment extending to the death penalty, the specific article is followed.

[17a] SUBCOMMENTARY: In adding, the number must be complete to be prosecuted. Suppose someone commits a robbery of goods lacking only one *ts'un* of being worth ten *p'i* of silk. According to the Articles on Violence and Robbery, robbery by stealth of goods worth five *p'i* of silk is punished by one year of penal servitude. One degree of punishment is added for each additional five *p'i*.[109] But since one *ts'un* was lacking, the punishment is only one year of penal servitude.

Further, adding punishment may not extend to the death penalty. According to the Articles on Arrests and Taking Flight: "If a guard is on duty and takes flight, the punishment is one hundred blows with the heavy stick for the first day, with one degree of punishment added for each further two days."[110] Even though the text gives no maximum punishment, this is limited to life exile to 3,000 *li* and may not extend to the death penalty. But where the specific article adds punishment extending to the death penalty, the specific article is followed. The Articles on Assaults and Accusations state that for beating a person so as to break two limbs, the punishment is life exile to 3,000 *li*.[111] Another

[108]Accessories usually have their punishment reduced one degree below that of the principals. See Article 42.

[109]Article 282.

[110]Article 460.

article states that if a personal retainer beats and wounds a commoner, one degree of punishment is added beyond that for the same crime committed by a commoner.[112] Thus in a specific article, adding punishment may extend to the death penalty.

COMMENTARY: 56.3c—Adding punishment may extend to strangulation but not to decapitation.

SUBCOMMENTARY: If a personal retainer strikes a commoner and breaks two limbs, the punishment is already strangulation. If the beating and breaking of limbs is deliberate, another degree of punishment is added. Here, however, additional punishment may only extend to strangulation, it may not extend further to decapitation.

ARTICLE: 56.4a—Where punishment is only one-half year of penal servitude and it is required to substitute blows with the heavy stick, the number is one hundred.
56.4b—If a reduction of punishment is required, ninety blows with the heavy stick is the next amount.

[17b] SUBCOMMENTARY: If a county clerk deliberately increases the circumstances affecting a prisoner so that one-half year of penal servitude is added, and the deputy magistrate knows of this and sentences an increase of punishment, then the clerk is the principal and is punished by one-half year of penal servitude. Should the clerk be the single adult member of his household, then one hundred blows with the heavy stick are administered. The deputy magistrate's punishment is required to be reduced one degree, so that he is sentenced to ninety blows with the heavy stick or payment of nine *chin* of copper.

Article 57
References to Taoist Priests and Nuns

ARTICLE: 57.1—All references to Taoist priests and nuns include Buddhist priests and nuns as well.

SUBCOMMENTARY: The Miscellaneous Articles state that cases of illicit sexual intercourse by Taoist priests and nuns have two degrees of pun-

[111]Article 305.
[112]Article 320.

ishment added beyond that for commoners.[113] In other articles, references to Taoist priests and nuns include Buddhist priests and nuns as well. In all cases where the crime of illicit sexual intercourse is committed at the time that one is a Taoist priest or nun and the crime is discovered after return to lay status, punishment is still added in accordance with the time that the crime was committed.

However, they are considered the same as commoners in that if sent into penal servitude they may not use their certificate of ordination (*kao-tieh* 告牒) to replace the punishment.[114]

ARTICLE: 57.2a—The relationship of Taoist and Buddhist priests and nuns to their masters is the same as for paternal uncles and aunts.

SUBCOMMENTARY: Masters refer to those who expound canonical texts and teachings in Taoist and Buddhist monasteries. Such persons are teaching masters. Crimes against them are punished the same as against paternal uncles and aunts. According to the Articles on Assaults and Accusations, cursing paternal uncles or aunts is punished by one year of penal servitude.[115] Cursing a teaching master is also punished by one year of penal servitude. Crimes against the teaching master in other articles all consider him to be of the same relationship as a paternal uncle or aunt.

[18a; 49] ARTICLE: 57.2b—The master's relationship to his disciples is the same as for nephews and nieces in the male line.

SUBCOMMENTARY: This refers to what has been explained in the text above. Crimes committed by a teaching master against his disciples are considered the same as those by a laymen against his nephews and nieces in the male line. According to the Articles on Assaults and Accusations, beating and killing nephews and nieces in the male line is punished by three years of penal servitude.[116]

The Articles on Violence and Robbery state that cases of intentionally killing relatives of the second degree of mourning or less, whether of a lower generation, or of the same generation but younger than oneself, because of greed, is punished by strangulation.[117] Nephews and nieces in

[113]Article 416.

[114]A photograph of a provisional certificate of ordination for a monk is given at the back of Jacques Gernet, *Les Aspects économiques du bouddhisme.*

[115]Article 329.

[116]Article 328.

[117]Article 287.

the male line are relatives of the second degree of mourning of a lower generation, or of the same generation but younger than oneself. Should a teaching master beat and kill a disciple because of anger, the punishment is three years of penal servitude. Cases of deliberate killing because of greed are sentenced to strangulation.

ARTICLE: 57.3a—The relationship of the Taoist or Buddhist monastery's personal retainers and slaves to the three authorities is the same as to a master's relatives of the second degree of mourning.

SUBCOMMENTARY: Taoist monasteries have abbots, chief administrators, and masters of ceremonies. Buddhist monasteries have abbots, chief administrators, and directors of prayers. These are the three authorities.

Should a personal retainer or slave commit a crime against one of the three authorities in their monastery, it is the same as that of a personal retainer or slave against his master's relatives of the second degree of mourning. According to the Articles on Assaults and Accusations, if a master beats and kills a personal retainer, the punishment is one year of penal servitude.[118] In another article, if a slave commits a crime and his master kills him without having asked the court's permission, the punishment is one hundred blows with the heavy stick.[119] The commentary states: "If the master's relatives of the one year degree of mourning . . . kill the slave, it is considered the same as the master's doing it. Articles below on personal retainers follow this law."

Another article states that personal retainers or slaves who beat their master's relatives of the second degree of mourning are punished by strangulation. If they curse them, the punishment is two years of penal servitude.[120]

If the three authorities beat and kill their monastery's personal retainers, this is punished by one year of penal servitude. If a slave commits a crime and they kill him without having asked the court's permission, the punishment is one hundred blows with the heavy stick. If a [18b] personal retainer or slave beats one of the three authorities, the punishment is strangulation. If he curses one of them, the punishment is two years of penal servitude.

ARTICLE: 57.3b—The relationship of the monastery's personal retainers and slaves to the other priests is the same as to a master's relatives of the fifth degree of mourning.

118 Article 322.
119 Article 321.
120 Article 323.

SUBCOMMENTARY: The Articles on Assaults and Accusations state: "A personal retainer or slave who beats his master's relatives of the fifth degree of mourning is punished by one year of penal servitude. If the wound is serious, one degree of punishment is added beyond that for the same crime committed by a commoner."[121]

Another article states that if they beat or break a limb, or wound or offend even more seriously against a personal retainer or slave of one of their master's relatives of the fifth degree of mourning, the punishment for each of these offenses is reduced two degrees below that for killing or wounding a personal retainer or slave of someone who is not kin to their master.[122]

Another article states: "If they beat, wound, or kill another person's personal retainers, the punishment is reduced one degree below that for killing a commoner. If the victim is a slave, the reduction of punishment is two degrees."[123]

Thus, if a personal retainer beats a Taoist or Buddhist priest or nun of the same monastery, each such offense is punished by one year of penal servitude. If the wound is serious, each such offense has one degree of punishment added beyond that for the same offense against a commoner. If the personal retainer beats a Taoist or Buddhist priest or another of those persons named above and breaks a tooth, the punishment is two years of penal servitude. If the offense is by a slave, another degree of punishment is added, the penalty being two and one-half years of penal servitude. . . .

COMMENTARY: Cases of illicit sexual intercourse and robbery are considered the same as against persons of non-kin status.

SUBCOMMENTARY: If Taoist or Buddhist priests or nuns commit illicit sexual intercourse or robbery, the law regards these crimes as being extremely serious. Therefore, even though they are committed against personal retainers or slaves of the same monastery, they are considered the same as if against commoners. This means that if the three authorities or lower officials commit illicit sexual intercourse [50] or robbery, the punishment is not different from that for these crimes committed against commoners.

If their slaves [19a] commit illicit sexual intercourse or robbery, the punishment is the same as if committed against a person of non-kin status. If a disciple robs his teaching master or a teaching master his

[121]Ibid.
[122]Article 324
[123]Article 320.

disciples, this also is treated the same as under the law on robbery of persons of non-kin status. If goods are held in common and a disciple takes them for his own use, this is considered the same as if someone of a lower generation, or of the same generation but younger than others who dwell together appropriated goods for his own use.[124] For goods worth ten *p'i* of silk, the punishment is ten blows with the light stick, with one degree of punishment added for each further ten *p'i* of silk. The maximum punishment is one hundred blows with the heavy stick. But if the goods are not worth ten *p'i* of silk, there is no prosecution.[125]

[124]Article 162.
[125]Article 56.

Appendix

Specific Articles Section

2. The Imperial Guard and Prohibitions (33 articles)

58. Unauthorized Entry of the Gates of the Imperial Ancestral Temple
59. Unauthorized Entry of the Gates of an Imperial Palace
60. Unauthorized Entry Means Passing over the Threshold
61. Those Who Are Not on the Name Registers at the Gates of an Imperial Palace or Imperial Audience Hall
62. Improper Substitution of the Imperial Guard
63. Those Who, Having Been Authorized to Enter the Imperial Palace, Improperly Spend the Night There
64. Those Who Enter an Imperial Palace or Imperial Audience without Signing the Name Registers
65. Those Who Do Not Leave an Imperial Palace or the Imperial Audience Hall after Their Work There Is Finished
66. Those Who Climb up to a High Place and Look into an Imperial Palace
67. Members of the Imperial Guard Who Are Accused in a Memorial to the Throne
68. Those Who Are Required to Leave an Imperial Palace or Imperial Audience Hall and Who Improperly Delay
69. Unauthorized Entry into Places where the Emperor Is Not Present
70. Changing the Assignments of Guards of Honor that Have Already Been Made
71. Reception of an Imperial Edict to Open the Gates of an Imperial Palace or the Imperial Audience Hall at Night
72. Leaving or Entering an Imperial Palace or Imperial Audience Hall at Night Is Forbidden
73. Shooting Arrows in the Direction of an Imperial Palace or Imperial Audience Hall
74. Breaking into the Imperial Cortege
75. Imperial Guardsmen Who Do Not Come to Take Their Turn at Duty
76. Weapons of the Imperial Guard
77. The Gates of the Imperial Lodges and Camps
78. Standing Night Duty inside or outside an Imperial Palace

79. Punishment for Crimes Involving the Imperial Ancestral Temple, the Temple of Earth, and the Imperial Gardens
80. Standing Guard under a False Name at Such Gates as That of an Imperial Palace
81. Climbing over the City Walls or Boundary Walls of Such Places as Prefectural Cities, Garrison Towns, and Frontier Garrisons
82. Illegally Passing through Boundary Gates
83. Improperly Passing through Boundary Gates
84. Guards at Boundary Gates Who Cause Difficulties
85. Those Illegally Passing through Boundary Gates Who Are Guilty of Other Crimes
86. Erroneously Allowing Persons and Weapons to Pass through the Boundary Gates
87. Illegally Sending Forbidden Articles through the Boundary Gates
88. Crossing Frontier Boundaries
89. Frontier Garrison Towns
90. Those in Charge of Beacon Fires Not Giving the Alarm

3. Administrative Regulations (58 articles)

91. The Number of Personnel in Government Offices
92. Recommending the Wrong Persons to the Examination for the Doctorate
93. Prefects and County Magistrates Who Illegally Leave Their Jurisdictions
94. Officials Who Are Required To Be but Are Not on Duty
95. Officials Who, without a Reason, Do Not Stand Duty
96. Time Limits on Moving to Take Office
97. Officials Who Do Not Follow the Time Schedule in Accompanying the Emperor
98. Failure to Make Advance Announcement of a Great *Chi* Sacrifice
99. Offering Condolences during Partial Abstinence for a Great *Chi* Sacrifice
100. Participation in Sacrifices or in Ceremonies at the Imperial Tombs
101. Participation in Court Celebrations during One's Mourning Period
102. Preparation of Medicine for the Emperor
103. Violation of the Dietary Proscriptions in Preparing the

Emperor's Food
104. Imperial Boats
105. Imperial Chariots, Clothing, and Articles
106. Officials in Charge Who Borrow the Imperial Clothing or Articles
107. Offenses Committed by Inspecting Officials and Those in Charge of the Emperor's Food
108. Food Presented to Officials
109. Divulging Important Matters
110. Astronomical Instruments
111. Delay of Imperial Decrees
112. Those Who Commit Violations in Carrying out Imperial Decrees
113. Omissions and Mistakes in Connection with Imperial Decrees
114. Improper Correction of Errors in Imperial Decrees
115. Violating Name Taboos in Memorials or Statements to the Throne
116. Making Errors in Memorials or in Statements to the Throne
117. Not Memorializing Matters that Ought to be Memorialized
118. Substitution of Signatures Giving Authorization of Administration or Endorsement on a Government Document when the Language Is Correct
119. Not Returning after Being Sent on a Mission with an Imperial Decree
120. Concealing and Not Mourning the Death of Parents or Husband
121. Violating Name Taboos in Administrative Designations and Official Titles
122. Criticizing the Emperor
123. Couriers Who Fall behind Schedule
124. Couriers Who Entrust Official Documents to Others
125. Documents That Are Required to be Sent by Courier
126. Couriers Who Do Not Follow the Address
127. Increasing the Number of Post Horses
128. Taking the Wrong Route while Riding Post Horses
129. Carrying Private Articles while Riding Post Horses
130. Offenses Committed by Senior Officials and Couriers
131. Completion of Matters in Which Tallies Have Been Used
132. Delay in Carrying out Official Matters
133. Hiring Persons for or Entrusting to Others What One Has Been Commanded to Do

134. Officials Who Improperly Set up Stone Monuments
135. Those Who Seek Favors
136. Officials Who Take Bribes for Favors Sought
137. Persons Who Offer Bribes in Seeking to Have a Matter Favorably Carried out
138. Supervisory and Custodial Officials Who Take Bribes and Subvert the Law
139. Officials Who Do Not Take Bribes before a Matter Has Been Administered
140. Officials Who Take Goods and Articles within Their Area of Jurisdiction
141. Officials Who Receive Presents because of a Commission
142. Officials Who Borrow Goods and Articles within Their Area of Jurisdiction
143. Officials Who Make Use of Labor within Their Area of Jurisdiction
144. Officials Who Receive Presents from Persons within Their Area of Jurisdiction
145. Officials Who Exact Goods and Articles from Persons within Their Area of Jurisdiction
146. Extortion by the Family Members of Officials within Their Area of Jurisdiction
147. Officials Who after Leaving Office Receive Presents from Their Former Subordinate Officials
148. Intimidation and Extortion
149. References to the *Code*, the *Statutes*, and the *Ordinances*

4. The Household and Marriage (46 articles)

150. Omitting to File a Household Register
151. Village Headmen Who Do Not Know that a Household Register Has Not Been Filed or that Household Members Have Been Left off of It
152. Prefects and County Magistrates Who Do Not Know that a Household Register Has Not Been Filed or that Household Members Have Been Left off of It
153. Village Headmen or Officials Who Erroneously Do Not File a Household Register or Who Leave Household Members off of It
154. Unauthorized Ordainment as a Buddhist or Taoist Priest
155. Sons and Grandsons in the Male Line Are Not Permitted to Have a Separate Household Register

156. Having a Child during the Period of Mourning for Parents
157. Adopted Sons Who Reject Their Foster Parents
158. Violation of the Law in Taking a Wife
159. Adoption of a General Bondsman as a Son or Grandson
160. Manumission of a Personal Retainer as a Commoner
161. Falsely Combining Households
162. Family Members of a Lower Generation or of the Same Generation but Younger than Other Family Members Who Improperly Make Use of Family Goods
163. Sale of Personal Share Land
164. Possession of More than the Permitted Amount of Land
165. Illegal Cultivation of Public or Private Land
166. Wrongfully Laying Claim to or Selling Public or Private Land
167. Officials Who Encroach upon Private Land
168. Illegal Cultivation of Other Person's Grave Plots
169. Drought, Flood, Frost, or Hail within an Area
170. Land Classified as Uncultivatable Land or Waste Land within an Area
171. Village Headmen's Allocation of Land and Plots for Mulberry Trees
172. Not Allowing Rightful Avoidance of Taxes and Labor Services
173. Violation of the Law in Assessment of Taxes and Labor Services
174. Violation of the Time Limit in Remitting Articles for Taxes
175. Betrothal of a Daughter and Announcement of the Marriage Contract
176. Wrongful Substitution by the Bride's Family in a Marriage
177. Taking a Second Wife
178. Making the Wife a Concubine
179. Marriage during the Period of Mourning for Parents or Husband
180. Marriage while Parents Are in Prison
181. Acting as Master of the Marriage during the Period of Mourning for Parents
182. Marriage by Those of the Same Surname
183. Taking a Wife within the Sixth Degree of Mourning
184. Remarriage of a Widow while Mourning Her Husband
185. Marrying a Runaway Wife
186. Marriage of Officials with Women within Their Area of Jurisdiction

187. Marrying Another Man's Wife by Consent
188. Family Members of a Higher Generation or of the Same Generation but Older than Other Family Members Making Engagements to Marry for Relatives of a Lower Generation or of the Same Generation but Younger than Themselves
189. Divorcing a Wife Who Has Not Given Any of the Seven Causes for Repudiation
190. Divorce
191. Slaves Who Take Commoners as Wives
192. General Bondsmen Are Not Permitted to Marry Commoners
193. Marriages that Violate the *Code*
194. Divorce and Correction of Status in Marriages that Violate the *Code*
195. Violation of the *Code* in Giving and Taking in Marriage

5. The Public Stables and Granaries (28 articles)

196. Shepherds in Charge of Domestic Animals Who Do Not Fulfill Their Assigned Number
197. Upon Examination the State of Domestic Animals Proving to be Unsatisfactory
198. Being in Charge of Government Domestic Animals that Are Weak or Sick
199. Using Government Animals for the Transportation of Private Articles
200. Sacrificial Animals for the Great *Chi* Sacrifice Not Conforming to the Law
201. Making Use of Government Animals in a Manner so that Their Backs Are Laid Bare or Their Throats Are Worn through by the Harness
202. Government Horses Not Being Trained
203. Deliberately Killing Government or Private Horses or Cattle
204. Government or Private Animals which Destroy or Eat Government or Private Articles
205. Killing the Horses or Cattle of a Relative of the Fifth Degree of Mourning
206. Dogs Wounding or Killing Domestic Animals
207. Domestic Animals that Gore, Kick, or Bite Persons
208. Supervisory or Custodial Officials Who Borrow Government Slaves or Domestic Animals
209. Government or Private Domestic Animals that Harm or Eat Articles
210. Inspection by Officials in Charge of Granaries

211. Borrowing Government Articles and Not Returning Them
212. Supervisory or Custodial Officials Who Borrow Government Articles
213. Supervisory or Custodial Officials Who Take Government Articles and Lend Them to Others
214. Damage to the Contents of a Granary
215. Goods or Articles that Are Required to Be Turned over to the Government or to Private Persons
216. Disposal of Government Articles
217. Required Collection of Taxes
218. Supervisory Officials Who Rent out the Collection of Taxes
219. Putting Obstacles in the Way of the Remittance and Collection of Taxes
220. Official Articles which Are Sealed
221. The Buying and Selling of Articles that Have Been Remitted for Taxes
222. Violations in the Taking in and Giving out of Government Articles
223. Government Articles that Are Required to Be Turned over to Private Persons

6. Unauthorized Levy (24 articles)

224. Unauthorized Dispatch of Troops
225. Transfer and Issuance of Military Supplies
226. Not Giving a Tally to Dispatch Troops
227. Selection of Imperial Guardsmen and Militiamen
228. Militiamen Replacing Each Other under False Names
229. Going beyond the Time Limit to Arrive for an Inspection
230. Delaying Army Levies
231. Militiamen Causing Delays
232. Informing the Enemy of an Attack
233. Commanders Who Are Guarding Cities
234. Commanders Who Retreat and Do Not Go into Battle
235. Release of Militiamen at a Garrison Town to Return Home
236. Militiamen Who Avoid Military Service through Craft or Fraud
237. Crimes Committed in Garrison Towns and Frontier Garrisons
238. Issuance of Weapons without an Official Document
239. Violation of the Time Limit in Sending up Men to Take Their Turn at Military Duty

240. Making Levies without Informing Superiors
241. Making Levies that Violate the Law
242. Work that Is Done Incorrectly
243. Private Possession of Forbidden Military Weapons
244. Employing Persons without Giving Them Work to Do
245. Unjust Selection of Laborers
246. Laborers and Artisans Who Make Delays
247. Officials Who Make Private Use of Laborers and Artisans

7. Violence and Robbery (54 articles)

248. Plotting Rebellion or Great Sedition
249. Collective Prosecution of Those Who Do Not Dwell Together
250. Speaking of Rebellion
251. Plotting Treason
252. Plotting to Kill One's Department Head or Other Officials
253. Plotting to Kill Relatives of the Second Degree of Mourning of a Higher Generation, or of the Same Generation but Older than Oneself
254. Personal Retainers or Slaves Who Kill Their Masters
255. Plotting to Kill a Late Husband's Parents
256. Plotting to Kill a Person
257. Breaking Open a Prison
258. Holding a Hostage to Get Goods or Evade Punishment
259. Killing Three Persons in One Family
260. Paternal Grandparents or Husband Being Killed by Someone
261. Pushing Articles into Persons' Ears or Noses
262. Making or Keeping *Ku* Poison
263. Treating Persons with Poisonous Medicine
264. Hatred and Sorcery
265. Killing Persons and Being Removed from the Community
266. Destruction of a Corpse
267. Digging in the Earth and Finding a Corpse
268. Making Magical Inscriptions and Magical Incantations
269. Entering a Person's House at Night without Reason
270. Robbery of Sacred Articles of the Spirits and the Great *Chi* Sacrifice
271. Robbery of the Imperial Seal
272. Robbery of Sealed Official Documents
273. Robbery of an Imperial Decree
274. Robbery of Tallies for the Gates of an Imperial Palace or

Imperial Audience Hall
275. Robbery of Forbidden Weapons and Instruments
276. Robbery or Destruction of Taoist or Buddhist Statues
277. Violation of Tombs
278. Robbery of Grass and Trees within the Imperial Tomb
279. Robbery or Killing of Government or Private Cattle and Horses
280. Determining the Punishment for Robbery When the Value of the Illicit Goods Cannot Be Calculated
281. Robbery by Force
282. Robbery by Stealth
283. Robbery by Supervisory and Custodial Officials within Their Areas of Jurisdiction
284. Intentionally Burning Persons' Homes
285. Obtaining Goods and Articles from Persons by Extortion or Intimidation
286. Plunder of Articles from Persons after Beating Them for Another Reason
287. Stealing Goods and Articles from Relatives in the Fifth and Fourth Degrees of Mourning
288. Family Members of a Lower Generation or of the Same Generation but Younger than Other Family Members Who Have Other Persons Rob Their Own Homes
289. Accidentally Killing or Wounding Persons Because of Robbery
290. Exchanging Private Goods and Slaves for Government Articles
291. Stealing Articles that Have Value Because of Other Persons' Efforts in Mountain and Wilderness Areas
292. Kidnapping and Selling Persons
293. Kidnapping or Misleading Persons to Become Slaves
294. Kidnapping and Selling Relatives of the Second Degree of Mourning of a Lower Generation or of the Same Generation but Younger Than Oneself
295. Taking Part in the Sale of Persons while Knowing that They Have Been Kidnapped or Mislead
296. Persons Who Have Some Connection with Kidnapping or Misleading Persons or Robbery by Force or by Stealth
297. Sentences for the Combined Amount of Illicit Goods in Robberies that Have Been Committed Collectively
298. Collectively Plotting Robbery by Force and Not Carrying It out

299. Committing Robbery Three Times
300. Both the Open and the Secret Taking of Goods Are Robbery
301. Concealment of Robbery within an Area

8. Assaults and Accusations (60 articles)

302. Beating or Wounding Persons in an Affray with Hands, Feet, or Other Articles
303. Beating Someone in an Affray so as to Break a Tooth or Injure an Ear or His Nose
304. To Cut Someone or Shoot at Someone with a Military Weapon
305. Beating Someone so as to Break a Limb or Blind an Eye
306. Beating or Deliberately Killing Someone with a Military Weapon
307. Responsibility for an Offense
308. Beating or Wounding a Person Whether or Not through a Collective Plot
309. To Use Threats or Force to Confine or to Tie up a Person
310. Both Parties to Beating or Wounding Will Be Sentenced According to the *Code*
311. Quarrels within an Imperial Palace
312. Beating Messengers Carrying Imperial Decrees, or Department Heads, or County Magistrates
313. Lower Officials or Subordinates Who Beat Their Senior Officers
314. Beating the Parents of One's Department Head or County Magistrate
315. The Emperor's Relatives of the Sixth or Closer Degree of Mourning
316. Government Employees without Official Rank Who Beat Officials of the Third Rank or Higher
317. Officials of the Ninth Rank or Higher Who Beat Officials of the Third Rank or Higher
318. Supervisory Officials Who Beat Their Subordinates
319. Resisting or Beating Messengers from a Prefecture or County
320. Personal Retainers, Slaves, and Commoners Who Beat Each Other
321. Masters Killing Their Slaves Who Have Committed an Offense
322. Punishment for Beating a Personal Retainer to Death
323. Personal Retainers or Slaves Who Kill Their Masters by

Mistake

324. Beating the Personal Retainer or Slaves of a Relative of the Fifth Degree of Mourning
325. Beating or Wounding a Wife or Concubine
326. Wives Who Beat or Curse Their Husbands
327. Beating Elder Cousins of the Fifth Degree of Mourning
328. Beating an Elder Brother or Sister
329. Beating or Cursing One's Paternal Grandparents or Parents
330. Wives or Concubines Who Beat or Curse Their Husband's Parents
331. Wives or Concubines Who Beat or Curse Their Late Husband's Parents
332. Beating One's Elder Brother's Wife or One's Husband's Younger Brothers or Sisters
333. Beating the Children of One's Wife's Former Husband
334. Beating or Cursing One's Husband's Relatives of the Second Degree of Mourning of a Higher Generation or of the Same Generation but Older Than Himself
335. Parents or Paternal Grandparents Being Beaten by Another Person
336. Mistakenly Killing a Bystander in an Affray
337. Personal Retainers or Slaves Who Curse Their Former Master
338. Killing or Wounding a Person in Play
339. Killing or Wounding a Person by Mistake
340. Secret Accusations to the Court of Plots of Rebellion or Great Sedition
341. False Accusations to the Court of Plots of Rebellion or Great Sedition
342. Reciprocal Punishment for False Accusations
343. Making an Accusation to the Court without Basis of a Minor Offense
344. Making a False Accusation to the Court without Basis for an Offense Punishable by Life Exile
345. Accusing Paternal Grandparents or Parents to the Court Is Punished by Strangulation
346. Accusing Relatives of the Second Degree of Mourning of a Higher Generation or of the Same Generation but Older than Oneself to the Court
347. Accusing Relatives of the Fifth Degree of Mourning of a Lower Generation or of the Same Generation but Younger than Oneself to the Court

348. Violations of Teachings and Commands by Sons and Grandsons in the Male Line
349. Personal Retainers and Slaves Who Accuse Their Masters to the Court
350. False Accusations to the Court of One's Department Head, Prefect, or County Magistrate
351. Anonymous Accusation of Criminals to the Court
352. Prisoners Are Not Permitted to Make Accusations of Other Crimes to the Court
353. Crimes Must Be Confessed to the Resident Official
354. Accusations to the Court of Crimes that Occurred before an Amnesty
355. In Making Accusations to the Court of a Person's Crime the Year and Month Must Be Clearly Indicated
356. Adding to the Circumstances in Making a Written Statement for a Person
357. Ordering a Person to Make an Accusation to the Court that Is without Basis
358. Appealing to the Emperor or Beating the Drum to Make an Accusation
359. Making Accusations to the Superior Court
360. Robbery by Force and Killing Persons
361. Supervisory Officials Who Know that a Crime Has Been Committed

9. Fraud and Counterfeit (27 articles)

362. Forging the Imperial Seals
363. Forging the Seal on Official Documents
364. Forging Tallies for the Gates of an Imperial Palace or Imperial Audience Hall
365. Forging Seals, Tallies, or Ensigns and Giving Them to Persons
366. The Robbery and Use of Imperial Seals, Official Seals, Tallies, or Ensigns
367. Falsifying an Imperial Decree
368. Not Being Truthful in Replying to an Imperial Decree or in Sending up a Memorial to the Emperor
369. Falsifying by Making Additions or Deletions to a Government Document
370. Fraudulently Falsifying Office or Falsely Giving Persons an Office
371. Falsely Making an Heir of a Son Not by the Legitimate Wife

372. Making False References to the Government and so Arresting Persons
373. Obtaining Government or Private Articles by Fraud or Cheating
374. Falsifying Government Documents or Making Additions or Deletions
375. Erroneously Stating that a Commoner Is a Slave
376. Falsely Excising the Names of Official Bondsmen and Slaves
377. Making False Predictions
378. Falsely Ordering or Enticing a Person to Commit a Crime
379. False Use of Post Horses
380. Fraudulent Avoidance of Taxes and Labor Services
381. Fraudulent Illness to Avoid Labor
382. Doctors Who Violate the Correct Prescriptions in Attempting to Cure Illness
383. Upon the Death of a Parent Stating that It Is Someone Else that Has Died
384. False Reports of Illness, Death, or Wounds
385. Causing a Person's Death or Injury through Deception
386. Guarantees of Performance that Fail
387. False Testimony
388. Falsely Stating that One Is an Official

10. Miscellaneous Articles (62 articles)

389. Crimes Involving Illicit Goods Obtained through Malfeasance
390. Making Music during Times of National Mourning
391. Private Coining of Money
392. Recklessly Driving Carts and Riding Horses through the Streets and Lanes of Cities
393. Shooting Arrows at a City Wall or at Government or Private Buildings
394. Firing Crossbows and Digging Pits
395. Doctors Compounding Medicine that Is Not According to the Prescription
396. Illness of Such Persons as Laborers, Artisans, and Frontier Guards
397. The Expenditure of Articles that Have Been Accepted from Other Persons
398. Violation of the Time Limit in a Contract without Repayment of the Debt

399. Seizure of Domestic Animals for Debt
400. Making a Commoner a Slave as Repayment for a Debt
401. Erroneously Stating that a Commoner Is a Slave
402. Betting Goods and Articles in Games of Chance
403. Buildings, Carts, Clothing, Utensils, and Articles
404. Encroaching upon Streets and Lanes
405. Getting Profit from Mountainsides and Lake Shores
406. Violating Curfew
407. Death while on Military or Government Services
408. Excessive Allowances beyond What Is Required
409. Wrongful Entry of a Government Post House
410. Illicit Sexual Intercourse Is Punished by One and One-Half Years of Penal Servitude
411. Illicit Sexual Intercourse with Relatives of the Fifth Degree of Mourning or Their Wives
412. Illicit Sexual Intercourse with Great Aunts in the Male Line and Female First Cousins once Removed in the Male Line
413. Illicit Sexual Intercourse with One's Father's or Paternal Grandfather's Concubines
414. Illicit Sexual Intercourse by Slaves with Commoners
415. Illicit Sexual Intercourse by Consent Where No Punishment Is Specified for the Woman
416. Illicit Sexual Intercourse by Supervisory and Custodial Officials within Their Area of Jurisdiction
417. Calibrating *Hu* and *Tou* Measures, Steelyards, and Measures of Length
418. Utensils and Goods
419. Market Officials Who Set the Price of Articles
420. Privately Making *Hu* and *Tou* Measures, Steelyards, and Measures of Length
421. Buyers and Sellers Not Reaching an Agreement and Attempts to Monopolize the Market
422. Making a Market Certificate to Buy Slaves, Cattle, and Horses
423. Making a Disturbance in a Market Place or Where There Are Crowds of People
424. Failure to Repair or Maintain Dikes
425. Cutting Dikes
426. Transport of Food and Grain while Traveling on Government Ships
427. Steering Ships Not in Accordance with the Law
428. Accidental Fires within the Imperial Tombs or the Imperial

Grave Area

429. It is Not Permitted to Light Fires within Government Warehouses and Graneries
430. Burning Fields and Wilderness Lands at the Wrong Season
431. Accidental Fires within Government Buildings, Graneries and Warehouses
432. Burning Government Buildings and Private Homes
433. Seeing a Fire without Giving the Alarm
434. Indemnification for Damage by Water and Fire
435. Destruction of the Articles of the Spirits
436. Destruction of the Altar Mound for the Great *Chi* Sacrifice
437. Destruction of Tallies, Incenses, and Seals
438. Destruction of Imperial Decrees and Official Documents
439. Illegal Circulation of Sealed Official Documents
440. Loss of the Registration Documents for Government Articles
441. Eating the Melons or Fruit from Government or Private Fields
442. Destruction of Utensils and Grain
443. Destruction of Persons' Grave Stones and Stone Animals
444. Delaying Requests for Military Stores
445. Destruction of Government or Private Utensils and Articles
446. Recovery of Lost Tallies and Seals
447. Requirements for Buried Treasure
448. Lost Articles
449. Violation of Statutes
450. Doing What Ought Not to Be Done

11. Arrest and Flight (18 articles)

451. Runners' Pursuit and Arrest of Criminals
452. Criminals Who Use Weapons to Resist Arrest
453. Arrest when Persons Are Being Beaten or Hit or when Illicit Sexual Intercourse or Robbery Are Being Committed
454. Arrest of Criminals by Passers By
455. Divulging His Crime to a Criminal Who Is Going to Be Arrested
456. Robbery by Force within a Neighborhood
457. Desertion from the Army
458. Militiamen on the March
459. Flight by Criminals Who Are Doing Labor for Sentences of Life Exile or Penal Servitude

460. Desertion by Imperial Guardsmen
461. Flight by Adult Males and Artisans
462. Vagrancy
463. Flight by Official Bondsmen and Slaves
464. Officials Who Desert Their Post
465. Resistance and Flight by Prisoners
466. Custodial Officials Who Are Not Aware of a Prisoner's Escape
467. Allowing Another Jurisdiction's Runaways to Stay
468. Knowingly Concealing a Criminal

12. Judgment and Prison (34 articles)

469. Not Imprisoning Persons Whose Imprisonment Is Required
470. Giving Prisoners Edged Tools that They Could Use to Free Themselves and Escape
471. Prisoners Whose Cases Have Ended and Who Have Been Condemned to Death
472. Custodial Officials Who Instruct Prisoners on How to Retract Their Testimony
473. Allowing Prisoners Clothing, Food, Medical Care, and Medicines
474. Those Who Have the Rights of the Eight Deliberations, Petition, or Reduction of Punishment or Are Aged or Juvenile
475. Prisoners Who Implicate Others as Accomplices
476. Examination of the Written Statement in Interrogation of the Prisoner
477. A Prisoner May Not Be Judicially Tortured More than Three Times
478. Completion of Judicial Torture without a Prisoner Confessing
479. Prison Officials' Detention of Prisoners Being Questioned
480. Interrogation According to the Circumstances of the Accusation
481. Moving Prisoners to One Location and Sentencing Them Together
482. Administering Punishment Not in Accordance with the Law
483. Supervisory Officials Having Persons Beaten with the Heavy Stick
484. Citation of the *Code*, the *Statutes*, the *Regulations*, and the *Ordinances* in Sentencing
485. Not Making Required Reports to Superiors

486. Sentencing in Accordance with an Imperial Decree or Imperial Edict
487. Officials Who Decrease or Increase a Person's Punishment
488. Incorrect Sentences Preceeding an Amnesty
489. Deliberately Committing an Offense Knowing that there Will Be an Amnesty
490. Getting the Prisoner to Accept His Sentence after Conviction
491. Releasing Persons Who Should Have Been Enslaved as a Result of Collective Prosecution
492. Delays in Sending Persons into Penal Servitude or Life Exile
493. Articles that Must Be Repaid, Paid as Redemption for Punishment, Confiscated by the State, or Turned over to the State
494. Capital Crimes Committed by Pregnant Women
495. Judicial Torture or Beating of Pregnant Women,
496. The Death Penalty Is Not to Be Administered after the Beginning of Spring
497. Repeated Memorials Concerning the Administration of the Death Penalty
498. Sentencing to Allow Redemption by Payment of Copper when Sentencing to Penal Servitude or Life Exile Is Required
499. Sentencing to Decapitation for a Crime that Requires Strangulation
500. Allowing Prisoners Not to Labor Who Are Required to Labor
501. Allowing Prisoners Who Have Been Condemned to Death to Escape
502. Doubtful Offenses

Glossary

cha-wei 詐僞 fraud and counterfeit
chan 斬 decapitation
chan-ts'ui 斬衰 the first degree of mourning
chang 杖 heavy stick
chang 長 relative of the same generation but older than oneself
ch'ang-hsing chang 常行杖 ordinary heavy stick
ch'ang-she 常赦 ordinary amnesty
ch'eng-chün 稱准 reference as comparable to
ch'eng-yi 稱以 reference to
chi 擊 to beat
chi 籍 household register
chi-chang 計帳 annual tax register
chi-ch'in 期親 the second degree of mourning
chi-nien 耆年 persons seventy years of age or older
ch'i 妻 wife
ch'i-ch'u 七出 the seven causes for repudiation
chia 家 household
chia-pan kuan 假版官 temporary official
chia-yi liu 加役流 exile with added labor
chiang 降 decrease of sentence; decrease of rank
chiang-so-pu-chih 降所不至 offices not reached by the demotion
ch'iang 強 by force
ch'iang-tao 強盜 robbery by force
chiao 絞 strangulation
ch'ieh 妾 concubine
ch'ieh-tao 竊盜 robbery by stealth
chien 姦 illicit sexual intercourse
chien 減 reduction of punishment
chien-lin 監臨 supervisory official
chien-lin chu-shou nei 監臨主守內 within the area of jurisdiction
chien-min 賤民 inferior classes
chih 制 imperial decree
chih-chih 職制 administrative regulations
ch'ih 笞 light stick
ch'ih 勅 imperial edict
ching-wen pu-ch'eng 經問不承 to undergo questioning without admitting the crime
ch'ing 請 right of petition
Chiu-chang chih lü 九章之律 *Statutes in Nine Sections*

chiu-hun 就婚 a type of marriage in which the husband goes to live with the wife's family
chiu-k'u 廐庫 public stables and granaries
chu 咒 to curse by means of spells
chu-hun 主婚 master of the marriage
chu-shou 主守 custodial official
chung 衆 a group
chü-ch'ing yi ming-chung 舉輕以明重 to bring up a lighter offense in order to make clear a heavier punishment
chü-chung yi ming-ch'ing 舉重以明輕 to bring up a heavier offense in order to make clear a lighter punishment
chü-tso 居作 forced labor in a fixed place
chü-wen 鞫問 to investigate and question
ch'u-ming 除名 disenrolled
ch'u-tsui 出罪 to reduce punishment
ch'ü-she 曲赦 amnesty for a particular section of the country
erh-mu so-pu-chi ssu-lü so-pu-tao 耳目所不及，思慮所不到 wherein eyes and ears could not have perceived such a result and where thought and planning could not have prevented it
Fa ching 法經 *Canon of Laws*
fa-li 法例 standards for the laws
fan-jen 蕃人 foreigners
fan-jen 凡人 persons of non-kin status; commoner
fan-ni yuan-tso 反逆緣坐 collective prosecution for rebellion or sedition
fang 放 to manumit
fei-chi 廢疾 disabled
ho 和 by consent
ho-yu 和誘 to mislead
hsia-shou 下手 to strike a blow
hsiang jung-yin 相容隱 mutual concealment
hsiao-kung 小功 the fourth degree of mourning
hsing 刑 punishment
hsing-ming 刑名 names of the punishments
hsü 叙 to resume office
hsün-ch'iu chang 訊囚杖 heavy stick used in interrogation
hu-hun 戶婚 household and marriage
kao 告 to accuse to the court
kao-shen 告身 certificate of appointment
kao-tieh 告牒 certificate of ordination
kao-yen 告言 accusingly speaking
k'o 課 general name for taxes

k'o-nü 客女 a female retainer
ku 蠱 a poison
ku 故 intentional
ku-sha 故殺 intentional killing
ku-tsung 故縱 to deliberately connive
kuan 貫 register of ancestry
kuan-hu 官戶 an official bondsman
kuan-tang 官當 to use office to replace punishment
kung 工 an artisan bondsman
kung-tso 公坐 public offense
kung-tsui 公罪 public offense
kuo-shih 過失 accidental
lan-ju 闌入 to enter without proper authorization
lei-chiang 累降 cumulative reduction in rank
lei-chien 累減 cumulative reduction of punishment
lei-k'o 累科 to sentence cumulatively
li 例 standard, principle
li 詈 to curse with bad language
lien-tso 連坐 collective responsibility
ling 令 statute
liu 流 life exile
liu-chu 留住 to remain and dwell at home
liu-kuan 留官 to retain office
lü 慮 revision of sentence
lüeh-jen 略人 to kidnap
ma 罵 to curse with bad language
mien-kuan 免官 to resign from office
mien-so-chü chih kuan 免所居之官 to resign from occupied office
ming 名 to name
mou 謀 to plan
mou fan 謀反 to plot rebellion
mou-p'an 謀叛 to plot treason
mou-sha 謀殺 to plot to kill
mou ta-ni 謀大逆 to plot great sedition
nei-luan 內亂 incest
nu-pei 奴婢 a slave
o-ni 惡逆 contumacy
ou 毆 to beat
pa-yi 八議 the eight deliberations
p'an 判 decision
pao-cheng 保證 to act as a guarantor
p'ei-liu 配流 to send into life exile

p'ei-yi 配役 to send to forced labor
pen-t'iao 本條 specific article
pi 比 to compare
pieh-chi 别籍 separate household register
p'in-fan 頻犯 repeated crimes
pu-ching 不敬 irreverence
pu-chang 簿帳 registration document
pu-ch'ü 部曲 a personal retainer
pu-hsiao 不孝 lack of filial piety
pu-mu 不睦 discord
pu-tao 不道 depravity
pu-yi 不義 unrighteousness
pu-wang 捕亡 arrest and flight
p'u-she 普赦 amnesty for the whole country
sha-jen 殺人 to kill
shan-hsing 擅興 unauthorized levies
shen 審 a hearing
shih 失 mistake
shih 式 ordinance
shih-o 十惡 the ten abominations
shih-ts'o chih-yi 失錯旨意 to make a mistake in the meaning of a decree
shou 首 a principal; to surrender
shou-ch'ing wang-fa 受請枉法 to subvert the law in receiving requests
shou so-chien-lin ts'ai-wu 受所監臨財物 to take goods and articles within one's area of jurisdiction
shou-ts'ai erh pu-wang-fa 受財而不枉法 to take bribes without subverting the law
shou-ts'ai erh wang-fa 受財而枉法 to take bribes and subvert the law
shu 贖 redemption by payment of copper
shu-yi 疏議 subcommentary
ssu-ma 緦麻 the fifth degree of mourning
ssu-tsui 私罪 private offense
ta 答 reply
ta-kung 大功 the third degree of mourning
ta pu-ching 大不敬 great irreverence
ta-she 大赦 great amnesty
t'an-wen 袒免 the lowest degree of mourning
tang 當 to replace
tang-chih chih kuan 當直之官 to take turns standing night duty
tao 盜 robbery

t'i-li 體例 structural standard
tiao 調 a tax paid in cloth
tou-sha 鬬殺 to kill in an affray
tou-sung 鬬訟 assault and accusation
tsa-hu 雜戶 a general bondsman
tsa-lü 雜律 miscellaneous articles
ts'an-chi 殘疾 persons who are maimed
tsang 贓 illicit goods
tsao-yi 造意 to formulate a plan
tse-pao ts'an-tui 責保參對 to require a guarantor while the criminal replies to questioning
tsei-tao 賊盜 violence and robbery
tso-tao 左道 ways of the left
tso-tsang 坐贓 illicit goods obtained through malfeasance
tsu 詛 to curse by means of spells
tsu 租 a tax paid in cloth
ts'ung 從 accessory
tu-chi 篤疾 incapacitated
t'u 徒 penal servitude
t'ung-chü 同居 to dwell together
t'ung-kuei 通貴 comprehensively honorable
tuan-yü 斷獄 judgement and prison
tzu-shou 自首 to confess
tz'u 辭 a written statement
wei 僞 false ones
wei-chin 衞禁 imperial guard and prohibitions
wen 問 query
wu-kao fan-tso 誣告反坐 reciprocal punishment for false accusation
yi 疑 doubtful
yi-chüeh 義絕 to divorce
yi-hsiang jen 移鄉人 a person removed from the community
yi-kuei 議貴 worthy of deliberation
yi-ts'ai 異財 separate goods
yin 蔭 protection
ying 媵 concubine
ying chüeh-p'ei 應決配 to require to be sent into penal servitude or life exile
yuan-tso 緣坐 collective prosecution
yüeh 樂 a musician bondsman

Bibliography

Premodern Works in Chinese

All citations to the dynastic histories are to the *Po-na* 百納 edition appended to the SPTK.

All citations to the thirteen classics are to the Nan-ch'ang fu hsüeh pen 南昌府學本 edition of the *Shih-san ching chu-shu* 十三經注疏 (1816), reprinted Taipei: Yi-wen yin-shu-kuan 藝文印書館, n.d., each of the classics separately paginated.

Ch'ung-k'an pu-chu hsi yüan-lu chi-cheng 重刊補注洗冤錄集證 (Instructions for Coroners, Reprinted with a Commentary), by Wang Yin-t'ing 王蔭庭 and others, Taipei: Wen-cheng ch'u-pan-she 文政出版社, 1970.

Feng-su t'ung-yi 風俗通義 (Treatise on Customs). Peking: Centre franco-chinois d'études sinologiques, 1943.

Hsün-tzu chi-chieh 荀子集解 (Collected Explanations of the *Book of Master Hsün*), by Wang Hsien-ch'ien 王先謙 (1842–1917). Taipei: Shih-chieh shu-chü 世界書局, 1960.

Ku T'ang-lü shu-yi 故唐律疏議 (The T'ang Code Explained), compiled in 653 by Ch'ang-sun Wu-chi 長孫無忌 (?–659) and others. Tai-nan-ko ts'ung-shu 岱南閣叢書 edition. The translation is based on this edition.

Ku T'ang-lü shu-yi. Chih-cheng 至正 edition. Ch'ung-hua 崇化, 1351.

Ku T'ang-lü shu-yi. SPTK edition.

Kuang ya 廣雅 (Broad Exposition), by Chang Yi 張揖 (fl. ca. 3rd century A.D.). Taipei: Hsin-hsing shu-chü 新興書局, n.d.

K'ung-tzu chia-yü 孔子家語 (The School Sayings of Confucius), compiler unknown. Taipei: Yi-wen yin-shu-kuan, n.d.

Kuo-yü 國語 (Discourses of the States), compiler unknown. Taipei: Yi-wen yin-shu-kuan, n.d.

Lü-yin yi 律音義 (Rhymes of the Code), by Sun She 孫奭 (962–1033). This work is included in the SPTK edition of the *Code*.

Po-hu t'ung 白虎通 (The Comprehensive Discussions in the White Tiger Hall), compiled by Pan Ku 班固 (A.D. 32–92). SPTK edition.

Pu Yüan shih yi-wen-chih 補元史藝文志 (Supplementary Bibliography of the Yüan History), compiled by Ch'ien Ta-hsin 錢大昕 (1728–1804), and included in the *Pa-shih ching-chi chih* 八史經籍志 (Bibliographical Records of the Eight Histories). Chang Shou-jung 張壽榮 recut block print edition, 1883.

Shang shu ta chuan 尚書大傳 (Great Commentary of the Book of History), by Fu Sheng 伏勝 (fl. ca. 3rd century B.C.). SPTK edition.

Shih-wen ting cheng 釋文訂正 (Revised Explanation of the Text), by Shen Ping 沈炳, dates unknown. Manuscript copy in the Japanese Imperial Library.

Shuo-wen chieh-tzu ku-lin 說文解字詁林 (Commentaries on the Analytical Dictionary of Characters), compiled by Ting Fu-pao 丁福保, in the twentieth century. Original compilation by Hsü Shen 許愼 (d. A.D. 120?). Taipei: Hsin-hsing shu-chü, 1960.

Ta T'ang liu-tien 大唐六典 (The T'ang Institutes), compiled under imperial auspices in the 8th century A.D. Taipei: Wen-hai ch'u-pan she 文海出版社, 1962.

T'ang hui-yao 唐會要 (Essential Documents of the T'ang Dynasty), compiled by Wang P'u 王溥 (922–982). Taipei: Shih-chieh shu-chü, 1960.

T'ang-lü chuan-li 唐律纂例 (Codification of Standards [for Applying Punishments]), by Wang Yüan-liang 王元亮 (fl. ca. 1300). This work is included in the Tai-nan ko ts'ung-shu edition of the *Code*.

T'ang-lü shu-yi 唐律疏議 (The T'ang Code Explained). KHCPTS edition. The translation gives volume and page numbers to this edition.

T'ang-lü shu-yi shih-wen 釋文 (Explanation of the Text of the T'ang Code), by Wang Yüan-liang. This work is included in all editions of the *Code* cited here.

Tao te ching 道德經 (The Book of the Way and Its Power), attributed to Lao-tzu 老子 SPTK edition.

Wen hsüan 文選 (Literary Selections), collected by Hsiao T'ung 蕭統 (501–531) Taipei: Yi-wen yin-shu-kuan, n.d.

Recent Works in Chinese and Japanese

Akitsuki Kanei 秋月觀映. "Tō-dai shukyō keihō ni kansuru kanken" 唐代宗教刑法に關する管見 (A Personal View of the Religious Penal Code of the T'ang Dynasty), *Tōhō shūkyō* 東方宗教, 4.5 (1954), 137–152.

Asai Torao 淺井虎夫 . *Shina ni okeru hōten hensan no enkaku* 支那に於ける法典編纂の沿革 (Development of Legal Codification in China). Kyoto: Hōgakukan 法學館 , 1911.

Ch'eng Shu-te 程樹德 . *Chiu-ch'ao lü-k'ao* 九朝律考 (Research on Law during the Nine Dynasties). Shanghai: Commercial Press, 1927.

Ch'ien Mu 錢穆 . *Chung-kuo li-tai cheng-chih te-shih* 中國歷代政治德失 (A History of the Merits and Deficiencies of Chinese Governments). Hong Kong: Tung-nan yin-wu ch'u-pan she 東南印務出版社 , 1952.

Chih-wu-hsüeh ta-tz'u-tien 植物學大辭典 (Botanical Dictionary), compiled by K'ung Ch'ing-lai 孔慶萊 and others. Shanghai: Commercial Press, 1918.

Chuang Wei-ssu 莊爲斯 [Wallace Johnson]. *T'ang-lü shu-yi yin-te* 唐律疏議引得 (A Concordance to *The T'ang Code*). Taipei: Wen-hai ch'u-pan she, 1965.

Hsü Shih-kuei 徐式圭 . *Chung-kuo ta-she k'ao* 中國大赦考 (Researches into Great Amnesties in China). Shanghai: Commercial Press, 1927.

Makino Tatsumi 牧野巽 , and Niida Noboru 仁井田陞 "Ko tōritsusogi seisaku nendai kō" 故唐律疏議制作年代考 (On the Compilation of the *Ku T'ang-lü shu-yi*, the Official Commentary on the Criminal Code of the T'ang Dynasty), *Tōhōgakuhō* 東方學報 , 1 (1931), 70–158; 2 (1932), 50–226.

Naitō Kenkichi 內藤乾吉 . "Bōkisaibon tōritsusogi no kankō nendai" 滂喜齋本唐律疏議の刋行年代 (On the Date of the Edition of *The T'ang Code* in the P'ang-hsi Chai), *Osaka shiritsu daigaku hōgaku zasshi* 大阪市立大學法學雜誌 , 4.3–4 (1958), 44–74.

Niida Noboru, 仁井田陞 . *Chūgoku hōseishi kenkyū: keihō* 中國法制史研究：刑法 (A Study of Chinese Legal History—Criminal Law). Tokyo: Tōkyō daigaku shuppankai 東京大學出版會 , 1959.

———. *Shina Mibunhō shi* 支那身分法史 (A History of Personal Status in Chinese Law). Tokyo: Tōkyō bunka gakuin 東京文化學院 , 1942.

———. *Tōryō shūi* 唐令拾遺 (The T'ang Statutes Re-collected). Tokyo: Tōkyō daigaku shuppankai, 1964 reprint of 1933 edition.

Riko Mitsuo 利光三津夫 "Waga kuni ni hakusai sareta tōritsu no chūsakusho to sono itsubun" 我が國に舶載された唐律の註釋書とその逸文 (Lost Commentaries on *The T'ang*

Code in Japanese Legal Writings), *Shigaku zasshi* 史學雜誌, 67 (1958), 1173–1193.

Shen Chia-pen 沈家本. *Shen Chi-yi hsien-sheng yi-shu, chia-pien* 沈寄簃先生遺書，甲編 (Bequeathed Writings of Mr. Shen Chi-yi [Shen Chia-pen], First Series). Taipei: Wen-hai ch'u-pan she, 1964 reprint in two volumes with continuous pagination of 1929 edition.

Shiga Shuzō 滋賀秀三. "Yakuchū tōritsusogi" 訳註唐律疏議 (*The T'ang Code*, Translated and Annotated), *Kokka gakkai zasshi* 國家學會雜誌, 72 (1958), 883–934; 73 (1959), 233–253; 74 (1961), 194–222; 75 (1962), 581–605; 78 (1964), 68–97.

Study Group for Ch'in Bamboo Slips from Yunmeng 云梦秦墓竹簡整理小組. "Yunmeng Ch'in-chien shih-wen" 云梦秦簡釋文 (A Transcription of Ch'in Dynasty Inscribed Bamboo Slips Unearthed at Yunmeng, Hupei Province), *Wen Wu* 文物, 6 (1976), 11–14; 7 (1976), 1–11; 8 (1976), 27–44.

Tai Yen-hui 戴炎輝. *T'ang-lü ko-lun* 唐律各論 (Specific Articles of *The T'ang Code*). Taipei: San-min shu-chü 三民書局, 1965.

———. *T'ang-lü t'ung-lun* 唐律通論 (General Principles of *The T'ang Code*). Taipei: Chung-hua shu-chü 中華書局, 1964.

Takigawa Masajirō 瀧川政次郎. "Ryō-no-shūge ni mieru tō no hōritsu shiryō" 令の集解に見える唐の法律史料 (T'ang Legal Material in the *Ryō-no-shūge*), in his *Shina hōseishi kenkyū* 支那法制史研究 (Researches into Chinese Legal History). Tokyo: Yuhikaku 有非閣, 1940.

Tōritsusogi kokanhyō 唐律疏議校勘表 (A Variorum to *The T'ang Code*), compiled by the Tōritsu kenkyūkai 唐律研究會 (T'ang Law Research Group) of the Jimbun kagaku kenkyūjo 人文科學研究所 (Institute of Humanistic Studies) of Kyōtō University. Kyoto: no publisher, 1963.

Tōritsusogi kokanhyō ho i 補遺 (A Supplement to a Variorum to *The T'ang Code*), compiled by the T'ang Law Research Group of the Institute of Humanistic Studies of Kyoto University. Kyoto: no publisher, 1964.

Yang Hung-lieh 楊鴻烈. *Chung-kuo fa-lü tsai Tung-ya chu-kuo chih ying-hsiang* 中國法律在東亞諸國之影響 (The Influence of Chinese Law in East Asia). Shanghai: Commercial Press, 1937.

Works in Western Languages

Balazs, Stephan [Etienne]. "Beiträge zur Wirtschaftsgeschichte der T'ang-

Zeit," *Mitteilungen des Seminars für Orientalische Sprachen zu Berlin*, 36 (1933), 1–62.

———, tr. *Le Traitè juridique du "Souei-chou"*. Bibliotèque de l'Institut des Hautes Etudes Chinoises, IX. Leiden: E. J. Brill, 1954.

Biot, Edouard. *Le Tcheou-li ou rites des Tcheou*. 2 vols. plus index. Paris: L'Imprimerie Nationale, 1851.

Bodde, Derk. *China's First Unifier*. Sinica Leidensia III. Leiden: E. J. Brill, 1938.

———. "The Chinese Cosmic Magic Known as Watching for the Ethers," in Søren Egerod and Else Glahn, eds., *Studia Serica Bernhard Karlgren Dedicata*. Copenhagen: Ejnar Munksgaard, 1959.

———. *Statesman, Patriot, and General in Ancient China*. New Haven: American Oriental Society, 1940.

——— and Clarence Morris. *Law in Imperial China, Exemplified by 190 Ch'ing Dynasty Cases (Translated from the* Hsing-an hui-lan*) with Historical, Social, and Juridical Commentaries*. Harvard Studies in East Asian Law, I. Cambridge: Harvard University Press, 1967.

Boulais, Gui. *Manuel du code chinois*. Variétés Sinologiques 55. Shanghai: Imprimerie de la Mission Catholique, 1924.

Broman, Sven. "Studies on the Chou Li," *Bulletin of the Museum of Far Eastern Antiquities*, 33 (1961), 1–89.

Bünger, Karl. "The Punishment of Lunatics and Negligents According to Classical Chinese Law," *Studia Serica*, 9 (1950), 1–16.

———. *Quellen zur Rechtsgeschichte der T'ang-Zeit*. Peking: Catholic University, 1946.

———. "Uber die Verantwortlichkeit der Beamten nach klassichem chinesischem Recht," *Studia Serica*, 6 (1947), 159–191.

Carter, Thomas F. *The Invention of Printing in China and Its Spread Westward*. 2nd ed. rev. L. Carrington Goodrich. New York: Ronald Press, 1955.

Chavannes, Edouard. *Les Mémoires historiques de Se-ma Ts'ien*. 5 vols. Paris: Ernest Leroux, 1895–1905.

———. *Le T'ai Chan*. Paris: Ernest Leroux, 1910.

Ch'ü, T'ung-tsu. *Law and Society in Traditional China*. Paris and The Hague: Mouton, 1961.

———. *Local Government in China under the Ch'ing*. Harvard East Asian Studies 9. Cambridge: Harvard University Press, 1962.

Couvreur, Séraphin. *I li, Cérémonial.* Hsien Hsien: Imprimerie de la Mission Catholique, 1916.

———. *Li ki ou Mémoires sur les bienséances et les cérémonies.* 2 vols. Hsien Hsien: Imprimerie de la Mission Catholique, 1913.

Creel, Herrlee G. *Confucius, The Man and the Myth.* New York: John Day, 1949.

———. *The Origins of Statecraft in China, Volume One: The Western Chou Empire.* Chicago: University of Chicago Press, 1970.

Deloustal, Raymond. "La Justice dans l'ancien Annam," *Bulletin de l'Ecole Française d'Extrême Orient,* 8 (1908), 177–220; 9 (1909), 91–122, 471–491, 765–796; 10 (1910), 1–60, 349–392, 461–505; 11 (1911), 25–66, 313–317; 12 (1912), 1–33; 13 (1913), 1–59; 19 (1919), 1–88; 22 (1922), 1–40.

Dien, Albert. "The Sa-pao Problem Re-examined," *Journal of the American Oriental Society,* 82.3 (1962), 1–19.

Dubs, Homer H. *The History of the Former Han Dynasty.* 3 vols. Baltimore: Waverly Press, 1938–1955.

———. *The Works of Hsüntze.* Probstain's Oriental Series, XVI. London: Arthur Probstain, 1928.

Duyvendak, J. J. L., tr. *The Book of Lord Shang.* Probstain's Oriental Series, XVIII. London: Arthur Probstain, 1928.

Elvin, Mark. *The Pattern of the Chinese Past.* Stanford: Stanford University Press, 1973.

Feifel, Eugene. *Po Chü-i as a Censor.* Paris and The Hague: Mouton, 1961.

Feng, Han-yi. "The Chinese Kinship System," *Harvard Journal of Asiatic Studies,* 2.2 (1937), 141–276.

——— and John Shryock. "The Black Magic in China Known as *Ku,*" *Journal of the American Oriental Society,* 55 (1935), 1–30.

Fitzgerald, C. P. *China: A Short Cultural History.* London: Cresset Press, 1961.

Forke, Alfred. *Lun Heng: Miscellaneous Essays of Wang Ch'ung.* 2 vols. New York: Paragon Book Gallery, 1962.

Fung, Yu-lan. *A History of Chinese Philosophy.* 2 vols., tr. by Derk Bodde. Princeton: Princeton University Press, 1952–1953.

Gernet, Jacques. *Les Aspects economiques du bouddhisme.* Publications de L'Eçole Française d'Extrême Orient XXXIX. Saigon: Ecole Française d'Extreme Orient, 1956.

———. "La Vente en Chine d'après des contrats de Touen-houang (IXe–Xe siècles)," *T'oung Pao*, 45 (1957), 295–391.

Giles, Herbert A. "The 'Hsi Yüan Lu' or Instructions to Coroners," *Proceedings of the Royal Society of Medicine*, 17 (1924), 59–107.

Herbert, Penelope A. "A Debate in T'ang China on the State Monopoly on Casting Coins," *T'oung Pao*, 65 (1977), 253–292.

Hoang, Pierre. *Le Mariage chinois au point de vue légal*. Variétés Sinologiques 14. Shanghai: Imprimerie de la Mission Catholique, 1898.

Hulsewé, A. F. P. *Periodieke executie- en slachtverboden in de T'ang tijd en hun oorsprong*. Leiden: E. J. Brill, 1948.

———. *Remnants of Han Law*, Vol. I. Sinica Leidensia IX. Leiden: E. J. Brill, 1955.

Ikeda, On. "T'ang Household Registers and Related Documents," in Arthur F. Wright and Denis Twitchett, eds., *Perspectives on the T'ang*. New Haven and London: Yale University Press, 1973, pp. 121–150.

Inoue, Mitsusada. "The *Ritsuryō* System in Japan," *Acta Asiatica*, 31 (1977), 83–112.

Karlgren, Bernhard. "Legends and Cults in Ancient China," *Bulletin of the Museum of Far Eastern Antiquities*, 18 (1946), 199–365.

Kennedy, George. *Die Rolle des Geständnisses im chinesischen Gesetz*. Berlin: no publisher, 1939.

Kracke, E. A. "Family vs. Merit in Chinese Civil Service Examinations under the Empire," *Harvard Journal of Asiatic Studies*, 10 (1947), 103–123.

Legge, James. *The Chinese Classics*. 5 vols. Oxford: Clarendon Press, 1893–1895; reprinted in Hong Kong: Hong Kong University Press, 1961.

———. *The Hsiao King*, in Max Müller, ed., Sacred Books of the East, Vol. III, 449–488. Oxford: Clarendon Press, 1879.

Needham, Joseph. *Science and Civilization in China*. 4 vols. to date. Cambridge: At the University Press, 1956.

Niida, Noboru. "Chinese Legal Institutions of the Sui and T'ang Periods and Their Influence on Surrounding East Asian Countries," in Comité internationale des sciences historiques: Congrés international des sciences historiques Vienne, 24 Aout–5 Septembre 1965. *Rapports, II Historie des Continents*. Horn/Vienna: Verlag Ferdinand Berger & Söhne, 1966, pp. 113–131.

Ou, Koei-hing. *La Peine d'après le code des T'ang*. Shanghai: Université L'Aurore, 1935.

Pokora, Timoteus. "The Canon of Laws by Li K'uei, A Double Falsification," *Archiv Orientalni*, 27 (1959), 96–121.

Pulleyblank, Edwin. "The Origins and Nature of Chattel Slavery in China," *Journal of the Economic and Social History of the Orient*, 1 and 2 (1958), 185–221.

Ratchnevsky, Paul. *Un Code des Yuan*. Paris: Librairie Ernest Leroux, 1937.

Reischauer, Edwin O. *Ennin's Diary*. New York: Ronald Press, 1955.

———. *Ennin's Travels in T'ang China*. New York: Ronald Press, 1955.

des Rotours, Robert. "Les Insignes en deux parties (*fou*) sous la dynastie des T'ang," *T'oung Pao*, 41 (1952), 1–148.

———. tr. *Le Traitè des examens*. Bibliothèque de l'Institut des Hautes Etudes Chinoises, II. Paris: Librairie Ernest Leroux, 1932.

———. tr. *Traité des fonctionnaires et traité de l'armée*. 2 vols. Bibliothèque de l'Institut des Hautes Etudes Chinoises, VI. Leiden: E. J. Brill, 1947.

Schafer, Edward A. *The Golden Peaches of Samarkand*. Berkeley and Los Angeles: University of California Press, 1963.

———. *The Vermillion Bird, T'ang Images of the South*. Berkeley and Los Angeles: University of California Press, 1967.

Tjan, Tjoe Som. *Po Hu T'ung: The Comprehensive Discussions in the White Tiger Hall*. 2 vols. Sinica Leidensia VI. Leiden: E. J. Brill, 1949, 1952.

Twitchett, Denis. "Chinese Social History from the Seventh to the Tenth Centuries," *Past & Present*, 35 (1966), 28–53.

———. *Financial Administration under the T'ang Dynasty*. 2nd ed. Cambridge: At the University Press, 1970.

———. "The Fragment of the T'ang Ordinances of the Department of Waterways Discovered at Tun-huang," *Asia Major*, New Series, 6.1 (1957), 23–79.

———. "A Note on the Tunhuang Fragments of the T'ang Regulations (*ko*)," *Bulletin of the School of Oriental and African Studies*, 30.2 (1967), 369–381.

———. "The T'ang Market System," *Asia Major*, New Series, 12 (1963), 202–248.

Waley, Arthur. *Monkey*. New York: John Day, 1943.

———. *The Real Tripitika and Other Pieces*. New York: Macmillan, 1952.

———. *The Way and Its Power*. Boston and New York: Houghton Mifflin, 1942.

Wang, Yi-t'ung. "Slaves and Other Comparable Groups during the Northern and Southern Dynasties," *Harvard Journal of Asiatic Studies*, 16 (1953), 293–364.

Watson, Burton. *Records of the Grand Historian of China*. 2 vols. New York: Columbia University Press, 1961.

Wilhelm, Richard. *Frühling und Herbst des Lü Bu We*. Jena: Eugen Diederichs Verlag: 1928.

———. *The I Ching or Book of Changes*. 2 vols., tr. by Cary Baynes. Bollingen Series XIX. New York: Pantheon Books, 1950.

Williams, Edward. "Witchcraft in the Chinese Penal Code," *Journal of the North China Branch of the Royal Asiatic Society*, New Series, 38 (1907), 61–95.

Wittfogel, Karl. "Public Office in the Liao Dynasty and the Chinese Examination System," *Harvard Journal of Asiatic Studies*, 10 (1947), 13–40.

Yang, Chung-i. "Evolution of the Status of 'Dependants,'" in E-Tu Zen Sun and John De Francis, eds., *Chinese Social History; Translations of Selected Studies*. Washington, D.C.: American Council of Learned Societies, 1956, pp. 142–156.

Yang, Lien-sheng. *Money and Credit in China, A Short History*. Harvard-Yenching Monograph Series, XII. Cambridge: Harvard University Press, 1952.

——— "Notes on Maspero's *Les Documents Chinois*," *Harvard Journal of Asiatic Studies*, 18 (1955), 142–158; reprinted in his *Excursions in Sinology*. Harvard-Yenching Institute Studies XXIV. Cambridge: Harvard University Press, 1969.

Yang, Martin C. *A Chinese Village: Taitou, Shantung Province*. London: Keagan Paul, 1947.

Index

Studies in East Asian Law Harvard University

Law in Imperial China Exemplified by 190 Ch'ing Dynasty Cases (translated from the Hsing-an hui-lan) *with Historical, Social, and Juridical Commentaries.* By Derk Bodde and Clarence Morris. Cambridge, Mass.: Harvard University Press, 1967.

The Criminal Process in the People's Republic of China, 1949-1963: An Introduction. By Jerome Alan Cohen. Cambridge, Mass.: Harvard University Press, 1968.

Agreements of the People's Republic of China, 1949-1967: A Calendar. By Douglas M. Johnston and Hungdah Chiu. Cambridge, Mass.: Harvard University Press, 1968.

Contemporary Chinese Law: Research Problems and Perspectives. Edited by Jerome Alan Cohen. Cambridge, Mass.: Harvard University Press, 1970.

The People's Republic of China and the Law of Treaties. By Hungdah Chiu. Cambridge, Mass.: Harvard University Press, 1972.

China's Practice of International Law: Some Case Studies. Edited by Jerome Alan Cohen. Cambridge, Mass.: Harvard University Press, 1972.

The Internal Organization of Ch'ing Bureaucracy—Legal, Normative, and Communication Aspects. By Thomas A. Metzger. Cambridge, Mass.: Harvard University Press, 1973.

People's China and International Law: a Documentary Study. By Jerome Alan Cohen and Hungdah Chiu. Princeton, N.J.: Princeton University Press, 1974.

The Chinese Communist Treatment of Counterrevolutionaries: 1924-1949. By Patricia E. Griffin. Princeton, N.J.: Princeton University Press, 1976.

Library of Congress Cataloging in Publication Data

Main entry under title:

The T'ang code.

(Studies in East Asian law, Harvard University; 10)

Translation of T'ang lü shu i.

CONTENTS: v. 1. General principles.

Bibliography: v.

Includes index.

1. Law—China. 2. Criminal law—China.
I. Johnson, Wallace Stephen, 1932- II. Series:
Harvard studies in East Asian law; 10.

Law 345'15'002632 78-51172

ISBN 0-691-09239-7

GPSR Authorized Representative: Easy Access System Europe - Mustamäe tee 50, 10621 Tallinn, Estonia, gpsr.requests@easproject.com

www.ingramcontent.com/pod-product-compliance
Lightning Source LLC
LaVergne TN
LVHW011113300926
849160LV00008B/364

* 9 7 8 0 6 9 1 6 0 6 3 2 3 *